Welcome to the CIA!

As you embark on this culinary journey, you might be wondering—how can I get the most out of my CIA experience? The answer, quite simply, is to get involved! I encourage you to immerse yourself in as many campus activities as your schedule will allow, and embrace as many experiences as you can.

Excellence, leadership, professionalism, ethics, and respect for diversity are the core values that drive everything we do at the CIA, and these will serve as important guides for you as you navigate through your education and campus life.

You'll find that, at the CIA, you share a special bond with your fellow students—here, everyone has the same incredible passion for food that you do. You'll have plenty of opportunities to express that passion as you strive for excellence in the kitchens, bakeshops, and classrooms. Our expert faculty will support you every day, serving as outstanding role models for professionalism.

I urge you to be a leader on campus, whether during classroom activities, through student organizations and events, or simply in your everyday campus life. Let your ethics guide your behavior, don't be afraid to speak your mind, and take full advantage of the many resources available to you—including the valuable support services offered on campus. Be open to sharing your talent, your ideas, your unique perspectives; they'll all serve to further enrich our diverse campus community.

Do as much as you can to be an active part of the college. It's the ideal way to fully prepare for your active and rewarding culinary career, and we're here to help you every step of the way. I wish you much success in all your endeavors.

Sincerely,

Dr. Tim Ryan
President

Thriving in College and Beyond

Research-Based Strategies
for Academic Success and Personal
Development

Second Edition

◆ Joseph B. Cuseo
Emeritus, Marymount College

◆ Viki Sox Fecas
University of South Carolina-Columbia

◆ Aaron Thompson
Eastern Kentucky University

With Foreword by Mary Stuart Hunter

Kendall Hunt
publishing company

Book Team

Chairman and Chief Executive Officer   Mark C. Falb
President and Chief Operating Officer   Chad M. Chandlee
Vice President, Higher Education   David L. Tart
Director of Publishing Partnerships   Paul B. Carty
Editorial Manager   Georgia Botsford
Senior Development Editor   Lynnette M. Rogers
Vice President, Operations   Timothy J. Beitzel
Assistant Vice President, Production Services   Christine E. O'Brien
Senior Production Editor   Charmayne McMurray
Permissions Editor   Renae Horstman
Cover Designer   Sandy Beck

Cover image © 2010, Shutterstock, Inc.

Kendall Hunt
publishing company
www.kendallhunt.com
Send all inquiries to:
4050 Westmark Drive
Dubuque, IA 52004-1840

Printed in the United States of America
10 9 8 7 6 5

Brief Contents

Contents

1 Touching All the Bases
An Overview and Preview of the Most Powerful Principles of College Success   1

2 Liberal Arts
The Meaning, Purpose, and Value of General Education   31

8 Social and Emotional Intelligence

Relating to Others and Regulating Emotions 191

9 Diversity

Learning About and from Human Differences 215

10 Educational Planning and Decision Making

Making Wise Choices About Your College Courses and College Major 241

11 Career Exploration, Planning, and Preparation

Foreword

The very fact that you have this book in your hands and are reading these words is evidence that you are well on your way to becoming a successful student—congratulations. You join hundreds of thousands of other undergraduate students who each year take important steps toward ensuring their success through enrolling in a first-year seminar, by participating in a learning community, or engaging in other special programs on college and university campuses. College can be an exciting experience with challenges and opportunities that you've never faced before. It is a time for personal growth and development far beyond simply the learning of facts and figures. How you choose to spend your time in college will impact your life for years to come. You will discover new ideas about the world and your place in it both in the classroom and beyond as you accept the challenges before you and take responsibility for your own educational experience. And along the way, you will certainly learn more about yourself as an individual.

My own work with college students over the past 25 years tells me that students of all types, ages, and abilities can succeed. But I have also, unfortunately, seen far too many very bright and capable students fail. The fact that your college accepted you for admission is evidence enough that you have the capacity to succeed. But, making the transition from a high school learning culture to that of college is not automatic. Simply being a college student on a college or university campus doesn't mean that you will be as successful as you were in high school or in the world of your pre-college experience. What worked for you before may not work for you in this new environment. Understanding the difference in teaching and learning cultures is key to student success.

This book is one of the many resources available to you as a college student. The title itself, *Thriving in College and Beyond*, should tell you that college is just the beginning of a life full of learning. The pages of this book address the critical and multi-faceted opportunities in front of you as a college student. Throughout the book you will find information that will assist you as you navigate the complex and often mysterious collegiate experience. The authors have masterfully constructed a book that contains a wide variety of elements including exercises, checklists, cartoons, "take action now" suggestions, quotes, reflection guides, and thought questions all carefully chosen to engage and inform you while at the same time providing meaningful material to help you find success in college.

As individuals, the authors have a wealth of experience in assisting college students and they are sharing their best information, ideas, and strategies with you. Joe Cuseo is a well-respected first-year educator and professor of psychology who has many years experience helping new students successfully transition from high school to college. An award-winning faculty member at Marymount College, his passion for student success and creativity in teaching are hallmarks of his teaching and can be easily witnessed in the pages of this book. Viki Sox Fecas has helped countless students at the University of South Carolina transition to college and her campus through teaching sections of the first-year seminar and through her good work as a career counselor. Her positive attitude and enthusiasm for the collegiate experience has made her a sought-after and valuable resource for students at all levels. Aaron

Thompson has many years of experience helping students attain educational success as well. With teaching and administrative experience at several public institutions, his contributions to this book are important and noteworthy. The partnership formed by these authors has resulted in a rich and practical book that will help countless students. You, too, can be one of these students.

So, read this book intentionally, apply what you read to yourself. Approach the exercises with vigor. Ask questions. Challenge the ideas. Discuss what you have read with your classmates and friends. Make the most of the generous resources in the book. But most of all, use what you learn in the book to help you be the very best student you can be. You'll be better for having done so. And then, you will be able to look back and appreciate all that this book has taught you!

Mary Stuart Hunter
Director
National Resource Center for The First-Year
Experience and Students in Transition
University of South Carolina

Welcome to Our Book

ACTIVATE YOUR THINKING   Journal Entry

What do you think are the key characteristics or features of a textbook that:

1. make you *want* to read it?

_____

_____

_____

2. enable you to *learn the most* from it?

_____

_____

_____

◆ Plan and Purpose of This Book

The primary purpose of this book is to help you make a smooth transition to college and equip you with strategies for success in college and beyond. The book is designed to promote the academic excellence and personal development of all students—whether you are transitioning directly from high school or from a full-time or part-time job, living on or off campus, or attending college on a full-time or part-time basis. Whatever your previous educational record may have been, college is a new ballgame played on a different field with different rules and expectations. If you haven't been a successful student in the past, this book will help you become a successful student in the future; if you have been a strong student, it will make an even stronger student.

The book's major goal is to help you put into practice one of the most powerful principles of human learning and personal success: *mindfulness*. When you're mindful, you remain aware of what you're doing while you're doing it to be sure that you're doing it effectively and to the best of your ability. Self-awareness is the critical first step toward self-improvement and success in any aspect of your life. If you develop the habit of watching yourself do college and maintain awareness of whether you're doing it effectively (e.g., using the key strategies identified in this book), you will have taken a huge step toward college success.

> "More than 30 years of research has shown that mindfulness is figuratively and literally enlivening. It's the way you feel when you're feeling passionate."
>
> –Dr. Ellen Langer, Harvard University, mindfulness researcher and author of *The Power of Mindful Learning*

Rather than trying to figure how to do college most effectively through trial and error, and hoping you'll eventually discover what works best, this book gives you a game plan for getting it right from the start. It provides a plan that's built on a solid foundation of research, which will equip you with well-documented strategies for doing college strategically and successfully.

Specific, action-oriented strategies make up the heart of this book. However, you'll find that these practical strategies aren't presented to you in the form of a laundry list of isolated and disconnected tips. Instead, strategies are accompanied by a research-based rationale for *why* they are effective and specific practices are organized into broader *principles*, which tie the strategies together into a meaningful plan. It's not only important to know *what* you should do in college, but also *why* you should do it. If you understand the reason behind a suggested strategy, you're more motivated to take it seriously and take action on it. Furthermore, when specific strategies are organized into general principles, they become more powerful because you're able to see how the same principle may be generalized and applied across different subjects and situations. When you understand a principle, you're also empowered to create specific strategies of you own that flow or follow from the same general principle.

Learning the underlying reasons why a specific strategy works and learning how specific strategies are embedded in larger principles represent deeper learning than simply acquiring tips about what you should or shouldn't do in college. We believe that you're ready and able to meet this challenge of deeper learning and will find it more stimulating than simply reading a compilation of tips and warnings, or completing a series of exercises and activities.

Since the strategies we recommend are research-based, you'll find references cited regularly throughout all the chapters and a sizable reference section at the end of the book. You'll also find that the references cited represent a balanced blend of older, "classic" studies and more recent "cutting edge" research from a wide variety of fields. This highlights the wide-ranging relevance of the ideas being discussed and their power to withstand the test of time. It also underscores the fact that the subject of college success, like any other subject in the college curriculum, is a scholarly field resting on a solid body of knowledge research that spans from past to present.

◆ Preview of Content

Introduction

In the introduction to this book, you'll find strong evidence why your college experience has the potential to be the most enriching experience of your life and one that will provide you with multiple benefits throughout life. The first year of college, in particular, is a critical stage of development during which students undergo the greatest amount of learning and personal growth. It's also the time when students experience the greatest challenges, the most stress, the most academic difficulties, and the highest dropout rate. This highlights the importance of the first-year experience, the importance of first-year courses designed to promote your college success, and the importance of this book. As documented in the Introduction, there are numerous studies show that new students who participate in first-year seminars (college-success

Student Perspectives

"I could really relate to everything we talked about. It is a great class because you can use it in your other classes."

–First-year student comment made when evaluating a first-year seminar (college success course)

"Everything we learned we will apply in our lives."

–First-year student comment made when evaluating a first-year seminar (college success course)

"This is the only course I've ever taken that was about me."

–First-year student comment made when evaluating a first-year seminar (college success course)

courses) are more likely to continue their enrollment in college, complete their college degree, and get the most of their college experience.

Chapter 1. Touching All the Bases

This chapter provides an overview and preview of the most powerful principles of college success. Its major goals are to equip you with "big picture" principles you can use on your own to promote success in college and raise your awareness of the wide range of campus resources you can use to support your quest for success. The chapter describes the services provided by various campus resources, why they're worth using, and how you can most effectively capitalize on them during your first year of college and throughout your college experience.

Chapter 2. Liberal Arts: The Meaning, Purpose, and Value of General Education

This chapter will help you gain a deeper understanding and appreciation of the liberal arts—the core component of the college experience that embodies the essence of a college education and provides the foundational, transferable skills needed for success in all college majors, careers, and life roles. You will acquire strategies for making the most of general education to gain a perspective on the whole world, to develop yourself as a whole person, and to enrich the quality (and marketability) of your college experience.

Chapter 3. Goal Setting, Motivation, and Character

The road to success starts with identifying a desired outcome (an end goal), and then continues with finding the means (succession of steps) to reach that goal. Studies show that setting specific goals is a more effective way to achieve success than simply telling ourselves that we're going to try hard or do your best. This chapter identifies the key steps involved in setting and reaching personal goals, self-motivational strategies for staying on track and moving toward your goals, and the inner qualities (virtues) associated not only with being a successful person, but also with being a person of character.

"Watch your thoughts. They become words. Watch your words. They become deeds. Watch your deeds. They become habits. Watch your habits. They become character. Character is everything."

—Ralph Waldo Emerson, American philosopher, public speaker, and advocate for the abolition of slavery

Chapter 4. Time Management

You will encounter an academic calendar and class schedule in college that differs radically from those of your previous years of schooling. You may be surprised by how much free time you seem to have because you'll be spending less time sitting in class; however, you'll be expected to spend more time outside of class on work related to class. Learning to use your out-of-class work time strategically and productively is critical to ensuring academic success in college, and you will learn ways to do so in this chapter. Furthermore, time is a valuable personal resource; if you gain greater control of it, you can greater control of your life. Managing your time well not only enables you to get your work done in a timely manner; it also enables you to attain and maintain balance in your life. This chapter offers a comprehensive set of strategies for managing time, combating procrastination, and ensuring that your time-spending habits are aligned with your educational goals and personal values.

Student Perspective

"In high school, a lot of the work was done while in school, but in college all of your work is done on your time. You really have to organize yourself in order to get everything done."

—First-year student's response to a question about what was most surprising about college life (Bates, 1994)

Chapter 5. Strategic Learning, Studying, and Test Taking

This chapter is intended to help you apply research on human learning and the human brain to become a more effective and efficient learner. It takes you through three key stages of the learning process—from the first stage of acquiring information through lectures and readings, through the second stage of studying and retaining the information you acquire, to the final stage of retrieving (recalling) the information you've studied. The ultimate goal of this chapter is to supply you with a set of powerful strategies that can be used to promote learning that's *deep* (not surface-level memorizing), *durable* (not short-term, but long-lasting), and retrievable (accessible to you when you need it).

Chapter 6. Achieving Peak Levels of Academic Performance

This chapter is designed to prepare you for the three key tasks that are most commonly used to evaluate your academic performance in college: tests, papers, and presentations. The chapter supplies a systematic set of test-taking strategies that can be used before, during, and after exams to improve your test performance by helping you become more "test wise" and less "test anxious." Also discussed are strategies for writing papers and reports, and how to use writing as a learning tool. Finally, strategies are shared for making effective oral presentations and for overcoming speech anxiety. Both writing and speaking are transferable skills that can be applied to improve academic performance in all majors and careers; and they're also portable skills you can use throughout life. This chapter is designed to "jump start" your development of these powerful skills, enabling you to use them immediately to achieve early success in your first year of college and beyond.

Chapter 7. Higher-Level Thinking

This chapter takes you beyond learning to acquire and retain information to higher levels of critical and creative thinking. Surveys indicate that teaching students how to think is the primary goal of college faculty; this chapter was written to help you understand the type of thinking that professors expect from you and empower you to think in this way. Specific forms of higher-level thinking are identified, self-questioning strategies that prompt your mind to use these forms of thinking are suggested, and practical strategies for demonstrating higher-level thinking on exams and assignments are provided.

Chapter 8. Social and Emotional Intelligence

Communicating and relating effectively with others is an important life skill and an important form of human intelligence. Similarly, emotional intelligence—the ability to identify and manage your emotions when dealing with others and to be aware of how your emotions are influencing your thoughts and actions—is an important life skill that has been found to promote personal success and improve academic performance. This chapter identifies effective ways to communicate, relate, and form meaningful relationships with others, as well as ways to understand and regulate key emotions—such as love, anger, stress and depression. The information included in this chapter should not only improve the quality of your performance in college; it should improve the overall quality of your life.

Chapter 9. Diversity

This chapter clarifies what "diversity" really means, demonstrates how experiencing diversity can deepen learning, promote critical and creative thinking, and contribute to your personal and professional development. Included in the chapter are ideas for overcoming cultural barriers and biases that interfere with developing rewarding relationships with diverse people, and it identifies ways to learn effectively from people whose prior personal experiences and cultural backgrounds are different than our own. Simply stated, we learn more from people who differ from us than we do from people similar to us.

Chapter 10. Educational Planning and Decision-Making

This chapter is designed to help you make wise choices about your college courses and your college major. Whether you're undecided about a college major or think you've reached a final decision, you need to be sure that you choose a path that's truly compatible with your personal interests, talents, and values. You should have a strategic plan in mind (and in hand) that enables you to strike a healthy balance between continuing to explore and making a final commitment. This chapter will help you strike this balance and make educational decisions that put you in the best position to reach your long-term goals.

Pause for Reflection

What percentage of beginning college students do you think have already made-up their mind about a major?

What percentage of these "decided" students do you think eventually change their mind and end up graduating with a different major?

(See Chapter 10. **p. 242** for answers to these questions.)

Chapter 11. Career Exploration, Planning, and Preparation

It may seem unusual or premature to find a chapter on career success in a book for beginning college students. However, career exploration and planning should begin in the first term of college because it gives you a practical, long-range goal to strive for; it also enables you to appreciate how the skills that you're using and developing in college are very similar to the skills sought by employers and promote career success after college. Since career planning is really a form of *life* planning, the sooner you start this process, the sooner you gain control of the future and start shaping a future life for yourself that finds you doing what interests you, what you do well, and what matters most to you.

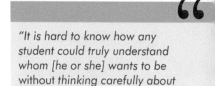

"It is hard to know how any student could truly understand whom [he or she] wants to be without thinking carefully about what career to pursue."

–Derek Bok, former president of Harvard University

Chapter 12. Managing Money and Minimizing Debt

Research shows that accumulating high levels of debt while in college is associated with higher levels of stress, lower academic performance, and greater risk of withdrawing from college. The good news is that research also shows that students who learn to use effective money-management strategies are able to minimize unnecessary spending, reduce accumulation of debt and stress, and improve the quality of their academic performance. This chapter identifies effective strategies and habits for tracking income and expenses, minimizing and avoiding debt, balancing time spent on school and work, and making wise decisions about spending, saving, and investing.

Chapter 13. Health and Wellness

No one can reach our full potential and achieve peak levels of performance without attending to our physical self. Sustaining health and attaining optimal levels of performance depend on how well you treat your *body*—what you put into it (healthy food), what you keep out of it (unhealthy substances), what you do with it (exercise), and how well you rejuvenate it (sleep). This chapter examines strategies for maintaining nutritional balance, attaining quality sleep, promoting total fitness, and avoiding risky behaviors that jeopardize and threaten our health.

Pause for Reflection

What does being a "well-rounded" person and leading a "well-balanced" life mean to you?

◆ Sequence of Chapter Topics

The chapters in this book have been arranged in an order that allows you to ask and answer the following sequence of questions:

1. Why am I here?
2. Where do I want to go?
3. What must I do to get there?
4. How do I know when I've arrived?

The early chapters are intended to help you get immediately situated and oriented to your new campus environment, reinforce your decision for being in college, and help you decide where you want college to take you. These initial chapters supply you with a mental map for your trip through college, helping you to set educational goals and become fully aware of the college environment that surrounds you that includes the wide array of campus resources available to you. Once you get a clear sense of why college is worth doing and where it will take you, you should become more enthused and motivated to take action on the strategies suggested throughout the remainder of the book.

The middle chapters of the text are devoted to helping you handle the more practical, day-to-day academic work responsibilities realities and how to get the job done. They focus on the core academic tasks of dealing with lectures, reading assignments, studying, and test-taking.

The final chapters shift to a focus on the future: planning for your major, your career, and your life beyond college.

Process and Style of Presentation

How information is delivered is as important as *what* information is delivered. When writing this text, we made an intentional attempt to deliver our message in a way that would:

- Stimulate your motivation to learn;
- Deepen your learning; and
- Strengthen your retention (memory) for what you've learned.

We attempted to do this by incorporating the following principles of motivation, learning and memory throughout the text.

- We begin each chapter with an **Activate Your Thinking** exercise designed to stimulate your thoughts and feelings about the upcoming topic. This prereading exercise is designed to "warm up" or "tune up" your brain, preparing it to relate the ideas you're about to encounter in the chapter with the ideas you already have in your head. It's an instructional strategy that implements one of the most powerful principles of human learning: we learn most effectively by connecting what we're going to learn with what we have already learned and stored in our brain.

Copyright © Harley Schwadron. Reprinted with permission.

"JUNIOR'S WRITING HAS IMPROVED. HIS LETTERS FROM COLLEGE, PLEADING FOR MORE MONEY, ARE FORCEFULLY AND FLAWLESSLY WRITTEN."

> Writing promotes deeper learning and higher-level thinking skills.

- Within each chapter, we periodically interrupt your reading with a **Pause for Reflection** and a **Journal Entry** that asks you to stop, reflect, and think deeply about the material you've just read. These timely pauses keep you mentally alert and active throughout the reading process. The pauses interrupt and intercept "attention drift" that normally takes place when the brain continually receives and processes information for an extended period—as it does while reading. The journal entries should also deepen your understanding of the material you read because you are *writing* in response to what you read. Writing encourages more thoughtful reflection, deeper learning, and a higher-level of thinking than simply underlining or highlighting sentences.

- **Exercises** are at the *end* of each chapter and ask you to reflect further on the knowledge you've acquired by reading the chapter and transform that knowledge into informed action. As discussed in Chapter 3, wisdom isn't achieved by simply acquiring knowledge, but by *applying* the knowledge you have acquired—i.e., using your knowledge by putting it into practice.

  The strategic positioning of the Activate Your Thinking exercises at the beginning of each chapter, the Pauses for Reflection interspersed during the chapter, and the Application Exercises at the end of the chapter, creates an effective learning sequence that keeps you actively involved in the reading process—from start to finish.

- In each chapter, information is delivered through a variety of formats that include diagrams, pictures, cartoons, advice from current and former college students, words of wisdom from famous and successful people, and personal stories drawn from the authors' experiences. Delivering information through multiple delivery formats allows you to receive it through multiple sensory modalities (input channels) and enables your brain to store it in multiple places. This deepens learning by allowing your brain to form multiple connections with the information and strengthens memory by recording multiple memory tracks (traces) of the information in your brain.

Here's a complete list of the book's key instructional features. As you read thee features, make a quick note in the side margin on how effectively you think this feature will motivate you to read the book and promote your learning from the book.

Snapshot Summary Boxes

At different points in the text, you'll find boxes containing summaries of key concepts and strategies. These boxed summaries are designed to connect major ideas related to the same concept and get them in the same place (physically), which, in turn, should help you get them in the same place (mentally).

Remember Cues

Periodically, you'll encounter a blue "Remember" box. This is a clue indicating it's a high-priority recommendation that deserves special attention and long-term retention.

Quotes

Throughout the book, quotes from famous and influential people appear in the side margins that relate to and reinforce the ideas being discussed at that point in the chapter. You'll find quotes from accomplished individuals who have lived in different historical periods and who have specialized in fields, including politics, philosophy, religion, science, business, music, art, and athletics. The wide-ranging time frames, cultures, and fields of study represented by the people who've been quoted testify that the wisdom of their words is timeless and universal. You can learn a lot from the first-hand experiences and actual words of "real people." It's our hope that the words of these highly successful and respected individuals will inspire you to aspire to similar levels of achievement.

Student Perspectives

Throughout the book, you'll find comments and advice from students at different stages of the college experience, including college graduates (alumni). Studies show that students can learn a great deal from other students—especially from students who've been there and experienced what you are about to experience. You can benefit from their experiences by hearing about their success stories and stumbling blocks.

Personal Stories

In each chapter, you'll find personal stories drawn from the authors' experiences. We've learned a lot from our own experiences as college students, from our professional experiences working with students as instructors and advisors, and from our life experiences. Studies show that sharing personal stories promotes understanding and memory for the concepts contained in the story. We share our personal stories with the intent of personalizing the book and with the hope that you'll learn from our experiences—even if it's learning not to make the same mistakes we made!

Pause for Reflection

Have you received any tips or advice from friends or family about what to do, or what not to do in college?

If yes, what was this advice? Do you think the advice is accurate and worth following?

If you haven't received any advice from anyone, why do you think no one has offered it?

Concept Maps: Verbal-Visual Aids

The book contains many concept (idea) maps that visually organize ideas into diagrams, charts, and figures. By representing key concepts in a visual-spatial format, you're more likely to retain them because two different memory traces are recorded in your brain: verbal (words) and visual (images).

Cartoons: Emotional-Visual Aids

You'll find a sizable supply of cartoons sprinkled throughout the text. These intended attempts at humor are included to provide you with a little entertainment, but more importantly, they should strengthen your retention of the concept depicted in the cartoon by reinforcing it with a visual image (drawing) and an emotional experience (humor). If the cartoon triggers at least a snicker, your body will release adrenalin—a hormone that facilitates memory formation. If the cartoon generates actual laughter, it's likely to stimulate release of endorphins—the brain's natural, morphine-like chemicals that lower stress (and elevate mood!).

Learning More Through the World Wide Web

To find additional information relating to the chapter's major ideas, Web-based resources are included at the end of the chapter. One of the major goals of a college education is to prepare you to become an independent, self-directed learner. Our hope is that the material presented for each chapter topic will stimulate your interest and motivation to learn more about the topic. If it does, you can use the online

Pause for Reflection

Quickly review the features of this book described on **pp. xviii–xx.** Which of these features do you think will be most effective for:

1. Stimulating your interest in reading the book, and

2. Promoting your learning from the book?

resources cited at the end of the chapter to access additional information relating to the major ideas presented within the chapter.

Summary and Conclusion

It's our hope that the content of this book, and the manner in which the content is presented, will motivated and empower you to make the most of your college experience. Don't forget that the skills and strategies discussed in this book are relevant to life beyond college. Effective planning and decision making, learning deeply and remembering longer, thinking critically and creatively, speaking and writing persuasively, managing time and money responsibly, communicating and relating effectively with others, and maintaining health and wellness are more than just college skills; they are life skills.

Learning doesn't stop after college; it's a lifelong process. If you strive to apply the ideas in this book, you should thrive in college and beyond.

Personal Story

I've learned a lot from teaching the first-year seminar (college success course) and from writing this book. Before teaching this course, I didn't have a clear idea about what the liberal arts were and how general education was so important for achieving personal and professional success. I also learned new strategies for managing my time, my money, and my health. The strategies and skills that I've learned from teaching the course and writing this book have convinced me that this course and this book go beyond developing skills for success in college; they develop skills for success in life.

—Joe Cuseo

!

Remember

This is more than just a textbook for first-term students. It's a *college-success* and *life-success* book; it contains principles and strategies that will promote your success in college *and* improve the quality of your life.

Sincerely,

Joe Cuseo, *Viki Sox Fecas*, and *Aaron Thompson*

Acknowledgments

I'd like to take this opportunity to thank several people who have played an important role in my life and whose positive influence made this book possible. My parents, Mildred (nee, Carmela) and Blase (nee, Biaggio) Cuseo for the many sacrifices they made to support my education. My wife, Mary, and my son, Tony, for their kindness, courage and love. James Vigilis, my uncle, for being a second father and life coach to me during my formative years. Jim Cooper, my best friend, for being a mentor to me in graduate school. My students, who taught me a lot and contributed their insightful perspectives, poignant poems, and humorous cartoons to this book.

—Joe Cuseo

If not for the love and support of my parents, Wyman and Fae Sox, and son, Matt Fecas, my involvement in this project would never have happened. Thanks also to Kendall/Hunt Publishing's Director of the National Book Program, Paul Carty, whose wisdom in assembling the writing team and assignment of a crackerjack editor, Tina Bower, made this idea a fun reality. I also tremendously value my colleagues for their encouragement and feedback through the writing and review process.

—Viki Sox Fecas

I would like to thank my wife Holly and my children, Sonya, Sara, Michael, Maya, Isaiah and Olivia for being my continual inspiration and source of unconditional love. I would also like to thank my father and mother (Big "A" and Margaret) for instilling in me that education is the key to most all that is valuable in our society. In addition, I would like to acknowledge the support that Eastern Kentucky University gave me with my education and with their support to write this book. This support largely came through Rhonda who made sure that I could get the time to do the work. I would also like to thank my co-authors (Joe and Viki) and Kendall/Hunt (Paul and Tina) for the opportunity to be part of a great team. Lastly, I would like to thank my mentors and students who gave me the encouragement and motivation.

—Aaron Thompson

We gratefully acknowledge the constructive criticism of the colleagues who provided reviews for individual chapters of this text, and who participated in the focus groups. They include:

Peg Adams
Northern Kentucky University

Linda Alvarez
University of Wisconsin—
River Falls

Stephanie Adams
William Woods University

Scott Amundsen
Eastern Kentucky University

Anita Adkins
Northern Kentucky University

Suzanne Ash
Cerritos College

Treva Barham
Le Tourneau University

Andrea Berta
University of Texas—El Paso

Paula Bradberry
Arkansas State University

Cynthia Burnley
Eastern Tennessee State University

Norma Campbell
Fayetteville State University

Jay Chaskes
Rowan University

Regina Clark
Tennessee State University

Karen Clay
Miami-Dade College

Geoff Cohen
University of California—Riverside

Amy D'Olivo
Centanary College of New Jersey

Donna Dahlgren
Indiana University Southeast

Rachelle Darabi
Indiana Purdue University—Fort Wayne

Michael Denton
University of North Carolina—Charlotte

Louise Ericson
University of South Carolina Upstate

Betsy Eudey
California State University—Stanislaus

Carlisa Finney
Anne Arundel Community College

Jennifer Gay
Fort Lewis College

Latty Goodwin
Rochester Institute of
Technology

Tracy Gottlieb
Seton Hall University

Virginia Granda
University of Texas—El Paso

Laurie Grimes
Lorain County Community
College

Allen Grove
Alfred University

Robert Guell
Indiana State University

Laurie Hazard
Bryant College

Marge Jaasma
California State University—
Stanislaus

Andrew Koch
Purdue University

Lora Lavery-Broda
St. Leo University

Deborah Lotsof
Mount Union College

Jane Owen
Waynesburg College

Denise Roade
Northern Illinois University

Chris Rubic
Grayslake North High School

Jane Snyder
Fontbonne University

Joe Cuseo holds a Ph.D. in Educational Psychology and Assessment from the University of Iowa. Currently, he is Professor Emeritus of Psychology at Marymount College (California) where for more than 25 years he directed the first-year seminar—taken by all new students. He is a columnist for a bimonthly newsletter published by the National Resource Center for The First-Year Experience & Students in Transition, and has received the Resource Center's "outstanding first-year advocate award." He is a 14-time recipient of the "faculty member of the year award" on his home campus, a student-driven award based on effective teaching and academic advising. He has made over 100 presentations at college campuses and conferences across the country, and has authored articles, chapters, and books on the first-year experience, academic advising, student diversity, and the senior-year experience.

Viki Sox Fecas has a Ph.D. in Educational Administration from the University of South Carolina (USC). In her current role as Program Manager for Freshman and Pre-Freshman Programs, she coordinates the career component for all of the 150+ sections of the number one ranked University 101 Program in the country. She serves as a career resource for international scholars visiting the National Resource Center (NRC). She also is an Adjunct Professor in the Higher Education and Student Affairs graduate program at USC. She was recognized as the *Outstanding Freshman Advocate* in 1996.

She took University 101 as a freshman at USC, and has been teaching for the past 18 years. Since 1995, she has taught the sole section dedicated to transfer students. Her research interests center around the transition of college students, with a special interest in transfer students. She has written a career chapter for both the U101 *Transitions book* as well as *Your College Experience*. She regularly presents at both the National First-Year Experience and Students in Transition Conferences sponsored by the NRC.

Aaron Thompson, Ph.D., is the Interim Vice President of Academic Affairs at the Kentucky Council on Postsecondary Education and a Professor of Sociology in the Department of Educational Leadership and Policy Studies at Eastern Kentucky University. Thompson has a Ph.D. in Sociology in areas of Organizational Behavior/Race and Gender relations. Thompson has researched, taught and/or consulted in areas of assessment, diversity, leadership, ethics, research methodology and social statistics, multicultural families, race and ethnic relations, student success, first-year students, retention, and organizational design. He is nationally recognized in the areas of educational attainment, academic success, and cultural competence. Dr. Thompson has worked in a variety of capacities within the two-year and four-year institutions. He got his start in college teaching within a community college. His latest co-authored books are *"Diversity and the College Experience," "Thriving in College and Beyond: Research-Based Strategies for Academic Success and Personal Development," "Focus on Success"* and *"Black Men and Divorce"*. His upcoming books are "*Infusing Diversity into Education: Research-Based Strategies for Appreciating and Learning Human Differences*" and "*Humanity, Diversity, & the Liberal Arts: The Foundation of a College Education.*" He has more than 30 publications and numerous research and peer reviewed presentations. Thompson has traveled over the U.S. and has given more than 500 workshops, seminars and invited lectures in areas of race and gender diversity, living an unbiased life, overcoming obstacles to gain success, creating a school environment for academic success, cultural competence, workplace interaction, organizational goal setting, building relationships, the first-year seminar, and a variety of other topics. He has been or is a consultant to educational institutions, corporations, nonprofit organizations, police departments, and other governmental agencies.

Introduction

Congratulations and welcome! We applaud your decision to continue your education. Your previous enrollment in school was required; however, you're decision to continue your education in college is entirely *your choice*. You've chosen to enter "higher education," where you will be learning and thinking at a higher level than you did in high school. You are about to begin a new and exciting journey; your time in college has the potential to be the most enriching experience of your life. It's probably safe to say that after your experience in college, you'll never again be a member of an organization or community with as many resources and services that are intentionally designed to promote your learning, development, and success. If you capitalize on the campus resources available to you, and if you utilize effective college-going strategies (such as those suggested in this book), you can create a life-changing experience for yourself that will enrich the quality of your life for the remainder of your life. (See **Box I.1** for a snapshot summary of the multiple, lifelong benefits of a college education and college degree.)

Snapshot Summary   I.1

Why College Is Worth It: The Economic and Personal Benefits of a College Education

Less than 30 percent of Americans have earned a 4-year college degree (U.S. Census Bureau). When individuals who attend college are compared with people from similar social and economic backgrounds who did not continue their education beyond high school, research reveals that college is well worth the investment. College graduates experience numerous long-lasting benefits, such as those summarized in the following list.

1. **Career Benefits**
   - Career Security and Stability—lower rates of unemployment
   - Career Versatility and Mobility—more flexibility to move out of a position and into other positions

   - Career Advancement—more opportunity to move up to higher professional positions
   - Career Interest—more likely to find their work stimulating and challenging
   - Career Autonomy—greater independence and opportunity to be their own boss
   - Career Satisfaction—enjoy their work more and feel that it allows them to use their special talents
   - Career Prestige—hold higher-status positions (i.e., careers that more socially desirable and respected)
2. **Economic Advantages**
   - Make better consumer choices and decisions
   - Make wiser long-term investments

- Receive greater pension benefits
- Earn higher income: The gap between the earnings of high school and college graduates is *growing*. Individuals with a bachelor's degree now earn an average annual salary of about $50,000 per year, which is 40 percent higher than high school graduates—whose average salary is less than $30,000 per year. When these differences are calculated over a lifetime, families head by people with a bachelor's degree will take in about 1.6 million more than families headed by people with a high school diploma.

"A bachelor's degree continues to be a primary vehicle of which one gains an advantaged socioeconomic position in American society."

–Ernest Pascarella & Patrick Terenzini, *How College Affects Students*

"If you think education is expensive, try ignorance."

–Derek Bok, former President, Harvard University

3. Advanced Intellectual Skills
- Greater knowledge
- More effective problem-solving skills
- Better ability to deal with complex and ambiguous (uncertain) problems
- Greater openness to new ideas

- More advanced levels of moral reasoning
- Clearer sense of self-identity—more awareness and knowledge of personal talents, interests, values, and needs
- Greater likelihood to continue learning throughout life

4. Better Physical Health
- Better health insurance—more comprehensive coverage and more likely to be covered
- Better dietary habits
- Exercise more regularly
- Lower rates of obesity
- Live longer and healthier lives

5. Social Benefits
- Higher social self-confidence
- Understand and communicate more effectively with others
- Greater popularity
- More effective leadership skills
- Greater marital satisfaction

6. Emotional Benefits
- Lower levels of anxiety
- Higher levels of self-esteem
- Greater sense of self-efficacy—believe they have more influence and control over their life
- Higher levels of psychological well-being
- Higher levels of personal happiness

7. Effective Citizenship
- Greater interest in national issues—both social and political
- Greater knowledge of current affairs
- Higher voting participation rates
- Higher rates of participation in civic affairs and community service

8. **Higher Quality of Life for Their Children**
   - Less likely to smoke during pregnancy
   - Provide better health care for their children
   - Spend more time with their children
   - More likely to involve their children in educational activities that stimulate their mental development
   - More likely to save money for their children to go to college
   - More likely that their children will graduate from college
   - More likely that their children will attain high-status and higher-paying careers

References

Astin, A. W. (1993). *What Matters in College?* San Francisco: Jossey-Bass.

Bowen, H. R. (1977, 1997). *Investment in Learning: The Individual & Social Value of American Higher Education.* Baltimore: The Johns Hopkins University Press.

College Board (2006). *Education pays update.* Washington, D. C.: Author.

Dee, T. (2004). Are there civic returns to education? *Journal of Public Economics,* 88, 1697-1720.

Feldman, K. A., & Newcomb, T. M. (1969, 1994). *The impact of college on students.* San Francisco: Jossey-Bass.

Pascarella, E. T., & Terenzini, P. T. (1991). *How college affects students: Findings and Insights from Twenty Years of Research.* San Francisco: Jossey-Bass.

Pascarella, E. T., & Terenzini, P. T. (2005). *How college affects students: A third decade of research* (volume 2). San Francisco: Jossey-Bass.

Tomasho, R. (2009, April 22.). Study tallies education gap's effect on GDP. *Wall Street Journal*

U.S. Census Bureau (2008). *Bureau of Labor Statistics.* Washington, D.C.: Author.

Student Perspectives

"My 3-month old boy is very important to me, and it is important that I graduate from college so my son, as well as I, live a better life."

—First-year student responding to the question, "What is most important to you?"

"Being a first-generation college student, seeing how hard my parents worked these past 18 years to give all that they can to get me to where I am now, I feel I cannot let them down. It is my responsibility to succeed in school and life and to take care of them in their old age."

—First-year college student, quoted in Nunez (2005)

"Getting the [college] degree meant more to me than an NCAA title, being named All-American or winning an Olympic gold medal."

—Patrick Ewing, Hall of Fame basketball player, and college graduate (Georgetown University)

◆ The Importance of the First Year of College

Your movement into higher education represents an important life transition. Somewhat similar to an immigrant moving to a new country, you're moving into a new culture with different expectations, regulations, customs, and language (Chaskes, 1996) (See the Glossary and Dictionary of College Vocabulary at the end of this book for "translations" of the new language that is used in the college culture.)

The *first* year of college is undoubtedly the most important year of the college experience because it's a stage of *transition*. During the first year of college, students report the most change, the most learning, and the most development (Flowers, et al., 2001; Doyle, Edison, & Pascarella, 1998; Light, 2001). Other research suggests that the academic habits students establish in their first year of college are likely to persist throughout their remaining years of college (Schilling, 2001). When graduating seniors look back at their college experience, many of them say that the first year was the time of greatest change and the time during which they made the most significant improvements in their approach to learning. Here is how one senior put it during a personal interview:

Pause for Reflection

Why have you decided to attend college?

Why did you decide to attend the college or university you're enrolled in now?

Interviewer: What have you learned about your approach to learning [in college]?

Student: I had to learn how to study. I went through high school with a 4.0 average. I didn't have to study. It was a breeze. I got to the university and there was no structure. No one took attendance to make sure I was in class. No one checked my homework. No one told me I had to do something. There were no quizzes on the readings. I did not work well with this lack of structure. It took my first year and a half to learn to deal with it. But I had to teach myself to manage my time. I had to teach myself how to study. I had to teach myself how to learn in a different environment (Chickering & Schlossberg, 1998, p. 47).

In many ways, the first-year experience in college is similar to ocean surfing or downhill skiing: it can be filled with many exciting thrills, but there's also a risk of taking some dangerous spills. The first year is also the stage of the college experience during which students experience the most stress, the most academic difficulties, and the highest withdrawal rate (American College Testing, 2009; Bartlett, 2002; Sax, Bryant, & Gilmartin, 2004). The ultimate goal of downhill skiing and surfing is to experience the thrills, avoid the spills, and finish the run while you're still standing. The same is true for the first year of college; studies show that if you can complete your first-year experience in good standing, your chances for successfully completing college improve dramatically (American College Testing, 2009).

In a nutshell, your college success will depend on what you for yourself and how you take advantage of what your college can do for you. You'll find that the research cited and the advice provided in this book point to one major conclusion: Success in college depends on you—you make it happen by what you do and how well you capitalize on the resources available to you.

After reviewing 40 years of research on how college affects students, two distinguished researched the following conclusion:

> The impact of college is largely determined by individual effort and involvement in the academic, interpersonal, and extracurricular [co-curricular] offerings on a campus. Students are not passive recipients of institutional efforts to "educate" or "change" them, but rather bear major responsibility for any gains they derive from their postsecondary [college] experience (Pascarella & Terenzini, 2005, p. 602).

> "What students do during college counts more than who they are or where they go to college."
>
> –George Kuh, author, *Student Success in College*

> "Some people make things happen, while others watch things happen or wonder what has happened."
>
> –Author unknown

Compared to your previous schooling, college will provide with a broader range of courses, more resources to capitalize on, more freedom of choice, and more decision-making opportunities. Your own college experience will differ from any other college student because you have the freedom to actively shape or create it in a way that is uniquely your own. Don't let college happen *to* you; make it happen *for* you—take charge of your college experience and take advantage of the college resources that are at your command.

Importance of a Student Success Course (also known as a First-Year Experience Course)

If you're reading this book, you are already beginning to take charge of your college experience because you're enrolled in a course that's designed to promote your college success. Research strongly indicates that new students who participate in student-success courses are more likely to stay continue in college until they complete their degree and perform at a higher level. These positive effects have been found for:

- All types of students (under-prepared and well-prepared, minority and majority, residential and commuter, male and female),
- Students at all types of colleges (2-year and 4-year, public and private),
- Students attending college of different sizes (small, mid-sized, and large), and
- Students attending college in different locations (urban, suburban, and rural).

(References: Barefoot et al., 1998; Boudreau & Kromrey, 1994; Cuseo & Barefoot, 1996; Fidler & Godwin, 1994; Glass & Garrett, 1995; Grunder & Hellmich, 1996; Hunter & Linder, 2005; Porter & Swing, 2006; Shanley & Witten, 1990; Sidle & McReynolds, 1999; Starke, Harth, & Sirianni, 2001; Thomson, 1998; Tobolowski, 2005).

There has been more carefully conducted research on student-success or college-success courses, and more evidence supporting their effectiveness for promoting success, than there is for any other course in the college curriculum. You're fortunate to be enrolled in this course, so give it your best effort and take full advantage of what it has to offer. If you do, you'll be taking an important first step toward thriving in college and beyond.

Enjoy the trip!

Touching All the Bases

An Overview and Preview of the Most Powerful
Principles of College Success

ACTIVATE YOUR THINKING | **Journal Entry** | **1.1**

1. How do you think college will be different from high school?

_____

_____

_____

2. What do you think it will take to be successful in college? (What personal
   characteristics, qualities, or strategies do you feel are most important for
   college success?)

_____

_____

_____

3. How well do you expect to do in your first term of college? Why?

_____

_____

_____

_____

LEARNING GOAL

To equip you with a set of
powerful success strategies
that you can use imme-
diately to get off to a fast
start in college and can
use continually throughout
your college experience to
achieve success.

The Most Powerful Research-Based
Principles of College Success

Research on human learning and student development indicates four powerful
principles of college success:

1. Active involvement;
2. Use of campus resources;
3. Interpersonal interaction and collaboration; and
4. Personal reflection and self-awareness (Astin, 1993; Kuh, 2000; Light,
   2001; Pascarella & Terenzini, 1991, 2005; Tinto, 1993).

These four principles represent the bases of college success. They are introduced and examined carefully in this opening chapter for two reasons:

1. You can put them into practice to establish good habits for early success in college.
2. These principles represent the foundational bases for the success strategies recommended throughout this book.

The four bases of college success can be represented visually by a baseball diamond (see **Figure 1.1**).

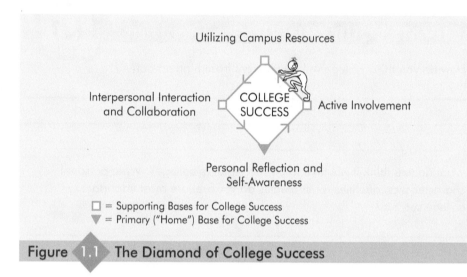

Utilizing Campus Resources

Interpersonal Interaction and Collaboration

COLLEGE SUCCESS

Active Involvement

Personal Reflection and Self-Awareness

☐ = Supporting Bases for College Success
▼ = Primary ("Home") Base for College Success

Figure   1.1   The Diamond of College Success

◆ Touching the First Base of College Success: Active Involvement

Research indicates that active involvement may be the most powerful principle of human learning and college success (Astin, 1993; Kuh, 2000). The bottom line is this: To maximize your success in college, you cannot be a passive spectator; you need to be an active player in the learning process.

The principle of active involvement includes the following pair of processes:

- The amount of personal time you devote to learning in the college experience;
- The degree of personal effort or energy (mental and physical) you put into the learning process.

Think of something you do with intensity, passion, and commitment. If you were to approach academic work in the same way, you would be faithfully implementing the principle of active involvement.

One way to ensure that you're actively involved in the learning process and putting forth high levels of energy or effort is to act on what you are learning. You can engage in any of the following actions to ensure that you are investing a high level of effort and energy:

- **Writing.** Express what you're trying to learn in print.
  Action: Write notes when reading rather than passively underlining sentences.

Student Perspective

"You don't have to be smart to work hard."

–24-year-old, first-year student who has returned to college

- **Speaking.** Express what you're trying to learn orally.
  Action: Explain a course concept to a study-group partner rather than just looking over it silently.
- **Organizing.** Group or classify ideas you're learning into logical categories.
  Action: Create an outline, diagram, or concept map (e.g., see Figure 1.1) to visually connect ideas.

The following section explains how you can apply both components of active involvement—spending time and expending energy—to the major learning challenges that you will encounter in college.

Time Spent in Class

Since the total amount of time you spend on learning is associated with how much you learn and how successfully you learn, this association leads to a straightforward recommendation: Attend all class sessions in all your courses. It may be tempting to skip or cut classes because college professors are less likely to monitor your attendance or take roll than your teachers were in high school. However, don't let this new freedom fool you into thinking that missing classes will have no effect on your grades. Over the past 75 years, many research studies in many types of courses have shown a direct relationship between class attendance and course grades—as one goes up or down, so does the other (Anderson & Gates, 2002; Devadoss & Foltz, 1996; Grandpre, 2000; Launius, 1997; Moore, 2003, 2006; Moore et al., 2003; Shimoff & Catania, 2001; Wiley, 1992; Wyatt, 1992). **Figure 1.2** represents the results of a study conducted at the City Colleges of Chicago, which shows the relationship between students' class attendance during the first 5 weeks of the term and their final course grades.

> "It is not so much what the individual thinks or feels but what the individual does, how he or she behaves, that defines and identifies involvement."
>
> –Alexander Astin, professor emeritus at University of California, Los Angeles, identified as the "most frequently cited author" in higher education and the person "most admired for creative insightful thinking"

© GreenstockCreative, 2010. Under license from Shutterstock, Inc.

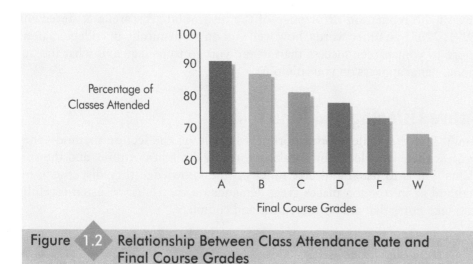

Figure **1.2** **Relationship Between Class Attendance Rate and Final Course Grades**

Student Perspective

"My biggest recommendation: GO TO CLASS. I learned this the hard way my first semester. You'll be surprised what you pick up just by being there. I wish someone would have informed me of this before I started school."

–Advice to new students from a college sophomore (Walsh, 2005)

Time Spent on Coursework Outside the Classroom

You will spend fewer hours per week sitting in class than you did in high school. However, you will be expected to spend more time on your own on academic work. Studies clearly show that when college students spend more time on academic work outside of class the result is better learning and higher grades (National Survey of Student Engagement, 2003). For example, one study of more than 25,000 college students found that the percentage of students receiving mostly A grades was almost three times higher for students who spent 40 or more hours per week on academic work than it was for students who spent between 20 and 40 hours. Among students who spent 20 or fewer hours per week on academic work, the percentage receiving grades that were mostly Cs or below was almost twice as high as it was for students who spent 40 or more hours on academic work (Pace, 1990a, 1990b).

Unfortunately, more than 80 percent of beginning college students report having studied 10 or fewer hours per week during their final year in high school and just 3 percent report studying more than 20 hours per week (Sax, Lindholm, Astin, Korn, & Mahoney, 2004). In addition, only 20 percent expect to spend more than 25 hours per week studying throughout college (National Survey of Student Engagement, 2005). This has to change if new college students are to earn good grades.

If you need further motivation to achieve good grades, keep in mind that higher grades during college result in higher chances of career success after college. Research on college graduates indicates that the higher their college grades, the higher

- The status (prestige) of their first job;
- Their job mobility (ability to change jobs or move into different positions); and
- Their total earnings (salary).

Thus, the more you learn, the more you'll earn. This relationship between college grades and career success exists for students at all types of colleges and universities regardless of the reputation or prestige of the institution (Pascarella & Terenzini, 1991, 2005). In other words, how well you do academically in college matters more to your career success than where you go to college and what institutional name appears on your diploma.

Active Listening and Note Taking

You'll find that college professors rely heavily on the lecture method—they profess their knowledge by speaking for long stretches of time, and the students' job is to listen and take notes on the knowledge they dispense. This method of instruction places great demands on the ability to listen carefully and take notes that are both accurate and complete.

Remember

Research shows that, in all subject areas, most test questions on college exams come from the professor's lectures and that students who take better class notes get better course grades (Brown, 1988; Kiewra, 2000).

The best way to apply the principle of active involvement during a class lecture is to engage in the physical action of writing notes. Writing down

Student Perspective

"In high school, you were a dork if you got good grades and cared about what was going on in your class. In college, you're a dork if you don't."

–College sophomore (Appleby, 2008)

Pause for Reflection

In high school, how many hours per week did you spend on schoolwork outside of class during your senior year?

Student Perspective

"I thought I would get a better education if the school had a really good reputation. Now, I think one's education depends on how much effort you put into it."

–First-year college student (Bates, 1994)

Student Perspective

"I never had a class before where the teacher just stands up and talks to you. He says something and you're writing it down, but then he says something else."

–First-year college student (Erickson & Strommer, 1991)

what your instructor is saying in class "forces" you to pay closer attention to what is being said and reinforces your retention of what was said. By taking notes, you not only hear the information (auditory memory) but also see it on paper (visual memory) and feel it in the muscles of your hand as you write it (motor memory).

> ### ! Remember
>
> Your role in the college classroom is not to be a passive spectator or an absorbent sponge that sits back and simply soaks up information through osmosis. Instead, your role is more like an aggressive detective or investigative reporter who's on a search-and-record mission. You need to actively search for information by picking your instructor's brain, picking out your instructor's key points, and recording your "pickings" in your notebook.

See **Box 1.1** for top strategies on classroom listening and note taking, which you should put into practice immediately.

> *"All genuine learning is active, not passive. It is a process in which the student is the main agent, not the teacher."*
>
> –Mortimer Adler, American professor of philosophy and educational theorist

Take Action!

Listening and Note Taking   1.1

One of the tasks that you will be expected to perform at the start of your first term in college is taking notes in class. Studies show that professors' lecture notes are the number one source of test questions (and test answers) on college exams. Get off to a fast start by using the following strategies to improve the quality of your note taking:

1. Get to every class. Whether or not your instructors take roll, you're responsible for all material covered in class. Remember that a full load of college courses (15 units) only requires that you be in class about 13 hours per week. If you consider your classwork to be a full-time job that only requires you to show up about 13 hours a week, that's a sweet deal, and it's a deal that allows more educational freedom than you had in high school. To miss a session when you're required to spend so little time in class per week is an abuse of your educational freedom. It's also an abuse of the money you, your family, or taxpaying American citizens pay to support your college education.

2. Get to every class on time. The first few minutes of a class session often contain valuable information, such as reminders, reviews, and previews.

© Joanne Harris and Daniel Bubnich, 2010. Under license from Shutterstock, Inc.

3. Get organized. Arrive at class with the right equipment; get a separate notebook for each class, write your name on it, date each class session, and store all class handouts in it.

4. Get in the right position.
   - The ideal place to sit—front and center of the room, where you can hear and see most effectively;
   - The ideal posture—upright and leaning forward, because your body influences your mind; if your body is in an alert and ready position, your mind is likely to follow;
   - The ideal position socially—near people who will not distract your focus of attention or detract from the quality of your note taking.

Remember

These attention-focusing strategies are particularly important during the first year of college, when class sizes tend to be larger. In a large class, individuals tend to feel more anonymous, which can reduce their sense of personal responsibility and their drive to stay focused and actively involved. Thus, in large-class settings, it's especially important to use effective strategies that eliminate distractions (such as those described in Chapter 4) and attention drift.

5. Get in the right frame of mind. Get psyched up; come to class with attitude—an attitude that you're going to pick your instructor's brain, pick up answers to test questions, and pick up your grade.

6. Get it down (in writing). Actively look, listen, and record important points at all times in class. Pay special attention to whatever information instructors put in writing, whether it is on the board, on a slide, or in a handout.

7. Don't let go of your pen. When in doubt, write it out; it's better to have it and not need it than to need it and not have it.

Remember

Most college professors do not write all important information on the board for you; instead, they expect you to listen carefully to what they're saying and write it down for yourself.

8. Finish strong. The last few minutes of class often contain valuable information, such as reminders, reviews, and previews.

9. Stick around. As soon as class ends, don't immediately bolt; instead, hang out for a few moments to briefly review your notes (by yourself or with a classmate). If you find any gaps, check them out with your instructor before he or she leaves the classroom. This quick end-of-class review will help your brain retain the information it just received.

Note: For more detailed information on listening and note taking, see Chapter 5.

Finish class with a rush of attention, not a rush out the door!

Active Class Participation

You can become actively involved in the college classroom by arriving at class prepared (e.g., having done the assigned reading), by asking relevant questions, and by contributing thoughtful comments during class discussions. When you communicate orally, you elevate the level of active involvement you invest in the learning process because speaking requires you to exert both mental energy (thinking about what you are going to say) and physical energy (moving your lips to say it). Thus, class participation will increase your ability to stay alert and attentive in class. It also sends a clear message to the instructor that you are a motivated student who takes the course seriously and wants to learn. Since class participation accounts for a portion of your final grade in many courses, your attentiveness and involvement in class can have a direct, positive effect on your course grade.

Pause for Reflection

When you enter a classroom, where do you usually sit?

Why do you sit there? Is it a conscious choice or more like an automatic habit?

Do you think that your usual seat places you in the best possible position for listening and learning in the classroom?

Active Reading

Writing not only promotes active listening in class but also can promote active reading out of class. Taking notes on information that you're reading, or on information you've highlighted while reading, helps keep you actively involved in the reading process because it requires more mental and physical energy than merely reading the material or passively highlighting sentences. (See **Box 1.2** for top strategies for reading college textbooks that you should put into practice immediately.)

Top Strategies: Improving Textbook-Reading Comprehension and Retention

If you haven't already acquired textbooks for your courses, get them immediately and get ahead on your reading assignments. Information from reading assignments ranks right behind lecture notes as a source of test questions on college exams. Your professors are likely to deliver class lectures with the expectation that you have done the assigned reading and can build on that knowledge when they're lecturing. If you haven't done the reading, you'll have more difficulty following and taking notes on what your instructor is saying in class. Thus, by not doing the reading you pay a double penalty. College professors also expect you to relate or connect what they talk about in class to the reading they have assigned. Thus, it's important to start developing good reading habits now. You can do so by using the following strategies to improve your reading comprehension and retention.

Student Perspective

"I recommend that you read the first chapters right away because college professors get started promptly with assigning certain readings. Classes in college move very fast because, unlike high school, you do not attend class five times a week but two or three times a week."

–Advice to new college students from a first-year student

1. Come fully equipped.
   - Writing tool and storage—Always bring a writing tool (pen, pencil, or keyboard) to record important information and a storage space (notebook or computer) in which you can save and retrieve information acquired from your reading for later use on tests and assignments.
   - Dictionary—Have a dictionary nearby to quickly find the meaning of unfamiliar words that may interfere with your ability to comprehend what you're reading. Looking up definitions of unfamiliar words does more than help you understand what you're reading; it's also an effective way to build your vocabulary. Building your vocabulary will improve your reading comprehension in all college courses, as well as your performance on standardized tests, such as those required for admission to graduate and professional schools.
   - Glossary of terms—Check the back of your textbook for a list of key terms included in the book. Each academic subject or discipline has its own vocabulary, and knowing the meaning of these terms is often the key to understanding the concepts covered in the text. Don't ignore the glossary; it's more than an ancillary or afterthought to the textbook. Use it regularly to increase your comprehension of course concepts. Consider making a photocopy of the glossary of terms at the back of your textbook so that you can have a copy of it in front of you while you're reading, rather than having to repeatedly stop, hold your place, and go to the back of the text to find the glossary.

2. **Get in the right position.** Sit upright and have light coming from behind you, over the side of your body opposite your writing hand. This will reduce the distracting and fatiguing effects of glare and shadows.

3. **Get a sneak preview.** Approach the chapter by first reading its boldface headings and any chapter outline, summary, or end-of-chapter questions that may be provided. This will supply you with a mental map of the chapter's important ideas before you start your reading trip and provide an overview that will help you keep track of the chapter's major ideas (the "big picture"), thereby reducing the risk that you'll get lost among the smaller, more details you encounter along the way.

4. **Use boldface headings and subheadings.** Headings are cues for important information. Turn them into questions, and then read to find their answers. This will launch you on an answer-finding mission that will keep you mentally active while reading and enable you to read with a purpose. Turning headings into questions is also a good way to prepare for tests because you're practicing exactly what you'll be expected to do on tests—answer questions.

5. **Pay attention to the first and last sentences.** Absorb opening and closing sentences in sections beneath the chapter's major headings and subheadings. These sentences often contain an important introduction and conclusion to the material covered within that section of the text.

1.2

6. Finish each of your reading sessions with a short review. Recall what you have highlighted or noted as important information (rather than trying to cover a few more pages). It's best to use the last few minutes of reading time to "lock in" the most important information you've just read because most forgetting takes place immediately after you stop processing (taking in) information and start doing something else.

Source: Underwood (1983).

> **Remember**
>
> Your goal while reading should be to discover or uncover the most important information contained in what you're reading; when you finish reading, your final step should be to reread (and lock in) the key information you discovered while reading.

Note: More detailed information on reading comprehension and retention is provided in Chapter 5.

◆ Touching the Second Base of College Success: Use of Campus Resources

Your campus environment contains multiple resources designed to support your quest for educational and personal success. Studies show that students who use campus resources report higher levels of satisfaction with college and get more out of the college experience (Pascarella & Terenzini, 1991, 2005).

> **Remember**
>
> Involvement with campus services is not just valuable but also "free"; the cost of these services has already been covered by your college tuition. By investing time and energy in campus resources, you not only increase your prospects for personal success but also maximize the return on your financial investment in college—that is, you get a bigger bang for your buck.

> "Do not be a PCP (Parking Lot→ Classroom→ Parking Lot) student. The time you spend on campus will be a sound investment in your academic and professional success."
>
> –Drew Appleby, professor of psychology

Your Campus Resources

Using your campus resources is an important, research-backed principle of college success, and it is a natural extension of the principle of active involvement. Successful students are active learners inside and outside the classroom, and this behavior extends to active use of campus resources. An essential first step toward putting this principle into practice is to become fully aware of all key support services that are available on campus.

> "The impact of college is not simply the result of what a college does for or to a student. Rather, the impact is a result of the extent to which an individual student exploits the people, programs, facilities, opportunities, and experiences that the college makes available."
>
> –Earnest Pascarella and Patrick Terenzini, *How College Affects Students*

◆ Offices and Centers on Campus

Several offices and centers at your college are designed to directly support your college experience. The following sections describe key campus services.

Learning Center (a.k.a. Academic Support or Academic Success Center)

An Academic Support or Learning Center is your campus resource for learning assistance to support and strengthen your academic performance. The personal and group tutoring provided by this campus service can help you master difficult course concepts and assignments, and the people working at this center are professionally trained to help you learn how to learn. While your professors may have expert knowledge of the subject matter they teach, learning resource specialists are experts on the process of learning. For instance, these specialists can show you how you could adjust or modify your learning strategies to meet the unique demands of different courses and teaching styles you encounter in college.

Studies show that college students who become actively involved with academic support services outside the classroom are more likely to attain higher grades and complete their college degree. This is particularly true if they began their involvement with these support services during the first year of college (Cuseo, 2003a). Also, students who seek and receive assistance from the Learning Center show significant improvement in academic self-efficacy—that is, they develop a stronger sense of personal control over their academic performance and higher expectations for academic success (Smith, Walter, & Hoey, 1992).

Despite the powerful advantages of using academic support services, these services are typically underused by college students, especially by those students who are likely to gain the most from using them (Knapp & Karabenick, 1988; Walter & Smith, 1990). This is probably because some students believe that seeking academic help is admitting they are not smart, self-sufficient, or unable to succeed on their own. Do not buy into this belief system. Using academic support services doesn't mean you're helpless or clueless; instead, it indicates that you're a motivated and resourceful student who is striving to achieve academic excellence.

Remember

The purpose of the Learning Center or Academic Support Center is not just to provide remedial repair work for academically underprepared learners or to supply academic life support for students on the verge of flunking out. It's a place where all learners benefit, including students who are well prepared and highly motivated.

Writing Center

Many college campuses offer specialized support for students who would like to improve their writing skills. Typically referred to as the Writing Center, this is the place where you can receive assistance at any stage of the writing process, whether it be collecting and organizing your ideas in outline form, composing your first draft, or proofreading your final draft. Since writing is an academic skill that you will use in many of your courses, if you improve your writing, you're likely to improve your overall academic performance. Thus, we strongly encourage you to capitalize on this campus resource.

Disability Services (a.k.a. Office for Students with Special Needs)

If you have a physical or learning disability that is interfering with your performance in college, or think you may have such a disability, Disability Services is the campus resource to consult for assistance and support. Programs and services typically provided by this office include:

- Assessment for learning disabilities;
- Verification of eligibility for disability support services;
- Authorization of academic accommodations for students with disabilities; and
- Specialized counseling, advising, and tutoring.

College Library

The library is your campus resource for finding information and completing research assignments (e.g., term papers and group projects). Librarians are professional educators who provide instruction outside the classroom. You can learn from them just as you can learn from faculty inside the classroom. Furthermore, the library is a place where you can acquire skills for locating, retrieving, and evaluating information that you may apply to any course you are taking or will ever take.

"

"The next best thing to knowing something is knowing where to find it."

–Dr. Samuel Johnson, English literary figure and original author of the *Dictionary of the English Language (1747)*

Your college library is your campus resource for developing research skills that let you access, retrieve, and evaluate information, which are skills for achieving both educational and occupational success.

Copyright © by Scott Arthur Masear. Reprinted with permission.

"WHEN DID THEY START USING A SEARCH ENGINE?"

Academic Advisement Center

Whether or not you have an assigned academic advisor, the Academic Advisement Center is a campus resource for help with course selection, educational planning, and choosing or changing a major. Studies show that college students who have developed clear educational and career goals are more likely to continue their

© Monkey Business Images, 2010. Under license from Shutterstock, Inc.

college education and complete their college degree (Willingham, 1985; Wyckoff, 1999). However, most beginning college students need help clarifying their educational goals, selecting an academic major, and exploring careers (Cuseo, 2005; Frost, 1991). As a first-year college student, being undecided or uncertain about your educational and career goals is nothing to be embarrassed about. However, you should start thinking about your future now. Connect early and often with an academic advisor to help you clarify your educational goals and choose a field of study that best complements your interests, talents, and values.

Office of Student Life (a.k.a. Office of Student Development)

The Office of Student Life is your campus resource for student development opportunities outside the classroom, including student clubs and organizations, recreational programs, leadership activities, and volunteer experiences. Learning experiences in college can occur inside or outside the classroom. Research consistently shows that out-of-class learning experiences are as important to your overall development as the course curriculum (Kuh, 1995; Kuh, Douglas, Lund, & Ramin-Gyurnek, 1994); hence, they are best referred to as "cocurricular" experiences rather than "extracurricular" activities. More specifically, studies show students who become actively involved in campus life are more likely to:

* Enjoy their college experience;
* Graduate from college; and
* Develop leadership skills that are useful in the world of work beyond college (Astin, 1993).

Devoting some out-of-class time to these cocurricular activities and programs should not interfere with your academic performance. Keep in mind that in college you'll be spending much less time in the classroom than you did in high school. As mentioned previously, a full load of college courses (15 units) only requires that you be in class about 13 hours per week. This leaves enough out-of-class time for other campus activities. Evidence indicates that college students who become involved in cocurricular, volunteer, and part-time work experiences outside the classroom that total *no more than 15 hours per week* earn higher grades than students who do not get involved in any out-of-class activities (Pascarella, 2001; Pascarella & Terenzini, 2005).

Try to get involved in cocurricular experiences on your campus, but limit yourself to participating in no more than two or three major campus organizations at any one time. Restricting the number of your out-of-class activities should enable you to keep up with your studies, and it's likely to be more impressive to future schools or employers, because a long list of involvement in numerous activities may suggest you're padding your resume with things you never did or did superficially.

"Just a [long] list of club memberships is meaningless; it's a fake front. Remember that quality, not quantity, is what counts."

—Lauren Pope, director of the National Bureau for College Placement

Remember

Cocurricular experiences are also resume-building experiences, and campus professionals with whom you interact regularly while participating in cocurricular activities (e.g., the director of student activities or dean of students) are valuable resources for personal references and letters of recommendation to future schools or employers.

Financial Aid Office

Consider the campus resource designed to help you finance your college education: the Financial Aid Office. If you have questions concerning how to obtain assistance in paying for college, the staff of this office is there to guide you through the application process. The paperwork needed to apply for and secure financial aid can sometimes be confusing or overwhelming. Don't let this intimidate you from seeking financial aid, because assistance is available to you from the knowledgeable staff in the Financial Aid Office. You can also seek help from this office to find:

- Part-time employment on campus through a work–study program;
- Low-interest student loans;
- Grants; and
- Scholarships.

If you have any doubt about whether you are using the most effective plan for financing your college education, make an appointment to see a profession in your Financial Aid Office.

Counseling Center

Counseling services can provide you with a valuable source of support in college, not only helping you cope with college stressors that may be interfering with your academic success but also helping you realize your full potential. Personal counseling can promote your self-awareness and self-development in social and emotional areas of your life that are important for mental health, physical wellness, and personal growth.

> **Remember**
>
> College counseling is not just for students who are experiencing emotional problems. It's for all students who want to enrich their overall quality of life.

Health Center

Making the transition from high school to college often involves adjustments and decisions affecting your health and wellness. In addition to making your own decisions about what to eat and when to sleep, your level of stress is likely to increase during times of change or transition in your life. Good health habits are one effective way to both cope with college stress and reach peak levels of performance. The Health Center on your campus is the resource for information on how to manage your health and maintain wellness. It is also the place to go for help with physical illnesses, sexually transmitted infections or diseases, and eating disorders.

Career Development Center (a.k.a. Career Center)

Research on college students indicates that they are more likely to stay in school and graduate when they have some sense of how their present academic experience relates to their future career goals (Levitz & Noel, 1989). Studies also show that most new students are uncertain about the career they would like to pursue (Gordon & Steele, 2003). If you are uncertain about a career,

"*Among any population of young adults who are just beginning in earnest their search for adult identity, it would be surprising indeed if one found that most were very clear about their long-term goals. The college years are an important growing period in which new social and intellectual experiences are sought as a means of coming to grips with the issue of adult careers. Students enter college with the hope that they will be able to formulate for themselves a meaningful answer to that important question.*"

–Vincent Tinto, nationally known scholar on student success

welcome to the club. This uncertainty is normal because you haven't had the opportunity for hands-on work experience in the real world of careers.

The Career Development Center is the place to go for help in finding a meaningful answer to the important question of how to connect your current college experience with your future career goals. This campus resource typically provides such services as personal career counseling, workshops on career exploration and development, and career fairs where you are able to meet professionals working in different fields. Although it may seem like the beginning of your career is light-years away because you're just starting college, the process of exploring, planning, and preparing for career success begins in the first year of college.

◆ Touching the Third Base of College Success: Interpersonal Interaction and Collaboration

Learning is strengthened when it takes place in a social context that involves interpersonal interaction. As some scholars put it, human knowledge is socially constructed, or built through interaction and dialogue with others. According to these scholars, your interpersonal conversations become mentally internalized (represented in your mind) and are shaped by the dialogue you've had with others (Bruffee, 1993). Thus, by having frequent, intelligent conversations with others, you broaden your knowledge and deepen your thinking.

Four particular forms of interpersonal interaction have been found to be strongly associated with student learning and motivation in college:

1. Student–faculty interaction
2. Student–advisor interaction
3. Student–mentor interaction
4. Student–student (peer) interaction

Pause for Reflection

Look back at the major campus resources that have been mentioned in this section. Which two or three of them do you think you should use immediately?

Why have you identified these resources as your top priorities at this time?

Consider asking your course instructor or academic advisor for recommendations about what campus resources you should consult during your first term on campus.

Interaction with Faculty Members

Studies repeatedly show that college success is influenced heavily by the quality and quantity of student–faculty interaction *outside the classroom*. Such contact is positively associated with the following positive outcomes for college students:

- Improved academic performance;
- Increased critical thinking skills;
- Greater satisfaction with the college experience;
- Increased likelihood of completing a college degree; and
- Stronger desire to seek education beyond college (Astin, 1993; Pascarella & Terenzini, 1991, 2005).

These positive results are so strong and widespread that we encourage you to seek interaction with college faculty outside of class time. Here are some of the most manageable ways to increase your out-of-class contact with college instructors during the first year of college.

1. Approach your instructors immediately after class.

If you are interested in talking about something that was just discussed in class, your instructor will likely be most interested in discussing it with you as soon as the class session ends. Furthermore, interaction with your instructor immediately after class can help the professor get to know you as an individual, which should increase your confidence and willingness to seek subsequent contact.

2. Seek interaction with your course instructors during their office hours.

One of the most important pieces of information on a course syllabus is your instructor's office hours. Make note of these office hours, and make an earnest attempt to capitalize on them. College professors spend most of their professional time outside the classroom preparing for class, grading papers, conducting research, and serving on college committees. However, some of their out-of-class time is reserved specifically for office hours during which they are expected to be available.

You can schedule an office visit with your instructor during the early stages of the course. You can use this time to discuss course assignments, term-paper topics, and career options in your instructor's field. Try to make at least one visit to the office of each of your instructors, preferably early in the term, when quality time is easier to find, rather than at midterm, when major exams and assignments begin to pile up.

Even if your early contact with instructors is only for a few minutes, it can be a valuable icebreaker that helps your instructors get to know you as a person and helps you feel more comfortable interacting with them in the future.

3. Contact your instructors through e-mail.

Electronic communication is another effective way to interact with an instructor, particularly if that professor's office hours conflict with your class schedule, work responsibilities, or family commitments. If you are a commuter student who does not live on campus, or if you are an adult student who is juggling family and work commitments and your academic schedule, e-mail communication may be an especially effective and efficient mode of interaction for you. If you're shy or hesitant about "invading" your professor's office space, e-mail can provide a less threatening way to interact and may give you the self-confidence to seek face-to-face contact with an instructor. In one national survey, almost half of college students reported that e-mail has allowed them to communicate their ideas with professors on subjects that they would not have discussed in person (Pew Internet & American Life Project, 2002).

Interaction with an Advisor

An academic advisor can be an effective referral agent who can direct you to, and connect you with, campus support services that best meet your needs. An advisor can also help you understand college procedures and navigate the bureaucratic maze of college policies and politics.

Student Perspective

"I wish that I would have taken advantage of professors' open-door policies when I had questions, because actually understanding what I was doing, instead of guessing, would have saved me a lot of stress and re-doing what I did wrong the first time."

—College sophomore (Walsh, 2005)

> ### ❗ Remember
>
> An academic advisor is not someone you see just once per term when you need to get a signature for class scheduling and course registration. An advisor is someone you should visit more regularly than your course instructors. Your instructors will change from term to term, but your academic advisor may be the one professional on campus with whom you have regular contact and a stable, ongoing relationship throughout your college experience.

Your academic advisor should be someone whom you feel comfortable speaking with, someone who knows your name, and someone who's familiar with your personal interests and abilities. Give your advisor the opportunity to get to know you personally, and seek your advisor's input on courses, majors, and personal issues that may be affecting your academic performance.

If you have been assigned an advisor and you find that you cannot develop a good relationship with this person, ask the director of advising or academic dean if you could be assigned to someone else. Ask other students about their advising experience and whether they know any advisors they can recommend to you.

If your college does not assign you a personal advisor but offers drop-by or drop-in advising, you may see a different advisor each time you visit the center. If you are not satisfied with this system of multiple advisors, find one advisor with whom you feel most comfortable and make that person your personal advisor by scheduling your appointments in advance. This will enable you to consistently connect with the same advisor and develop an ongoing relationship.

Pause for Reflection

Do you have a personally assigned advisor?

If yes, do you know who this person is and where he or she can be found?

If no, do you know where to go if you have questions about your class schedule or academic plans?

Interaction with a Mentor

A mentor may be described as an experienced guide who takes personal interest in you and the progress you're making toward your goals. (For example, in the movie *Star Wars*, Yoda served as a mentor for Luke Skywalker.) Research in higher education demonstrates that a mentor can make first-year students feel significant and enable them to stay on track until they complete their college degree (Campbell & Campbell, 1997; Knox, 2008). A mentor can assist you in troubleshooting difficult or complicated issues that you may not be able to resolve on your own and is someone with whom you can share good news, such as your success stories and personal accomplishments. Look for someone on campus with whom you can develop this type of trusting relationship. Many people on campus have the potential to be outstanding mentors, including the following:

- Your instructor in a first-year seminar or experience course
- Faculty in your intended major
- Juniors, seniors, or graduate students in your intended field of study
- Working professionals in careers that interest you

- Academic support professionals (e.g., professional tutors in the Learning Center)
- Career counselors
- Personal counselors
- Learning assistance professionals (e.g., from the Learning Center)
- Student development professionals (e.g., the director of student life or residential life)
- Campus minister or chaplain
- Financial aid counselors or advisor

Interaction with Peers (Student–Student Interaction)

Studies of college students repeatedly point to the power of the peer group as a source of social and academic support (Pascarella, 2005). One study of more than 25,000 college students revealed that when peers interact with one another while learning they achieve higher levels of academic performance and are more likely to persist to degree completion (Astin, 1993). In another study that involved in-depth interviews with more than 1,600 college students, it was discovered that almost all students who struggled academically had one particular study habit in common: They always studied alone (Light, 2001).

Peer interaction is especially important during the first term of college. At this stage of the college experience, new students have a strong need for belongingness and social acceptance because many of them have just left the lifelong security of family and hometown friends. As a new student, it may be useful to view your early stage of the college experience and academic performance in terms of the classic hierarchy model of human needs, developed by American psychologist Abraham Maslow (see **Figure 1.3**).

According to Maslow's model, humans cannot reach their full potential and achieve peak performance until their more basic emotional and social needs have been met (e.g., their needs for personal safety, social acceptance, and self-esteem). Making early connections with your peers helps you meet these basic human needs, provides you with a base of social support to ease your integration into the college community, and prepares you to move up to higher levels of the need hierarchy (e.g., achieving educational excellence and fulfilling your potential).

Studies repeatedly show that students who become socially integrated or connected with other members of the college community are more likely to complete their first year of college and continue on to complete their college degree (Tinto, 1993). (For effective ways to make these interpersonal connections, see **Box 1.3**.)

Pause for Reflection

Four categories of people have the potential to serve as mentors for you in college:

1. Experienced peers (to be discussed in the next section)

2. Faculty (instructors)

3. Administrators (e.g., office and program directors)

4. Staff (e.g., student support professionals and administrative assistants)

Think about your first interactions with faculty, staff, and administrators on campus. Do you recall anyone who impressed you as being approachable, personable, or helpful? If you did, make a note of that person's name in case you would like to seek out the person again. (If you haven't met such a person yet, when you do, be sure you remember that person because he or she may be an effective mentor for you.)

© Monkey Business Images, 2010. Under license from Shutterstock, Inc.

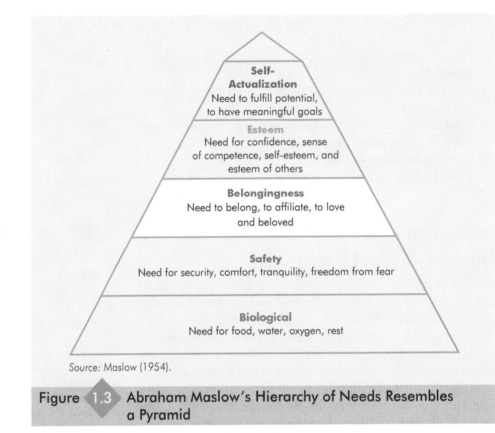

Source: Maslow (1954).

Figure 1.3   Abraham Maslow's Hierarchy of Needs Resembles a Pyramid

Take Action!

Making Connections with Members of Your College Community

Consider 10 tips for making important interpersonal connections in college. Start making these connections now so that you can begin constructing a base of social support that will strengthen your performance during your first term and, perhaps, throughout your college experience.

1. Connect with a favorite peer or student development professional that you may have met during orientation.
2. Connect with peers who live near you or who commute to school from the same commu-

nity in which you live. If your schedules are similar, consider carpooling together.

3. Join a college club, student organization, campus committee, intramural team, or volunteer-service group whose members may share the same personal or career interests as you.
4. Connect with a peer leader who has been trained to assist new students (e.g., peer tutor, peer mentor, or peer counselor) or with a peer who has more college experience than you (e.g., sophomore, junior, or senior).
5. Look for and connect with a motivated classmate in each of your classes, and try working as a team to take notes, complete reading assignments, and study for exams. (Look especially to team up with a peer who may be in more than one class with you.)

1.3

6. Connect with faculty members in a field that you're considering as a major by visiting them during office hours, conversing briefly with them after class, or communicating with them via e-mail.
7. Connect with an academic support professional in your college's Learning Center for personalized academic assistance or tutoring related to any course in which you'd like to improve your performance.
8. Connect with an academic advisor to discuss and develop your educational plans.

9. Connect with a college librarian to get early assistance and a head start on any research project that you've been assigned.
10. Connect with a personal counselor or campus minister to discuss any college-adjustment or personal-life issues that you may be experiencing.

Note: For more information on meeting people and forming friendships, see Chapter 8, **pp. 195–196.**

Getting involved with campus organizations or activities is one way to connect you with other students. Also, try to interact with students who have spent more time at college than you. Sophomores, juniors, and seniors can be valuable social resources for a new student. You're likely to find that they are willing to share their experiences with you because you have shown an interest in hearing what they have to say. You may even be the first person who has bothered to ask them what their experiences have been like on your campus. You can learn from their experiences by asking them which courses and instructors they would recommend or what advisors they found to be most well informed and personable.

!

Remember

Your peers can be more than competitors or a source of negative peer pressure; they can also be collaborators, a source of positive social influence, and a resource for college success. Be on the lookout for classmates who are motivated to learn and willing to learn with you, and keep an eye out for advanced students who are willing to assist you. Start building your social-support network by surrounding yourself with success-seeking and success-achieving students. They can be a stimulating source of positive peer power that drives you to higher levels of academic performance and heightens your motivational drive to complete college.

Collaboration with Peers

Simply defined, collaboration is the process of two or more people working interdependently toward a common goal (as opposed to working independently or competitively). Collaboration involves true teamwork, in which teammates support one another's success and take equal responsibility for helping the team move toward its shared goal. Research on students from kindergarten through college shows that when students collaborate in teams their academic performance and interpersonal skills improve dramatically (Cuseo, 1996).

"

"TEAM = Together Everyone Achieves More"

–Author unknown

Research shows that when peers work collaboratively to reach a common goal, they learn more effectively and achieve "higher levels" of thinking.

"Surround yourself with only people who are going to lift you higher."

–Oprah Winfrey, actress and talk-show host

To maximize the power of collaboration, use the following guidelines to make wise choices about teammates who will contribute positively to the quality and productivity of your learning team:

1. Observe your classmates with an eye toward identifying potentially good teammates. Look for fellow students who are motivated and who will likely contribute to your team's success, rather than those whom you suspect may just be hitchhikers looking for a free ride.

2. Don't team up exclusively with peers who are similar to you in terms of their personal characteristics, backgrounds, and experiences. Instead, include teammates who differ from you in age; gender; ethnic, racial, cultural or geographical background; learning style; and personality characteristics. Such variety brings different life experiences, styles of thinking, and learning strategies to your team, which enrich not only its diversity but its quality as well. If your team consists only of friends or classmates whose interests and lifestyles are similar to your own, this familiarity can interfere with your team's focus and performance because your common experiences can get you off track and on to topics that have nothing to do with the learning task (e.g., what you did last weekend or what you are planning to do next weekend).

Remember

Seek diversity; capitalize on the advantages of collaborating with peers with varied backgrounds and lifestyles. Simply stated, studies show that we learn more from people who are different from us than we do from people who are similar to us (Pascarella, 2001).

Keep in mind that learning teams are not simply study groups formed the night before an exam. Effective learning teams collaborate more regularly and work on more varied academic tasks than late-night study groups. For example, you can form note-taking teams, reading teams, or test results-reviews teams.

◆ Touching the Fourth (Home) Base of College Success: Personal Reflection and Self-Awareness

The final steps in the learning process, whether it be learning in the classroom or learning from experience, are to step back from the process, thoughtfully review it, and connect it to what you already know. Reflection may be defined as the flip side of active involvement; both processes are necessary for learning to be complete. Learning requires not only effortful action but also thoughtful reflection. Active involvement gets and holds your focus of attention, which enables information to reach your brain, and personal reflection promotes consolidation, which locks that information into your brain's long-term memory (Bligh, 2000; Broadbent, 1970). Brain research reveals that two brain-wave patterns are associated with the mental states of involvement and reflection (Bradshaw, 1995). The brain-wave pattern on the left in **Figure 1.4** reveal faster activity, indicating that the person is actively involved in the learning task and attending to it. The slower brain-wave pattern on the right in the figure indicates that the person is thinking deeply about information taken in, which will help consolidate or lock that information into long-term memory. Thus, effective learning combines active mental involvement (characterized by faster, shorter brain waves) with thoughtful reflection (characterized by slower, longer brain waves).

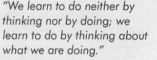

Faster Brain-Wave Pattern Associated with a Mental State of *Active Involvement*

Slower Brain-Wave Pattern Associated with a Mental State of *Reflective Thinking*

Figure 1.4

Personal reflection involves introspection—turning inward and inspecting yourself to gain deeper self-awareness of what you've done, what you're doing, or what you intend to do. Two forms of self-awareness are particularly important for success in college:

1. Self-assessment
2. Self-monitoring

Self-Assessment

Simply defined, self-assessment is the process of reflecting on and evaluating your personal characteristics, such as your personality traits, learning habits, and strengths or weaknesses. Self-assessment promotes self-awareness, which

Pause for Reflection

Think about the students in your classes this term. Are there any students who you might want to join with to form learning teams?

Do you have any classmates who are in more than one class with you and who might be good peer partners for the courses you have in common?

"

"We learn to do neither by thinking nor by doing; we learn to do by thinking about what we are doing."

–George Stoddard, former professor of psychology and education at the University of Iowa

is the critical first step in the process of self-improvement, personal planning, and effective decision making. The following are important target areas for self-assessment and self-awareness because they reflect personal characteristics that play a pivotal role in promoting success in college and beyond:

- **Personal interests.** What you like to do or enjoy doing;
- **Personal values.** What is important to you and what you care about doing;
- **Personal abilities or aptitudes.** What you do well or have the potential to do well;
- **Learning habits.** How you go about learning and the usual approaches, methods, or techniques you use to learn;
- **Learning styles.** How you prefer to learn; that is, the way you like to:
  - Receive information—which learning format you prefer (e.g., reading, listening, or experiencing);
  - Perceive information—which sensory modality you prefer (e.g., vision, sound, or touch);
  - Process information—how you mentally deal with information once you have taken it in (e.g., think about it on your own or discuss it with others).
- **Personality traits.** Your temperament, emotional characteristics, and social tendencies (e.g., whether you lean toward being outgoing or reserved);
- **Academic self-concept.** What kind of student you think you are and how you perceive yourself as a learner (e.g., your level of self-confidence and whether you believe success is within your control or depends on factors beyond your control).

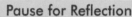

Pause for Reflection

How would you rate your academic self-confidence at this point in your college experience? (Circle one.)

very confident   somewhat confident
somewhat unconfident   very unconfident

Why did you make this choice?

Self-Monitoring

Research indicates that one characteristic of successful learners is that they monitor or watch themselves and maintain self-awareness of:

- Whether they are using effective learning strategies (e.g., they are aware of their level of attention or concentration in class);
- Whether they are comprehending what they are attempting to learn (e.g., they're understanding it at a deep level or merely memorizing it at a surface level); and
- How to regulate or adjust their learning strategies to meet the demands of different tasks or subjects (e.g., they read technical material in a science textbook more slowly and stop to test their understanding more often than when they're reading a novel; Pintrich, 1995; Weinstein, 1994; Weinstein & Meyer, 1991).

"*Successful students know a lot about themselves.*"

—Claire Weinstein and Debra Meyer, professors of educational psychology at the University of Texas

Remember

Successful students are self-aware learners who know their learning strategies, styles, strengths, and shortcomings.

You can begin to establish good self-monitoring habits by getting in the routine of periodically pausing to reflect on how you're going about learning and how you're "doing" college. For instance, consider these questions:

- Am I listening attentively to what my instructor is saying in class?
- Do I comprehend what I am reading outside of class?
- Am I effectively using campus resources that are designed to support my success?
- Am I interacting with campus professionals who can contribute to my current success and future development?
- Am I interacting and collaborating with peers who can contribute to my learning and increase my level of involvement in the college experience?
- Am I effectively implementing the success strategies identified in this book?

◆ Summary and Conclusion

Research reviewed in this chapter points to the conclusion that successful students are:

1. **Involved.** They invest time and effort in the college experience;
2. **Resourceful.** They capitalize on their surrounding resources;
3. **Interactive.** They interact and collaborate with others; and
4. **Reflective.** They are self-aware learners who assess and monitor their own performance.

> **Pause for Reflection**
>
> How would you rate your academic self-confidence at this point in your college experience? (Circle one.)
>
> very confident   somewhat confident
> somewhat unconfident   very unconfident
>
> Why?

Successful students are students who could honestly check almost every box in the following self-assessment checklist of success-promoting principles and practices.

A Checklist of Success-Promoting Principles and Practices

1. **Active Involvement**
   Inside the classroom:
   - ☑ **Get to class.** Treat it like a job; if you cut, your pay (grade) will be cut.
   - ☑ **Get involved in class.** Come prepared, listen actively, take notes, and participate.

   Outside the classroom:
   - ☑ **Read actively.** Take notes while you read to increase attention and retention.
   - ☑ **Double up.** Spend twice as much time on academic work outside the classroom than you spend in class—if you're a full-time student, that makes it a 40-hour academic workweek (with occasional "overtime").

2. **Use of Campus Resources**
   Capitalize on academic and student support services:
   - ☑ Learning Center
   - ☑ Writing Center

- ☑ Disability Services
- ☑ College library
- ☑ Academic Advisement Center
- ☑ Office of Student Life
- ☑ Financial Aid Office
- ☑ Counseling Center
- ☑ Health Center
- ☑ Career Development Center
- ☑ Experiential Learning Resources

3. **Interpersonal Interaction and Collaboration**
   Interact with the following people:
   - ☑ **Peers.** Join student clubs and participate in campus organizations.
   - ☑ **Faculty members.** Connect with professors and other faculty members immediately after class, in their offices, or via e-mail.
   - ☑ **Academic advisors.** See an advisor for more than just a signature to register; find an advisor you can relate to and with whom you can develop an ongoing relationship.
   - ☑ **Mentors.** Try to find experienced people on campus who can serve as trusted guides and role models.

   Collaborate by doing the following:
   - ☑ **Form learning teams.** Join not only last-minute study groups but also teams that collaborate more regularly to work on such tasks as taking lecture notes, completing reading and writing assignments, conducting library research, and reviewing results of exams or course assignments.
   - ☑ **Participate in learning communities.** Enroll in two or more classes with the same students during the same term.

4. **Personal Reflection and Self-Awareness**
   - ☑ **Self-Assessment.** Reflect on and evaluate your personal traits, habits, strengths and weaknesses.
   - ☑ **Self-Monitoring.** Maintain self-awareness of how you're learning, what you're learning, and whether you're learning.

Pause for Reflection

Before exiting this chapter, look back at the Checklist of Success-Promoting Principles and Practices and see how these ideas compare with those you recorded at the start of this chapter, when we asked you how you thought college would be different from high school and what it would take to be successful in college.

What ideas from your list and our checklist tend to match?

Were there any ideas on your list that were not on ours, or vice versa?

Learning More Through the World Wide Web

Internet-Based Resources for Further Information on Liberal Arts Education

For additional information related to the ideas discussed in this chapter, we recommend the following Web sites:

Learning Strategies: www.dartmouth.edu/~acskills/success/index.html

Academic Success Strategies: www.uni.edu/walsh/linda7.html

www.lifehack.org/articles/lifehack/from-a-freshman-five-tips-for-success-in-college.html

1.1 Constructing a Master List of Campus Resources

1. Use each of the following sources to gain more in-depth knowledge about the support services available on your campus:

   - Information published in your college catalog and student handbook

   - Information posted on your college's Web site

   - Information gathered by speaking with a professional in different offices or centers on your campus

2. Using the preceding sources of information, construct a master list of all support services that are available to you on your campus. Your final product should be a list that includes the following:

   - The names of different support services your campus offers

   - The types of support each service provides

   - A short statement indicating whether you think you would benefit from each particular type of support

   - The name of a person whom you could contact for support from each service

Notes

- You can pair up with a classmate to work collaboratively on this assignment. Working together with a peer on any research task can reduce your anxiety, increase your energy, and generate synergy—which results in a final product that is superior to what could have been produced by one person working alone (independently).
- After you complete this assignment, save your master list of support services for future use. You might not have an immediate need for some of these services during your first term in college, but all of them are likely to be useful to you at some point in your college experience.

1.2 Support Services

Learning Center

Types of Support

_____

Will I benefit?   Contact Person:

_____

Will I benefit?   Contact Person:

_____

Will I benefit?   Contact Person:

Writing Center

Types of Support

_____

Will I benefit?   Contact Person:

_____

Will I benefit?   Contact Person:

_____

Will I benefit?   Contact Person:

Disability Services

Types of Support

_____

Will I benefit?   Contact Person:

_____

Will I benefit?   Contact Person:

_____

Will I benefit?   Contact Person:

College Library

Types of Support

_____

Will I benefit?   Contact Person:

_____

Will I benefit?   Contact Person:

_____

Will I benefit?   Contact Person:

Academic Advisement Center

Types of Support

_____

Will I benefit?   Contact Person:

_____

Will I benefit?   Contact Person:

_____

Will I benefit?   Contact Person:

Office Of Student Life

Types of Support

_____

Will I benefit?   Contact Person:

_____

Will I benefit?   Contact Person:

_____

Will I benefit?   Contact Person:

Financial Aid Office

Types of Support

_____

Will I benefit?   Contact Person:

_____

Will I benefit?   Contact Person:

_____

Will I benefit?   Contact Person:

Counseling Center

Types of Support

_____

Will I benefit?   Contact Person:

_____

Will I benefit?   Contact Person:

_____

Will I benefit?   Contact Person:

Health Center
Types of Support

_____

Will I benefit?   Contact Person:

_____

Will I benefit?   Contact Person:

_____

Will I benefit?   Contact Person:

Career Development Center
Types of Support

_____

Will I benefit?   Contact Person:

_____

Will I benefit?   Contact Person:

_____

Will I benefit?   Contact Person:

Experiential Learning Resources
Types of Support

_____

Will I benefit?   Contact Person:

_____

Will I benefit?   Contact Person:

_____

Will I benefit?   Contact Person:

Other
Types of Support

_____

Will I benefit?   Contact Person:

_____

Will I benefit?   Contact Person:

_____

Will I benefit?   Contact Person:

Alone and Disconnected: Feeling Like Calling It Quits

Josephine is a first-year student in her second week of college. She doesn't feel like she's fitting in with other students on her campus. She also feels guilty about the time she's taking time away from her family and her old high school friends who are not attending college, and she fears that her ties with them will be weakened or broken if she continues spending so much time at school and on schoolwork. Josephine is feeling so torn between college and her family and old friends that she's beginning to have second thoughts about whether she should have gone to college.

Reflection and Discussion Questions

1. What would you say to Josephine that might persuade her to stay in college?

2. Could the college have done more during her first 2 weeks on campus to make Josephine (and other students) feel more connected with college and less disconnected from family?

3. Do you see anything that Josephine could do now to minimize the conflict she's experiencing between her commitment to college and her commitment to family and old friends?

Liberal Arts

The Meaning, Purpose, and Value of General Education

ACTIVATE YOUR THINKING   **Journal Entry**   **2.1**

Before you launch into this chapter, do your best to answer the following question:

Which one of the following statements represents the most accurate meaning of the term *liberal arts*?

1. Learning to be less politically conservative
2. Learning to be more artistic
3. Learning ideas rather than practical skills
4. Learning to spend money more freely
5. Learning skills for freedom

LEARNING GOAL

To appreciate the meaning, purpose, and benefits of the liberal arts and to develop a strategic plan for making the most out of general education.

Personal Story   I was once advising a first-year student (Laura) who intended to major in business. While helping her plan the courses she needed to complete her degree, I pointed out to Laura that she still needed to take a course in philosophy. Here's how our conversation went after I made this point.

Laura (in a somewhat irritated tone): Why do I have to take philosophy? I'm a business major.

Dr. Cuseo: Because philosophy is an important component of a liberal arts education.

Laura (in a very agitated tone): I'm not liberal and I don't want to be a liberal. I'm conservative and so are my parents; we all voted for Ronald Reagan in the last election!

—Joe Cuseo

◆ The Meaning and Purpose of a Liberal Arts Education

If you're uncertain about what the term "liberal arts" means, you're not alone. Most first-year students don't have the foggiest idea what a liberal arts education represents (Hersh, 1997). If they were to guess, they may mistakenly say that it's something impractical or related to liberal politics.

Laura probably would have picked option 1 as her answer to the multiple-choice question posed at the start of this chapter. That would not have been the right choice; option 5 is the correct answer. Literally translated, the term "liberal arts" derives from the Latin words liberales—meaning to "liberate" or "free," and artes—meaning "skills." Thus, "skills for freedom" is the most accurate meaning of the term "liberal arts."

The roots of the term "liberal arts" date back to the origin of modern civilization—to the ancient Greeks and Romans, who argued that political power in a democracy rests with the people because they choose (elect) their own leaders. In a democracy, people are liberated from uncritical dependence on a dictator or autocrat. To preserve their political freedom, citizens in a democracy must be well educated and critical thinkers so that they can make wise choices about whom they elect as their leaders and lawmakers (Bishop, 1986; Cheney, 1989).

Many students (and their parents) do not know what the term "liberal arts" truly means.

> "Knowledge will forever govern ignorance; and a people who mean to be their own governors must arm themselves with the power which knowledge gives."
>
> –James Madison, fourth president of the United States and cosigner of the American Constitution and first author of the Bill of Rights

> "It is such good fortune for people in power that people do not think."
>
> –Adolf Hitler, German dictator

The political ideals of the ancient Greeks and Romans were shared by the founding fathers of the United States who also emphasized the importance of an educated citizenry for preserving America's new democracy. As Thomas Jefferson, third president of the United States, wrote in 1801 (Ford, 1903, p. 278):

I know of no safe depository of the ultimate powers of a society but the people themselves; and if we think them not enlightened enough to exercise control with a wholesome discretion [responsible decision-making], the remedy is not to take power from them, but to inform their discretion by education.

Thus, the liberal arts are rooted in the belief that education is the essential ingredient for preservation of democratic freedom. When people are educated in the liberal arts, they gain the breadth of knowledge and depth of thinking to vote wisely, preserve democracy, and avoid autocracy (dictatorship).

The importance of a knowledgeable, critical-thinking citizenry for making wise political choices is still relevant today. Contemporary political campaigns are using more manipulative media advertisements. These ads rely on short sound bites, one-sided arguments, and powerful visual images that are intentionally designed to appeal to emotions and discourage critical thinking (Goleman, 1992).

Over time, the term "liberal arts" has acquired the more general meaning of liberating or freeing people to be self-directed individuals who make personal choices and decisions that are determined by their own, well-reasoned ideas and values, rather than blind conformity to the ideas and values of others (Gamson, 1984). Self-directed critical thinkers are empowered to resist manipulation by politicians and other societal influences, including:

- Authority figures (e.g., they question excessive use or abuse of authority by parents, teachers, or law enforcers);
- Peers (e.g., they resist peer pressure that's unreasonable or unethical); and
- Media (e.g., they detect and reject forms of advertisements designed to manipulate their self-image and material needs).

A liberal arts education encourages you to be your own person and to ask "Why?" It's the component of your college education that supplies you with the mental tools needed to be an independent thinker with an inquiring mind that questions authority and resists conformity.

> "In a nation whose citizens are to be led by persuasion and not by force, the art of reasoning becomes of the first importance."
> —Thomas Jefferson

> **Student Perspective**
>
> "I want knowledge so I don't get taken advantage of in life."
> —First-year college student

◆ The Liberal Arts Curriculum

The first liberal arts curriculum (collection of courses) was designed with the belief that individuals who experienced these courses would be equipped with (a) a broad base of knowledge that would ensure they would be well informed in various subjects and (b) a range of mental skills that would enable them to think deeply and critically. Based on this educational philosophy of the ancient Greeks and Romans, the first liberal arts curriculum was developed during the Middle Ages and consisted of the following subjects: logic, language, rhetoric (the art of argumentation and persuasion), music, mathematics, and astronomy (Ratcliff, 1997; Association of American Colleges & Universities, 2002).

The purpose of the original liberal arts curriculum has withstood the test of time. Today's colleges and universities continue to offer a liberal arts curriculum designed to provide students with a broad base of knowledge in multiple subject areas and equip them with critical skills. The liberal arts curriculum today is often referred to as general education—representing skills and knowledge that are general rather than narrowly specialized. General education is what all college students learn, no matter what their major or specialized field of study may be (Association of American Colleges & Universities, 2002).

On some campuses, the liberal arts are also referred to as the core curriculum, with "core" standing for what is central or essential for all students to know and do because of their importance for effective performance in any field, or as breadth requirements, referring the their broad scope that spans a range of subject areas.

> **! Remember**
>
> Whatever term is used to describe the liberal arts, the bottom line is that they are the foundation of a college education upon which all academic specializations (majors) are built; they are what all college graduates should be able to know and do for whatever occupational path they choose to pursue; they are what distinguishes college education from vocational preparation; and they define what it means to be a well-educated person.

◆ Major Divisions of Knowledge and Subject Areas in the Liberal Arts Curriculum

The divisions of knowledge in today's liberal arts curriculum have expanded to include more subject areas than those included in the original curriculum that was based on the work of the ancient Greeks and Romans. The liberal arts' divisions, and the courses that make up each division, vary somewhat from campus to campus. Campuses also vary in terms of the nature of courses required within each division of knowledge and the range of courses from which students can choose to fulfill their general educational requirements. On average, about one-third of a college graduate's course credits were required general education courses selected from the liberal arts curriculum (Conley, 2005).

Despite campus-to-campus variation in the number and nature of courses required, the liberal arts curriculum on every college campus represents the areas of knowledge and the types of skills that all students should possess, no matter what their particular major may be. It allows you to stand on the shoulders of intellectual giants from a range of fields and capitalize on their collective wisdom.

On most campuses today, the liberal arts curriculum typically consists of general divisions of knowledge and related subject areas similar to those listed in the sections that follow. As you read through these divisions of knowledge, highlight any subjects in which you've never had a course.

> **Pause for Reflection**
>
> For someone to be successful in any major and career, what do you think that person should:
>
> 1. Know; and
>
> 2. Be able to do?

Humanities

Courses in the humanities division of the liberal arts curriculum focus on the human experience and human culture, asking the important questions that arise in the life of humans, such as "Why are we here?" "What is the meaning or purpose of our existence?" "How should we live?" "What is the good life?" and "Is there life after death?"

The following are the primary subject areas in the humanities division:

- **English Composition.** Writing clearly, critically, and persuasively;
- **Speech.** Speaking eloquently and persuasively;
- **Literature.** Reading critically and appreciating the artistic merit of various literary genres (forms of writing), such as novels, short stories, poems, plays, and essays;
- **Languages.** Listening, speaking, reading and writing languages other than the student's native tongue;

- **Philosophy.** Thinking rationally, developing wisdom (the ability to use knowledge prudently), and living an ethically principled life;
- **Theology.** Understanding how humans conceive of and express their faith in a transcendent (supreme) being.

Fine Arts

Courses in the fine arts division focus largely on the art of human expression, asking such questions as "How do humans express, create, and appreciate what is beautiful?" and "How do we express ourselves aesthetically (through the senses) with imagination, creativity, style, and elegance?"

The primary subject areas of the fine arts division are as follows:

- **Visual Arts.** Creating and appreciating human expression through visual representation (drawing, painting, sculpture, photography, and graphic design);
- **Musical Arts.** Appreciating and creating rhythmical arrangements of sounds;
- **Performing Arts.** Appreciating and expressing creativity through drama and dance.

Mathematics

Courses in the mathematics division are designed to promote skills in numerical calculation, quantitative reasoning and problem solving.

Mathematics has the following primary subject areas:

- **Algebra.** Mathematical reasoning involving symbolic representation of numbers in a language of letters that vary in size or quantity;
- **Statistics.** Mathematical methods for summarizing; estimating probabilities; representing and understanding numerical information depicted in graphs, charts, and tables; and drawing accurate conclusions from quantitative data;
- **Calculus.** Higher mathematical methods for calculating the rate at which the quantity of one entity changes in relation to another and for calculating the areas enclosed by curves.

Natural Sciences

Courses in the natural sciences division of the liberal arts curriculum are devoted to systematic observation of the physical world and the explanation of natural phenomena, asking such questions as "What causes physical events that take place in the natural world?" "How can we predict and control these events?" and "How do we promote symbiotic interaction between humans and the natural environment that sustains the survival of both?"

The following are the primary subject areas of the natural sciences division:

- **Biology.** Understanding the structure and underlying processes of all living things;
- **Chemistry.** Understanding the composition of natural and synthetic (manmade) substances and how these substances may be changed or developed;
- **Physics.** Understanding the properties of physical matter, the principles of energy and motion, and electrical and magnetic forces;

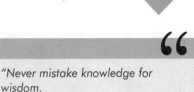

"Never mistake knowledge for wisdom.

One helps you make a living; the other helps you make a life."

—Sandra Carey, lobbyist to the California State Assembly

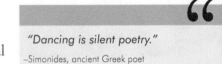

"Dancing is silent poetry."

—Simonides, ancient Greek poet

© El Greco, 2010. Under license from Shutterstock, Inc.

"The universe is a grand book which cannot be read until one learns to comprehend the language and become familiar with the characters of which it is composed. It is written in the language of mathematics."

—Galileo Galilei, seventeenth-century Italian physicist, mathematician, astronomer, and philosopher

© Laurence Gough, 2010. Under license from Shutterstock, Inc.

The natural sciences division of the liberal arts curriculum focuses on the observation of the physical world and the explanation of natural phenomena.

> "Science is an imaginative adventure of the mind seeking truth in a world of mystery."
>
> –Cyril Herman Hinshelwood, Nobel Prize–winning English chemist

> "Man, the molecule of society, is the subject of social science."
>
> –Henry Charles Carey, nineteenth-century American economist

> "To eat is a necessity, but to eat intelligently is an art."
>
> –La Rochefoucauld, seventeenth-century French author

- **Geology.** Understanding the composition of the earth and the natural processes that have shaped its development;
- **Astronomy.** Understanding the makeup and motion of celestial bodies that comprise the universe.

Social and Behavioral Sciences

Courses in the division of social and behavioral sciences focus on the observation of human behavior, individually and in groups, and ask such questions as "What causes humans to behave the way they do?" and "How can we predict, control, or improve human behavior and human interaction?"

This division has the following primary subject areas:

- **Psychology.** Understanding the human mind, its conscious and subconscious processes, and the underlying causes of human behavior;
- **Sociology.** Understanding the structure, interaction, and collective behavior of organized social groups and institutions or systems that comprise human society (e.g., families, schools, and social services);
- **Anthropology.** Understanding the cultural and physical origin, development, and distribution the human species;
- **History.** Understanding past events, their causes, and their influence on current events;
- **Political Science.** Understanding how societal authority is organized and how this authority is exerted to govern people, make collective decisions, and maintain social order;
- **Economics.** Understanding how the monetary needs of humans are met through allocation of limited resources and how material wealth is produced and distributed;
- **Geography.** Understanding how the place (physical location) where humans live influences their cultural and societal development and how humans have shaped and been shaped by their surrounding physical environment.

Physical Education and Wellness

Courses in the physical education and wellness division of the liberal arts curriculum focus on the human body, how to best maintain health, and how to attain peak performance levels of performance. They ask such questions as "How does the body function most effectively?" and "What can we do to prevent illness, promote wellness, and improve the physical quality of our lives?"

These primary subject areas fall under this division:

- **Physical Education.** Understanding the role of human exercise for promoting health and peak performance;
- **Nutrition.** Understanding how the body uses food as nourishment to promote health and generate energy;
- **Sexuality.** Understanding the biological, psychological, and social aspects of sexual relations;
- **Drug Education.** Understanding how substances that alter the body and mind affect physical health, mental health, and human performance.

Most of your liberal arts requirements will be taken during your first 2 years of college. Don't be disappointed if some of these requirements seem similar to courses you recently had in high school, and don't think you'll be bored because these are subjects you've already studied. College courses will not be video-tape replays of high school courses because you will examine these subjects in greater depth and breadth and at a higher level of thinking (Conley, 2005). Research shows that most of the higher-level thinking gains that students make in college take place during their first 2 years—the years during which they're taking most of their liberal arts courses (Pascarella & Terenzini, 2005).

> **Pause for Reflection**
>
> Look back at the subject areas in which you've never had a course. Which of these courses strike you as particularly interesting or useful?
>
> Why?

◆ Transferable Learning Skills That Last a Lifetime

A liberal arts education promotes success in your major, career, and life by equipping you with a set of lifelong learning skills with two powerful qualities:

- **Transferability.** These skills can be transferred and applied to a range of subjects, careers, and life situations.
- **Durability.** These skills are long lasting and can be continually used throughout your lifetime.

To use an athletic analogy, what the liberal arts do for the mind is similar to what cross-training does for the body. Cross-training engages the body in a range of exercises to promote total physical fitness and develop a range of physical skills (e.g., strength, endurance, flexibility, and agility), which can be applied to improve performance in any sport or athletic endeavor. Similarly, the liberal arts engage the mind in a range of subject areas (e.g., arts, sciences, and humanities), which develop a range of mental skills that can be applied to improve performance in any academic field or professional career.

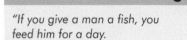

> *"You know you've got to exercise your brain just like your muscles."*
>
> –Will Rogers, Native American humorist and actor

! **Remember**

The liberal arts not only provide you with academic skills needed to succeed in your chosen major but also equip you with skills to succeed in whatever career or careers you decide to pursue. Don't underestimate the importance of these transferable and durable skills. Work hard at developing them, and take seriously the general education courses that promote their development.

A major difference exists between learning factual knowledge and learning transferable skills. A transferable skill can be applied to different situations or contexts. The mental skills developed by the liberal arts are transportable across academic subjects you'll encounter in college and work positions you'll assume after college. It could be said that these lifelong learning skills are a mental gift that keeps on giving.

The transferable skills developed by the liberal arts are summarized in **Box 2.1**.

As you read them, rate yourself on each of the skills using the following scale:

> *"If you give a man a fish, you feed him for a day.*
>
> *If you teach a man how to fish, you feed him for life."*
>
> –Author unknown

4 = very strong, 3 = strong, 2 = needs some improvement,
1 = needs much improvement

Take Action!

Transferable Lifelong Learning Skills Developed by the Liberal Arts

1. **Communication Skills.** Accurate comprehension and articulate expression of ideas. Five particular types of communication skills are essential for success in any specialized field of study or work:

- **Written communication skills.** Writing in a clear, creative, and persuasive manner;
- **Oral communication skills.** Speaking concisely, confidently, and eloquently;
- **Reading skills.** Comprehending, interpreting, and evaluating the literal meaning and connotations of words written in various styles and subject areas;
- **Listening skills.** Comprehending spoken language accurately and sensitively;
- **Electronic communication skills.** Using computer and technology-mediated communication skills effectively.

2. **Information literacy skills.** Effectively and efficiently accessing, retrieving, and evaluating information from various sources, including in-print and online (technology-based) systems.

2.1

> "Ability to recognize when information is needed and have the ability to locate, evaluate, and use it effectively."
>
> —Definition of "information literacy," American Library Association Presidential Committee on Information Literacy

3. **Computation skills.** Accurate calculation, analysis, summary, interpretation, and evaluation of quantitative information or statistical data.
4. **Higher-level thinking skills.** Learning deeply and thinking at a more advanced level than simply acquisition and memorization of factual information.

Pause for Reflection

Reflect on the four skill areas developed by a liberal arts education (communication, information literacy, computation, and higher-level thinking). Which one do you think is most important or most relevant to your future success?

Write a one-paragraph explanation about why you chose this skill.

Students often see general education as something to get out of the way and get behind them so they can get into their major and career (Association of American Colleges & Universities, 2007). Don't take the view that general education as a series of obstacles along the way to a degree; instead, view it as a learning process from which you can take a set of powerful skills that are:

1. **Portable.** Travel well across work situations and life roles; and
2. **Stable.** Remain relevant and useful across changing times.

Remember

When you acquire lifelong *learning* skills, you're also acquiring lifelong *earning* skills.

The skills developed by a liberal arts education are strikingly similar to the types of skills that employers seek in new employees. In numerous national surveys and in-depth interviews, employers and executives in both industry and government consistently report that they seek employees with skills that fall into the following three categories:

1. **Communication skills** (e.g., listening, speaking, writing, and reading; Business–Higher Education Forum, 1999; National Association of Colleges & Employers, 2003; Peter D. Hart Research Associates, 2006):

   "There is such a heavy emphasis on effective communication in the workplace that college students who master these skills can set themselves apart from the pack when searching for employment." Marilyn Mackes, executive director of the National Association of Colleges and Employers (Mackes, 2003, p. 1).

2. **Thinking skills** (e.g., problem solving and critical thinking; Business–Higher Education Forum, 1999; Peter D. Hart Research Associates, 2006; Van Horn, 1995):

"We look for people who can think critically and analytically. If you can do those things, we can teach you our business." Paul Dominski, store recruiter for the Robinson-May Department Stores Company (Indiana University, 2004, p. 1).

3. **Lifelong learning skills** (e.g., learning how to learn and how to continue learning; Conference Board of Canada, 2000):

"Employers are virtually unanimous that the most important knowledge and skills the new employee can bring to the job are problem solving, communication, and 'learning to learn' skills. The workers of the future need to know how to think and how to continue to learn." David Kearns, former chief executive officer (CEO) for the Xerox Corporation (Kearns, 1989, p. 8).

The remarkable resemblance between the work skills sought by employers and the academic skills developed by a liberal arts education isn't surprising when you think about the typical duties or responsibilities of working professionals. They need good communication skills because they must listen, speak, describe, and explain ideas to co-workers and customers. They read and critically interpret written and statistical reports, and they write letters, memos, and reports. They need highly developed thinking skills to analyze problems, construct well-organized plans, generate innovative ideas and solutions to problems (creative thinking), and evaluate whether their plans and strategies will be effective (critical thinking).

Student Perspective

"They asked me during my interview why I was right for the job and I told them because I can read well, write well and I can think. They really liked that because those were the skills they were looking for."

—English major hired by a public relations firm (*Los Angeles Times,* 2004)

"

"At State Farm, our [employment] exam does not test applicants on their knowledge of finance or the insurance business, but it does require them to demonstrate critical thinking skills and the ability to calculate and think logically. These skills plus the ability to read for information, to communicate and write effectively need to be demonstrated."

—Edward B. Rust Jr., chairman and chief executive officer of State Farm Insurance Companies (Association of American Colleges & Universities, 2007)

A Liberal Arts Education Is Preparation for Your Major

Don't assume that liberal arts courses you're taking as general education requirements have nothing to do with your specialized field of interest. Liberal arts courses provide a relevant foundation for success in your major. Recall our story at the start of the chapter about Laura, the first-year student with a business major who questioned why she had to take a course in philosophy. Laura needed to take philosophy because she will encounter topics in her business major that relate either directly or indirectly to philosophy. In her business courses, she will likely encounter philosophical issues relating to (a) the logical assumptions and underlying values of capitalism, (b) business ethics (e.g., hiring and firing practices), and (c) business justice (e.g., how profits should be fairly or justly distributed to workers and shareholders). Philosophy will equip her with the fundamental logical thinking and ethical reasoning skills to understand these issues deeply and respond to them humanely.

As with the field of business, liberal arts subjects are relevant to successful performance in any major and career. For example, historical and ethical perspectives are needed for all fields because all of them have a history and none of them are value free.

Pause for Reflection

During your college experience, you might hear students say that they need to get their general education (liberal arts) courses out of the way so that they can get into courses that relate to their major and career. Would you agree or disagree with this argument?

Why?

"

"The unexamined life is not worth living."

—Socrates, classic Greek philosopher and one of the founding fathers of Western philosophy

The academic skills developed by a liberal arts education are also *practical* skills that contribute to successful performance in *any career.*

Calvin and Hobbes © 1992 Watterston. Dist. By Universal Press Syndicate. Reprinted with permission. All rights reserved.

Learning from the collective wisdom of diverse disciplines provides you with a broad base of knowledge that enables you to view issues and solve problems from multiple angles or vantage points. Although you may specialize in a particular field of study in college (your major), real-life issues and challenges are not divided neatly into specialized majors. Important and enduring issues, such as effective leadership, improving race relations, and preventing international warfare, can neither be fully understood nor effectively solved by using the thinking tools of a single academic discipline. Approaching multidimensional issues such as these from the perspective of a single, specialized field of study is likely to result in single-minded and over-simplified attempt to solve a complex problem.

Figure 2.1 Key Elements of Holistic (Whole-Person) Development

The Liberal Arts Promote Self-awareness and Development of the Whole Person

One of the most emphasized intended outcomes of a liberal arts education is to "know thyself" (Cross, 1982). The ability to turn inward and become aware of your self is a form of intelligence that has been referred to as intrapersonal intelligence (Gardner, 1999), and it's essential for beginning any quest for personal growth and self-fulfillment.

To become self-aware requires awareness of all elements that comprise the self. As illustrated in **Figure 2.1**, the human self is composed of multiple dimensions that join together to form the whole person.

◆ Key Dimensions of the Self

Each of the following elements of self plays an influential role in promoting human health, success, and happiness:

1. **Intellectual.** Knowledge, perspectives, and ways of thinking;
2. **Emotional.** Feelings, self-esteem, emotional intelligence, and mental health;
3. **Social.** Interpersonal relationships;
4. **Ethical.** Values, character, and moral convictions;
5. **Physical.** Bodily health and wellness;
6. **Spiritual.** Beliefs about the meaning or purpose of life and the hereafter;

7. **Vocational.** Occupational or career development and satisfaction;

8. **Personal.** Identity, self-concept, and self-management.

Research strongly suggests that quality of life depends on attention to and development of all elements of the self. It's been found that people who are healthy (physically and mentally) and successful (personally and professionally) are those who attend to and integrate dimensions of their self, enabling them to lead well-rounded and well-balanced lives (Covey, 1990; Goleman, 1995; Heath, 1977).

In Figure 2.1, these diverse dimensions of the self are joined or linked to represent how they are interrelated and work not independently but interdependently to affect an individual's development and well-being (Love & Love, 1995).

These elements are discussed separately in this chapter to keep them clear in your mind. In reality, they do not operate independently of one another; they are interconnected and influence one another. (This is why the elements the self in Figure 2.1 are depicted as links in an interconnected chain.) Thus, the self is a diverse, multidimensional entity that has the capacity to develop along various interdependent dimensions.

One of the primary goals of the liberal arts is to provide a well-rounded education that promotes development the whole person (Kuh, Shedd, & Whitt, 1987). Research on college students confirms that their college experience affects them in multiple ways and promotes the development of multiple dimensions of self (Bowen, 1997; Feldman & Newcomb, 1994; Pascarella & Terenzini, 1991).

Since wholeness is essential for wellness, success, and happiness, carefully read the following descriptions and skills associated with each of the eight elements of holistic development. As you are read the skills and qualities listed beneath each of the eight elements, place a checkmark in the space next to any skill that is particularly important to you. You may check more than one skill within each area.

Know Thyself

Self-awareness is the first step to overcoming personal prejudices and developing intrapersonal intelligence.

"The research portrays the college student as changing in an integrated way, with change in any one area appearing to be part of a mutually reinforcing network or pattern of change in other areas."

—Ernest Pascarella and Pat Terenzini, *How College Affects Students* (XXXX)

◆ Skills and Qualities Associated with Each Element of Holistic (Whole-Person) Development

1. **Intellectual development.** Acquiring knowledge and learning how to learn deeply and think at a higher level.

   Goals and skills:

   ☑ Becoming aware of your intellectual abilities, interests, and learning styles

   ☑ Maintaining attention and concentration

   ☑ Improving your ability to retain knowledge (long-term memory)

   ☑ Moving beyond memorization to higher levels of thinking

   ☑ Acquiring effective research skills for accessing information from various sources and systems

   ☑ Viewing issues from multiple angles or viewpoints (psychological, social, political, economic, etc.) to attain a balanced, comprehensive perspective

   ☑ Evaluating ideas critically in terms of their truth and value

   ☑ Thinking creatively or imaginatively

   ☑ Responding constructively to differing viewpoints or opposing arguments

   ☑ Detecting and rejecting persuasion tactics that appeal to emotions rather than reason

"Intellectual growth should commence at birth and cease only at death."

—Albert Einstein, Nobel Prize–winning physicist

2. **Emotional development.** Strengthening skills for understanding, controlling, and expressing emotions.
Goals and skills:
☑ Dealing with personal emotions in an honest, nondefensive manner
☑ Maintaining a healthy balance between emotional control and emotional expression
☑ Responding with empathy and sensitivity to emotions experienced by others
☑ Dealing effectively with depression
☑ Dealing effectively with anger
☑ Using effective stress-management strategies to control anxiety and tension
☑ Responding effectively to frustrations and setbacks
☑ Dealing effectively with fear of failure and poor performance
☑ Accepting feedback in a constructive, nondefensive manner
☑ Maintaining optimism and enthusiasm

3. **Social development.** Enhancing the quality and depth of interpersonal relationships.
Goals and skills:
☑ Developing effective conversational skills
☑ Becoming an effective listener
☑ Relating effectively to others in one-to-one, small-group, and large-group situations
☑ Collaborating effectively with others when working in groups or teams
☑ Overcoming shyness
☑ Developing more meaningful and intimate relationships
☑ Resolving interpersonal conflicts assertively, rather than in aggressively or passively
☑ Providing feedback to others in a constructive and considerate manner
☑ Relating effectively with others from different cultural backgrounds and lifestyles
☑ Developing leadership skills

4. **Ethical development.** Developing a clear value system for guiding life choices and decisions and building moral character, or the ability to make and act on ethical judgments and to demonstrate consistency between convictions (beliefs) and commitments (actions).
Goals and skills:
☑ Gaining deeper self-awareness of personal values and ethical assumptions
☑ Making personal choices and life decisions based on a meaningful value system
☑ Developing the capacity to think and act with personal integrity and authenticity
☑ Using electronic technology in an ethical and civil manner
☑ Resisting social pressure to act in ways that are inconsistent with personal values
☑ Treating others in an ethical manner
☑ Knowing how to exercise individual freedom without infringing on the rights of others
☑ Developing concern and commitment for human rights and social justice
☑ Developing the courage to confront those who violate the rights of others
☑ Becoming a responsible citizen

5. **Physical development.** Applying knowledge about how the human body functions to prevent disease, preserve wellness, and promote peak performance.
   Goals and skills:
   - ☑ Maintaining awareness of your physical condition and state of health
   - ☑ Applying knowledge about exercise and fitness training to promote physical and mental health
   - ☑ Understanding how sleep patterns affect health and performance
   - ☑ Maintaining a healthy balance among work, recreation and relaxation
   - ☑ Applying knowledge of nutrition to reduce the risk of illness and promote optimal performance
   - ☑ Becoming knowledgeable about nutritional imbalances and eating disorders
   - ☑ Developing a positive physical self-image
   - ☑ Becoming knowledgeable about the effects of drugs and their impact on physical and mental well-being
   - ☑ Being knowledgeable about human sexuality and sexually transmitted diseases
   - ☑ Understanding how biological differences between the sexes affect male–female relationships and gender orientation

6. **Spiritual development.** Searching for answers to the big questions, such as the meaning or purpose of life and death, and exploring nonmaterial issues that transcend human life and the physical world.
   Goals and skills:
   - ☑ Developing a personal philosophy or worldview about the meaning and purpose of human existence
   - ☑ Appreciating what cannot be completely understood
   - ☑ Appreciating the mysteries associated with the origin of the universe
   - ☑ Searching for the connection between the self and the larger world or cosmos
   - ☑ Searching for the mystical or supernatural—that which transcends the boundaries of the natural world
   - ☑ Being open to examining questions relating to death and life after death
   - ☑ Being open to examining questions about the possible existence of a supreme being or higher power
   - ☑ Being knowledgeable about different approaches to spirituality and their underlying beliefs or assumptions
   - ☑ Understanding the difference and relationship between faith and reason
   - ☑ Becoming aware and tolerant of religious beliefs and practices

7. **Vocational development.** Exploring career options, making career choices wisely, and developing skills needed for lifelong career success.
   Goals and skills:
   - ☑ Understanding the relationship between college majors and careers
   - ☑ Using effective strategies for exploring and identifying potential careers
   - ☑ Selecting career options that are consistent with your personal values, interests, and talents
   - ☑ Acquiring work experience in career fields that relate to your occupational interests
   - ☑ Developing an effective résumé and portfolio

> "A man too busy to take care of his health is like a mechanic too busy to take care of his tools."
>
> –Spanish proverb

Student Perspective

"You may think I'm here, living for the 'now' . . . but I'm not. Half of my life revolves around the invisible and immaterial. At some point, every one of us has asked the Big Questions surrounding our existence: What is the meaning of life? Is my life inherently purposeful and valuable?"

–College student (Dalton, Eberhardt, Bracken, & Echols, 2006)

> "Everyone is a house with four rooms: a physical, a mental, an emotional, and a spiritual. Most of us tend to live in one room most of the time but unless we go into every room every day, even if only to keep it aired, we are not complete."
>
> –Native American proverb

> "Your work is to discover your work and then with all your heart to give yourself to it."
>
> –Hindu Siddhartha Prince Gautama Siddharta, a.k.a. Buddha, founder of the philosophy and religion of Buddhism

☑ Adopting effective strategies for identifying individuals to serve as personal references and for improving the quality of personal letters of recommendation

☑ Acquiring effective job-search strategies

☑ Using effective strategies for writing letters of inquiry and applications to potential employers

☑ Developing strategies for performing well in personal interviews

☑ Acquiring effective networking skills for developing personal contacts with potential employers

8. **Personal development.** Developing positive self-beliefs, personal attitudes, and personal habits.
Goals and skills:

☑ Developing a strong sense of personal identity and a coherent self-concept (e.g., "Who am I?")

☑ Finding a sense of purpose direction in life (e.g., "Who will I become?")

☑ Developing self-respect and self-esteem

☑ Increasing self-confidence

☑ Developing self-efficacy, or the belief that events and outcomes in life are influenced or controlled by personal initiative and effort

☑ Setting realistic personal goals and priorities

☑ Becoming self-motivated and self-disciplined

☑ Developing the perseverance and persistence to reach long-range goals

☑ Acquiring practical skills for managing personal affairs effectively and efficiently

☑ Becoming independent and self-reliant

> "Remember, no one can make you feel inferior without your consent."
>
> –Eleanor Roosevelt, UN diplomat and humanitarian

> "I'm a great believer in luck and I find the harder I work, the more I have of it."
>
> –Thomas Jefferson

◆ The Cocurriculum: Using the Whole Campus to Develop the Whole Person

To maximize the impact of a liberal arts education, you need to take advantage of the total college environment. This includes not only the courses you take in the college curriculum, but also the learning experiences you have outside the classroom, known as the cocurriculum. Cocurricular experiences include all educational discussions you have with your peers and professors outside the classroom, as well as your participation in the various events and programs offered on your campus. As mentioned in Chapter 1, research clearly indicates that out-of-class learning experiences are as important to your overall development as the course curriculum (Kuh, 1995; Kuh, Douglas, Lund, & Ramin-Gyurnek, 1994), hence the term "co"-curriculum.

The learning that takes place in college courses is primarily vicarious—that is, you learn from or through somebody else—by listening to professors in class and by reading outside of class. While this type of academic learning is valuable, it needs to be complemented by experiential learning (i.e., learning directly through firsthand experiences). For example, leadership cannot be developed solely by listening to lectures and reading books about

Pause for Reflection

Look back and count the number of checkmarks you've placed by each of the eight areas of self-development. Did you find that you placed roughly the same number of checkmarks in all eight areas, or were there large discrepancies across the eight areas?

Based on the checkmarks that you placed in each area, would you say that your interests in self-development are balanced across elements of the self, or do they suggest a strong interest in certain dimensions of yourself, with little interest in others?

Do you think you will eventually develop a more balanced set of interests across these different dimensions of self-development?

leadership. To fully develop your leadership skills, you need to have leadership experiences, such as those developed by "leading a [discussion] group in class, holding office in student government or by being captain of a sports team" (Association of American Colleges & Universities, 2002, p. 30). Fully using campus resources is one of the keys to college success, so take advantage of your whole college to develop yourself as a whole person.

Listed in **Snapshot Summary 2.1** are some programs and services included in a cocurriculum, accompanied by the primary dimension of the self that they are designed to develop.

> *"To educate liberally, learning experiences must be offered which facilitate maturity of the whole person. These are goals of student development and clearly they are consistent with the mission and goals of liberal education."*
>
> —Theodore Berg, "Student Development and Liberal Education"

Snapshot Summary   2.1

Cocurricular Programs and Services Promoting Dimensions of Holistic Development

Intellectual Development
- Academic advising
- Learning center services
- College library
- Tutoring services
- Information technology services
- Campus speakers
- Concerts, theater productions, and art shows

Emotional and Social Development
- Student activities
- Student clubs and organizations
- Counseling services
- Peer counseling
- Peer mentoring
- Residential life programs
- Commuter programs

Ethical Development
- Judicial Review Board
- Student government
- Integrity committees and task forces

Physical Development
- Student health services
- Wellness programs
- Campus athletic activities and intramural sports

Spiritual Development
- College chaplain
- Campus ministry
- Peer ministry

Vocational Development
- Career development services
- Internships programs
- Service learning experiences
- Work–study programs
- Major and career fairs

Personal Development
- Financial aid services
- Campus workshops on self-management (e.g., managing time or money)

Note: This list represents just a sample of the total number of programs and services that may be available on your campus. As you can see from the list's length, colleges and universities are organized to promote your development in multiple ways. The power of the liberal arts is magnified when you combine coursework and cocurricular experiences to create a college experience that contributes to your development as a whole person.

◆ Broadening Your Perspective of the World Around You

You should know more than yourself; you should know your world. The liberal arts education helps you move beyond yourself and expands your perspective to include the wider world around you (Braskamp, 2008). The components of this larger perspective are organized and illustrated in **Figure 2.2**.

In Figure 2.2, the center circle represents the self. Fanning out to the right of the self is a series of arches that encompasses the *social–spatial perspective*; this perspective includes increasingly larger social groups and more distant places, ranging from the narrowest perspective (the individual) to the widest perspective (the universe). The liberal arts liberate you from the narrow tunnel vision of a self-centered (egocentric) perspective, providing a panoramic perspective of the world that enables you to move outside yourself and see yourself in relation to other people and other places.

To the left of the self in Figure 2.2 are three arches labeled the *chronological perspective*; this perspective includes the three dimensions of time: past (historical), present (contemporary), and future (futuristic). The liberal arts not only widen your perspective but also lengthen it by stretching your vision beyond the present—enabling you to see yourself in relation to humans who've lived before you and will live after you. The chronological perspective gives you hindsight to see where the world has been, insight into the world's current condition, and foresight to see where the world may be going.

It could be said that the chronological perspective provides you with a mental time machine for flashing back to the past and flashing forward to the future, and the social–spatial perspective provides you with a conceptual telescope for viewing people and places that are far away. Together, these two

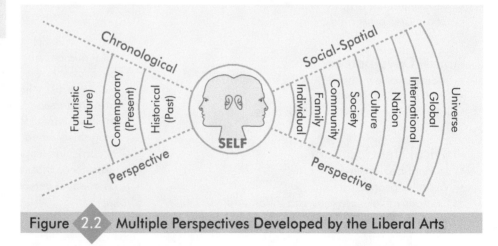

Figure 2.2 Multiple Perspectives Developed by the Liberal Arts

broadening perspectives of the liberal arts enable to you to appreciate the experience of anyone living anywhere at any time.

The elements that comprise each of these broadening perspectives are provided in the next sections.

◆ Elements of the Social–Spatial Perspective

The Family Perspective

Moving beyond the perspective of your individual self, you are part of a larger social unit—your family. The people with whom you were raised have almost certainly influenced the person you are today and how you got to be that way. Moreover, your family hasn't only influenced you; you've also influenced your family. For example, your decision to go to college may make your parents and grandparents proud and may influence the decision of other members of your family to attend college. In addition, if you have children, graduating from college will have a positive influence on their future welfare. As mentioned in the introduction to this book, children of college graduates experience improved intellectual development, better physical health, and greater economic security (Bowen, 1977, 1997; Pascarella & Terenzini, 1991, 2005).

The Community Perspective

Moving beyond the family, you are also a member of a larger social unit—your community. This wider social circle includes friends and neighbors at home, at school, and at work. These are communities where you can begin to take action to improve the world around you. If you want to make the world a better place, this is the place to start—through civic engagement in your local communities.

Civically responsible people also demonstrate civic concern by stepping beyond their narrow self-interests to selflessly volunteer time and energy to help members of their community, particularly those in need. They demonstrate their humanity by being humane (they show genuine compassion for others who are less fortunate than they are) and by being humanitarian (they work to promote the welfare of other humans).

> "Think globally, act locally."
> –Patrick Geddes, Scottish urban planner and social activist

> "Get involved. Don't gripe about things unless you are making an effort to change them. You can make a difference if you dare."
> –Richard C. Holbrooke, former director of the Peace Corps and American ambassador to the United Nations

The Societal Perspective

Moving beyond our local communities, we are also members of a larger society that includes people from different regions of the country, cultural backgrounds, and social classes.

In human societies, groups of people are typically stratified into social classes with unequal levels of resources, such monetary wealth. According to U.S. Census (2000) figures, the wealthiest 20 percent of the American population controls approximately 50 percent of the total American income, while the 20 percent with the lowest level of income controls 4 percent of the nation's wealth. Sharp differences in income level exist among people of different race, ethnicity, and gender. A recent survey revealed that Black households had the lowest median income in 2007 ($33,916), compared to a median income of $54,920 for non-Hispanic White households (Current Population Survey Annual Social and Economic Supplement, 2008).

> "[Liberal arts education] shows you how to accommodate yourself to others, how to throw yourself into their state of mind, how to come to an understanding of them. You are at home in any society; you have common ground with every class."
> –John Henry Newman

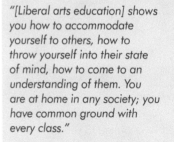

The Cultural Perspective

Culture can be broadly defined as a distinctive pattern of beliefs and values that are learned by a group of people who share the same social heritage and traditions. In short, culture is the whole way in which a group of people has learned to live (Peoples & Bailey, 2008); it includes their customary style of speaking (language), fashion, food, art, music, values, and beliefs.

Intercultural awareness is one of the outcomes of a liberal arts education (Wabash National Study, 2007). Being able to step outside of your own culture and see issues from a broader worldview enables you to perceive reality and evaluate truth from diverse vantage points. This makes your thinking more comprehensive and less ethnocentric (centered on your own culture).

The National Perspective

Besides being a member of society, you're also a citizen of a nation. Having the privilege of being a citizen in a free nation brings with it the responsibility of participating in your country's governance through the process of voting. As a democracy, the United States is a nation that has been built on the foundation of equal rights and freedom of opportunity, which are guaranteed by its constitution.

Exercise your right to vote, and when you do vote, be mindful of political leaders who are committed to ensuring equal rights, social justice, and political freedom. When the personal rights and freedom of any of our fellow citizens are threatened by prejudice and discrimination, the political stability and survival of any democratic nation is threatened.

The International Perspective

Moving beyond your particular country of citizenship, you are also a member of an international world that includes close to 200 nations (Rosenberg, 2009). Communication and interaction among citizens of different nations is greater today than at any other time in world history, largely because of rapid advances in electronic technology (Dryden & Vos, 1999; Smith, 1994). The World Wide Web is making today's world a small one indeed, and success in today's world requires an international perspective. Our lives are increasingly affected by events beyond our national borders because boundaries between nations are breaking down as a result of international travel, international trading, and multinational corporations. Employers of college graduates are placing higher value on prospective employees with international knowledge and foreign language skills (Fixman, 1990; Office of Research, 1994). By learning from and about different nations, you become more than a citizen of your own country: you become cosmopolitan—a citizen of the world.

The Global Perspective

Broader than an international perspective is the global perspective. It extends beyond the relations among citizens of different nations to include all life forms that inhabit the earth and the relationships between these diverse life forms and the earth's natural resources (minerals, air, and water). Humans share the earth and its natural resources with approximately 10 million animal species (Myers, 1997) and more than 300,000 forms of vegetative life (Knoll, 2003).

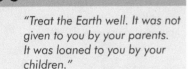

Pause for Reflection

What would you say is the factor that is most responsible for poverty in human societies?

> "It is difficult to see the picture when you are inside the frame."
>
> –Author unknown

> "A progressive society counts individual variations as precious since it finds in them the means of its own growth. A democratic society must, in consistency with its ideal, allow intellectual freedom and the play of diverse gifts and interests."
>
> –John Dewey, U.S. educator, philosopher, and psychologist

> "A liberal [arts] education frees a person from the prison-house of class, race, time, place, background, family, and nation."
>
> –Robert Hutchins, former dean of Yale Law School and president of the University of Chicago

> "Treat the Earth well. It was not given to you by your parents. It was loaned to you by your children."
>
> –Kenyan proverb

As inhabitants of this planet and as global citizens, we have an environmental responsibility to address global warming and other issues that require balancing our industrial–technological progress with the need to sustain the earth's natural resources and preserve the life of our planet's cohabitants.

The Universal Perspective

Beyond the global perspective is the broadest of all perspectives—the universe. The earth is just one planet that shares a solar system with seven other planets and is just one celestial body that shares a galaxy with millions of other celestial bodies, including stars, moons, meteorites, and asteroids (Encrenaz et al., 2004).

Just as we should guard against being ethnocentric (thinking that our culture is the center of humanity), we should guard against being geocentric (thinking that we are at the center of the universe). All heavenly bodies do not revolve around the earth; our planet revolves around them. The sun doesn't rise in the east and set in the west; our planet rotates around the sun to produce our earthly experiences of day and night.

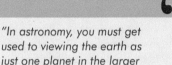

"In astronomy, you must get used to viewing the earth as just one planet in the larger context of the universe."

–Physics professor (Donald, 2002)

"The sun, with all those planets revolving around it and dependent on it, can still ripen a bunch of grapes as if it had nothing else in the universe to do."

–Galileo Galilei

◆ Elements of the Chronological Perspective

The Historical Perspective

A historical perspective is critical for understanding the root causes of our current human condition and world situation. Humans are products of both a social and a natural history. Don't forget that the earth is estimated to be more than 4.5 billion years old and our human ancestors date back more than 250,000 years (Knoll, 2003). Thus, our current lives represent a small frame of time in a long chronological reel. Every modern convenience we now enjoy reflects the collective efforts and cumulative knowledge of diverse human groups that have accumulated over thousands of years of history. By studying the past, we can build on our ancestors' achievements and avoid their mistakes. For example, by understanding the causes and consequences of the Holocaust, we can reduce the risk that an atrocity of that size and scope will ever happen again.

Pause for Reflection

Look back at the broadening perspectives developed by a liberal arts education. What college course would develop each perspective? If you're unsure or cannot remember whether a course is designed to develop any of these perspectives, look at the course's goals described in your college catalog (in print or online).

The Contemporary Perspective

The contemporary perspective focuses on understanding the current world situation and the events that comprise today's news. One major goal of a liberal arts education is to increase your understanding the contemporary human condition so that you may have the wisdom to improve it (Miller, 1988). For example, despite historical progress in the nation's acceptance and appreciation of different ethnic and racial groups, the Unites States today remains a nation that is deeply divided with respect to culture, religion, and social class (Brooking Institute, 2008).

The current technological revolution is generating information and new knowledge at a faster rate than at any other time in human history (Dryden &

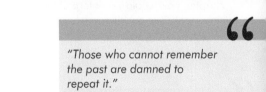

"Those who cannot remember the past are damned to repeat it."

–George Santayana, Spanish-born American philosopher

"Yesterday is gone. Tomorrow has not yet come. We have only today. Let us begin."

–Mother Teresa of Calcutta, Albanian, Catholic nun and winner of the Nobel Peace Prize

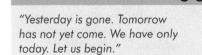

> "The only person who is educated is the one who has learned how to learn and change."
>
> –Carl Rogers, humanistic psychologist and Nobel Peace Prize nominee

> "In times of change, learners inherit the Earth . . . [they] find themselves beautifully equipped to deal with a world that no longer exists."
>
> –Eric Hoffer, author of The Ordeal of Change (XXXX) and recipient of the Presidential Medal of Freedom

> "The future is literally in our hands to mold as we like. But we cannot wait until tomorrow. Tomorrow is now."
>
> –Eleanor Roosevelt

> "We all inherit the past. We all confront the challenges of the present. We all participate in the making of the future."
>
> –Ernest Boyer and Martin Kaplan, Educating for Survival

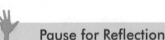

Pause for Reflection

In light of the information you've read in this chapter, how would you interpret the following statement: "We can't know where we're going until we know where we've been"?

> "A truly great intellect is one which takes a connected view of old and new, past and present, far and near, and which has an insight into the influence of all these on one another, without which there is no whole, and no center."
>
> –John Henry Newman, The Idea of a University (1852)

Vos, 1999). Knowledge quickly becomes obsolete when there is rapid creation and communication of new information (Naisbitt, 1982). Workers in the today's complex, fast-changing world need to continually update their skills to perform their jobs and advance in their careers (Niles & Harris-Bowlsbey, 2002). This creates a demand for workers who have learned how to learn, a hallmark of the liberal arts.

The Futuristic Perspective

The futuristic perspective allows us to flash forward and envision what our world will be like years from now. This perspective focuses on such questions as "Will we leave the world a better or worse place for humans who will inhabit after our departure, including our children and grandchildren?" and "How can humans living today avoid short-term, shortsighted thinking and adopt a long-range vision that anticipates the consequences of their current actions on future generations of humans?"

To sum up, a comprehensive chronological perspective brings the past, present, and future into focus on a single screen. It enables us to see how the current world is a single segment of a temporal sequence that's been shaped by events that preceded it and will shape future events.

Remember

By embracing the perspectives of different times, places, and people, you're embracing the diversity promoted by a liberal arts education. These diverse perspectives liberate or emancipate you from the here and now and empower you to see things long ago and far away.

◆ The Synoptic Perspective: Integrating Diverse Perspectives to Form a Unified Whole

A liberal arts education helps you not only appreciate multiple perspectives but also integrate them into a meaningful whole (King, Brown, Lindsay, & VanHencke, 2007). Understanding of how the perspectives of time, place, and person interrelate to form a unified whole is sometimes referred to as a synoptic perspective (Cronon, 1998; Heath, 1977). The word derives from a combination of two roots: syn, meaning "together" (as in the word "synthesize"), and optic, meaning "to see." Thus, a "synoptic" perspective literally means to "see things together" or "see the whole." It enables you to see how all the trees come together to form the forest.

A liberal arts education helps you step beyond yourself to see the wider world and connects you with it. By seeing yourself as an integral part of humankind, you become integrated with the whole of humanity; you're able to see how you, as an individual, fit into the big picture—the larger scheme of things (Heath, 1968). When we view ourselves as nested within a web of interconnections with other places, cultures, and times, we become aware of the common humanity we all share. This increased sense of connection with humankind decreases our feelings of personal isolation or alienation (Bellah, Madsen, Sullivan, Swidler, & Tipton, 1985). In his book The Perfect Education, Kenneth Eble (1966, pp. 214–215) skillfully describes this benefit of a liberal arts education:

> *It can provide that overarching life of a people, a community, a world that was going on before the individual came onto the scene and that will continue on after [s]he departs. By such means we come to see the world not alone. Our joys are more intense for being shared. Our sorrows are less destructive for our knowing universal sorrow. Our fears of death fade before the commonness of the occurrence.*

!

Remember

A liberal arts education launches you on a quest for two forms of wholeness: (a) an *inner* wholeness in which elements of self become connected to form a *whole person*, and (b) an *outer* wholeness in which your individual self becomes connected with the *whole world*. This inner and outer quest will enable you to lead a richer, more fulfilling life that's filled with greater breadth, balance, and wholeness.

> "Without exception, the observed changes [during college] involve greater breadth, expansion, and appreciation for the new and different. These changes are eminently consistent with values of a liberal [arts] education, and the evidence for their presence is compelling."
>
> –Ernest Pascarella and Pat Terenzini, How College Affects Students

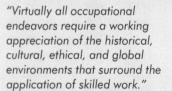

Pause for Reflection

In light of the knowledge you've acquired thus far in this chapter, what points or arguments would you make to counter the claim that the liberal arts are impractical?

◆ Educating You for Life

Research shows that the primary reasons students go to college are to prepare for a career and get a better job (Sax, Lindholm, Astin, Korn, & Mahoney, 2004). While these are important reasons and your career is an important element of your life, a person's vocation or occupation represents just one element of the self. It also represents just one of many roles or responsibilities that you are likely to have in life.

Similar to global issues, personal issues and challenges that individuals face in their everyday lives are multidimensional, requiring perspectives and skills that go well beyond the boundaries of a single academic field or career specialization. Your occupational role represents just one of many roles you assume in life, which include the roles of family member, friend, co-worker, community member, citizen, and possibly, mother or father. A liberal arts education provides you with the breadth of knowledge and the variety skills needed to successfully accommodate the multiple roles and responsibilities you face in life.

> "Virtually all occupational endeavors require a working appreciation of the historical, cultural, ethical, and global environments that surround the application of skilled work."
>
> –Robert Jones, "Liberal Education for the Twenty-First Century: Business Expectations"

> "The finest art, the most difficult art, is the art of living."
>
> –John Albert Macy, American author, poet, and editor of Helen Keller's autobiography

Personal Story

One life role that a liberal arts education helped prepare me for was the role of parent. Courses that I took in psychology and sociology proved to be useful in helping me understand how children develop and how a parent can best support them at different stages of their development. Surprisingly, however, there was one course I took in college that I never expected would ever help me as a parent. That course was statistics, which I took to fulfill a general education requirement in mathematics. It was not a particularly enjoyable course; some of my classmates sarcastically referred to it as "sadistics" because they felt it was a somewhat painful or torturous experience. However, what I learned in that course became valuable to me many years later when, as a parent, my 14-year-old son (Tony) developed a life-threatening disease, leukemia, which is a form of cancer that attacks blood cells. Tony's form of leukemia was a particularly perilous one because it had only a 35 percent average cure rate; in other words, 65 percent of those who develop the disease don't recover and eventually die from it. This statistic was based on patients that received the traditional treatment of chemotherapy, which was the type of treatment that my son began receiving when his cancer was first detected.

Another option for treating Tony's cancer was a bone-marrow transplant, which involved using radiation to destroy all of his own bone marrow (that was making the abnormal blood cells) and replace it with bone marrow donated to him by another person. My wife and I got opinions from doctors at two major cancer centers—one from a center that specialized in chemotherapy, and one from a center that specialized in bone-marrow transplants. The chemotherapy doctors felt strongly that drug treatment would be the better way to treat and cure Tony, and the bone-marrow transplant doctors felt strongly that his chances of survival would be much better if he had a transplant. So, my wife and I had to decide between two opposing recommendations, each made by a respected group of doctors.

To help us reach a decision, I asked both teams of doctors for research studies that had been done on the effectiveness of chemotherapy and bone-marrow transplants for treating my son's particular type of cancer. I read all of these studies and carefully analyzed their statistical findings. I remembered from my statistics course that when an average is calculated for a general group of people (e.g., average cure rate for people with leukemia), it tends to lump together individuals from different subgroups (e.g., males and females or young children and teenagers). Sometimes, when separate statistics are calculated for different subgroups, the results may be different from the average statistic for the whole group. So, when I read the research reports, I looked for any subgroup statistics that may have been calculated. I found two subgroups of patients with my son's particular type of cancer that had a higher rate of cure with chemotherapy than the general (whole-group) average of 35 percent. One subgroup included people with a low number of abnormal cells at the time when the cancer was first diagnosed, and the other subgroup consisted of people whose cancer cells dropped rapidly after their first week of chemotherapy. My son belonged to both of these subgroups, which meant that his chance for cure with chemotherapy was higher than the overall 35 percent average. Furthermore, I found that the statistics showing higher success rate for bone-marrow transplants were based only on patients whose body accepted the donor's bone marrow and did not include those who died because their body rejected the donor's bone marrow. So, the success rates for bone-marrow patients were not actually as high as they appeared to be, because the overall average did not include the subgroup of patients who died because of transplant rejection. Based on these statistics, my wife and I decided to go with chemotherapy and not the transplant operation.

Our son has now been cancer free for more than 5 years, so we think we made the right decision. However, I never imagined that a statistics course, which I took many years ago to fulfill a general education requirement, would help me fulfill my role as a parent and help me make a life-or-death decision about my own son.

—Joe Cuseo

! **Remember**

The liberal arts education not only prepares you for a career but also prepares you for life.

◆ Summary and Conclusion

General education represents the foundation of a college education upon which all academic majors are built. It promotes success in any major and career by supplying students with a set of lifelong learning skills that can be applied in multiple settings and that can be continually used throughout life.

General education promotes development of the whole person (intellectual, emotional, social, physical, spiritual, etc.) and broadens your perspective on the world by expanding (a) your social–spatial perspective to include increasingly larger social groups and more distant places, from the individual to the universe; and (b) your chronological perspective to include the past, present, and future.

Despite popular beliefs the contrary, the liberal arts have many practical benefits, including promoting career mobility and career advancement. Most importantly, a liberal arts education prepares you for life roles other than an occupation, including roles such as family member, community member, and citizen. In short, a liberal arts education prepares you for than a career; it prepares you for life.

Learning More Through the World Wide Web

Internet-Based Resources for Further Information on Liberal Arts Education

For additional information related to the ideas discussed in this chapter, we recommend the following Web sites:

Liberal Arts Education: www.aacu.org/resources/liberaleducation/index.cfm

Liberal Arts Resources: www.eace.org/networks/liberalarts.html

2.1 Planning Your Liberal Arts Education

Since general education is an essential component of your college experience, it should be intentionally planned. This exercise will leave you with a flexible plan that capitalizes on your educational interests while ensuring that your college experience has both breadth and balance.

1. Use your course catalog (bulletin) to identify the general education requirements at your college. The requirements should be organized into general divisions of knowledge similar to those discussed in this chapter (humanities, fine arts, natural sciences, etc.) Within each of these liberal arts divisions, you'll find specific courses listed that fulfill the general education requirements for that particular division. (Catalogs can sometimes be difficult to navigate; if you encounter difficulty or doubt about general education requirements, seek clarification from an academic advisor on campus).

2. You'll probably have some freedom to choose courses from a larger group of courses that fulfill general education requirements within each division. Use your freedom of choice to choose courses whose descriptions capture your curiosity or pique your interest. You can take liberal arts courses not only to fulfill general education requirements but also to test your interest and talent in fields that you may end up choosing as a college major or minor.

3. Highlight the courses in the catalog that you plan to take to fulfill your general education requirements in each division of the liberal arts, and use the form that follows to pencil in the courses you've chosen. (Use pencil because you will likely make some adjustments to your plan.) Remember that the courses you're taking this term may be fulfilling certain general education requirements, so be sure to list them on your planning form.

2.2 General Education Planning Form

Division of the Liberal Arts Curriculum: _____

General education courses you're planning to take to fulfill requirements in this division (record the course number and course title):

_____   _____

_____   _____

_____   _____

Division of the Liberal Arts Curriculum: _____

General education courses you're planning to take to fulfill requirements in this division (record the course number and course title):

_____   _____

_____   _____

_____   _____

Division of the Liberal Arts Curriculum: _____

General education courses you're planning to take to fulfill requirements in this division (record the course number and course title):

_____   _____

_____   _____

_____   _____

Division of the Liberal Arts Curriculum: _____

General education courses you're planning to take to fulfill requirements in this division (record the course number and course title):

_____   _____

_____   _____

_____   _____

Division of the Liberal Arts Curriculum: _____

General education courses you're planning to take to fulfill requirements in this division (record the course number and course title):

_____   _____

_____   _____

_____   _____

4. Look back at the general education courses you've listed and identify the broadening perspectives developed by the liberal arts that each course appears to be developing. (See **pp. 46–49** for a description of these perspectives.) Use the form that follows to ensure that your overall perspective is comprehensive and that you have no blind spots in your liberal arts education. For any perspective that's not covered in your plan, find a course in the catalog that will enable you to address the missing perspective.

Broadening Social–Spatial Perspectives

Perspective   **Course Developing This Perspective**
(See **pp. 46–49** for further
descriptions of these perspectives.)

    Self _____

    Family _____

    Community _____

    Society _____

    Culture _____

    Nation _____

    International _____

    Global _____

    Universe _____

Broadening Chronological Perspectives

Perspective   **Course Developing This Perspective**
(See **pp. 49–50** for detailed
description of these perspectives.)

    Historical _____

    Contemporary _____

    Futuristic _____

5. Look back at the general education courses you've listed and identify what element of holistic (whole-person) development each course appears to be developing. (See **pp. 41–44** for a description of each of these elements.) Use the form that follows to ensure that your course selection didn't overlook any element of the self. For any element that's not covered in your plan, find a course in the catalog or a cocurricular experience program that will enable you to address the missing area. For cocurricular learning experiences (e.g., leadership and volunteer experiences), consult your student handbook or contact someone in the Office of Student Life.

Dimensions of Self (See **pp. 41–44** for further description of these dimensions.)	**Course or Cocurricular Experience Developing This Dimension of Self** (Consult your student handbook for cocurricular experiences.)
Intellectual	_____
Emotional	_____
Social	_____
Ethical	_____
Physical	_____
Spiritual	_____
Vocational	_____
Personal	_____

!

Remember

This general education plan is not set in stone; it may be modified as you gain more experience with the college curriculum and campus life. Its purpose is not to restrict your educational exploration or experimentation but to give it some direction, breadth, and balance.

Dazed and Confused: General Education versus Career Specialization

Joe Tech was really looking forward to college because he thought he would have freedom to select the courses he wanted and the opportunity to get into the major of his choice (computer science). However, he's shocked and disappointed with his first-term schedule of classes because it consists mostly of required general education courses that do not seem to relate in any way to his major. He's frustrated further because some of these courses are about subjects that he already took in high school (English, history, and biology). He's beginning to think he would be better off quitting college and going to a technical school where he could get right into computer science and immediately begin to acquire the knowledge and skills he'll need to prepare him for his intended career.

Reflection and Discussion Questions

1. Can you relate to this student, or do you know of students who feel the same way as Joe does?

2. If Joe decides to leave college for a technical school, how do you see it affecting his future: (a) in the short run and (b) in the long run?

3. Do you see any way Joe might strike a balance between pursuing his career interest and obtaining his college degree so that he could work toward achieving both goals at the same time?

Goal Setting, Motivation, and Character

3

1. How would you define the word "successful"?

_____

_____

_____

LEARNING GOAL

To develop meaningful goals to strive for, along with strategies for maintaining motivation and building character to achieve those goals.

◆ What Does Being "Successful" Mean to You?

The word "success" means to achieve a desired outcome; it derives from the Latin root *successus*, which means "to follow or come after" (as in the word "succession"). Thus, by definition, success involves an order or sequence of actions that lead to a desired outcome. The process starts with identifying an end (goal) and then finding a means (sequence of steps) to reach that goal (achieving success). Goal setting is the first step in the process of becoming successful because it gives you something specific to strive for and ensures that you start off in the right direction. Studies consistently show that setting goals is a more effective self-motivational strategy than simply telling yourself that you should try hard or do your best (Boekaerts, Pintrich, & Zeidner, 2000; Locke & Latham, 1990).

By setting goals, you show initiative—you initiate the process of gaining control of your future and taking charge of your life. By taking initiative, you demonstrate what psychologists call an internal locus of control—you believe that the locus (location or source) of control for events in your life is *internal*, and thus inside of you and within your control, rather than *external*, or outside of you and beyond your control (controlled by such factors as luck, chance, or fate; Rotter, 1966).

Research has revealed that individuals with a strong internal locus of control display the following characteristics:

1. Greater independence and self-direction (Van Overwalle, Mervielde, & De Schuyer, 1995);
2. More accurate self-assessment (Hashaw, Hammond, & Rogers, 1990; Lefcourt, 1982);
3. Higher levels of learning and achievement (Wilhite, 1990); and
4. Better physical health (Maddi, 2002; Seligman, 1991).

❝

"You've got to be careful if you don't know where you're going because you might not get there."

—Yogi Berra, Hall of Fame baseball player

"There is perhaps nothing worse than reaching the top of the ladder and discovering that you're on the wrong wall."

—Joseph Campbell, American professor and writer

"Success is getting what you want. Happiness is wanting what you get."

—Dale Carnegie, author of the best-selling book *How to Win Friends and Influence People* (1936) and founder of The Dale Carnegie Course, a worldwide program for business based on his teachings

❝

"The future is literally in our hands to mold as we like. But we cannot wait until tomorrow. Tomorrow is now."

—Eleanor Roosevelt, UN diplomat and humanitarian

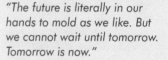

An internal locus of control also contributes to the development of another positive trait that psychologists call self-efficacy—the belief that you have power to produce a positive effect on the outcomes of your life (Bandura, 1994). People with low self-efficacy tend to feel helpless, powerless, and passive; they think (and allow) things to happen to them rather than taking charge and making things happen for them. College students with a strong sense of self-efficacy believe they're in control of their educational success, regardless of their past or current circumstances.

If you have a strong sense of self-efficacy, you initiate action, put forth effort, and sustain that effort until you reach your goal. If you encounter setbacks or bad breaks along the way, you don't give up or give in; you persevere or push on (Bandura, 1986, 1997).

Students with a strong sense of academic self-efficacy have been found to:

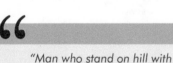

Pause for Reflection

You are not required by law or by others to attend college; you've made the decision to continue your education. Do you believe you are in charge of your educational destiny?

Why or why not?

1. Put great effort into their studies;
2. Use active-learning strategies;
3. Capitalize on campus resources; and
4. Persist in the face of obstacles (Multon, Brown, & Lent, 1991; Zimmeman, 1995).

Students with self-efficacy also possess a strong sense of personal responsibility. As the breakdown of the word "responsible" implies, they are "response" "able"—that is, they think they're able to respond effectively to personal challenges, including academic challenges.

Students with self-efficacy don't have a false sense of entitlement. They don't feel they're entitled to, or owed, anything; they believe that success is earned and is theirs for the taking. For example, studies show that students who convert their college degree into a successful career have two common characteristics: personal initiative and a positive attitude (Pope, 1990). They don't take a passive approach and assume a good position will fall into their lap; nor do they believe they are owed a position simply because they have a college degree or credential. Instead, they become actively involved in the job-hunting process and use various job-search strategies (Brown & Krane, 2000).

Strategies for Effective Goal Setting

Motivation begins with goal setting. Studies show that people who neglect to set and pursue life goals are prone to feelings of "life boredom" and a belief that one's life is meaningless (Bargdill, 2000).

Goals may be classified into three general categories: long range, midrange, and short range, depending on the length of time it takes to reach them and the order in which they are to be achieved. Short-range goals need to be completed before a mid-range goal can be reached, and mid-range goals must be reached before a long-range goal can be achieved. For example, if your long-range goal is a successful career, you must complete the courses required for a degree that will allow you entry into a career (mid-range goals); to reach your mid-range goal of a college degree, you need to successfully complete the courses you're taking this term (short-range goals).

Setting Long-Range Goals

Setting effective long-range goals involves two processes: (a) self-awareness, or insight into who you are now, and (b) self-projection, or a vision of what you want to become. When you engage in both of these processes, you're able to see a connection between your short- and your long-range goals.

Long-range goal setting enables you to take an approach to your future that is proactive—acting beforehand to anticipate and control your future life rather than putting it off and being forced to react to it without a plan. Research shows that people who neglect to set goals for themselves are more likely to experience boredom with life (Bargdill, 2000). Setting long-range goals and planning ahead also help reduce feelings of anxiety about the future because you've given it forethought, which gives you greater power to control it (i.e., it gives you a stronger sense of self-efficacy). As the old saying goes, "To be forewarned is to be forearmed."

Remember that setting long-range goals and developing long-range plans doesn't mean you can't adjust or modify them. Your goals can undergo change as you change, develop skills, acquire knowledge, and discover interests or talents. Finding yourself and discovering your path in life are among the primary purposes of a college education. Don't think that the process of setting long-range goals means you will be locked into a premature plan and reduced options. Instead, it will give you something to reach for and some momentum to get you moving in the right direction.

Pause for Reflection

In what area or areas of your life do you feel that you've been able to exert the most control and achieve the most positive results?

In what area or areas of your life do you wish you had more control and were achieving better results?

What have you done in those areas of your life in which you've taken charge and gained control that might be transferred or applied to those areas in which you need to gain more control?

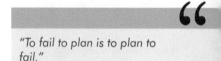

"To fail to plan is to plan to fail."

—Robert Wubbolding, internationally known author, psychologist, and teacher

◆ Steps in the Goal-Setting Process

Effective goal setting involves a four-step sequence:

1. **Awareness of yourself.** Your personal interests, abilities and talents, and values;

   ↓

2. **Awareness of your options.** The choices available to you;

   ↓

3. **Awareness of the options that best fit you.** The goals most compatible with your personal abilities, interests, values, and needs;

   ↓

4. **Awareness of the process.** The steps that you need to take to reach your chosen goal.

Discussed in the next sections are strategies for taking each of these steps in the goal-setting process.

You have brains in your head. You have feet in your shoes. You can steer yourself any direction you choose.

—Theodore Seuss Giesel, a.k.a. Dr. Seuss, author of children's books including *Oh the Places You'll Go*

Step 1. Gain Awareness of Yourself

The goals you choose to pursue say a lot about who you are and what you want from life. Thus, self-awareness is a critical first step in the process of goal setting. You must know yourself before you can choose the goals you want to achieve. While this may seem obvious, self-awareness and self-discovery are often overlooked aspects of the goal-setting process. Deepening your self-awareness puts you in a better position to select and choose goals and to pursue a personal path that's true to who you are and what you want to become.

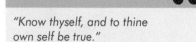

"Know thyself, and to thine own self be true."

—Plato, ancient Greek philosopher

> **Remember**
>
> Self-awareness is the first, most important step in the process of making any important life choice or decision. Good decisions are built on a deep understanding of one's self.

No one is in a better position to know who you are, and what you want to be, than *you*. One effective way to get to know yourself more deeply is through self-questioning. You can begin to deepen your self-awareness by asking yourself questions that can stimulate your thinking about your inner qualities and priorities. Effective self-questioning can launch you on an inward quest or journey to self-discovery and self-insight, which is the critical first step to effective goal setting. For example, if your long-range goal is career success, you can launch your voyage toward achieving this goal by asking yourself thought-provoking questions related to your personal:

- **Interests.** What you like to do;
- **Abilities and talents.** What you're good at doing; and
- **Values.** What you believe is worth doing.

The following questions are designed to sharpen your self-awareness with respect to your interests, abilities, and values. As you read each question, briefly note what thought or thoughts come to mind about yourself.

> "In order to succeed, you must know what you are doing, like what you are doing, and believe in what you are doing."
>
> —Will Rogers, Native American humorist and actor

Your Personal Interests

1. What tends to grab your attention and hold it for long periods?

2. What sorts of things are you naturally curious about or tend to intrigue you?

3. What do you enjoy and do as often as you possibly can?

4. What do you look forward to or get excited about?

5. What are your favorite hobbies or pastimes?

6. When you're with your friends, what do you like to talk about or spend time doing together?

7. What has been your most stimulating or enjoyable learning experience?

8. If you've had previous work or volunteer experience, what jobs or tasks did you find most enjoyable or stimulating?

9. When time seems to fly by for you, what are you usually doing?

10. What do you like to read about?

11. When you open a newspaper or log on to the Internet, what do you tend to read first?

12. When you find yourself daydreaming or fantasizing about your future life, what do you most find yourself doing?

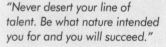

Pause for Reflection

From your responses to the preceding questions, identify a long-range goal you could pursue that's compatible with your personal interests. In the space that follows, note the goal and the interests that are compatible with it.

Your Personal Abilities and Talents

1. What seems to come easily or naturally to you?

2. What would you say is your greatest or talent or personal gift?

3. What do you excel at when you apply yourself and put forth your best effort?

4. What are your most advanced or well-developed skills?

5. What would you say has been the greatest accomplishment or achievement in your life thus far?

6. What about yourself are you most proud of or do you take the most pride in doing?

7. When others come to you for advice or assistance, what is it usually for?

8. What would your best friend or friends say is your best quality, trait, or characteristic?

> "Never desert your line of talent. Be what nature intended you for and you will succeed."
>
> –Sydney Smith, eighteenth-century English writer and defender of the oppressed

9. When you had a strong feeling of being successful after you had done something, what was it that you did?

10. If you've received awards or other forms of recognition, what have you received them for?

Pause for Reflection

From your responses to the preceding questions, identify a long-range goal you could pursue that's compatible with your personal abilities and talents. In the space that follows, note the goal and the abilities and talents that are compatible with it.

11. On what types of learning tasks or activities have you experienced the most success?

12. In what types of courses do you tend to earn the highest grades?

Your Personal Values

1. What matters most to you?

2. If you were to single out one thing you stand for or believe in, what would it be?

3. What would you say are your highest priorities in life?

4. What makes you feel good about what you're doing when you're doing it?

5. If there were one thing in the world you could change, improve, or make a difference in, what would it be?

6. When you have extra spending money, what do you usually spend it on?

7. When you have free time, what do you usually find yourself doing?

8. What does living a "good life" mean to you?

9. How would you define success? (What would it take for you to feel that you were successful?)

10. How would you define happiness? (What would it take for you to feel happy?)

11. Do you have any heroes or anyone you admire, look up to, or feel has set an example worth following? If yes, who and why?

12. How would you like others to see you? Rank these characteristics in the order of their priority for you (1 = highest, 4 = lowest).

    • Smart _____

    • Wealthy _____

    • Creative _____

    • Caring _____

> "Do what you value; value what you do."
>
> –Sidney Simon, author of *Values Clarification* (XXXX) and *In Search of Values*

Pause for Reflection

From your responses to the preceding questions, identify a long-range goal you could pursue that's compatible with your personal values. In the space that follows, note the goal and the values that are compatible with it.

Step 2. Gain Awareness of Your Options

The second critical step in the goal-setting process is to become aware of your long-range goal choices. For example, to effectively choose a career goal, you need to be aware of the careers options available to you and have a realistic understanding of the type of work done in these careers. To gain this knowledge, you'll need to capitalize on available resources, such as by doing the following:

1. Reading books about different careers
2. Taking career development courses
3. Interviewing people in different career fields
4. Observing (shadowing) people working in different careers

One characteristic of effective goal setting is to create goals that are realistic. In the case of careers, getting firsthand experience in actual work settings (e.g., shadowing, internships, volunteer services, and part-time work) would allow you to get a realistic view of what work is like in certain careers—as opposed to the idealized or fantasized way careers are portrayed on TV and in the movies.

> "Students [may be] pushed into careers by their families, while others have picked one just to relieve their anxiety about not having a career choice. Still others may have picked popular or lucrative careers, knowing nothing of what they're really like or what it takes to prepare for them."
>
> –Lee Upcraft, Joni Finney, and Peter Garland, student development specialists

Step 3. Gain Awareness of the Options That Best Fit You

In college, you'll have many educational options and career goals from which to choose. To deepen your awareness of what fields may be a good fit for you, take a course in that field to test out how well it matches your interests, values, talents, and learning style. Ideally, you want to select a field that closely taps into, or builds on, your strongest skills and talents. Choosing a field that's compatible with your strongest abilities should enable you to master the skills required by that field more deeply and efficiently. You're more likely to succeed or excel in a field that draws on your talents, and the success you experience will, in turn, strengthen your self-esteem, self-confidence, and drive to continue with it. You've probably heard of the proverb "If there's a will, there's a way" (i.e., when you're motivated, you're more likely to succeed). However, it's also true that "If there's a way, there's a will" (i.e., when you know how to do something well, you're more motivated to do it).

Student Perspective

"Making good grades and doing well in school helps my ego. It gives me confidence, and I like that feeling."

–First-year college student (Franklin, 2002)

Pause for Reflection

Think about a career you're considering and answer the following questions:

1. Why are you considering this career? What led or caused you to become interested in this choice? Why or why not?

2. Would you say that your interest in this career is motivated primarily by intrinsic factors (i.e., factors "inside" of you, such as your personal abilities, interests, needs, and values)? Or would you say that your interest in the career is motivated more heavily by extrinsic factors (i.e., factors "outside" of you, such as starting salary, pleasing parents, and meeting family expectations or societal expectations for your gender or ethnicity)?

Step 4. Gain Awareness of the Process

The fourth and final step in an effective goal-setting process is becoming aware of the steps needed to reach your goal. For example, if you've set the goal of achieving a college degree in a particular major, you need to be aware of the course requirements for a degree in that major. Similarly, to set a career goal, you need to know what major or majors lead to that career because some careers require a specific major but other careers may be entered through various majors.

! Remember

The four-step process for effective goal setting applies to more than just educational goals. It's a strategic process that could and should be applied to any goal you set for yourself in life, at any stage of your life.

◆ Motivation: Moving Toward Your Long-Range Goals

The word "motivation" derives from the Latin *movere*, meaning "to move." Success comes to those who exert effort to move toward their goal. Knowledge of all kinds of success-promoting strategies, such as those discussed this text, provides only the potential for success; turning this potential into reality requires motivation, which converts knowledge into action. If you have all the knowledge, strategies, and skills for being successful but don't have the will to succeed, there's no way you will succeed. Studies show that without a strong personal commitment to attain a goal it will not be reached, no matter how well designed the goal and the plan to reach it are (Locke & Latham, 1990).

Motivation consists of three elements that may be summarized as the "three Ds" of motivation:

1. Drive
2. Discipline
3. Determination

Drive

Drive is the force within you that supplies you with the energy needed to overcome inertia and initiate action. Much like shifting into the drive gear is necessary to move your car forward, it takes personal drive to move forward and toward your goals.

People with drive aren't just dreamers: They're dreamers and doers. They take action to convert their dreams into reality, and they hustle—they go all out and give it their all, all of the time, to achieve their goals. College students with drive approach college with passion and enthusiasm. They don't hold back and work halfheartedly; they give 100 percent and put their whole heart and soul into the experience.

Discipline

Discipline includes such positive qualities as commitment, devotion, and dedication. These personal qualities enable you to keep going over an extended period. Successful people think big but start small—they take all the small steps and diligently do all the little things that need to be done, which in the long run add up to a big accomplishment: the achievement of their long-range goal.

People who are self-disciplined accept the day-to-day sweat, toil, and perspiration needed to attain their long-term aspirations. They're willing to tolerate short-term strain or pain for long-term gain. They have the self-control and self-restraint needed to resist the impulse for instant gratification or the temptation to do what they feel like doing instead of what they need to do. They're willing to sacrifice their immediate needs and desires in the short run to do what is necessary to put them where they want to be in the long run.

> "Mere knowledge is not power; it is only possibility. Action is power; and its highest manifestation is when it is directed by knowledge."
>
> —Francis Bacon, English philosopher, lawyer, and champion of modern science

> "You can lead a horse to water, but you can't make him drink."
>
> —Author unknown

> "Education is not the filling of a pail, but the lighting of a fire."
>
> —William Butler Yeats, Irish poet and playwright

> "Success comes to those who hustle."
>
> —Abraham Lincoln, 16th U.S. president and author of the Emancipation Proclamation, which set the stage for the abolition of slavery in the United States

Pause for Reflection

Think about something that you do with drive, effort, and intensity. What thoughts, attitudes, and behaviors do you display when you do it?

Do you see ways in which you could apply the same approach to your college experience?

Remember

Sacrifices made for a short time can bring benefits lasting a lifetime.

> "I long to accomplish some great and noble task, but it is my chief duty to accomplish small tasks as if they were great and noble."
>
> —Helen Keller, seeing- and hearing-impaired author and activist for the rights of women and the handicapped

The ability to delay short-term (and short-sighted) gratification is a distinctively human characteristic that differentiates people from other animals. As you can see in **Figure 3.1**, the upper frontal part of the brain that's responsible for long-range planning and controlling emotions and impulses is much larger in humans than it is in one of the most intelligent and human-like animals, the chimpanzee.

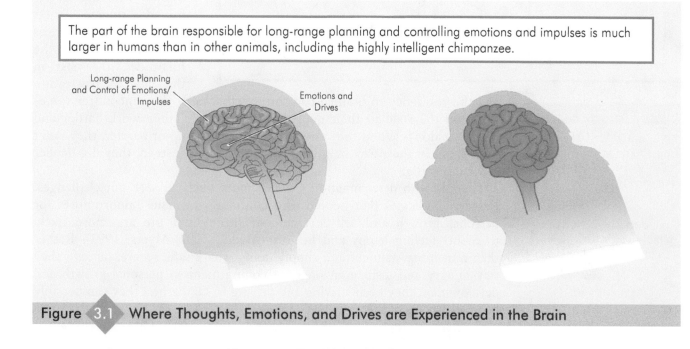

The part of the brain responsible for long-range planning and controlling emotions and impulses is much larger in humans than in other animals, including the highly intelligent chimpanzee.

Long-range Planning and Control of Emotions/Impulses

Emotions and Drives

Figure 3.1   Where Thoughts, Emotions, and Drives are Experienced in the Brain

Remember

Sometimes you've got to do what you have to do in order to get to do what you want to do.

Personal Story

When I entered college in the mid-1970s, I was a first-generation student from an extremely impoverished background. Not only did I have to work to pay for part of my education, but I also needed to assist my family financially. I stocked grocery store shelves at night during the week and waited tables at a local county club on the weekends. Managing my life, time, school, and work required full-time effort. However, I always understood that my purpose was to graduate from college and all of my other efforts supported that goal. Thus, I went to class and arrived on time even when I did not feel like going to class. One of my greatest successes in life was to keep my mind and body focused on the ultimate prize of getting a college education. That success has paid off many times over.

—Aaron Thompson

Postponing immediate or impulsive satisfaction of material desires is a key element of effective college financing and long-term financial success.

Studies show that individuals with dedication—who are deeply committed to what they do—are more likely to report that they are healthy and happy (Maddi, 2002; Myers, 1993).

Determination

People who are determined pursue their goals with a relentless tenacity. They have the fortitude to persist in the face of frustration and the resiliency to bounce back after setbacks. If they encounter something on the road to their goal that's hard to do, they work harder and longer to do it. When they encounter a major bump or barrier, they don't let it stand in their way by giving up or giving in; instead, they dig deeper and keep going.

People with determination are also more likely to seek out challenges. Research indicates that people who continue to pursue opportunities for personal growth and self-development throughout life are more likely to report feeling happy and healthy (Maddi, 2002; Myers, 1993). Rather than remaining stagnant and simply doing what's safe, secure, or easy, they stay hungry and display an ongoing commitment to personal growth and development; they keep striving and driving to be the best they can possibly be in all aspects of life.

Student Perspective

"Why is it so hard when I *have* to do something and so easy when I *want* to do something?"

—First-year college student

"Self-discipline is the ability to make yourself do the thing you have to do, when it ought be done, whether you like it or not."

—Thomas Henry Huxley, nineteenth-century English biologist

"If you are going through hell, keep going."

-Winston Churchill

"*SUCCESS is peace of mind which is a direct result of self-satisfaction in knowing you made the effort to become the best that you are capable of becoming.*"

—John Wooden, college basketball coach and author of the *Pyramid of*

Remember

On the highway to success, you can't be a passive passenger; you're the driver and at the wheel. Your goal setting will direct you there, and your motivation will drive you there.

Strategies for Maintaining Motivation and Progress Toward Your Goals

Reaching your goals requires will and energy; it also requires skill and strategy. Listed here are strategies for maintaining your motivation and commitment to reaching your goals.

Put your goals in writing. When you put your goals in writing, they become visible and memorable. Doing so can provide you with a sense of direction, a source of motivation for putting your plan into action, or a written contract with yourself that makes you more accountable to following through on your commitment.

Create a visual map of your goals. Lay out your goals in the form a flowchart to show the steps you'll be taking from your short- through your mid- to your long-range goals. Visual diagrams can help you "see" where you want to go, enabling you to connect where you are now and where you want to be. Diagramming can be energizing because it gives you a sneak preview of the finish line and a maplike overview of how to get there.

Keep a record of your progress. Research indicates that the act of monitoring and recording progress toward goals can increase motivation to continue pursuing them (Matsui, Okada, & Inoshita, 1983). The act of keeping records of your progress probably increases your motivation by giving you frequent feedback on your progress and positive reinforcement for staying on track and moving toward your target (long-range goal) (Bandura & Cervone, 1983; Schunk, 1995). For example, you can keep a journal of the goals you've reached. Your entries can keep you motivated by supplying you with concrete evidence of your progress and commitment. You can also chart or graph your progress, which can sometimes provide a powerful visual display of your upward trends and patterns. Place it where you see it regularly to keep your goals in your sight and on your mind.

Develop a skeletal résumé of your goals. Include your goals as separate sections or categories that will be fleshed out as you complete them. Your to-be-completed résumé can provide a framework or blueprint for organizing, building, and tracking progress toward your goals. It can also serve as a visual reminder of the things you plan to accomplish and eventually showcase to potential employers. Furthermore, every time you look at your growing résumé, you'll be reminded of your past accomplishments, which can energize and motivate you to reach your goals. As you fill in and build up your résumé, you can literally see how much you've achieved, which boosts your self-confidence and motivation to continue achieving. (See Chapter 11, **p. 284**, for a sample skeletal résumé.)

Reward yourself for making steady progress toward your long-range goals. Reward is already built into reaching your long-range goal because it represents the end of your trip, which lands you at your desired destination (e.g., in a successful career). However, short- and mid-range goals may not be desirable ends in themselves but rather means to a desirable end (your long-range goal). Consequently, you need to intentionally reward yourself for landing on these smaller stepping stones up the path to your long-range goal. When you complete these short- and mid-range goals, record and reward your accomplishments (e.g., celebrate your successful completion of midterms or finals by treating yourself to something you enjoy).

A habit of perseverance and persistence through all intermediate steps needed to reach a long-range goal, like any other habit, is more likely to continue if it's followed by a reward (positive reinforcement). Setting small goals, moving steadily toward them, and rewarding yourself for reaching them are components of a simple but powerful strategy. This strategy will help you maintain motivation over the extended period needed to reach a long-range goal.

Capitalize on available campus resources that can help you stay on track and move toward your goal. Research indicates that college success results from a combination of what students do for themselves (personal responsibility) and what they do to capitalize on the resources available to them (resourcefulness; Pascarella & Terenzini, 1991, 2005). Successful college students are resourceful students; they seek out and take advantage of college resources to help them reach their goals.

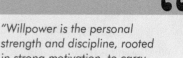

"Life isn't a matter of milestones but of moments."

–Rose Fitzgerald Kennedy, philanthropist and mother of John F. and Robert F. Kennedy

"Willpower is the personal strength and discipline, rooted in strong motivation, to carry out your plans. 'Waypower' is the exertion of willpower that helps you find resources and support."

–Jerry Pattengale, history professor and author of *The Purpose-Guided Student: Dream to Succeed*

Don't only see your advisor during the mad rush of registration for the short-range purpose of scheduling next term's classes; schedule advisor appiontments at less hectic times to discuss your long-range educational goals.

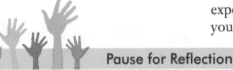

> "Develop an inner circle of close associations in which the mutual attraction is not sharing problems or needs. The mutual attraction should be values and goals."
>
> —Denis Waitley, former mental trainer for U.S. Olympic athletes and author of *Seeds of Greatness*

> "I make progress by having people around who are smarter than I am."
>
> —Henry Kaiser, successful industrialist known as the father of American shipbuilding

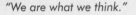

Pause for Reflection

What would you say is the biggest setback or obstacle you've overcome in your life thus far?

How did you overcome it? (What enabled you to get past it or prevented you from being blocked by it?)

> "We are what we think."
>
> —Hindu Prince Siddhartha Gautama, a.k.a. Buddha, founder of the philosophy and religion of Buddhism

For example, a resourceful student who's having trouble deciding what field of study to pursue for a degree will seek assistance from an academic advisor on campus. A resourceful student who's interested in a particular career but is unclear about the best educational path to take toward that career will use the Career Development Center as a resource.

Use your social resources. The power of social support groups for helping people achieve personal goals is well documented by research in various fields (Ewell, 1997; Moeller, 1999). You can use the power of people by surrounding yourself with peers who are committed to successfully achieving their educational goals and by avoiding "toxic" people who are likely to poison your plans or dampen your dreams.

For example, find a supportive and motivating friend and make a mutual pact to help each other reach your respective goals. This step could be taken to a more formal level by drawing up a "social contract" whereby you and your partner are "cowitnesses" or designated social-support agents whose role is to help each other stay on track and move toward long-range goals. Studies show that making a public commitment to a goal increases your commitment to it, probably because it becomes a matter of personal pride and integrity that's seen not only through your own eyes but also through the eyes of others (Hollenbeck, Williams, & Klein, 1989).

Convert setbacks into comebacks. The type of thoughts you have after experiencing a setback can affect your emotional reaction to it and the action you take in response. For instance, what you think about a poor performance (e.g., a poor test grade) can affect your emotional reaction to that grade and what action, or lack of action, you take in response to it. You can react to the poor grade by knocking yourself down with a putdown ("I'm a loser") or by building yourself back up with a positive pep talk ("I'm going to learn from my mistakes on this test and rebound with a stronger performance on the next one").

If a poor past performance is seen not as a personal failure but as learning opportunity, the setback may be turned into a comeback. Here are some notable people who turned early setbacks into successful comebacks:

- Louis Pasteur, famous bacteriologist, who failed his admission test to the University of Paris;
- Albert Einstein, Nobel Prize–winning physicist, who failed math in elementary school;

- Thomas Edison, prolific inventor, who was once expelled from school as "uneducable";
- Johnny Unitas, Hall of Fame football player, who was cut twice from professional football teams early in his career.

In response to their early setbacks, these successful people didn't get bitter; they got better. Getting mad or sad about a setback is likely to make you stressed or depressed and leave you focused on a past event that you can no longer control. By reacting rationally to a poor performance and using the results as feedback to improve your future performance, you gain control of it. You put yourself in the position to convert the setback into a comeback and turn a liability into an opportunity.

This can be a challenging task because when you have an experience, your response to it passes through emotional areas of the brain before it reaches areas of the brain involved in rational thinking and reasoning (see **Figure 3.2**; LeDoux, 1998).

Thus, your brain reacts to events emotionally before it does rationally. If the experience triggers intense emotions (e.g., anger, anxiety, or sadness after receiving a bad test grade), your emotional reaction has the potential to short-circuit or wipe out rational thinking. Thus, if you find yourself beginning to feel overwhelmed by negative emotions following a setback, you need to consciously and quickly block them by rational thoughts (e.g., thinking or saying to yourself, "Before I get carried away emotionally, let me think this through rationally"). This involves more than simply saying, "I have to think positively." Instead, you should develop a set of specific counterthinking strategies ready to use as soon as you begin to think negatively. Described here are thinking strategies that you can use to maintain motivation and minimize negative thinking in reaction to setbacks.

Whatever you do, don't let setbacks make you mad or sad, particularly at early stages in your college experience, because you're just beginning to learn what it takes to be successful in college. A bad performance can be turned into a good learning experience by using the results as an error detector for identifying sources or causes of your mistakes and as feedback for improving your future performance.

> "What happens is not as important as how you react to what happens."
>
> –Thaddeus Golas, *Lazy Man's Guide to Enlightenment*

> "When written in Chinese, the word 'crisis' is composed of two characters. One represents danger, and the other represents opportunity."
>
> –John F. Kennedy, 35th U.S. president

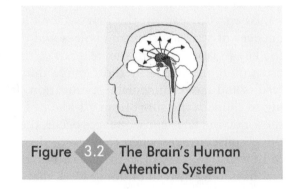

Figure 3.2 The Brain's Human Attention System

Information passes through the emotional center of the brain (lower, shaded area) before reaching the center responsible for rational thinking (upper area). Thus, people need to counteract their tendency to respond emotionally and irrationally to personal setbacks by making a conscious attempt to respond rationally and reflectively.

Remember

Don't let past mistakes bring you down emotionally or motivationally; however, don't ignore or neglect them either. Instead, inspect them, reflect on them, and correct them so that they don't happen again.

Maintain positive expectations. Just as your thoughts in reaction to something that's already taken place can affect your motivation, so can thoughts

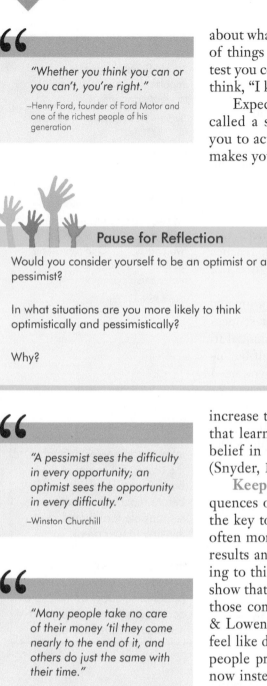

"Whether you think you can or you can't, you're right."

–Henry Ford, founder of Ford Motor and one of the richest people of his generation

Pause for Reflection

Would you consider yourself to be an optimist or a pessimist?

In what situations are you more likely to think optimistically and pessimistically?

Why?

"A pessimist sees the difficulty in every opportunity; an optimist sees the opportunity in every difficulty."

–Winston Churchill

"Many people take no care of their money 'til they come nearly to the end of it, and others do just the same with their time."

–Johann Wolfgang von Goethe, German poet, dramatist, and author of the epic Faust

"You've got to think about 'big things' while you're doing small things, so that all the small things go in the right direction."

–Alvin Toffler, American futurologist and author who predicted the future effects of technology on our society

about what you expect to happen next affect what will occur. Your expectations of things to come can be either positive or negative. For example, before a test you could think, "I'm poised, confident, and ready to do it." Or you could think, "I know I'm going to fail this test; I just know it."

Expectations can lead to what sociologists and psychologists have called a self-fulfilling prophecy—a positive or negative expectation leads you to act in a way that is consistent with your expectation, which, in turn, makes your expectation come true. For instance, if you expect you're going to fail an exam ("What's the use? I'm going to fail anyway."), you're less likely to put as much effort into studying for the test. During the test, your negative expectation is likely reduce your test confidence and elevate you test anxiety; for example, if you experience difficulty with the first item on a test, you may get anxious and begin to think you're going to have difficulty with all remaining items and flunk the entire exam. All of this negative thinking is likely to increase the probability that your expectation of doing poorly on the exam will become a reality.

In contrast, positive expectations can lead to a positive self-fulfilling prophecy: If you expect to do well on an exam, you're more likely to demonstrate higher levels of effort, confidence, and concentration, all of which combine to increase the likelihood that you'll earn a higher test grade. Research shows that learning and practicing positive self-talk increase a sense of hope—a belief in the ability to reach goals and the ability to actually reach them (Snyder, 1994).

Keep your eye on the prize. Don't lose sight of the long-term consequences of your short-term choices and decisions. Long-range thinking is the key to reaching long-range goals. Unfortunately, however, humans are often more motivated by short-range thinking because it produces quicker results and more immediate gratification. It's more convenient and tempting to think in the short term ("I like it. I want it. I want it now."). Studies show that the later consequences occur, the less likely people are to consider those consequences when they make their decisions (Ainslie, 1975; Elster & Lowenstein, 1992; Lewin, 1935). For example, choosing to do what you feel like doing instead of doing work that needs to be done is why so many people procrastinate, and choosing to use a credit card to get something now instead of saving money to buy it later is why so many people pile up credit-card debt.

To be successful in the long run, you need to keep your focus on the big picture—your long-range goals and dreams that provide your motivation. At the same time, you need to focus on the details—the due dates, to-do lists, and day-to-day duties that require perspiration but keep you on track and going in the right direction.

Thus, setting an important life goal and steadily progressing toward that long-range goal requires two means of focusing. One is a narrow-focus lens that allows you to view the details immediately in front of you. The other is a wide-focus lens that gives you a big-picture view of what's further ahead of you (your long-range goal). Success involves seeing the connection between the small, short-term chores and challenges (e.g., completing an assignment that's due next week) and the large, long-range picture (e.g., college graduation and a successful future). Thus, you need to periodically shift from a wide-focus lens that gives you a vision of the bigger, more distant picture to a narrow-focus lens that shifts your attention to completing the smaller tasks immediately ahead of you and keeping on the path to your long-range goal: future success.

> *"Whoever wants to reach a distant goal must take many small steps."*
>
> –Helmut Schmidt, former chancellor of West Germany

Personal Story

When I was an assistant coach for a youth soccer team, I noticed that many of the less successful players tended to make one of two mistakes when they were trying to move with the ball. Some spent too much time looking down, focusing on the ball at their feet and trying to be sure that they did not lose control of it. By not lifting their head and looking ahead periodically, they often missed open territory, open teammates, or an open goal. Other unsuccessful players made the opposite mistake: They spent too much time with their heads up, trying to see saw where they were headed. By not looking down at the ball immediately in front of them, they often lost control of the ball, moved ahead without it, or sometimes stumbled over it and fell flat on their face. Successful soccer players on the team were in the habit of shifting their focus between looking down to maintain control of the ball immediately in front of them and lifting their eyes to see where they were headed.

The more I thought about how successful players alternate between handling the ball in front of them and viewing the goal further ahead, it struck me that this was a metaphor for success in life. Successful people alternate between both of these perspectives so that they don't lose sight of how completing the short-range tasks in front of them connects with the long-range goal ahead of them.

—Joe Cuseo

! Remember

Keep your future dreams and current tasks in clear focus. Integrating these two perspectives will produce an image that can provide you with the inspiration to complete your college education and the determination to complete your day-to-day tasks.

◆ Personal Character

Reaching your goals depends on acquiring and using effective strategies, but it takes something more. Ultimately, success emerges from the inside out; it flows from positive qualities or attributes found within you, which, collectively, form your personal character.

> *"If you do not find it within yourself, where will you go to get it?"*
>
> –Zen saying (Zen is a branch of Buddhism that emphasizes seeing deeply into the nature of things and ongoing self-awareness)

We become successful and effective humans when our actions and deeds become a natural extension of who we are and how we live. At first, developing the habits associated with achieving success and leading a productive life may require effort and intense concentration because these behaviors may be new to you. However, if these actions occur consistently enough, they're transformed into natural habits.

When you engage in effective habits regularly, they become virtues. A virtue may be defined as a characteristic or trait that is valued as good or admirable, and someone who possesses a collection of important virtues is said to be a person of character (Peterson & Seligman, 2004).

> *"We are what we repeatedly do. Excellence, then, is not an act, but a habit."*
>
> –Aristotle, ancient Greek philosopher

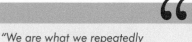

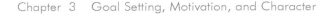

Three virtues in particular are important for success in college and beyond:

1. Wisdom
2. Integrity
3. Civility

Wisdom

When you use the knowledge you acquire to guide your behavior toward doing what is effective or good, you demonstrate wisdom (Staudinger & Baltes, 1994). For example, if you apply your knowledge of the four research-based principles found in this book (i.e., active involvement, resourcefulness, collaboration, and reflection) to guide your behavior in college, you are exhibiting wisdom.

Integrity

The word "integrity" comes from the same root as the word "integrate," which captures a key characteristic of people with integrity: their outer self is integrated or in harmony with their inner self. For example, "outer-directed" people decide on their personal standards of conduct by looking outward to see what others are doing (Riesman, Glazer, & Denney, 2001). In contrast, individuals with integrity are "inner directed"—their actions reflect their inner qualities and are guided by their conscience.

People with character are not only wise but also ethical. Besides doing what effective, they do what is good or right. They don't pursue success at any ethical cost. They have a strong set of personal values that guide them in the right moral direction.

For example, college students with integrity don't cheat and then rationalize that their cheating is acceptable because "others are doing it." They don't look to other people to determine their own values, and they don't conform to the norm if the norm is wrong; instead, they look inward and let their conscience be their guide.

Pause for Reflection

Thus far in your college experience, which of the following four principles of success have you put into practice most effectively? (Circle one.)

active involvement resourcefulness
collaboration reflection

Which of the four principles do you think will be the most difficult for you to put into practice? (Circle one.)

active involvement resourcefulness
collaboration reflection

Why?

Student Perspective

"To achieve success through deceitful actions is not success at all. In life, credibility is more important than credentials, and if honesty is not valued personally, others will not value you. Lack of self-respect results in lack of respect from others."

—First-year college student's reflection on an academic integrity violation

Civility

People of character are personally and socially responsible. They model what it means to live in a civilized community by demonstrating civility—they respect the rights of other members of their community, including members of their college community. In exercising their own rights and freedoms, they don't step (or stomp) on the rights and freedoms of others. People with civic character not only behave civilly but also treat other members of their community in a sensitive and courteous manner and are willing to confront others who violate the rights of their fellow citizens. They are model citizens whose actions visibly demonstrate to others that they oppose any attempt to disrespect or interfere with the rights of fellow members of their community.

Insensitive Use of Personal Technology in the Classroom: A Violation of Civility

Behavior that interferes with the rights of others to learn or teach in the college classroom represents a violation of civility. Listed here are behaviors illustrating classroom incivility that involve student use of personal technology. These behaviors are increasing in college, as is the anger of college instructors who witness them, so it is wise to avoid engaging in them.

1. **Leave your cell phone off or outside the classroom.** Keeping a cell phone on in class is a clear example of classroom incivility because if it rings it will interfere with the right of others to learn. In a study of college students who were exposed to a cell phone ringing during a class session and were later tested for their recall of information presented in class, they scored approximately 25 percent worse when attempting to recall information that was presented at the time a cell phone rang. This attention loss occurred even when the material was covered by the professor before the cell phone rang and was projected on a slide during the call. This study showed that students were further distracted when classmates frantically searched through a bag or pockets to find and silence a ringing (or vibrating) phone (Shelton, Elliot, Eaves, & Exner, 2009). These findings clearly suggest that the civil thing to do is turn your cell phone off before entering the classroom or keep it out of the classroom altogether.

2. **Save text messaging until after class.** Just as answering a cell phone during class represents a violation of civility because it interferes with the learning of other members of the classroom community, so too does text messaging. Although messaging is often viewed it as a quick and soundless way to communicate, it can momentarily disrupt learning if it takes place when the instructor is covering critical or complex information. Text messaging while driving a car can take your eyes and mind off the road, thereby putting yourself and others in danger. Similarly, messaging in the classroom takes your eyes and mind off the instructor and any visual aids being displayed at the time. It's also discourteous or disrespectful to instructors when you put your head down and turn your attention from them while they're speaking to the class. Finally, it can be distracting or disturbing to classmates who see you messaging instead of listening and learning.

> "There is no pillow as soft as a clear conscience."
>
> –French proverb

> "Our character is what we do when we think no one is looking."
>
> –Henry David Thoreau, American philosopher and lifelong abolitionist who championed the human spirit over materialism and conformity

> Emollit mores nec sinit esse feros. ("Learning humanizes character and does not permit it to be cruel.")
>
> –Motto of the University of South Carolina

Pause for Reflection

Have you observed an example of personal integrity that you thought was exceptionally admirable or particularly despicable?

What was the situation, and what was done that demonstrated integrity or an integrity violation?

Snapshot Summary   3.1

Guidelines for Civil and Responsible Use of Personal Technology in the College Classroom

- Turn your cell phone completely off or leave it out of the classroom. In the rare case of an emergency when you think you need to leave it on, inform you instructor.
- Don't check your cell phone during the class period by turning it on and off.
- Don't text message during class.
- Don't surf the Web during class.
- Don't touch your cell phone during any exam because this may be viewed by the instructor as a form of cheating.

◆ Summary and Conclusion

Goal setting only becomes meaningful if you have motivation to reach the goals you set. Motivation may be said to consist of three Ds: drive, discipline, and determination. Drive is the internal force that gives you the energy to overcome inertia and initiate action. Discipline consists of positive, personal qualities such as commitment, devotion, and dedication that enable you to sustain your effort over time. Determination enables you to relentlessly pursue your goals, persist in the face of frustration, and bounce back after any setback.

Reaching your goals requires all three Ds; it also involves the use of effective self-motivational strategies, such as:

- Visualizing reaching your long-range goals;
- Putting goals in writing;
- Creating a visual map of your goals;
- Keeping a record of your progress;
- Developing a skeletal résumé;
- Rewarding yourself for progress toward long-range goals;
- Capitalizing on available campus and social resources;
- Converting setbacks into comebacks by using positive self-talk, maintaining positive expectations, and avoiding negative self-fulfilling prophecies; and
- Keeping your eye on the long-term consequences of your short-term choices and decisions.

To reach your goals you must acquire and use effective strategies, but you also need character. Three character traits or virtues are particularly important for college and life success:

- **Wisdom.** Using knowledge to guide your behavior toward effective or good actions.
- **Integrity.** Doing what is ethical. Plagiarism, or giving readers the impression (intentionally or not) that someone else's work is your own, is a violation of academic integrity.
- **Civility.** Respecting the rights of other members of your college and larger communities. Violations of civility include insensitive use of personal technology in the classroom (e.g., using cell phones and text messaging).

Studies of highly successful people, whether scientists, musicians, writers, chess masters, or basketball stars, consistently show that achieving high levels of skill and success requires practice (Levitin, 2006). This is true even of people whose success is thought to be to be due to natural gifts or talents. For example, during the Beatles' first 4 years as a band and before they burst into musical stardom, they performed live an estimated 1,200 times, and many of these performances lasted 5 or more hours a night. They performed (practiced) for more hours during those first 4 years than most bands perform during their entire career. Similarly, before Bill Gates became a computer software giant and creator of Microsoft, he logged almost 1,600 hours of computer time during one 7-month period alone, averaging 8 hours a day, 7 days a week (Gladwell, 2008).

What these extraordinary success stories show is that it takes time and practice for effective skills to take hold and take effect. Reaching long-range goals means making small steps; they aren't achieved in one quick, quantum leap. If you are patient and persistent and consistently practice effective strategies, their positive effects will gradually accumulate and eventually have a significant impact on your success in college and beyond.

> ### Remember
>
> Success isn't a short-range goal; it's not a sprint but a long-distance run that takes patience and perseverance to complete. What matters most is not how fast you start but where you finish.

Learning More Through the World Wide Web

Internet-Based Resources for Further Information on Liberal Arts Education

For additional information related to the ideas discussed in this chapter, we recommend the following Web sites:

Goal Setting: www.siue.edu/SPIN/activity.html

Self-Motivational Strategies: www.selfmotivationstrategies.com

Academic Integrity and Character Development: www.academicintegrity.org/useful_links/index.php

3.1 Prioritizing Important Life Goals

Consider the following life goals. Rank them in the order of their priority for you (1 = highest, 5 = lowest).

___ Emotional well-being

___ Spiritual growth

___ Physical health

___ Social relationships

___ Rewarding career

Self-Assessment Questions

1. What were the primary reasons behind your first- and last-ranked choices?

2. Have you established any short- or mid-range goals for reaching your highest-ranked choice? If yes, what are they? If no, what could they be?

3.2 Setting Goals for Reducing the Gap Between the Ideal Scenario and the Current Reality

Think of an aspect of your life with a gap between what you hoped it would be (the ideal) and what it is (the reality). On the lines that follow, identify goals you could purse that would reduce this gap.

Long-range goal: _____

Mid-range goal: _____

Short-range goal: _____

Use the form that follows to identify strategies for reaching each of these three goals. Consider the following areas for each goal:

- Actions to be taken
- Available resources
- Possible roadblocks
- Potential solutions to roadblocks

Long-range goal: _____

- Actions to be taken:

- Available resources:

- Possible roadblocks:

- Potential solutions to roadblocks:

Mid-range goal: _____

- Actions to be taken:

- Available resources:

- Possible roadblocks:

- Potential solutions to roadblocks:

Short-range goal: _____

- Actions to be taken:

- Available resources:

- Possible roadblocks:

- Potential solutions to roadblocks:

3.3 Converting Setbacks into Comebacks: Transforming Pessimism into Optimism

In Hamlet, Shakespeare wrote: "There is nothing good or bad, but thinking makes it so." His point was that experiences have the potential to be positive or negative, depending on how people interpret them and react to them.

Listed here is a series of statements representing negative interpretations and reactions to a situation or experience:

1. "I'm just not good at this."

2. "There's nothing I can do about it."

3. "Things will never be the same."

4. "Nothing is going to change."

5. "This always happens to me."

6. "This is unbearable."

7. "Everybody is going to think I'm a loser."

8. "I'm trapped, and there's no way out."

For each of the preceding statements, replace the negative statement with a statement that represents a more positive interpretation or reaction.

No Goals, No Direction

Amy Aimless decided to go to college because it seemed like that's what she was expected to do. All of her closest friends were going and her parents have talked to her about going to college as long as she can remember.

Now that she's in her first term, Amy isn't sure she made the right decision. She has no educational or career goals, nor does she have any idea about what her major might be. None of the subjects she took in high school and none of the courses she's taking in her first term of college have really sparked her interest. Since she has no goals or sense of purpose, she's beginning to think that being in college is a waste of time and money, so she's considering withdrawing at the end of her first term.

Reflection and Discussion Questions

1. What advice would you give Amy about whether she should remain in college or withdraw?

2. What suggestion would you have for Amy that might help her find some sense of educational purpose or direction?

3. How could you counter Amy's claim that no subjects interest her as a possible college major?

4. Would you agree that Amy is currently wasting her time and her parents' money? Why?

5. Would you agree that Amy shouldn't have begun college in the first place? Why?

Time Management

ACTIVATE YOUR THINKING | **Journal Entry** | **4.1**

Complete the following sentence with the first thought that comes to your mind:

For me, time is . . .

_____

_____

_____

LEARNING GOAL

To help you appreciate the significance of managing time and supply you with a powerful set of time-management strategies that can be used to promote your success in college and beyond.

◆ The Importance of Time Management

For many first-year students, the beginning of college means the beginning of more independent living and self-management. Even if you've lived on your own for some time, managing time is an important skill to possess because you're likely juggling multiple responsibilities, including school, family, and work.

In college, the academic calendar and your class schedule differ radically from those during high school. You have less "seat time" in class each week and more "free time" outside of class, which you have the freedom to self-manage; it is not closely monitored by school authorities or family members, and you are expected to do more academic work on your own outside of class. Time-management skills grow in importance when a person's time is less structured or controlled by others, leaving the individual with more decision-making power about how to spend personal time. Thus, it is no surprise that research shows the ability to manage time effectively as playing a crucial role in college success (Erickson, Peters, & Strommer, 2006).

Simply stated, college students who have difficulty managing their time have difficulty managing college. In one study, sophomores who had an outstanding first year in college (both academically and socially) were compared with another group of sophomores who struggled during the prior year. Interviews conducted with these students revealed one key difference between the two groups: The sophomores who experienced a successful first year repeatedly brought up the topic of time during the interviews. The successful

Student Perspective

"The major difference [between high school and college] is time. You have so much free time on your hands that you don't know what to do for most of the time."

—First-year college student (Erickson & Strommer, 1991)

Student Perspective

"I cannot stress enough that you need to intelligently budget your time."

—Advice to new college students from a first-year student

students said they had to think carefully about how they spent their time and that they needed to budget their time because it was a scarce resource. In contrast, the sophomores who experienced difficulty in their first year of college hardly talked about the topic of time during their interviews, even when they were specifically asked about it (Light, 2001).

Studies also indicate that managing time plays a pivotal role in the lives of working adults. Setting priorities and balancing multiple responsibilities (e.g., work and family) that compete for limited time and energy can be a juggling act and a source of stress for people of all ages (Harriott & Ferrari, 1996).

For these reasons, time management should be viewed not only as a college-success strategy but also as a life-management and life-success skill. Studies show that people who manage their time well report they are more in control of their life and are happier (Myers, 1993). In short, when you gain greater control of your time, you become more satisfied with your life.

Personal Story

I started the process of earning my doctorate a little later in life than other students. I was a married father with a preschool daughter (Sara). Since my wife left for work early in the morning, it was always my duty to get up and get Sara's day going in the right direction. In addition, I had to do the same for me—which was often harder than doing it for my daughter. Three days of my week were spent on campus in class or in the library. (We did not have quick access to research on home computers then as you do now.) The other two days of the workweek and the weekend were spent on household chores, family time, and studying.

I knew that if I was going to have any chance of finishing my Ph.D in a reasonable amount of time and have a decent family life I had to adopt an effective schedule for managing my time. Each day of the week, I held to a strict routine. I got up in the morning, drank coffee while reading the paper, took a shower, got Sara ready for school, and took her to school. Once I returned home, I put a load of laundry in the washer, studied, wrote, and spent time concentrating on what I needed to do to be successful from 8:30 a.m. to 12:00 p.m. every day. At lunch, I had a pastrami and cheese sandwich and a soft drink while rewarding myself by watching *Perry Mason* reruns until 1:00 p.m. I then continued to study until it was time to pick up Sara from school. Each night I spent time with my wife and daughter and prepared for the next day. I lived a life that had a preset schedule. By following this schedule, I was able to successfully complete my doctorate in a decent amount of time while giving my family the time they needed. (By the way, I still watch *Perry Mason* reruns.)

—*Aaron Thompson*

Strategies for Managing Time

You can use a series of strategies to manage your time:

1. **Analyzing.** Breaking down time into segments and work into specific tasks;
2. **Itemizing.** Identifying what you need to accomplish and when it needs to be done;
3. **Prioritizing.** Organizing your tasks based on their importance.

The following steps can help you discover time you did not know you had and use the time you have more wisely.

1. Break down your time and become more aware about how it's spent.

Have you ever asked yourself "Where did all the time go?" or told yourself "I just can't seem to find the time"? One way to find out where your time went is by taking a time inventory (Webber, 1991). To do this, you conduct a time analysis by breaking down and tracking your time, recording what you do and when you do it. By mapping out how you spend time, you become more aware of how much total time you have available to you and how its component parts are used, including patches of wasted time in which you get little or nothing accomplished. You don't have to do this time analysis for more than a week or two. This should be long enough to give you some sense of where your time is going and allow you to start developing strategies for using your time more effectively and efficiently.

Pause for Reflection

Do you have time gaps between your classes this term? If you do, what have you been doing during those periods?

What would you say is your greatest time waster?

Do you see a need to stop or eliminate it?

If no, why not? If yes, what would you like to see yourself doing instead?

2. Identify which tasks you need to accomplish and when you need to accomplish them.

People make lists to be sure they don't forget items they need from the grocery store or people they want to be sure are invited to a party. You can use the same list-making strategy for work tasks so that you don't forget to do them or forget to do them on time. Studies of effective people show that they are list makers and they write out lists not only for grocery items and wedding invitations but also for things they want to accomplish each day (Covey, 1990).

You can itemize your tasks by listing them in either of the following time-management tools:

- **Small, portable planner.** List all your major assignments and exams for the term, along with their due dates. By pulling all work tasks from different courses in one place, it is easier to keep track of what you have to do and when you have to do it.
- **Large, stable calendar.** Record in the calendar's date boxes your major assignments for the academic term and when they are due. Place the calendar in a position or location where it's in full view and you can't help but see it every day (e.g., on your bedroom or refrigerator door). If you regularly and literally "look" at the things you have to do, you're less likely to "overlook" them, forget about them, or subconsciously push them out of your mind.

"Doesn't thou love life? Then do not squander time, for that is the stuff life is made of."

—Benjamin Franklin, eighteenth-century inventor, newspaper writer, and cosigner of the *Declaration of Independence*

© Gary Woodward, 2010. Under license from Shutterstock, Inc.

Using a personal planner is an effective way to itemize your academic commitments.

3. Rank your tasks in order of their importance.

Once you've itemized your work by listing all tasks you need to do, prioritize them—determine the order in which you will do them. Prioritizing basically involves ranking your tasks in terms of their importance, with the highest-ranked tasks appearing at the top of your list to ensure that they are tackled first. How do you determine which tasks are most important and should be ranked highest? Two criteria or standards of judgment can be used to help determine which tasks should be your priorities:

- **Urgency.** Tasks that are closest to their deadline or due date should receive high priority. For example, finishing an assignment that's due tomorrow should receive higher priority than starting an assignment that's due next month.

Personal Story

My mom was the person who ensured I got up for school on time. Once I got to school the bell would ring to let me know to move on to the next class. When I returned home I had to do my homework and chores. My daily and weekly schedules were dictated by someone else.

When I entered college, I quickly realized that I needed to develop my own system for being organized, focused, and productive without the assistance of my mother. Since I came from a modest background, I had to work my way through college. Juggling schedules became an art and science for me. I knew the things that I could not miss, such as work and school, and the things I could miss—TV and girls. (OK, TV, but not girls.)

After college, I spent 10 years in business—a world where I was measured by being on time and a productive "bottom line." It was during this time that I discovered a scheduling book. When I became a professor, I had other mechanisms to make sure I did what I needed to do when I needed to do it. This was largely based on when my classes were offered. Other time was dedicated to working out and spending time with my family. Now, as an administrator, I have an assistant who keep my schedule for me. She tells me where I am going, how long I should be there, and what I need to accomplish while I am there. Unless you take your parents with you or have the luxury of a personal assistant, it's important to determine which activities are required and to allow time in your schedule for fun. Use a planner!

—Aaron Thompson

Pause for Reflection

Do you have a calendar for the current academic term that you carry with you?

If yes, why? If no, why not?

If you carry neither a calendar nor a work list, why do you think you don't?

Student Perspective

"I like to get rid of my stress by doing what I have to do first, like if it's a paper."

—First-year college student

- **Gravity.** Tasks that carry the heaviest weight (count the most) should receive highest priority. For example, if an assignment worth 100 points and another worth 10 points are due at the same time, the 100-point task should receive higher priority. You want to be sure you invest your work time on tasks that matter most. Just like investing money, you want to invest your time on tasks that yield the greatest dividends or payoff.

One strategy for prioritizing your tasks is to divide them into A, B, and C lists (Lakein, 1973). The A list is for *essential* tasks—what you *must* do now. The B list is for *important* tasks—what you *should* do soon. Finally, the C list is for *optional* tasks—what you *could* or *might* do if there is time remaining after you've completed the tasks on the A and B lists. Organizing your tasks in this fashion can help you decide how to divide your labor in a way that ensures you put first things first. What you don't want to do is waste time doing unimportant things and deceive yourself into thinking that you're keeping busy and getting things done when actually you're doing things that just take your time (and mind) away from the more important things that should be done.

At first glance, itemizing and prioritizing may appear to be rather boring chores. However, if you look at these mental tasks carefully, they require many higher-level thinking skills, such as

1. **Analysis.** Dividing time into component elements or segments and breaking down work into specific tasks;
2. **Evaluation.** Critically evaluating the relative importance or value of tasks; and
3. **Synthesis.** Organizing individual tasks into classes or categories based on their level of priority.

Thus, developing self-awareness about how you spend time is more than a menial, clerical task; when done with thoughtful reflection, it's an exercise in higher-level thinking. It's also a good exercise in values clarification because what people choose to spend their time on is a more accurate indicator of what they truly value rather than what they say they value.

Develop a Time-Management Plan

Humans are creatures of habit. Routines help you organize and gain control of your lives. Doing things by design, rather than leaving them to chance or accident, is the first step toward making things happen for you rather than allowing them to happen you—by chance or accident. By developing an intentional plan for how you're going to spend your time, you're developing a plan to gain greater control of your life.

Don't buy into the myth that you don't have time to plan because it takes too much time that could be spent getting started and getting things done. Time-management experts estimate that the amount of time you spend planning your work reduces your total work time by a factor of three (Lakein, 1973). In other words, for every one unit of time you spend planning, you save three units of work time. Thus, 5 minutes of planning time will typically save you 15 minutes of total work time, and 10 minutes of planning time will save you 30 minutes of work time. This saving of work time probably occurs because you develop a clearer game plan or plan of attack for identifying what needs to be done and the best order in which to get it done. A clearer sense of direction reduces the number of mistakes you may make due to false starts—starting the work but then having to restart it because you started off in the wrong direction. If you have no plan of attack, you're more likely to go off track; when you discover this at some point after you've started, you're then forced to retreat and start over.

As the proverb goes, "A stitch in time saves nine." Planning your time represents the "stitch" (unit of time) that saves you nine additional stitches (units of time). Similar to successful chess players, successful time managers plan ahead and anticipate their next moves.

>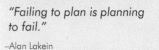
> "Time = Life. Therefore waste your time and waste your life, or master your time and master your life."
>
> –Alan Lakein, international expert on time management and author of the best-selling book *How to Get Control of Your Time and Your Life* (1973)

> "Failing to plan is planning to fail."
>
> –Alan Lakein

Elements of a Comprehensive Time-Management Plan

Once you've accepted the notion that taking the time to plan your time saves you time in the long run, you're ready to design a time-management plan. The following are elements of a comprehensive, well-designed plan for managing time.

1. A good time-management plan should have several time frames.

Your academic time-management plan should include:

- A *long-range* plan for the entire academic term that identifies deadline dates for reports and papers that are due toward the end of the term;

- A *mid-range* plan for the upcoming month and week; and
- A *short-range* plan for the following day.

The preceding time frames may be integrated into a total time-management plan for the term by taking the following steps:

- Identify deadline dates of all assignments, or the time when each of them must be completed (your long-range plan).
- Work backward from these final deadlines to identify dates when you plan to begin taking action on these assignments (your short-range plan).
- Identify intermediate dates when you plan to finish particular parts or pieces of the total assignment (your mid-range plan).

This three-stage plan should help you make steady progress throughout the term on college assignments that are due later in the term. At the same time, it will reduce your risk of procrastinating and running out of time.

Here's how you can put this three-stage plan into action this term

a. **Develop a long-range plan for the academic term.**

- Review the *course syllabus (course outline)* for each class you are enrolled in this term, and highlight all major exams, tests, quizzes, assignments, and papers and the dates on which they are due.

! **Remember**

College professors are more likely than high school teachers to expect you to rely on your course syllabus to keep track of what you have to do and when you have to do it.

- Obtain a *large calendar* for the academic term (available at your campus bookstore or learning center) and record all your exams, assignments, and so on, for all your courses in the calendar boxes that represent their due dates. To fit this information within the calendar boxes, use creative abbreviations to represent different tasks, such as E for exam and TP for term paper (not toilet paper). When you're done, you'll have a centralized chart or map of deadline dates and a potential master plan for the entire term.

b. **Plan your week.**

- Make a map of your *weekly schedule* that includes times during the week when you are in class, when you typically eat and sleep, and if you are employed, when you work.
- If you are a full-time college student, find *at least 25 total hours per week* when you can do academic work outside the classroom. (These 25 hours can be pieced together in any way you like, including time between daytime classes and work commitments, evening time, and weekend time.) When adding these 25 hours to the time you spend in class each week, you will end up with a 40-hour workweek, similar to any full-time job. If you are a part-time student, you should plan on spending at least 2 hours on academic work outside of class for every 1 hour that you're in class.
- Make good use of your *free time between classes* by working on assignments and studying in advance for upcoming exams. See **Box 4.1** for a summary of how you can use your out-of-class time to improve your academic performance and course grades.

Student Perspective

"The amount of free time you have in college is much more than in high school. Always have a weekly study schedule to go by. Otherwise, time slips away and you will not be able to account for it."

–Advice to new college students from a first-year student (Rhoads, 2005)

c. **Plan your day.**
- Make a *daily to-do list*.

> ! **Remember**
>
> If you write it out, you're less likely to block it out and forget about it.

- Attack daily tasks in *priority order*.

> ! **Remember**
>
> "First things first." Plan your work by placing the most important and most urgent tasks at the top of your list, and work your plan by attacking tasks in the order in which you have listed them.

- Carry a *small calendar*, *planner*, *or appointment book* at all times. This will enable you to record appointments that you may make on the run during the day and will allow you to jot down creative ideas or memories of things you need to do—which sometimes pop into your mind at the most unexpected times.
- Carry *portable work* with you during the day,—that is, work you can take with you and do in any place at any time. This will enable you to take advantage of "dead time" during the day. For example, carry material with you that you can read while sitting and waiting for appointments or transportation, allowing you to resurrect this dead time and convert it to "live" work time. (This isn't only a good time-management strategy; it's a good stress-management strategy because it puts you in control of "wait time," enabling you use it to save time later rather than making you feel frustrated about losing time or bored about having nothing do with your time while you're waiting.)
- Wear a *watch* or carry a cell phone that can accurately and instantly tell you what time it is and what date it is. You can't even begin to manage time if you don't know what time it is, and you can't plan a schedule if you don't know what date it is. Set the time on your watch or cell phone slightly ahead of the actual time; this will help ensure that you arrive to class, work, or meetings on time.

2. A good time-management plan should include reserve time to take care of the unexpected.

You should always hope for the best but be prepared for the worst. Your time-management plan should include a buffer zone or safety net, building in extra time that you can use to accommodate unforeseen developments or unexpected emergencies. Just as you should plan to save money in your bank for unexpected extra costs (e.g., emergency medical expenses), you should plan to save time in your schedule for unexpected events that cost you time (e.g., dealing with unscheduled tasks or taking longer than expected to complete already-planned tasks).

Student Perspective

"I was constantly missing important meetings during my first few weeks because I did not keep track of the dates and times. I thought I'd be told again when the time was closer, just as had been done in high school. Something I should have done to address that would have been to keep a well-organized planner for reference."

–College sophomore
(Walsh, 2005)

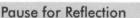

Pause for Reflection

Do you make a to-do list of things you need to get done each day? (Circle one.)

never   seldom   often   almost always

If you circled "never" or "seldom," why don't you?

"
Murphy's Laws:

1. Nothing is as simple as it looks.
2. Everything takes longer than it should.
3. If anything can go wrong, it will.

–Author unknown (Murphy's Laws were named after Captain Edward Murphy, naval engineer, in 1949)

Making Productive Use of Free Time Outside the Classroom

Unlike high school, homework in college often does not involve turning things in to your instructor daily or weekly. The academic work you do outside the classroom may not even be collected and graded. Instead, it is done for your own benefit as you prepare yourself for upcoming exams and major assignments (e.g., term papers or research reports). Rather than formally assigning work to you as homework, your professors expect that you will do this work on your own and without supervision. Listed here are strategies for working independently and in advance of college exams and assignments, which will increase the quality of your preparation and performance.

Independent Work in Advance of Exams

Use the following strategies to prepare for exams:

- Complete reading assignments in advance of lectures that relate to the same topic as the reading. This will make lectures easier to understand and will prepare you to ask intelligent questions and make relevant comments in class.
- Review your class notes between class periods so that you can construct a mental bridge from one class to the next and make each upcoming lecture easier to follow. When reviewing your notes before the next class, rewrite any class notes that may be sloppily written. If you find notes related to the same point all over the place, reorganize them by combining them into one set of notes. Lastly, if you find any information gaps or confusing points in your notes, seek out the course instructor or a trusted classmate to clear them up before the next class takes place.
- Review information that you have highlighted in your reading assignments to improve your memory of the information. If certain points are confusing to you, discuss

them with your course instructor or a fellow classmate.
- Integrate key ideas in your class notes with information that you have highlighted in your assigned reading and that is related to the same major point or general category. In other words, put related information from your lecture notes and your reading in the same place.
- Use a part-to-whole study method whereby you study material from your class notes and reading in small parts during short, separate study sessions that take place well in advance of the exam (the parts); then make your last study session before the exam a longer review session during which you restudy all the small parts together (the whole). The belief that studying in advance is a waste of time because you will forget it all anyway is a myth. As you'll see in Chapter 5, information studied in advance of an exam remains in your brain and is still there when you later review it. Even if you cannot recall the previously studied information when you first start reviewing it, you will relearn it faster than you did the first time, thus proving that some memory of it was retained.

Independent Work in Advance of Term Papers or Research Reports

Work on large, long-term assignments by breaking them into the following smaller, short-term tasks:

1. Search for and select a topic.
2. Locate sources of information on the topic.
3. Organize the information obtained from these sources into categories.
4. Develop an outline of the report's major points and the order or sequence in which you plan to discuss them.
5. Construct a first draft of the paper (and, if necessary, a second draft).
6. Write a final draft of the paper.
7. Proofread the final draft of your paper for minor mechanical mistakes, such as spelling and grammatical errors, before submitting it to your instructor.

3. A good time-management plan should include a balance of work and recreation.

Don't only plan work time; plan time to relax, refuel, and recharge. Your overall plan shouldn't turn you into an obsessive-compulsive workaholic. Instead, it should represent a balanced blend of work and play, which includes activities that promote your mental and physical wellness—such as relaxation, recreation, and reflection. You could also arrange your schedule of work and play as a self-motivation strategy by using your play time to reward your work time.

A good time-management plan includes a balanced blend of time planhed for both work and recreation.

Remember

A good time-management plan should help you stress less, learn more, and earn higher grades while leaving you time for other important aspects of your life. A good plan not only enables you to get your work done on time but also enables you to attain and maintain balance in your life.

Pause for Reflection

What activities do you engage in for fun or recreation?

What do you do to relax or relieve stress?

Do you intentionally plan to engage in these activities?

4. A good time-management plan should have some flexibility.

Some people are immediately turned off by the idea of developing a schedule and planning their time because they feel it overstructures their lives and limits their freedom. It's only natural for you to prize your personal freedom and resist anything that appears to restrict your freedom in any way. A good plan preserves your freedom by helping you get done what must be done, reserving free time for you to do what you want and like to do.

A good time-management plan shouldn't enslave you to a rigid work schedule. It should be flexible enough to allow you to occasionally bend it without having to break it. Just as work commitments and family responsibilities can crop up unexpectedly, so, too, can opportunities for fun and enjoyable activities. Your plan should allow you the freedom to modify your schedule so that you can take advantage of these enjoyable opportunities and experiences. However, you should plan to make up the work time you lost. In other words, you can borrow or trade work time for play time, but don't "steal" it; you should plan to pay back the work time you borrowed by substituting it for a play period that existed in your original schedule.

> ### ! Remember
>
> When you create a personal time-management plan, remember that it is *your* plan—you own it and you run it. It shouldn't run you.

Converting Your Time-Management Plan into an Action Plan

Once you've planned the work, the next step is to work the plan. A good action plan is one that gives you a preview of what you intend to accomplish and an opportunity to review what you actually accomplished. You can begin to implement an action plan by constructing a daily to-do list, bringing that list with you as the day begins, and checking off items on the list as you get them done. At the end of the day, review your list and identify what was completed and what still needs to be done. The uncompleted tasks should become high priorities for the next day.

At the end of the day, if you find many unchecked items remain on your daily to-do list, this could mean that you're spreading yourself too thin by trying to do too many things in a day. You may need to be more realistic about the number of things you can reasonably expect to accomplish per day by shortening your daily to-do list.

Being unable to complete many of your intended daily tasks may also mean that you need to modify your time-management plan by adding work time or subtracting activities that are drawing time and attention away from your work (e.g., taking phone calls during your planned work times).

Pause for Reflection

By the end of a typical day, how often do you find that you accomplished most of the important tasks you hoped to accomplish? (Circle one.)

never   seldom   often   almost always

Why?

◆ Dealing with Procrastination

Procrastination Defined

The word "procrastination" derives from two roots: *pro* (meaning "forward") plus *crastinus* (meaning "tomorrow.") As these roots suggest, procrastinators don't abide by the proverb "Why put off to tomorrow what can be done today?" Their philosophy is just the opposite: "Why do today what can be put off until tomorrow?" Adopting this philosophy promotes a perpetual pattern of postponing what needs to be done until the last possible moment, which results in rushing frantically to get it done (and compromising its quality), getting it only partially done, or not finishing it.

Research shows that 75 percent of college students label themselves as procrastinators (Potts, 1987), more than 80 percent procrastinate at least

A procrastinator's idea of planning ahead and working in advance often boils down to this scenario.

List of Things To Do TODAY	List of Things DUE TODAY
1. Write Paper	1. Turn in Paper
2. Study for Math Test	2. Take Math Test
3. Prepare Speech	3. Deliver Speech

Next time, I'll start sooner!

occasionally (Ellis & Knaus, 1977), and almost 50 percent procrastinate consistently (Onwuegbuzie, 2000). Furthermore, the percentage of people reporting that they procrastinate is on the rise (Kachgal, Hansen, & Nutter, 2001).

Procrastination is such a serious issue for college students that some colleges and universities have opened "procrastination centers" to provide help exclusively for students who are experiencing problems with procrastination (Burka & Yuen, 1983).

Myths That Promote Procrastination

Before there can be any hope of putting a stop to procrastination, procrastinators need to let go of two popular myths (misconceptions) about time and performance.

Myth 1. "I work better under pressure" (e.g., on the day or night before something is due).

Procrastinators often confuse desperation with motivation. Their belief that they work better under pressure is often just a rationalization to justify or deny the truth, which is that they *only* work when they're under pressure—that is, when they're running out of time and are under the gun to get it done just before the deadline.

It's true that some people will only start to work and will work really fast when they're under pressure, but that does not mean they're working more *effectively* and producing work of better *quality*. Because they're playing "beat the clock," procrastinators' focus no longer is on doing the job *well* but is on doing the job *fast* so that it gets done before they run out of time. This typically results in a product that turns out to be incomplete or inferior to what could have been produced if the work process began earlier.

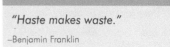

"Haste makes waste."
–Benjamin Franklin

Although you may work quickly under pressure, you are probably not working better.

Myth 2. "Studying in advance is a waste of time because you will forget it all by test time."

The misconception that information learned early will be forgotten is commonly used to justify procrastinating with respect to preparing for upcoming exams. As will be discussed in Chapter 5, studying that is distributed (spread out) over time is more effective than massed (crammed) studying. Furthermore, last-minute studying that takes place the night before exams often results in lost sleep time due to the need to pull late-nighters or all-nighters. This fly-by-night strategy interferes with retention of information that has been studied and elevates test anxiety because of lost dream sleep (a.k.a. rapid eye movement, or REM), which enables the brain to store memories and cope with stress (Hobson, 1988; Voelker, 2004). Research indicates that procrastinators experience higher rates of stress-related physical disorders, such as insomnia, stomach problems, colds, and flu (McCance & Pychyl, 2003).

Working under time pressure adds to performance pressure because procrastinators are left with no margin of error to correct mistakes, no time to seek help on their work, and no chance to handle random catastrophes that may arise at the last minute (e.g., an attack of the flu or a family emergency).

Psychological Causes of Procrastination

Sometimes, procrastination has deeper psychological roots. People may procrastinate for reasons related not directly to poor time-management habits but more to emotional issues involving self-esteem or self-image. For instance, studies show that procrastination is sometimes used as a psychological strategy to protect self-esteem, which is referred to as self-handicapping. This strategy may be used by some procrastinators (consciously or unconsciously) to give themselves a "handicap" or disadvantage. Thus, if their performance turns out to be less than spectacular, they can conclude (rationalize) that it was because they were performing under a handicap—lack of time (Smith, Snyder, & Handelsman, 1982).

For example, if the grade they receive on a test or paper turns out to be low, they can still "save face" (self-esteem) by concluding that it was because they waited until the last minute and didn't put much time or effort into it. In other words, they had the ability or intelligence to earn a good grade; they just didn't try very hard. Better yet, if they happened to luck out and get a good grade—despite doing it at the last minute—then they can think the grade just shows how intelligent they are. Thus, self-handicapping creates a fail-safe scenario that's guaranteed to protect the procrastinators' self-image: If the work performance or product is less than excellent, it can be blamed on external factors (e.g., lack of time); if it happens to earn them a high grade, then they can attribute the result to themselves—their extraordinary ability enabled them to do so well despite working at the last minute.

In addition to self-handicapping, other psychological factors have been found to contribute to procrastination, including the following:

- **Fear of failure.** Feeling that it's better to postpone the job, or not do it, than to fail at it (Burka & Yuen, 1983; Soloman & Rothblum, 1984);

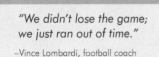

Pause for Reflection

Do you tend to put off work for so long that getting it done turns into an emergency or panic situation?

If your answer is yes, why do you think you find yourself in this position? If your answer is no, what is it that prevents this from happening to you?

"
"We didn't lose the game; we just ran out of time."

–Vince Lombardi, football coach

"
"Procrastinators would rather be seen as lacking in effort than lacking in ability."

–Joseph Ferrari, professor of psychology and procrastination researcher

- **Perfectionism.** Having unrealistically high personal standards or expectations, which leads to the belief that it's better to postpone work or not do it than to risk doing it less than perfectly (Flett, Blankstein, Hewitt, & Koledin, 1992; Kachgal et al., 2001);

- **Fear of success.** Fearing that doing well will show others that the procrastinator has the ability to achieve success and will allow others to expect the procrastinator to maintain those high standards by repeating the performance (Beck, Koons, & Milgram, 2000; Ellis & Knaus, 1977);

- **Indecisiveness.** Having difficulty making decisions, including decisions about what to do or how to begin doing it (Anderson, 2003; Steel, 2003);

- **Thrill seeking.** Enjoying the adrenaline rush triggered by hurrying to get things done just before a deadline (Szalavitz, 2003).

If these or any other issues are involved, their underlying psychological causes must be dealt with before procrastination can be overcome. Because they have deeper roots, it may take some time and professional assistance to uproot them. A good place to get such assistance is the Counseling Center. Personal counselors on college campuses are professional psychologists who are trained to deal with psychological issues that can contribute to procrastination.

> "Striving for excellence motivates you; striving for perfection is demoralizing."
> –Harriet Braiker, psychologist and best-selling author

Pause for Reflection

How often do you procrastinate? (Circle one.)

rarely   occasionally   frequently   consistently

When you do procrastinate, what is the usual reason?

Self-Help Strategies for Beating the Procrastination Habit

Once inaccurate beliefs or emotional issues underlying procrastination have been identified and dealt with, the next step is to move from gaining self-insight to taking direct action on the procrastination habit itself. Listed here are our top strategies for minimizing or eliminating the procrastination habit.

1. Continually practice effective time-management strategies.

If effective time-management practices, such as those previously cited in this chapter, are implemented consistently, they can turn into a habit. Studies show that when people repeatedly practice effective time-management strategies these practices gradually become part of their routine and develop into habits. For example, when procrastinators repeatedly practice effective time-management strategies with respect to tasks that they procrastinate on, their procrastination tendencies begin to fade and are gradually replaced by good time-management habits (Ainslie, 1992; Baumeister, Heatherton, & Tice, 1994).

2. Make the start of work as inviting or appealing as possible.

Getting started can be a stumbling block for many procrastinators. They experience what's called "start-up stress" when they're about to begin a task they expect will be unpleasant, difficult, or boring (Burka & Yuen, 1983). If you have trouble starting your work, one way to give yourself a jump start is to arrange your work tasks in an order that allows you to start on tasks that you're likely to find most interesting or are most likely to experience success with. Once you've overcome the initial inertia and get going, you can ride the momentum you've created to attack the tasks that you find less appealing and more daunting.

> "Just do it."
> –Commercial slogan of Nike, the athletic equipment company named after the Greek goddess of victory

You're also likely to discover that the dreaded work wasn't as difficult, boring, or time consuming as it appeared to be. When you sense that you're making some progress toward getting work done, your anxiety begins to decline. Like many experiences in life that are dreaded and avoided, the anticipation of the event turns out to be worse than the event itself. Research on students who hadn't started a project until it was about to be due indicates that these students experience anxiety and guilt about delaying their work but that once they begin working these negative emotions decline and are replaced by more positive feelings (McCance & Pychyl, 2003).

Student Perspective

"Did you ever dread doing something, then it turned out to take only about 20 minutes to do?"

—Conversation between two college students overheard in a coffee shop

For many procrastinators, getting *started* is often their biggest obstacle.

"To eat an elephant, first cut it into small pieces."

—Author unknown

3. Make the work manageable.

Work becomes less overwhelming and less stressful when it's handled in small chunks or pieces. You can conquer procrastination for large tasks by using a "divide and conquer" strategy: Divide the large task into smaller, more manageable units, and then attack and complete them one at a time.

Don't underestimate the power of short work sessions. They can be more effective than longer sessions because it's easier to maintain momentum and concentration for shorter periods. If you're working on a large project or preparing for a major exam, dividing your work into short sessions will enable you to take quick jabs and poke small holes in it, reducing its overall size with each successive punch. This approach will also give you the sense of satisfaction that comes with knowing that you're making steady progress toward completing a big task—continually chipping away at it in short strokes and gradually taking away the pressure associated with having to go for a big knockout punch right before the final bell (deadline).

Personal Story

The two biggest projects I've had to complete in my life were writing my doctoral thesis and writing this textbook. The strategy that enabled me to keep going until I competed both of these large tasks was to make up short-term deadlines for myself (e.g., complete 5-10 pages each week). I psyched myself into thinking that these make-believe due dates were real, drop-dead deadlines and that if I didn't meet them by completing these smaller tasks on time I was going to fall so far behind that I'd never get the whole thing done. I think these self-imposed deadlines worked for me because they gave me short, more manageable tasks to work on that allowed me to make steady progress toward my larger, long-term task. It was as if I took a huge, hard-to-digest meal and broke it into small, bite-sized pieces that I could easily swallow and gradually digest over time—as opposed to trying to consume a large meal right before bedtime (the final deadline).

—Joe Cuseo

4. Understand that organization matters.

Research indicates that disorganization is a factor that contributes to procrastination (Steel, 2003). How well you organize your workplace and manage your work materials can reduce your risk of procrastination. Having the right materials in the right place at the right time can make it easier to get to and get going on your work. Once you've made a decision to get the job done, you don't want to waste time looking for the tools you need to begin doing it. For procrastinators, this time delay may be just the amount of time they need to change their mind and not start their work.

> **Remember**
>
> The less effort it takes to start doing something, the more likely you are to do it.

One simple yet effective way to organize your college work materials is by developing your own file system. You can begin to create an effective file system by filing (storing) materials from different courses in different colored folders or notebooks. This will allow you to keep all materials related to the same course in the same place and give you direct and immediate access to the materials you need as soon as you need them. Such a system helps you get organized, reduces stress associated with having things all over the place, and reduces the risk of procrastination by reducing the time it takes for you to start working.

5. Recognize that location matters.

Where you work can influence when or whether you work. Research demonstrates that distraction is a factor that can contribute to procrastination (Steel, 2003). Thus, it may be possible for you to minimize procrastination by working in an environment whose location and arrangement prevent distraction and promote concentration.

Distractions tend to come in two major forms: social distractions (e.g., people nearby who are not working) and media distractions (e.g., cell phones, e-mails, text messages, CDs, and TV). Research indicates that the number of hours per week that college students spend watching TV is *negatively* associated with academic success, including lower grade point average, less likelihood of graduating with honors, and lower levels of personal development (Astin, 1993).

Pause for Reflection

List your two most common sources of distraction while working. Next to each distraction, identify a strategy that you might use to reduce or eliminate it.

Source of Distraction	Strategy for Reducing this Distraction
1.	
2.	

> **Remember**
>
> Select a workplace and arrange your workspace to minimize distraction from people and media. Try to remove everything from your work site that's not directly relevant to your work.

Student Perspective

"To reduce distractions, work at a computer on campus rather than using one in your room or home."

—Advice to new college students from a first-year student

Lastly, keep in mind that you can arrange your work environment in a way that not only disables distraction but also enables concentration. You can enable or empower your concentration by working in an environment that allows you easy access to work-support materials (e.g., class notes, textbooks, and a dictionary) and easy access to social support (e.g., working with a group of motivated students who will encourage you to get focused, stay on task, and keep on track to complete you work tasks).

6. Arrange the order or sequence of your work tasks to intercept procrastination when you're most likely to experience it.

While procrastination often involves difficulty starting work, it can also involve difficulty continuing and completing work (Lay & Silverman, 1996). As previously mentioned, if you have trouble starting work, it might be best to first do tasks that you find most interesting or easiest. However, if you have difficulty maintaining or sustaining your work until it's finished, you might try to schedule work tasks that you find easier and more interesting *in the middle or toward the end* of your planned work time. If you're performing tasks of greater interest and ease at a point in your work when you typically lose interest or energy, you may be able to sustain your interest and energy long enough to continue working until you complete them, which means that you'll have completed your entire list of tasks. Also, doing your most enjoyable and easiest tasks later can provide an incentive or reward for completing your less enjoyable tasks first.

7. Learn that momentum matters.

It's often harder to restart a task than it is to finish a task that you've already started; this occurs because you've overcome come the initial inertia associated with getting started and can ride the momentum that you've already created. Furthermore, finishing a task can give you a sense of closure—the feeling of personal accomplishment and self-satisfaction that comes from knowing that you "closed the deal." Placing a checkmark next to a completed task and seeing that it's one less thing you have to do can motivate you to continue working on the remaining tasks on your list.

◆ Summary and Conclusion

To manage time effectively, you need to

- **Analyze.** Break down time and become aware of how you spend it;
- **Itemize.** Identify the tasks you need to accomplish and their due dates; and
- **Prioritize.** Tackle your tasks in their order of importance.

Developing a comprehensive time-management plan involves long-, mid-, and short-range plans, such as

- Planning the total term (long-range);
- Planning your week (mid-range); and
- Planning your day (short-range).

A good time-management plan also has the following features:

- It sets aside time to take care of unexpected developments.
- It takes advantage of your natural peak periods and down times.

- It balances work and recreation.
- It gives you the flexibility to accommodate unforeseen opportunities.

The enemy of effective time management is procrastination, which often relies on the following myths:

- Better work occurs on the day or night before something is due.
- Advance studying wastes time because everything learned will be forgotten by test time.

Effective strategies for beating the procrastination habit include the following:

- Start with the work that is the most inviting or appealing.
- Divide a large task into manageable units.
- Organize work materials.
- Work in a location that minimizes distractions and temptations not to work.
- Intentionally arrange work tasks so that more enjoyable or stimulating tasks are the focus when you're vulnerable to procrastination.
- Maintain momentum, because it's often harder to restart a task than to finish one.

Mastering the skill of managing time is critical for success in college and in life beyond college. Time is one of the most powerful personal resources; the better use you make of it, the greater control you gain over your priorities and your life.

Learning More Through the World Wide Web

Internet-Based Resources for Further Information on Time Management

For additional information related to the ideas discussed in this chapter, we recommend the following Web sites:

Procrastination Elimination: **www.time-management-guide.com/procrastination.html**

Time-Management Strategies for All Students: **www.studygs.net/timman.htm**

Time-Management Strategies for Non-Traditional-Age Students:
www.essortment.com/lifestyle/timemanagement_sjmu.htm

4.1 Term at a Glance

Term _____, Year _____

Review the syllabus (course outline) for all classes you're enrolled in this term, and complete the following information for each course.

Course ↓	Professor ↓	Exams ↓	Projects & Papers ↓	Other Assignments ↓	Attendance Policy ↓	Late & Makeup Assignment Policy ↓

Self-Assessment Questions

1. Is the overall workload what you expected? Are your surprised by the amount of work required in any particular course or courses?

2. At this point in the term, what do you see as your most challenging or demanding course or courses? Why?

3. Do you think you can handle the total workload required by the full set of courses you're enrolled in this term?

4. What adjustments or changes could you make to your personal schedule that would make it easier to accommodate your academic workload this term?

4.2 Taking a Personal Time Inventory

On the blank Week-at-a-Glance Grid that follows, map out your typical or average week for this term. Start by recording what you usually do on these days, including when you have class, when you work, and when you relax or recreate. You can use abbreviations (e.g., use J for job and R&R for rest and relaxation) or write tasks out in full if you have enough room in the box. List the abbreviations you created at the bottom of the page so that your instructor can follow them.

If you're a *full-time* student, find 25 *hours* in your week that you could devote to homework (HW). These 25 hours could be found between classes, during the day, in the evenings, or on the weekends. If you can find 25 hours per week for homework, in addition to your class schedule, you'll have a 40-hour workweek for coursework, which research has shown to result in good grades and success in college.

If you're a *part-time* student, find 2 *hours* you could devote to homework *for every hour* that you're in class (e.g., if you're in class 9 hours per week, find 18 hours of homework time).

Week-at-a-Glance Grid

	Sunday	Monday	Tuesday	Wednesday	Thursday	Friday	Saturday
7:00 a.m.							
8:00 a.m.							
9:00 a.m.							
10:00 a.m.							
11:00 a.m.							
12:00 p.m.							
1:00 p.m.							
2:00 p.m.							
3:00 p.m.							
4:00 p.m.							
5:00 p.m.							
6:00 p.m.							
7:00 p.m.							
8:00 p.m.							
9:00 p.m.							
10:00 p.m.							
11:00 p.m.							

1. Go to the following Web site: www.ulc.psu.edu/studyskills/time_management.html#monitoring_your_time

2. Complete the time management exercise at this site. The exercise asks you to estimate the hours per day or week that you spend doing various activities (e.g., sleeping, employment, and commuting). As you enter the amount of time you engage in these activities, the total number of remaining hours available in the week for academic work will be automatically computed.

3. After completing your entries, look at your week-at-a-glance grid and answer the following questions, or provide your best estimate.

Self-Assessment Questions

1. How many hours per week do you have available for academic work?

2. Do you have 2 hours available for academic work outside of class for each hour you spend in class?

3. What time wasters do you detect that might be easily eliminated or reduced to create more time for academic work outside of class?

Procrastination: The Vicious Cycle

Delilah has a major paper due at the end of the term. It's now past midterm, and she still hasn't started to work on her paper. She tells herself, "I should have started sooner."

However, Delilah continues to postpone starting her work on the paper and begins to feel anxious and guilty about it. To relieve her growing anxiety and guilt, she starts doing other tasks instead, such as cleaning her room and returning e-mails. This makes Delilah feel a little better because these tasks keep her busy, take her mind off the term paper, and give her the feeling that at least she's getting something accomplished. Time continues to pass, and the deadline for the paper is growing dangerously close. Delilah now finds herself in the position of having lots of work to do and little time in which to do it.

Source: Burka & Lenora (1983).

Reflection and Discussion Questions

1. What do you predict Delilah will do at this point?

2. Why did you make this prediction?

3. What grade do you think Delilah will receive on her paper?

4. What do you think Delilah will do on the next term paper she's assigned?

5. Other than starting sooner, what recommendations would you have for Delilah (and other procrastinators like her) to break this cycle of procrastination and prevent it from happening repeatedly?

Strategic Learning, Studying, and Test Taking

5

Deep-Learning Strategies

ACTIVATE YOUR THINKING Journal Entry **5.1**

What do you think is the key difference between learning and memorizing?

_____

_____

_____

_____

LEARNING GOAL

To develop a set of effective strategies that will enable you to learn deeply and remember longer.

◆Stages in the Learning and Memory Process

Learning deeply, and remembering what you've learned, is a process that involves three stages:

1. **Sensory input (perception).** Taking information into the brain;
2. **Memory formation (storage).** Saving that information in the brain;
3. **Memory recall (retrieval).** Bringing information back to mind when you need it.

You can consider these stages of the learning and memory process to be similar to the way information is processed by a computer: (a) information is typed onto the screen (perceptual input), (b) the information is saved in a file (memory storage), and (c) the saved information is recalled and used when it's needed (memory retrieval).

These three stages in the learning–memory process are summarized visually in **Figure 5.1**.

This three-stage process can be used to create a systematic set of strategies for effectively using the two major routes through which you acquire information and knowledge in college:

• Taking notes as you listen to lectures, and
• Reading textbooks.

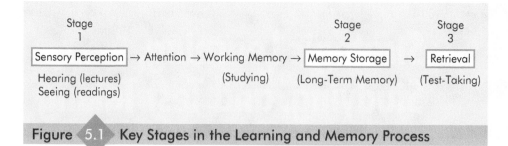

Figure 5.1   Key Stages in the Learning and Memory Process

◆ Effective Lecture-Listening and Note-Taking Strategies

The importance of effective listening skills in the college classroom is highlighted by a study of more than 400 first-year students who were given a listening test at the start of their first term in college. At the end of their first year, 49 percent of those students who scored low on the listening test were on academic probation, compared to only 4.4 percent of students who scored high on the listening test. On the other hand, 68.5 percent of students who scored high on the listening test were eligible for the honors program at the end of their first year, compared to only 4.17 percent of those students who had low listening test scores (Conaway, 1982).

Pause for Reflection

Do you think writing notes in class helps or hinders your ability to pay attention and learn from your instructors' lectures?

Why?

Studies show that information delivered during lectures is the number one source of test questions (and answers) on college exams (Brown, 1988; Kuhn, 1988). When lecture information appears on a test and hasn't been recorded in students' notes, it has only a 5 percent chance of being recalled (Kiewra, Hart, Scoular, Stephen, Sterup, & Tyler, 2000). When you write down information presented in lectures, rather than just listen to it, you're more likely to remember that information. For example, students who write notes during lectures achieve higher course grades than students who just listen to lectures (Kiewra, 1985), and students with a more complete set of notes are more likely to demonstrate higher levels of overall academic achievement (Johnstone, & Su, 1994; Kiewra & Fletcher, 1984).

Contrary to popular belief that writing while listening interferes with the ability to listen, students report that taking notes actually increases their attention and concentration in class (Hartley, 1998; Hartley & Marshall, 1974). Studies also show that when students write down information that's presented to them, rather than just listening to it, they're more likely to remember the most important aspects of that information when tested later (Bligh, 2000; Kiewra et al., 1991). For instance, one study discovered that successful students with grade point averages (GPAs) of 2.53 or higher record more information in their notes and retain a larger percentage of the most important information than do students with GPAs of less than 2.53 (Einstein, Morris, & Smith, 1985). These findings are not surprising when you consider that *hearing* lecture information, *writing* it, and *seeing* it while you write it lay down three different memory traces or tracks in the brain that combine to improve memory for that information.

Furthermore, students with a good set of notes have a written record of that information, which can be reread and studied later.

This research suggests that you should view each lecture as if it were a test-review session during which your instructor is giving out test answers and you're given the opportunity to write all those answers in your notes. Come to class with the attitude that your instructors are dispensing answers to test questions as they speak; your purpose for being there is to pick out and pick up these answers.

!

Remember

If important points your professors make in class make it into your notes, they can become points learned, and these learned points will turn into earned points on your exams (and higher grades in your courses).

The next sections give strategies for getting the most out of lectures at three stages in the learning process: before lectures, during lectures, and after lectures.

Prelecture Strategies: What You Can Do Before Hearing Lectures

1. Check your syllabus to see where you are in the course and determine how the upcoming class fits into the total course picture.

By checking your syllabus before individual class sessions, you will strengthen your learning because you will see how each part (individual class session) relates to the whole (the entire course). This also capitalizes on the human brain's natural tendency to seek larger patterns and the "big picture." Rather than seeing things in separate parts, the brain is naturally inclined to perceive parts as interconnected and forming a meaningful whole (Caine & Caine, 1991). It looks for meaningful patterns and connections rather than isolated bits and pieces of information (Nummela & Rosengren, 1986). In **Figure 5.2**, notice how your brain naturally ties together and fills in the missing information to perceive a meaningful whole pattern.

You perceive a white triangle in the middle of this figure. However, if you use three fingers to cover up the three corners of the white triangle that fall outside the other (background) triangle, the white triangle suddenly disappears. What your brain does is take these corners as starting points and fills in the rest of the information on its own to create a complete or whole pattern that has meaning to you. (Notice also how you perceive the background triangle as a complete triangle, even though parts of its left and right sides are missing.)

Figure 5.2   Triangle Illusion

2. Get to class early so that you can look over your notes from the previous class session and from any reading assignment that relates to the day's lecture topic.

Research indicates that when students preview information related to an upcoming lecture topic it improves their ability to take more accurate and complete lecture notes (Ladas, 1980). Thus, a good strategy to help you learn from lectures is to review your notes from the previous class session and read textbook information related to an upcoming lecture topic—before hearing the lecture. This strategy will help you better understand and take more detailed notes on the lecture. Reviewing previously learned information activates your previous knowledge, enabling you to build a mental bridge from one class session to the next and connect new information to what you already know, which is the key to deep learning (Piaget, 1978; Vygotsky, 1978). Acquiring knowledge isn't a matter of simply pouring information into the brain as if it were an empty jar. It's a matter of attaching or connecting new ideas to ideas that are already stored in the brain. When you learn deeply, you make a biological connection between nerve cells in the brain (Alkon, 1992), as illustrated in **Figure 5.3**.

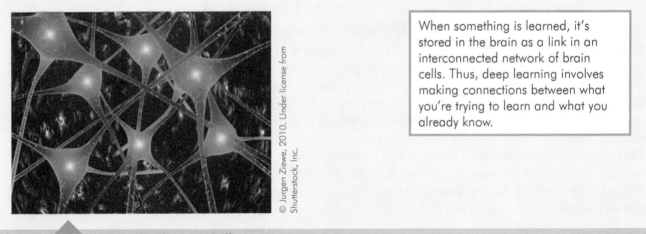

© Jurgen Ziewe, 2010. Under license from Shutterstock, Inc.

When something is learned, it's stored in the brain as a link in an interconnected network of brain cells. Thus, deep learning involves making connections between what you're trying to learn and what you already know.

Figure 5.3 Network of Brain Cells

3. Adopt a seating location that maximizes your focus of attention and minimizes sources of distraction.

Studies show that students who sit in the front and center of class tend to earn higher exam scores (Rennels & Chaudhair, 1988). These results are found even when students are assigned seats by their instructor, so it's not just a matter of more motivated and studious students tending to sit in the front of the classroom; instead, the academic performance of students sitting front and center is likely higher because a learning advantage is provided by this seating location. Front-and-center seating probably aids academic performance by improving vision of the board and hearing of the instructor's words—as well as allowing better eye contact with the instructor, which increases students' attention and heightens their sense of personal responsibility in the classroom. There's another advantage to sitting up front: It increases your comfort level about speaking in class because if you ask a question or contribute a comment you will not have numerous classmates sitting in front of you who turn around to look at you when you speak.

When you enter the classroom, get in the habit of heading for a seat in the front and center of class. In large classes, it is particularly important that you get "up close and personal" with your instructors. This not only will improve your attention, note taking, and participation in class but also should improve your instructors' ability to remember who you are and how well you performed in class, which will work to your advantage when you ask for letters of recommendation.

4. Be aware of the people who sit near you.

Intentionally sit near classmates who will not distract you or interfere with the quality of your note taking. Attention comes in degrees or amounts; you can give all of it or part of it to whatever task you're performing. Trying to grasp complex information in class is a task that demands your undivided attention.

Student Perspective
"[In high school] the teacher knows your name. But in college they don't know your name; they might see your face, but it means nothing to them unless you make yourself known." —First-year college student

Student Perspective
"I like to sit up front so I am not distracted by others and I don't have to look around people's heads to see the chalkboard." —First-year college student

! Remember
When you enter a class, you have a choice about where you're going to sit. Choose wisely by selecting a location that will maximize your attentiveness to the instructor and the aggressiveness of your note taking.

The evolution of student attention from the back to the front of class.

5. Adopt a seating posture that screams attention.

Sitting upright and leaning forward are more likely to increase your attention because these signals of bodily alertness will reach your brain and increase mental alertness. If your body is in an alert and ready position, your mind tends to pick up these bodily cues and follow your body's lead by also becoming alert and ready (to learn). Just as baseball players assume a ready position in the field before a pitch is delivered to put their body in position to catch batted balls, learners who assume a ready position in the classroom put themselves in a better position to catch ideas batted around in the classroom. Studies show that when humans are ready and expecting to capture an idea greater amounts of the brain chemical C-kinase are released at the connection points between brain cells, which increases the likelihood that a learning connection is formed between them (Howard, 2000).

There's another advantage to being attentive in class: You send a clear message to your instructor that you're a conscientious and courteous student. This can influence your instructor's perception and evaluation of your academic performance, which can earn you the benefit of the doubt at the end of the term if you're on the border between a higher and a lower course grade.

Listening and Note-Taking Strategies: What You Can Do During Lectures

1. Take your own notes in class.

Don't rely on someone else to take notes for you. Taking your own notes in your own words ensures they make sense and have personal meaning to you. You can collaborate with classmates to compare one another's notes for completeness and accuracy or to get notes if you happen to miss class. However, do not routinely rely on others to take notes for you. Studies show that students who record and review their own notes earn higher scores on memory tests for that information than do students who review the notes of others (Fisher, Harris, & Harris, 1973). These findings point to the importance of taking and studying your own notes because they will be most meaningful to you.

© JupiterImages Corporation.

Students who take notes during lectures have been found to achieve higher class grades than those who just listen.

2. Focus your attention on important information.

Attention is the critical first step to successful learning and memory. Since the human attention span is limited, it's impossible to attend to and make note of every piece of given information.

Thus, you need to use your attention *selectively* to focus on and choose the most important information. Here are some strategies for attending to and recording the most important information delivered by professors in the college classroom:

- Pay attention to information your instructors put in writing—on the board, on a slide, or in a handout. If your instructor takes the time and energy to write it out, that's usually a good clue the information is important and you're likely to see it again—on an exam.
- Pay attention to information presented during the first and last few minutes of class. Instructors are more likely to provide valuable reminders, reviews, and previews at the start and end of class.

- Use your instructor's verbal and nonverbal cues to detect important information. Don't just to tune in when the instructor is writing something down and tune out at other times. It's been found that students record almost 90 percent of information that is written on the board (Locke, 1977) but less than 50 percent of important ideas that professors state but don't write on the board (Johnstone & Su, 1994). Don't fall into the reflex-like routine of just writing something in your notes when you see your instructor writing on the board. You also have to listen actively to record important ideas in your notes that you hear your instructor saying. In **Box 5.1**, you'll find strategies for detecting important information that professors deliver orally during lectures.

3. Take organized notes.

Keep taking notes in the same paragraph if the instructor is continuing on the same point or idea. When the instructor shifts to a new idea, skip a few lines and shift to a new paragraph. Be alert to phrases that your instructor may use to signal a shift to a new or different idea (e.g., "Let's turn to . . ." or "In addition to . . ."). Use these phrases as cues for taking notes in paragraph form. By using

Take Action!

Detecting When Instructors Are Delivering Important Information During Class Lectures

5.1

1. Verbal cues
   - Phrases signal important information (e.g., "The point here is . . ." or "What's most significant about this is . . .").
   - Information is repeated or rephrased in a different way (e.g., "In other words, . . .").
   - Stated information is followed with a question to check understanding (e.g., "Is that clear?" "Do you follow that?" "Does that make sense?" or "Are you with me?").
2. Vocal (tone of voice) cues
   - Information is delivered in a louder tone or at a higher pitch than usual, which may indicate excitement or emphasis.
   - Information is delivered at a slower rate or with more pauses than usual, which may

be your instructor's way of giving you more time to write down these important ideas.

3. Nonverbal cues
   - Information is delivered by the instructor with more than the usual
     a. facial expressiveness (e.g., raised or furrowed eyebrows);
     b. body movement (e.g., more gesturing and animation); or
     c. eye contact (e.g., looking more directly and intently at the faces of students to see whether they are following or understanding what's being said).
   - The instructor moves closer to the students (e.g., moving away from the podium or blackboard).
   - The instructor's body is oriented directly toward the class (i.e., both shoulders directly or squarely face the class).

paragraphs, you improve the organizational quality of your notes, which will improve your comprehension and retention of them. Leave an extra space between successive paragraphs (ideas) to give yourself room to add information that you may have missed or to translate the professor's words into your own words, making them more meaningful to you.

Another strategy for taking organized notes, the called the Cornell Note-Taking System, is summarized in **Box 5.2**.

4. If you don't immediately understand what your instructor is saying, don't stop taking notes.

Keep taking notes, even if you are temporarily confused, because this will at least leave you with a record of the information that you can review later—when you have more time to think about it and grasp it. If you still don't understand it after taking time to review it, check it out in your text-book, with your instructor, or with a classmate.

> **! Remember**
>
> Your primary goal during lectures is to get important information into your brain long enough to note it mentally and then physically by recording it in your notes. Making sense of that information often has to come later, when you have time to reflect on the notes you took in class.

Postlecture Strategies: What You Can Do After Lectures

Pause for Reflection

What do you tend to do immediately after a class session ends?

Why?

1. As soon as class ends, quickly check your notes for missing information or incomplete thoughts.

Since the information is likely to be fresh in your mind immediately after class, a quick check of your notes at this time will allow you take advantage of your short-term memory. By reviewing and reflecting on it, you can help move the information into long-term memory before forgetting takes place. This quick review can be done alone or, better yet, with a motivated classmate. If you both have gaps in your notes, check them out with your instructor before he or she leaves the classroom. Even though it may be weeks before you will be tested on the material, the quicker you address missed points and clear up sources of confusion, the better, because you'll be able to use your knowledge to help you understand and learn upcoming material. Catching confusion early in the game also enables you to avoid the last-minute, mad rush of students seeking help from the instructor just before test time. You want to reserve the critical time just before exams for studying a set of notes that you know are complete and accurate, rather than rushing around and trying to find missing information and getting fast-food help on concepts that were presented weeks ago.

2. Before the next class session meets, reflect on and review your notes to make sense of them.

Your professors will often lecture on information that you may have little prior knowledge about, so it is unrealistic to expect that you will understand

Take Action!

The Cornell Note-Taking System

1. On the page on which you're taking notes, draw a horizontal line about 2 inches from the bottom edge of the paper.
2. If there's no vertical line on the left side of the page, draw one line about 2½ inches from the left edge of the paper (as shown in the scaled-down illustration here).

```
                    ← 8½" →

  ← 2½" →                    ← 6" →




                      ↑
  Area C              9"          Area A
                      ↓



  ↑
  2"                           Area B
  ↓
```

3. When your instructor is lecturing, use the large space to right of the vertical line (area A) to record your notes.
4. After a lecture, use the space at the bottom of the page (area B) to summarize the main points you recorded on that page.
5. Use the column of space on the left side of the page (area C) to write questions that are answered in the notes on the right.
6. Quiz yourself by looking at the questions listed in the left margin while covering the answers to them found in the class notes on the right.

Note: You can use this note-taking and note-review method on your own, or you could team up with two or more students and do it collaboratively.

everything that's being said the first time you hear it. Instead, you'll need to set aside time for making notes or taking notes on your own notes (i.e., rewriting them in your own words so that they make sense to you).

During this reflect-and-rewrite process, we recommend that you take notes on your notes by:

- Translating technical information into your own words to make it more meaningful to you; and
- Reorganizing your notes to get ideas related to the same point in the same place.

Studies show that when students organize lecture information into meaningful categories they show greater recall on a delayed memory test for that information than do students who simply review their notes (Howe, 1970).

> **!**
>
> **Remember**
>
> Look at note taking as a two-stage process: Stage 1 is aggressively taking notes in class (active involvement), and stage 2 occurs later—when you think about those notes more deeply (personal reflection).

Personal Story   My first year in college was mainly spent trying to manipulate my schedule to find some free time. I took all of my classes in a row without a break to save some time at the end of the day for relaxation and hanging out with friends before I went to work. Seldom did I look over my notes and read the material that I was assigned on the day I took the lecture notes and received the assignment. Thus, on the day before the test I was in a panic trying to cram the lecture notes into my head for the upcoming test. Needless to say, I did not perform well on many of these tests. Finally, I had a professor who told me that if I spent time each day after a couple of my classes catching up on reading and rewriting my notes I would retain the material longer, increase my grades, and decrease my stress at test time. I employed this system, and it worked wonderfully.

—Aaron Thompson

◆ Reading Strategically to Comprehend and Retain Textbook Information

Second only to lecture notes is information from reading assignments as a source of test questions on college exams (Brown, 1988). You're likely to find exam questions that your professors haven't talked about directly, or even mentioned, in class but that were drawn from your assigned reading. College professors often expect you to relate or connect what they are lecturing about in class with material that you've been assigned to read. Furthermore, they often deliver class lectures with the assumption that you have done the assigned reading, so if you haven't done it, you're likely to have more difficulty following what your instructor is talking about in class.

> **! Remember**
>
> Do the assigned reading and do it according to the schedule your instructor has established. It will help you better understand class lectures, improve the quality of your participation in class, and raise your overall grade in the course.

What follows is a series of strategies for effective reading at three stages in the learning process: before reading, while reading, and after reading. When completing your reading assignments, use effective reading strategies that are based on sound principles of human learning and memory, such as those listed here.

Prereading Strategies: What You Can Do Before Reading

1. Before jumping into your assigned reading, look at how it fits into the overall organizational structure of the book and course.

You can do this efficiently by taking a quick look at the book's table of contents to see where the chapter you're about to read is placed in the overall sequence of chapters, particularly in relation to chapters that immediately precede and follow the assigned chapter. This will give you a sense of how the particular part you're focusing on connects with the bigger picture. Research shows that if learners have advance knowledge of how the information they're about to learn is organized—if they see how the parts relate to the whole *before* they attempt to start learning the specifics—they're better able to comprehend and retain the material (Ausubel, 1978; Kintsch, 1994). Thus, the first step toward improving reading comprehension and retention of a textbook chapter is to see how its parts relate to the whole—before you begin to examine the chapter part by part.

2. Preview a chapter by reading its boldface headings and any chapter outline, objectives, summary, or end-of-chapter questions.

Get in the habit of previewing what's in a chapter to gain an overall sense of its organization before jumping right into the content. If you dive into details too quickly, you lose sight of how the smaller details relate to the larger picture. The brain's natural tendency is to perceive and comprehend whole patterns rather than isolated bits of information. Start by seeing how the parts of the chapter are integrated into the whole. This will enable you to better connect the separate pieces of information you encounter while you read, much like seeing the whole picture of a completed jigsaw puzzle helps you connect its separate pieces while assembling the puzzle.

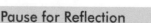

Pause for Reflection

Rate yourself in terms of how frequently you use these note-taking strategies according to the following scale:

4 = always, 3 = sometimes, 2 = rarely, 1 = never

1. I take notes aggressively in class.   4 3 2 1
2. I sit near the front of the room during class.   4 3 2 1
3. I sit upright and lean forward while in class.   4 3 2 1
4. I take notes on what my instructors say, not just what they write on the board.   4 3 2 1
5. I pay special attention to information presented at the start and end of class.   4 3 2 1
6. I take notes in paragraph form.   4 3 2 1
7. I review my notes immediately after class to check that they are complete and accurate.   4 3 2 1

Pause for Reflection

When you open a textbook to read a chapter, how do you start the reading process? That is, what's the first thing you do?

3. Take a moment to think about what you already know that relates to the material in the chapter.

By thinking about knowledge you possess about the topic you're about to read, you activate the areas of your brain where that knowledge is stored, thereby preparing it to make meaningful connections with the material you're about to read.

Strategies to Use While Reading
Read Selectively to Find Important Information

Rather than jumping into reading and randomly highlighting, effective reading begins with a plan or goal for identifying what should be noted and remembered. Here are three strategies to use while reading to help you determine what information should be noted and retained.

1. **Use boldface or dark-print headings and subheadings as cues for identifying important information.** These headings organize the chapter's major points; thus, you can use them as "traffic" signs that direct you to the most important information in the chapter. Better yet, turn the headings into questions and then read to find answers to these questions. This question-and-answer strategy will ensure that you read actively and with a purpose. (You can do this when you preview the chapter by placing a question mark after each heading contained in the chapter.) Creating and answering questions while you read also keeps you motivated; the questions help stimulate your curiosity, and finding answers as you read rewards you for reading (Walter, Knudsbig, & Smith, 2003). Lastly, this strategy is an effective way to prepare for tests because you are practicing exactly what you'll be expected to do on exams—answer questions. You can quickly write the heading questions on separate index cards and use them as flash cards to review for exams. Use the question on the flash card to flashback and attempt to recall the information from the text that answers the question.

2. **Pay special attention to words that are *italicized*, underlined, or appear in boldface print.** These usually represent building-block terms whose meanings must be understood before you can grasp the meanings of higher-level ideas and more general concepts covered in the reading. Don't simply highlight these words because their special appearance suggests they are important. Read these terms carefully and be sure you understand their meaning before you continue reading.

3. **Pay special attention to the first and last sentences in each paragraph.** These sentences contain an important introduction and conclusion to the ideas covered in that passage. When reading sequential or cumulative material that requires comprehension of what was previously covered to understand what will be covered next, it's a good idea to reread the first and last sentences of each paragraph before you move on to the next paragraph.

4. **Reread the chapter after you've heard your instructor lecture on the material contained in the chapter.** You can use your lecture notes as a guide to help you focus on what information in the chapter your instructor feels is most important. If you adopt this strategy, your reading before lectures will help you understand the lecture and take better class notes, and your reading after lectures will help you locate and learn the most important information contained in your textbook.

> **⚠ Remember**
>
> Your goal when reading is not merely to cover the assigned pages but to uncover the most important information and ideas contained in those pages.

Take Written Notes on What You're Reading

Just as you write notes in response to your instructor's lectures in class, take notes in response to the author's words in the text. For example, write short answers to the boldface heading questions in the text itself by using its side, top, and bottom margins or in a reading journal organized by chapters or units. Writing requires more active thinking than highlighting because you're creating your own words rather than passively highlighting words written by someone else. Don't get into the habit of using your textbook as a coloring book in which the artistic process of highlighting what you're reading with spectacular kaleidoscopic colors distracts you from the more important process of learning actively and thinking deeply.

> ❝
>
> *"I would advise you to read with a pen in your hand, and enter in a little book of short hints of what you find that is curious, or that might be useful; for this will be the best method of imprinting such particulars in your memory, where they will be ready."*
>
> –Benjamin Franklin, eighteenth-century inventor, newspaper writer, and cosigner of the Declaration of Independence

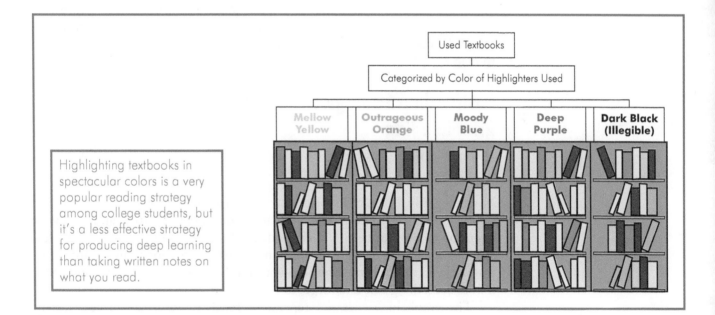

Highlighting textbooks in spectacular colors is a very popular reading strategy among college students, but it's a less effective strategy for producing deep learning than taking written notes on what you read.

Pause Periodically to Summarize and Paraphrase What You're Reading in Your Own Words

If you can express what someone else has written in words that make sense to you, this means that you understand what you're reading and can relate it to what you already know—which is a telltale sign of deep learning (Demmert & Towner, 2003). A good time to pause and paraphrase is when you encounter a boldface heading that indicates you're about to be introduced to a new concept. This may be the ideal place to stop and summarize what you read in the section you just completed.

> **! Remember**
>
> Effective reading isn't a passive or mechanical process in which you just follow printed words on a page. Instead, it's a reflective process in which you actively search for and find meaning in the words you read.

Pause for Reflection

When reading a textbook, do you usually have the following tools on hand?

Highlighter:	yes	no
Pen or pencil:	yes	no
Notebook:	yes	no
Class notes:	yes	no
Dictionary:	yes	no
Glossary:	yes	no

Use the Visual Aids Included in Your Textbook

Don't fall into the trap of thinking that visual aids can or should be skipped because they're merely add-ons that are secondary to the written words of the text. Visual aids, such as charts, graphs, diagrams, and concept maps, are powerful learning and memory tools for a couple of reasons:

1. They enable you to "see" the information in addition to reading (hearing) it.
2. They organize separate pieces of information into an integrated picture.

Furthermore, visual aids allow you to periodically experience a mode of information input other than repeatedly reading words. This occasional change of pace brings variety to the reading process, which can recharge your attention and motivation to read.

Postreading Strategies: What Should Be Done After Reading

End a Reading Session With a Short Review of the Information You've Noted or Highlighted

Most forgetting that takes place after you receive and process information occurs immediately after you stop focusing on the information and turn your attention to another task (Underwood, 1983). (See **Figure 5.4.**) Taking a few minutes at the end of your reading time to review the most important information locks that information into your memory before you turn your attention to something else and forget it.

The graph in Figure 5.4 represents recall of information at different intervals after it was originally learned. As you can see, most forgetting of information occurs right after learning (e.g., after 20 minutes, the participants in the study forgot more than 60 percent of it). This suggests that reviewing information from reading or a lecture immediately after it's been acquired is an effective strategy for intercepting the forgetting curve and improving memory.

Seek Outside Help From Informed Sources

If you find you can't understand a concept explained in your text, even after rereading and repeatedly reflecting on it, try the following strategies:

1. **Look at how another textbook explains it.** Not all textbooks are created equally; some do a better job of explaining certain concepts than others. Check to see whether your library has other texts in the same subject as your course, or check your campus bookstore for textbooks in the same subject area as the course you're taking. A different text may be able to

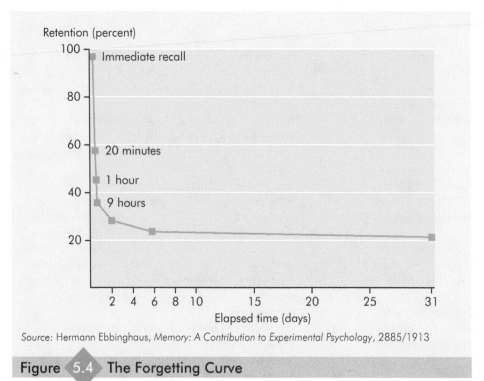

Source: Hermann Ebbinghaus, *Memory: A Contribution to Experimental Psychology*, 2885/1913

Figure 5.4   The Forgetting Curve

explain a hard-to-understand concept much better than the textbook you purchased for the course.

2. **Seek help from your instructor.** If you read carefully and made every effort to understand a particular concept but still can't grasp it, your instructor should be willing to assist you. If your instructor is unavailable or unwilling to assist you, seek help from the professionals and peer tutors in the Learning Center or Academic Support Center on campus.

Another technique for organizing and remembering strategies for improving reading comprehension and retention is the SQ3R method. See **Box 5.3** for a summary of steps involved in this reading method.

Take Action!

The SQ3R Method

SQ3R is an acronym of the five steps you can take to increase textbook-reading comprehension and retention, particularly when reading highly technical or complex material. The sequence in this method is as follows:

1. Survey
2. Question
3. Read
4. Recite
5. Review

S = Survey: *Get a preview and overview of what you're about to read.*

5.3

1. Read the title to activate your thoughts about the subject and prepare your mind to receive information related to it.
2. Read the introduction, chapter objectives, and chapter summary to become familiar with the author's purpose, goals, and most important points.
3. Note the boldface headings and subheadings to get a sense of the chapter's organization before you begin to read. It will help you understand or create a mental structure for the information to come.
4. Notice any graphics, such as charts, maps, and diagrams. They provide valuable visual support and reinforcement for the material you're reading, so don't ignore them.
5. Pay special attention to reading aids (e.g., italics and boldface font) that you can use to identify, understand, and remember key concepts.

Q = **Q**uestion: *Stay active and curious.*
As you read, use the boldface headings to formulate questions you think will be answered in that particular section. When your mind is actively searching for answers to questions, it becomes more engaged in the learning process.

As you continue to read, add any questions that you have about the reading.
R = **R**ead: *Find the answer to the question or questions.*
Read one section at a time, with your questions in mind, and search for answers to these questions. Also, keep an eye out for new questions that need to be asked.
R = **R**ecite: *Rehearse your answers.*
After you read each section, recall the questions you asked and see whether you can answer them from memory. If not, look at the questions again and practice your answers to them until you can recall them without looking. Don't move onto the next section until you're able to answer all questions in the section you've just completed.
R = **R**eview: *Look back and get a second view of the whole picture.*
Once you've finished the chapter, review all the questions you've created for different parts or sections. See whether you can still answer them all without looking. If not, go back and refresh your memory.

◆ Study Strategies for Learning Deeply and Remembering Longer

Learning gets information into your brain; the next step is to save that information in your brain (memory storage) and bring it back to mind at test time (memory retrieval). Described here is a series of effective study strategies for acquiring knowledge (learning) and keeping that knowledge in your brain (memory).

The Importance of Undivided Attention

Attention comes in a fixed amount. You only have so much of it available to you at any point in time, and you can give all or part of it to whatever task you're working on. If study time is spent on multiple tasks that provide sources of external stimulation (e.g., listening to music, watching TV, or text-messaging friends), the total attention time available for studying is subtracted and divided among the other tasks. In other words, studying doesn't receive your undivided attention.

Studies show that when people multitask they don't pay equal attention to all tasks at the same time. Instead, they divide their attention by shifting it back and forth between tasks (Howard, 2000), and their performance on the task that demands the most concentration or deepest thinking is the one that suffers the most (Crawford & Strapp, 1994). Furthermore, research shows that multitasking can increase boredom with tasks that involve concentration. One study found that with even a low level of distraction, such as a TV turned on a low volume in the next room, students were more likely to describe the mental task they were concentrating on as "boring" (Damrad-Frye & Laird, 1989).

When performing tasks that cannot be done automatically (mindlessly), including complex mental tasks, other tasks and sources of external stimulation interfere with the quiet, internal reflection needed for permanent connections to form between brain cells (Jensen, 1998)—which is what has to happen biologically for deep, long-lasting learning to take place.

Remember

Without attention first, there can be no retention later.

Meaningful Association

Relating what you're trying to learn to something you already know is a powerful learning strategy because learning is all about making connections in the brain. People tend to perceive meaningful patterns in information because knowledge is stored in the form of a connected network of brain cells (Coward, 1990).

The brain's natural tendency to seek meaningful, whole patterns applies to words, as well as images. The following passage once appeared (anonymously) on the Internet. See whether you can read it and grasp its meaning.

Pause for Reflection

Rate yourself in terms of how frequently you use these reading strategies according to the following scale:

4 = always, 3 = sometimes, 2 = rarely, 1 = never

1. I read the chapter outlines and summaries before I start reading the chapter content.   4 3 2 1

2. I preview a chapter's boldface headings and subheadings before I begin to read the chapter.   4 3 2 1

3. I adjust my reading speed to the type of subject I am reading.   4 3 2 1

4. I look up the meaning of unfamiliar words and unknown terms that I come across before I continue reading.   4 3 2 1

5. I take written notes on information I read.   4 3 2 1

6. I use the visual aids included in my textbooks.   4 3 2 1

7. I finish my reading sessions with a review of important information that I noted or highlighted.   4 3 2 1

Studies show that doing challenging academic work while multi-tasking divides up attention and drives down comprehension and retention.

Aoccdrnig to rscheearch at Cmabridge Uinverstisy, it deos't mattaer in what order the ltteers in a word are, the only iprmoetnt thing is that the frist and lsat ltteer be at the rghit pclae. The rset can be a total mses and you can still raed it wouthit a porbelm. This is bcusae the human mind deos not raed ervey lteter by istlef, but the word as a wlohe. Amzanig huh?

Notice how easily you found the meaning of the misspelled words by naturally transforming them into correctly spelled words—which you knew because they were stored in your brain. Thus, whenever you learn something, you do so by connecting what you're trying to understand to what you already know.

Learning by making meaningful connections is referred to as deep learning (Entwistle & Ramsden, 1983). It involves moving beyond shallow memorization to deeper levels of understanding. This is a major a shift from the old view that learning occurs by passively absorbing information like a sponge, for example, by receiving it from the teacher or text and studying it in the same, prepackaged form as you received it. Instead, you want to adopt an approach to learning that involves actively transforming the information you receive into a form that's meaningful to you (Entwistle & Marton, 1984; Feldman & Paulsen, 1994). This enables you to move beyond surface-level memorization of information to deeper learning and acquisition of knowledge.

Before you start to repeatedly pound what you're learning into your head like a hammer hitting a nail, first look for a hook to hang it on by relating it to something you already know that's stored in your brain. It may take a little while to discover the right hook, but once you've found it, the information will store in your brain quickly and remain there a long time. For example, consider a meaningful way to learn and remember how to correctly spell one of the most frequently misspelled words in the English language: "separate" (not "seperate"). By remembering that "to par" means to divide, as in the words *par*ts or *par*tition, it makes sense that the word "separate" should be spelled se*par*ate because its meaning is "to divide into parts."

> "The extent to which we remember a new experience has more to do with how it relates to existing memories than with how many times or how recently we have experienced it."
>
> —Morton Hunt, *The Universe Within: A New Science Explores the Human Mind*

! Remember

The more meaningful you make what you're learning, the deeper you learn it and the longer you remember it.

Personal Story

Some time ago, I had to give up running because of damage to my right hip, so I decided to start riding a stationary bike instead. My wife found an inexpensive, used stationary bike at a garage sale. It was an old and somewhat rusty bike that made a repeated noise that sounded like "ee-zoh" as the wheel spun. One evening I was riding it and, after about 10 minutes, I noticed that I was hearing the words "zero," "rosy," and "Rio" off and on in my head. My brain was taking a meaningless sound ("ee-zoh"), which it apparently grew bored of hearing as the wheels spun, and transforming that sound into words that provided it with variety and meaning. Perhaps this was a classic case of how the human brain naturally prefers to seek meaning rather than mindless repetition.

—Joe Cuseo

Meaning in Academic Terms

Each academic field has specialized vocabulary that can sound like a foreign language to someone who has no experience with the subject area. Before you start to brutally beat these terms into your brain through sheer repetition, try to find some meaning in them. You can make a term more meaningful to you by looking up its word root in the dictionary or by identifying its prefix or suffix, which may give away the term's meaning. For instance, suppose you were studying the autonomic nervous system in biology, which is the part of the nervous system that operates without your conscious awareness or voluntary control (e.g., your heart beating and lungs breathing). The meaning of the phrase is given away by the prefix "auto," which means self-controlling—as in the word "automatic" (e.g., automatic transmission).

If the term's root, prefix, or suffix doesn't give away its meaning, then see whether you can make it more meaningful to you in some other way. For instance, suppose you looked up the root of the term "artery" and nothing about the origins of this term suggested its meaning or purpose. You could then create your own meaning for this term by taking its first letter (a), and have it stand for "*a*way"—to help you remember that arteries carry blood away from the heart. Thus, you've taken a biological term and made it personally meaningful (and memorable).

Compare and Contrast

When you're studying something new, get in the habit of asking yourself the following questions:

1. Is this idea similar or comparable to something that I've already learned? (Compare)
2. How does this idea differ from what I already know? (Contrast)

Research indicates that this simple strategy is one of the most powerful ways to promote learning of academic information (Marzano, Pickering, & Pollock, 2001). The power of the compare-and-contrast strategy probably stems from asking the question, "How is this similar to and different from concepts that I already know?" By working to answer this question, you make learning more personally meaningful because you are relating what you're trying to learn to what you already know.

Integration and Organization

Pull together or integrate information from your class notes and assigned reading related to the same major concept or category. For example, get this information in the same place by recording it on the same index card under the same category heading. Index cards are a good tool for such purposes; you can use each card as a miniature file cabinet for a separate category of information. The category heading on each card functions like the hub of a wheel, around which individual pieces of related information are attached like spokes. Integrating information related to the same topic in the same place and studying it at the same time

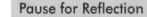

© JupiterImages Corporation.

Spreading out your studying into shorter sessions improves your memory by reducing loss of attention due to fatigue.

helps divide the total material you need to learn into more identifiable and manageable parts. In contrast, when ideas pertaining to the same point or concept are spread all over the place, they're more likely to take that form in your mind—leaving them mentally disconnected and leaving you confused (as well as feeling stressed and overwhelmed).

Divide and Conquer

Effective learning depends not only on *how* you learn (your study method); it also depends on *when* you learn (your study timing). Although cramming just before exams is better than not studying, it is far less effective than studying that's spread out across time. Rather than cramming all your studying into one long session, use the distributed practice method, which spreads study time over several shorter sessions. Research consistently shows that short, periodic practice sessions are more effective than a single marathon session.

Distributing your study time over several shorter sessions improves your learning and memory by:

- Reducing loss of attention due to fatigue or boredom; and
- Reducing mental interference by giving the brain some downtime to cool down and lock in information that it's received without being interrupted by the need to deal with additional information (Murname & Shiffrin, 1991).

If the brain's downtime is interfered with by the arrival of additional information, it gets overloaded and its capacity for handling information becomes impaired. This is what cramming does—it overloads the brain with lots of information in a limited period. In contrast, distributed study does just the opposite—it uses shorter sessions with downtime between sessions, thereby giving the brain the time and opportunity to save (retain) the information that it's processing (studying).

Another major advantage of distributed study is that it's less stressful and more motivating than cramming. Shorter sessions can be an incentive to study because you know that you're not going to be doing it for a long stretch of time or lose any sleep over it. It's easier to maintain your interest and motivation for any task that's done for a shorter rather than a longer period. Furthermore, you should feel more relaxed because if you run into difficulty understanding anything you know there's still time to get help with it before you're tested and graded on it.

The Part-to-Whole Study Method

The part-to-whole method of studying is a natural extension of the distributed practice just discussed. With the part-to-whole method, you break the material you need to study into separate parts and study those parts in separate sessions in advance of the exam. You then use your last study session just before the exam to review (restudy) all the parts that you previously studied in separate sessions. Thus, your last study session is a review session, rather than a study session, because you're not trying to learn information for the first time.

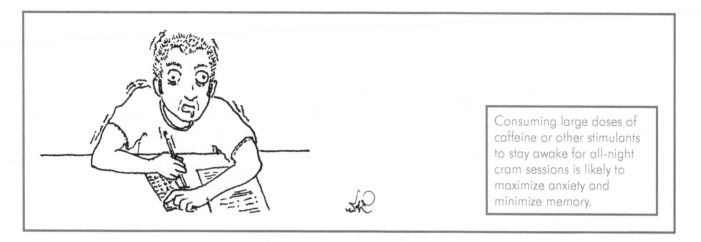

Consuming large doses of caffeine or other stimulants to stay awake for all-night cram sessions is likely to maximize anxiety and minimize memory.

Don't buy into the myth that studying in advance is a waste of time because you'll forget it all by test time. This is the myth that procrastinators use to put off studying until the last moment, when they cram for their exams. Do not underestimate the power of breaking material to be learned into smaller parts and studying those parts some time before a major exam. Even if you cannot recall what you previously studied, when you start reviewing it you'll find that you will relearn it much faster than when you studied it the first time. This proves that studying in advance is not pointless, because it takes less time to relearn the material. The memory of it remains in your brain from the time you studied it earlier (Kintsch, 1994).

Reviewing

For sequential or cumulative subjects that build on understanding of previously covered material to learn new concepts (e.g., math), it's especially important to begin each study session with a quick review of what you learned in your previous study session.

Research shows that students of all ability levels learn material in college courses more effectively when it's studied in small units and when progression to the next unit takes place only after the previous unit has been mastered or understood (Pascarella & Terenzini, 1991, 2005). This strategy has two advantages: (a) it reinforces your memory for what you previously learned and (b) it builds on what you already know to help you learn new material. This is particularly important in cumulative subjects that require memory for problem-solving procedures or steps, such as math and science. By repeatedly practicing these procedures, they become more automatic and you're able to retrieve them quicker (e.g., on a timed test) and use them efficiently without having to expend a lot of mental effort and energy (Newell & Rosenbloom, 1981). This frees your working memory for more important tasks, such as critical thinking and creative problem solving (Schneider & Chein, 2003).

Variety in the Study Process

The following strategies can be used to infuse variety and a change of pace into your study routine, which can increase your concentration and motivation.

1. Periodically vary the type of academic work you do while studying.

Changing the nature of your work activities or the type of mental tasks you're performing while studying increases your level of alertness and concentration by reducing habituation—a psychological term referring to the attention loss that occurs after repeated engagement in the same type of mental task (McGuiness & Pribram, 1980). To combat attention loss due to habituation, occasionally vary the type of study task you're performing. For instance, shift periodically among tasks that involve reading, writing, studying (e.g., rehearsing or reciting), and practicing skills (e.g., solving problems).

2. Study different subjects in different places.

Studying in different locations provides different environmental contexts for learning, which reduces the amount of interference that normally builds up when all information is studied in the same place (Anderson & Bower, 1974). Thus, in addition to spreading out your studying at different times, it's a good idea to spread it out in different places. The great public speakers in ancient Greek and Rome used this method of changing places to remember long speeches by walking through different rooms while rehearsing their speech, learning each major part of their speech in a different room (Higbee, 1998).

Changing the nature of the learning task and the learning environment provides changes of pace that infuse variety into the learning process, which improves attention and concentration. Although it's useful to have a set time and place to study for getting you into a regular work routine, this doesn't mean that learning occurs best by habitually performing all types of academic tasks in the same place. Instead, research suggests that you should periodically change the learning tasks you perform and the environment in which you perform them to maximize attention and minimize interference (Druckman & Bjork, 1991).

> **Remember**
>
> Change of pace and place while studying can stimulate your attention to, and your interest in, what you're studying.

3. Mix long study sessions with short study breaks that involve physical activity (e.g., a short jog or brisk walk).

Study breaks that include physical activity not only refresh the mind by giving it a rest from studying but also stimulate the mind by increasing blood flow to your brain, which will help you retain what you've already studied and regain concentration for what you'll study next.

4. Use all of your senses.

When studying, try to use as many sensory channels as possible. Research shows that information perceived through

Pause for Reflection

Would you say that you're more of a visual learner or verbal learner?

How do you think most people would answer this question?

multiple sensory modalities or channels is remembered better (Bjork, 1994; Schacter, 1992) because it forms more interconnections in long-term memory areas of the brain (Zull, 2002). When a memory is formed in the brain, different sensory aspects of it are stored in different areas. For example, when your brain receives visual, auditory (hearing), and motor (movement) stimulation that accompany with what you're learning, each of these associations is stored in a different part of the brain. See **Figure 5.5** for a map of the surface of the human brain; you can see how different parts of the brain are specialized to receive input from different sensory modalities. When you use all of these sensory modalities while learning, multiple memory traces of what you're studying are recorded in different parts of your brain, which leads to deeper learning and stronger memory (Education Commission of the States, 1996).

5. Learn visually.

The human brain consists of two hemispheres (half rounds): the left and the right hemispheres (see **Figure 5.6**).

Each hemisphere of the brain specializes in a different type of learning. In most people, the left hemisphere specializes in verbal learning, dealing primarily with words. In contrast, the right hemisphere specializes in visual–spatial learning, dealing primarily with images and objects that occupy physical space. If you use both hemispheres while studying, you lay down two different memory traces in your brain: one in left hemisphere, where words are stored, and one in the right hemisphere, where images are stored. This process of laying down a double memory trace (verbal and visual) is referred to as dual

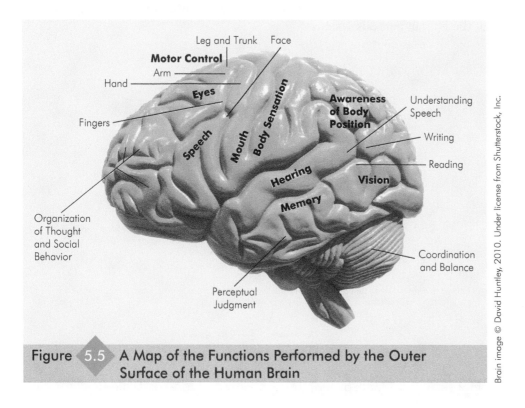

Brain image © David Huntley, 2010. Under license from Shutterstock, Inc.

Figure 5.5   **A Map of the Functions Performed by the Outer Surface of the Human Brain**

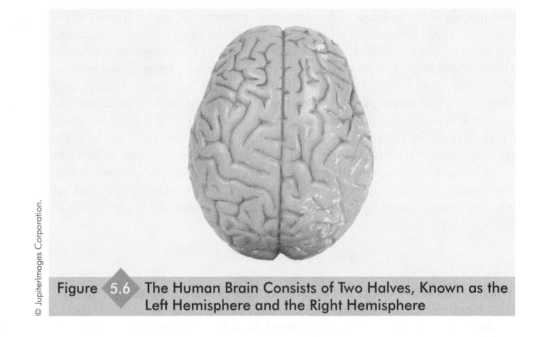

© JupiterImages Corporation.

Figure 5.6 The Human Brain Consists of Two Halves, Known as the Left Hemisphere and the Right Hemisphere

coding (Paivio, 1990). When this happens, memory for what you're learning is substantially strengthened, primarily because two memory traces are better than one.

To capitalize on the advantage of dual coding, use any visual aids that are available to you. Use the visual aids provided in your textbook and by your instructor, or create your own by drawing pictures, symbols, and concept maps, such as flowcharts or branching tree diagrams. See **Figure 5.7** for a concept map that could be used to help you remember the parts and functions of the human nervous system.

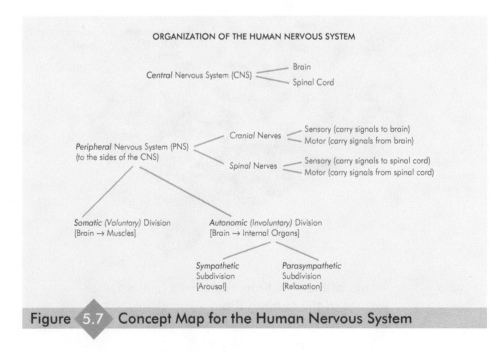

ORGANIZATION OF THE HUMAN NERVOUS SYSTEM

Central Nervous System (CNS) — Brain
Spinal Cord

Peripheral Nervous System (PNS) (to the sides of the CNS)

Cranial Nerves — Sensory (carry signals to brain)
Motor (carry signals from brain)

Spinal Nerves — Sensory (carry signals to spinal cord)
Motor (carry signals from spinal cord)

Somatic (Voluntary) Division [Brain → Muscles]

Autonomic (Involuntary) Division [Brain → Internal Organs]

Sympathetic Subdivision [Arousal]

Parasympathetic Subdivision [Relaxation]

Figure 5.7 Concept Map for the Human Nervous System

Remember

Drawing and other forms of visual illustration are not just artistic exercises; they also can be powerful learning tools (i.e., you can draw to learn). Drawing keeps you actively involved with the material you're trying to learn. By representing the material in visual form, you're able to dual-code the information you're studying, thus doubling its number of memory traces in your brain. As the old saying goes, "A picture is worth a thousand words."

Pause for Reflection

Think of a course you're taking this term in which you're learning related pieces of information that could be joined together to form a concept map. In the space that follows, make a rough sketch of this map that includes the information you need to remember.

6. Learn by moving or using motor learning (a.k.a. muscle memory).

In addition to hearing and seeing, movement is a sensory channel. When you move, your brain receives kinesthetic stimulation—the sensations generated by your muscles when your body moves. Research shows that memory traces for movement are commonly stored in an area of your brain that plays a major role for all types of learning (Middleton & Strick, 1994). Thus, associating movement with what you're learning can improve your ability to retain it because you record an additional muscle memory trace of it to another area of your brain.

Personal Story

I was talking about memory in class one day and mentioned that when I temporarily forget how to spell a word its correct spelling comes back to me once I start to write it. One of my students raised her hand and said the same thing happens to her when she forgets a phone number—it comes back to her when she starts dialing it. In both of these cases, motor memory brings information back to mind that was temporarily forgotten, which points to the power of movement for promoting learning and memory.

—Joe Cuseo

You can use movement to help you learn and retain academic information by using your body to act out what you're studying or to symbolize it with your hands (Kagan & Kagan, 1998). For example, if you're trying to remember five points about something (e.g., five consequences of the Civil War), when you're studying these points, count them on your fingers as you try to recall each of them. Also, remember that talking involves muscle movement of your lips and tongue. Thus, by speaking aloud when you're studying, either to a friend or to yourself, your memory of what you're studying may be improved by adding kinesthetic stimulation to your brain (in addition to the auditory or sound stimulation your brain receives from hearing what you're saying).

Student Perspective

"When I have to remember something, it is better for me to do something with my hands so I could physically see it happening."

–First-year college student

7. Learn with emotion.

Information reaches the brain through your senses and can be stored in the brain as a memory trace. The same is true of emotions. Numerous connections occur between brain cells in the emotional and memory centers (Zull, 1998). For instance, when you're experiencing emotional excitement about what you are learning, adrenaline is released and is carried through the bloodstream to your brain. Once adrenaline reaches the brain, it increases blood flow and glucose production, which can stimulate learning and strengthen memory (LeDoux, 1998; Rosenfield, 1988). If you have an emotionally intense experience, such a substantial amount of adrenaline is released in your body that it can lead to immediate, long-term storage of that memory; you'll remember the experience for the rest of your life. For instance, most people remember exactly what they were doing at the time they experienced such emotionally intense events as the September 11 terrorist attack on the United States, their first kiss, or their favorite team winning a world championship.

What does this emotion–memory link have to do with helping you remember academic information that you're studying? Research indicates that emotional intensity, excitement, and enthusiasm affect memory of academic information just as they affect memory for life events and personal experiences. If you get psyched up about what you're learning, you have a much better chance of learning and remembering it. Even telling yourself that it's important to remember what you're learning can increase your memory of it (Howard, 2000; Minninger, 1984).

> **!**
>
> **Remember**
>
> You will learn most effectively when you actively involve all your senses (including bodily movement) and when you learn with passion and enthusiasm. In other words, learning grows deeper and lasts longer when you put your whole self into it—your heart, your mind, and your body.

8. Learn with others.

One way to put the power of group learning into practice is by forming study groups. Research indicates that college students who work regularly in small groups of four to six become more actively involved in the learning process and learn more (Light, 2001).

To maximize the power of study groups, each member should study individually *before* studying in a group and should come prepared with specific information or answers to share with teammates, as well as questions or points of confusion that the team can attempt to help answer or clarify.

> "
>
> *"We are born for cooperation, as are the feet, the hands, the eyelids, and the upper and lower jaws."*
>
> —Marcus Aurelius, Roman emperor

Personal Story

When I was in my senior year of college, I had to take a theory course by independent study because the course would not be offered again until after I planned to graduate. Another senior found himself in the same situation. The instructor allowed both of us to take this course together and agreed to meet with us every 2 weeks. My fellow classmate and I studied independently for the first 2 weeks. I prepared for the biweekly meetings by reading thoroughly, yet I had little understanding of what I had read. After our first meeting, I left with a strong desire to drop the course but decided to stick with it. Over the next 2 weeks, I spent many sleepless nights trying to prepare for our next meeting and was feeling pretty low about not being the brightest student in my class of two. During the next meeting with the instructor, I found out that the other student was also having difficulty. Not only did I notice, so did the instructor. After that meeting, the instructor gave us study questions and asked us to read separately and then get together to discuss the questions. During the next 2 weeks, my classmate and I met several times to discuss what we were learning (or attempting to learn). By being able to communicate with each other about the issues we were studying, we both ended up gaining greater understanding. Our instructor was delighted to see that he was able to suggest a learning strategy that worked for both of us.

—*Aaron Thompson*

Self-Monitoring Learning

Successful learners reflect and check on themselves to see whether they really understand what they're attempting to learn. They monitor their comprehension as they go along by asking themselves questions such as "Am I following this?" "Do I really understand it?" and "Do I know it for sure?"

How do you know if you really know it? Probably the best answer to this question is "I find *meaning* in it—that is, I can relate to it personally or put it in terms that make sense to me" (Ramsden, 2003). When you really understand a concept, you learn it at a deeper level than by merely memorizing it. You're also more likely to remember that concept because the deeper its roots, the more durable its memory trace that enables you to retain it long term (Kintsch, 1970).

Discussed here are some strategies for checking whether you truly understand what you're trying to learn. They help you answer the question, "How do I know if I really know it?" These strategies can be used as indicators or checkpoints for determining whether you're just memorizing information or you're learning deeply and acquiring knowledge.

- **Can you restate or translate what you're learning into your own words?** When you can paraphrase what you're learning, you're able to complete the following sentence: "In other words, . . ." If you can complete that sentence in your own words, this is a good indication that you've moved beyond memorization to comprehension because you've transformed what you're learning into words that are meaningful to you. Thus, you learn deeply not by simply stating what your instructor or textbook states but by restating the information in words that are your own.
- **Can you explain what you're learning to someone who is unfamiliar with it?** If you can explain to a friend what you've learned, this is a good sign that you've moved beyond memorization to comprehension because you are able to translate it into less technical language that someone hearing it for the first time can understand. Often, you won't realize how well you know or don't know something until you have to explain it to someone who's never heard it before (just ask any teacher). Simply put, if you can't explain it to someone else, you don't really understand it yourself. Studies show that students gain deeper levels of understanding for what they're learning when they're asked to explain it to someone else (Chi, de Leeuw, Chiu, & LaVancher, 1994). If you cannot find someone else to explain it to, then explain it aloud as if you were talking to an imaginary friend.
- **Can you think of an example of what you've learned?** If you can come up with an instance of what you're learning that is your own example—not one given by your instructor or textbook—this is a good sign that you truly comprehend it. It shows you're able to take a general, abstract concept and apply it to a specific, real-life experience (Bligh, 2000). Furthermore, a personal example is a powerful memory tool. Studies show that when people retrieve a concept from memory they first

Student Perspective

"I learn best through teaching. When I learn something and teach it to someone else, I find that it really sticks with me a lot better."

–College sophomore

Pause for Reflection

Rate yourself in terms of how frequently you use these study strategies according to the following scale:

4 = always, 3 = sometimes, 2 = rarely, 1 = never

1. I block out all distracting sources of outside stimulation when I study.   4 3 2 1

2. I try to find meaning in technical terms by looking at their prefix or suffix or by looking up their word root in the dictionary.   4 3 2 1

3. I compare and contrast what I'm currently studying with what I've already learned.   4 3 2 1

4. I organize the information I'm studying into categories or classes.   4 3 2 1

5. I integrate or pull together information from my class notes and readings that relate to the same concept or general category.   4 3 2 1

6. I distribute or spread out my study time over several short sessions in advance of the exam, and I use my last study session before the test to review the information I previously studied.   4 3 2 1

7. I participate in study groups with my classmates.   4 3 2 1

recall an example of it, which then serves a memory-retrieval cue to trigger their memory of other details about the concept, such as its definition and relationship to other concepts (Norman, 1982; Park, 1984).

- **Can you represent or describe what you've learned in terms of an analogy or metaphor that compares it to something that has similar meaning or that works in a similar way?** Analogies and metaphors are basically ways of learning something new by understanding it in terms of its similarity to something you already understand. For instance, the computer can be used as a metaphor for the human brain to get a better understanding of learning and memory as a three-stage process in which information is (a) perceived or received (through lectures and readings), (b) stored or saved (through studying), and (c) retrieved (recalled at test time). If you can use an analogy or metaphor to represent what you're learning, you're grasping it at a deep level because you're able to build a mental bridge that connects it to what you already know (Cameron, 2003).

- **Can you apply what you're learning to solve a new problem that you haven't previously seen?** The ability to use your knowledge shows deep learning (Erickson & Strommer, 2005). Learning specialists refer to this mental process as decontextualization—taking what you learned in one context (situation) and applying it to another (Bransford, Brown, & Cocking, 1999). For instance, you know that you've learned a mathematical concept when you can use that concept to solve math problems that are different from the ones initially used by your instructor or textbook to help you learn it. This is why your math instructors rarely include on exams the exact problems solved in class or in your textbook. They're not trying to trick you at test time; they're trying to test your comprehension to determine whether you've learned the concept or principle deeply or just memorized it superficially.

◆ Summary and Conclusion

Information delivered during lectures is most likely to form questions and answers on college tests. At exam time, students who did not record lectures in notes have a slim chance of recalling the information presented. Thus, effective note taking is critical to successful academic performance in college.

Information from reading assignments is the next most common source of test questions on college exams. Professors often won't discuss these assignments in detail in class and sometimes don't even bring up the information from this reading. Thus, doing the assigned reading, and doing it in a way that's most effective for promoting comprehension and retention, plays an important role in your academic success.

The most effective strategies for promoting effective classroom listening, textbook reading, and higher-level thinking are those that reflect three of the college-success principles discussed in Chapter 1: (a) active involvement, (b) interpersonal interaction and collaboration, and (c) personal reflection and self-awareness.

Active involvement is critical for learning from lectures (e.g., actively taking notes while listening to lectures) and learning from reading (e.g., actively taking notes while reading). While active involvement is necessary for learning because it engages your attention and thus enables information to reach your brain, personal reflection is necessary for deep learning because it promotes consolidation, retaining information in your brain by locking it into long-term memory. Reflection also encourages deep learning by promoting self-awareness. By periodically pausing to reflect on whether you are truly attending to and understanding the words you're hearing in lectures and the words you're seeing while reading, you become a more self-aware learner and a more effective learner.

Lastly, learning from note taking, reading, and higher-level thinking can all be magnified if they're done collaboratively. You can collaborate with peers to take better notes in class, to identify what's most important in your assigned reading, and to ask questions of one another that promote higher-level thinking.

Learning More on Your Own Through the World Wide Web

Internet-Based Resources for Further Information on Liberal Arts Education

For additional information related to the ideas discussed in this chapter, we recommend the following Web sites:

www.Dartmouth.edu/~acskills/success/index.html

www.utexas.edu/student/utlc

www.muskingum.edu/~cal/database/general/

www.pima.edu/library/online-distance/study-guides/StudySkills.shtml

Learning Math and Overcoming Math Anxiety:

www.mathacademy.com/pr/minitext/anxiety

www.onlinemathlearning.com/math-mnemonics.html

5.1 Self-Assessment of Note-Taking and Reading Habits

Look back at the ratings you gave yourself for effective note-taking (**p. 106**), reading (**p. 114**), and studying (**p. 120**) strategies. Add up your total score for these three sets of learning strategies (the maximum score for each set is 28):

Note Taking = _____

Reading = _____

Studying = _____

Total Learning Strategy Score = _____

Self-Assessment Questions

1. In which learning strategy area did you score lowest?

2. Do you think that the strategy area in which you scored lowest has anything to do with your lowest course grade at this point in the term?

3. Of the seven strategies listed within the area in which you scored lowest, which ones could you immediately put into practice to improve your lowest course grade this term?

4. What is the likelihood that you will put the preceding strategies into practice this term?

5.2 Consultation with a Learning Center or Academic Development Specialist

Make an appointment to visit your Learning Center or Academic Support Center on campus to discuss the results of your note-taking, reading, and studying self-assessment in Exercise 5.1 (or any other learning self-assessment you may have taken). Ask for recommendations about how you can improve your learning habits in your lowest-score area. Following your visit, answer the following questions.

Learning Resource Center Reflection

1. Date of appointment _____

2. Who did you meet with in the Learning Center? _____

3. Was your appointment useful (e.g., did you gain any insights or acquire any new learning or test-taking strategies)?

4. What steps were recommended to you for improving your academic performance?

5. How likely is it that you will take the steps mentioned in the previous question: (a) definitely, (b) probably, (c) possibly, or (d) unlikely? Why?

6. Do you plan to visit the Learning Center again? If yes, why? If no, why not?

Too Fast, Too Frustrating: A Note-Taking Nightmare

Joanna Scribe is a first-year student who is majoring in journalism, and she's enrolled in an introductory course that is required for her major (Introduction to Mass Media). Her instructor for this course lectures at a rapid rate and uses vocabulary words that go right over her head. Since she cannot get all the instructor's words down on paper and cannot understand half the words she does manage to write down, she becomes frustrated and stops taking notes. She wants to do well in this course because it's the first course in her major, but she's afraid she will fail it because her class notes are so pitiful.

Reflection and Discussion Questions

1. Can you relate to this case personally, or do know any students who are in the same boat as Joanna?

2. What would you recommend that Joanna do at this point?

3. Why did you make the preceding recommendation?

Achieving Peak Levels of Academic Performance

6

Taking Tests, Writing Papers, and Making Presentations

ACTIVATE YOUR THINKING | **Journal Entry** | **6.1**

1. In which of the following academic-performance situations do you tend to perform best? (Circle one.) In which do you perform worst? (Circle one.)

   Taking multiple-choice tests
   Taking essay tests
   Writing papers
   Making oral presentations

2. What do you think accounts for the fact you perform better in one situation than the other?

_____

_____

_____

LEARNING GOAL

To strengthen your performance on three tasks used to evaluate students' academic achievement in college: tests, papers, and presentations.

◆ Test-Taking Strategies

Academic learning in college involves three stages: acquiring information from lectures and readings; studying that information and storing it in your brain as knowledge; and demonstrating that knowledge on exams.

What follows is a series of strategies related to stage three of the learning: test taking. The strategies are divided into three categories:

- Strategies to use in advance of test day,
- Strategies to use during the test, and
- Strategies to use after test results are returned.

Pretest Strategies: What to Do in Advance of Test Day

Your ability to remember what you've studied will depend not only on how much and how well you studied but also on how your memory will be tested (Stein, 1978). You may be able to remember what you've studied if you are tested in one format (e.g., multiple-choice questions) but may not remember the material as well if the test is in a different format (e.g., essay questions). You need to be aware of the type of test you'll be taking and adjust your study strategy accordingly.

College test questions fall into two major categories: (1) recognition questions and (2) recall questions. Each of these types of questions requires a different type of memory and a different study strategy.

- **Recognition test questions.** Recognition questions ask you to select or choose the correct answer from choices that are provided for you. Falling into this category are multiple-choice, true–false, and matching questions. These test questions don't require you to supply or produce the correct answer on your own; instead, you're asked to recognize or pick out the correct answer—similar to picking out the "correct" criminal from a lineup of potential suspects.

Mutiple-choice questions require recognition memory similar to that used to identify the correct criminal from a line-up of possible suspects.

"It's NUMBER THREE, MR. HUGO, OUR SEVENTH GRADE TEACHER--THE ONE WHOSE EXAMS CONTAINED QUESTIONS NOT COVERED IN THE ASSIGNED READING."

- **Recall test questions.** Recall questions require you to retrieve information you've stored in your brain and reproduce it on your own at test time. As the word "recall" implies, you have to recall or "call back" back to mind the information you need and supply it yourself, rather than selecting it or picking it out from information that's supplied for you. Recall test questions include essay and short-answer questions, which require a written response.

Since recognition test questions ask you to recognize or identify the correct answer from among answers that are provided for you, repeatedly reading over your class and textbook notes to identify important concepts may be an effective study strategy for multiple-choice and true–false test questions. Doing so matches the type of mental activity you'll be asked to perform on the exam—read over and identify correct answers.

On the other hand, recall test questions, such as essay questions, require you to retrieve information and generate correct answers on your own. Studying for essay tests by looking over your class notes and highlighted reading will not prepare you to retrieve and recall information on your own because it does not simulate what you'll be doing on the test itself. However, if you prepare for essay tests by writing out answers on your own, you ensure that your practice (study) sessions match your performance (test) situation because you are be rehearsing what you'll be expected to do on the test—write essays.

Two strategies that are particularly effective for practicing the type of memory retrieval you will need to perform on recall tests are reciting and creating retrieval cues.

Reciting

Recitation involves saying the information you need to recall—without looking at it. Research indicates that memory for information is significantly strengthened when students study by trying to generate that information on their own, rather than reviewing or rereading it (Graf, 1982). Reciting strengthens recall memory in three ways:

- Reciting forces you to actively retrieve information, which is what you will have to do on the test, rather than passively reviewing information that's in front of you and in full view, which is not what you will do on the test.
- Reciting gives you clear feedback on whether you can recall the information you're studying. If you cannot retrieve and recite it without looking at it, you know for sure that you will not be able to recall it at test time and that you need to study it further. One way to provide yourself with this feedback is to put the question on one side of an index card and the answer on the flip side. If you find yourself flipping over the index card to look at the answer in order to state it, you clearly cannot retrieve the information on your own and need to study it further.
- Reciting encourages you to use your own words; this gives you feedback on whether you can paraphrase it. If you can paraphrase it (rephrase it in your own words), it's a good indication you really understand it; and if you really understand it, you're more likely to recall it at test time.

Reciting can be done silently, by speaking aloud, or by writing what you are saying. We recommend speaking or writing out what you're reciting because these strategies involve physical action, which keeps you more actively involved when you're studying.

Creating Retrieval Cues

Suppose you're trying to remember the name of a person you know but just cannot recall it. If a friend gives you a clue (e.g., the first letter of the person's name or a name that rhymes with it), then it may suddenly trigger your memory of the person's entire name. What your friend did was provide you with a retrieval cue. A retrieval cue is a type of memory reminder (like a string tied around your finger) that brings back to your mind what you've temporarily forgotten. Human memories are stored as parts in an interconnected network

(Pribram, 1991). If you're able to recall one piece or segment of the network (the retrieval cue), it can trigger recall of the other pieces of information linked to it in the same organizational network (Collins & Loftus, 1975).

Studies show that students who are unable to remember previously studied information are better able to recall that information if they are given retrieval cue. For instance, suppose students have studied a list of items that includes different animals (e.g., giraffe, coyote, and turkey) but are unable to recall all these animals on a later memory test. If a retrieval cue is provided at the time of the recall test (e.g., if the word "animals" is written on top of the answer sheet), the students often are able to recall many animals they couldn't name before the retrieval cue was provided (Kintsch, 1968). These research findings suggest that category names can serve as powerful retrieval cues. By taking information that you'll need to recall on an essay test and organizing it into categories, you can then use the category names as retrieval cues at the time of the test.

Another strategy for creating retrieval cues is to create catchwords or catchphrases that you can use as a net to "catch" related ideas that you need to recall. For example, an acronym can serve as a catchword, with each letter acting as a retrieval cue for a set of related ideas. Suppose you're studying for a test in abnormal psychology that is likely to include essay questions that will test your knowledge about types of mental illness. You could create the acronym SCOT as a retrieval cue to help you remember to include each of the following elements of mental illness in your answers: symptoms (S), causes (C), outcomes (O), and therapies (T).

Pause for Reflection

Think of material in a course you're taking this term that could be easily grouped into categories to help you remember that material. What is the course?

What categories could you use to organize information that's been covered in the course?

! Remember

Unlike multiple-choice questions on which you choose from answers given to you, on essay questions your mind can go blank because you're facing a blank sheet of paper that requires you to provide answers. To avoid drawing blanks on essay questions, you need to study differently—you need to recite (rehearse) your answers while studying and bring retrieval cues with you to the test.

Students can go "completely blank" on essay tests because they face a blank sheet that requires them to provide information on their own—as opposed to multiple-choice tests, which ask students to recognize or pick-out a correct answer from information that is provided for them.

"When I looked at the first essay question, my whole life flashed before my eyes, then my whole mind went totally blank!"

Strategies to Use Immediately Before the Test

1. **Before exams, take a brisk walk.** Physical activity will increase mental alertness by increasing oxygen flow to the brain; it will also decrease tension by increasing the brain's production of emotionally "mellowing" brain chemicals (e.g., serotonin and endorphins).

2. **Arrive at the test room fully equipped with all the test-taking tools you'll need.** In addition to the required supplies (e.g., No. 2 pencil, pen, blue book, Scantron, calculator, etc.), bring backup equipment in case you experience equipment failure (e.g., an extra pen in case your first one runs out of ink or extra pencils in case your original one breaks).

3. **Try to get to the test a few minutes early.** Arriving at the test ahead of time will give you a chance to review any terms, formulas, and equations you may have struggled to remember and any recall shortcuts you may have created (e.g., acronyms). You want to be sure that you have this information in your working memory when you receive the exam so that you can get it down on paper—before you forget it. Arriving early will also allow you to take a few minutes to get into a relaxed pretest state of mind by thinking positive thoughts; taking slow, deep breaths; and stretch your muscles. Try to avoid discussing the test with other students immediately before it begins because their last-minute questions, confusion, and anxiety may rub off on you. (Anxiety can be contagious.)

4. **Sit in the same seat that you normally occupy in class.** Research indicates that memory is improved when information is recalled in the same place where it was originally received or reviewed (Sprenger, 1999). Thus, taking the test in the same seat you normally occupy during lectures, which is the place where you originally heard much of the information appearing on the test, may improve your test performance.

> **Student Perspective**
>
> "Avoid flipping through notes (cramming) immediately before a test. Instead, do some breathing exercises and think about something other than the test."
>
> –Advice to first-year students from a college sophomore (Walsh, 2005)

> **! Remember**
>
> Popular energy drinks typically contain a significant amount of caffeine, which can increase nervousness, blood pressure, and the tendency to crash (experience a sharp drop in energy) after the drink's effects wear off.

Strategies to Use During the Test

1. **As soon as you receive a copy of the test, write down key information.** Writing down any hard-to-remember terms, formulas, and equations and any memory-improvement shortcuts you may have created as soon as you start the exam will ensure that you don't forget this information once you get involved with answering test questions.

2. **Answer the easier test questions first.** As soon as you receive the test, before launching into the first question, check out the layout of the test. Note the questions that are worth the most points and the questions that you know well. One way to implement this recommendation is to first survey the test and put a checkmark by difficult questions and come back to them later—after you've answered the easier ones.

3. **Prevent "memory block" from setting in.** If you experience memory block for information that you

> **Pause for Reflection**
>
> During tests, if I experience memory block, I usually . . .
>
> I am most likely to experience memory block in the following subject areas:

know you've studied and have stored in your brain, use the following strategies:

- Mentally put yourself back in the environment or situation in which you studied the information. Recreate the steps in which you learned the information that you've temporarily forgotten by mentally picturing the place where you first heard or saw it and where you studied it, including the sights, sounds, smells, and time of day. This memory-improvement strategy is referred to as guided retrieval, and research supports its effectiveness for recalling information, including information recalled by eye witnesses to a crime (Glenberg, Bradley, Kraus, & Renzaglia, 1983).

- Think of any idea or piece of information that may be related to the information you cannot remember. Studies show that when students experience temporary forgetting they're more likely to suddenly recall that information if they first recall partial information that relates to it in some way (Reed, 1996). This related piece of information may trigger your memory for the forgotten information because related pieces of information are likely to be stored as memory traces within the same network of brain cells.

- Take your mind off the question and turn to another question. This allows your subconscious to work on the problem, which may trigger your memory of the information you've forgotten. Also, by turning to other test questions, you may find some information included in those questions that can trigger memory for the information you forgot.

Strategies for Answering Multiple-Choice Questions

Multiple-choice questions are commonly used on college tests, on exams to be admitted to graduate school (e.g., for master's and doctoral degree programs) or professional school (e.g., law school and medical school), and on certification or licensing exams to practice in particular professions (e.g., nursing and teaching). Since multiple-choice tests are so common in college and beyond, this section of the text is devoted to a detailed discussion of strategies for answering such test questions.

1. **Read all choices listed and use a process-of-elimination approach.** You can find an answer by eliminating choices that are clearly wrong and continuing doing so until you're left with one answer that seems to be the most accurate option. Keep in mind that the correct answer is often the one that has the highest probability or likelihood of being true; it doesn't have to be absolutely true—just truer than the other choices listed.

2. **Use *test-wise* strategies when you don't know the correct answer.** Your first strategy on any multiple-choice question should be to choose an answer based on your knowledge of the material, not to try to outsmart the test or the test maker by guessing the correct answer based on how the question is worded. However, if you've relied on your knowledge and used the process-of-elimination strategy to eliminate clearly wrong choices but you're still left you with two or more answers that appear to be correct, then you should turn to being test wise, which refers your ability to use the

Pause for Reflection

How would you rate your general level of test anxiety during most exams? (Circle one.)

high   moderate   low

What types of tests or subjects tend to produce the most test stress or test anxiety for you?

Why?

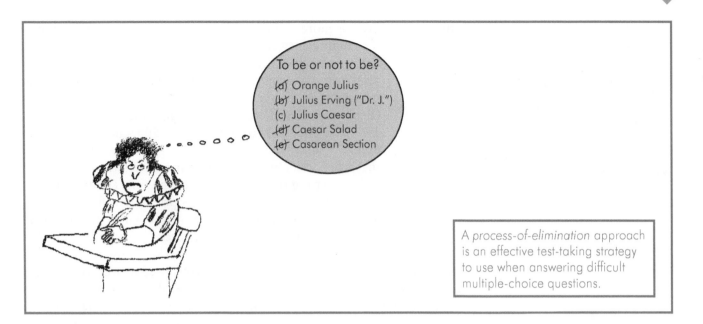

To be or not to be?

~~(a)~~ Orange Julius
~~(b)~~ Julius Erving ("Dr. J.")
(c) Julius Caesar
~~(d)~~ Caesar Salad
~~(e)~~ Casarean Section

A *process-of-elimination* approach is an effective test-taking strategy to use when answering difficult multiple-choice questions.

characteristics of the test question itself (such as its wording or format) to increase your chances of selecting the correct answer (Millman, Bishop, & Ebel, 1965). Listed here are three test-wise strategies for multiple-choice questions whose answer you don't know or can't remember:

- **Pick an answer that contains qualifying words.** Look for words such as "usually," "probably," "likely," "sometimes," "perhaps," or "may." Truth often doesn't come neatly wrapped in the form of a definitive statement, so choices that are stated as broad generalizations or absolute truths are more likely to be false. For example, answers containing words such as "always," "never," "only," "must," and "completely" are more likely to be false than true.

- **Pick the longest answer.** True statements often require more words to make them true.

- **Pick a middle answer rather than the first or last answer.** For example, on a question with four choices, select answer "b" or "c" rather than "a" or "d." Studies show that many instructors have a tendency to place correct answers as middle choices rather than as the first or last choice (Linn & Gronlund, 1995)—perhaps because they think the correct answer will be too obvious or stand out if it's listed as the beginning or end.

3. **Check that your answers are in line.** When looking over your test before turning it in, search carefully for questions you may have skipped and intended to go back to later. Sometimes you may skip a test question on a multiple-choice test and forget to skip the number of that question on the answer form, which will throw off all the other answers by one space or line. On a computer-scored test, this means that you may get multiple items marked wrong because your answers are misplaced. This can produce a domino effect of wrong answers that will severely damage your test score. As a damage-prevention measure, check all of your answers to be sure no blank lines or spaces on your answer sheet could set off this domino effect.

4. **Don't feel locked in to your answers.** When checking your answers on multiple-choice or true–false tests, don't be afraid to change an answer

Pause for Reflection

On exams, do you ever change your original answers?

If you do change answers, what's the usual reason you make changes?

after you've given it more thought. There have been numerous studies on the topic of changing answers on multiple-choice and true–false tests dating back to 1928 (Kuhn, 1988). These studies consistently show that most changed test answers go from being incorrect to correct, resulting in improved test scores (Benjamin, Cavell, & Shallenberger, 1984; Shatz & Best, 1987). In one study of more than 1,500 students' midterm exams in an introductory psychology course, it was found that when students changed their answers they went from right to wrong only 25 percent of the time (Kruger, Wirtz, & Miller, 2005). These findings probably reflect that students may catch a mistake they made when they read the question the first time or discover some information later in the test that causes them to reconsider their first answer. So, don't buy into the common belief that your first answer is always your best answer. If you have good reason to think a change should be made, don't be afraid to make it. However, if you find yourself changing many of your original answers, this may indicate that you were not well prepared for the exam and are just doing a lot of guessing (and second guessing).

Strategies for Answering Essay Questions

Along with multiple-choice questions, essay questions are among the most commonly used forms on college exams. Listed here are strategies that will help you reach peak levels of performance on essay questions.

1. **Focus on the main ideas.** Make a brief outline or list of bullet points to represent the main ideas you will include in your answers before you begin to write them. This strategy is effective for several reasons:
   - **An outline will help you remember major points.** In addition to reminding you of the points you intend to make, an outline will give you the order in which you intend to make them. This should help prevent you from forgetting the big picture and the most important concepts when you become wrapped up in the details of constructing sentences and choosing words for your answers.
   - **An outline improves your answer's organization.** One factor that instructors will consider when determining an answer's grade is its organization. (You can make your answer's organization clearer by underlining your major sections or numbering your major points.)
   - **Having an advanced idea of what you will write can reduce your test anxiety.** The outline will take care of the answer's organization in advance so that you don't have the added stress of organizing your answer and explaining it while you're writing it.
   - **An outline can add points to an incomplete answer's score.** If you run out of test time, your instructor will be able to see your outline for any questions that you didn't have time to complete. Even if you didn't have the opportunity to convert it into sentence form, your outline should earn you points because it demonstrates your knowledge of the major ideas called for by the question. In contrast, if you skip an outline and just starting writing answers to test questions one at a time, you run the risk of not getting to questions you know well before your time is up; you'll then have nothing written on your test to show what you know about those unfinished questions.

Exhibit 1

Identical twins
Adoption
Parents/family tree

$\frac{6}{6}$

1. There are several different studies that scientists conduct, but one study that they conduct is to find out how genetics can influence human behavior in <u>identical twins</u>. Since they are identical, they will most likely end up very similar in behavior because of their identical genetic make up. Although environment has some impact, genetics are still a huge factor and they will, more likely than not, behave similarly. Another type of study is with <u>parents and their family trees</u>. Looking at a subject's family tree will alleviate why a certain person is bi-polar or depressed. It is most likely a cause of a gene in the family tree, even if it was last seen decades ago. Lastly, another study is with adopted children. If an <u>adopted child</u> acts a certain way that is unique to that child, and researchers find the parents' family tree, they will most likely see similar behavior in the parents and siblings as well.

No freewill
No afterlife

$\frac{6}{6}$

2. The monistic view of the mind-brain relationship is so strongly opposed and criticized because there is a belief or assumption that <u>freewill</u> is taken away from people. For example, if a person commits a horrendous crime, it can be argued "monastically" that the chemicals in the brain were the reason, and that a person cannot think for themselves to act otherwise. This view limits responsibility.
Another reason that this view is opposed is because it has been said that <u>there is no afterlife</u>. If the mind and brain are one and the same, and there is <u>NO</u> difference, then once the brain is dead and is no longer functioning, so is the mind. Thus, is cannot continue to live beyond what we know today as life. <u>And</u> this goes against many religions, which is why this reason, in particular, is heavily opposed.

> Written answers to two short essay questions given by a college sophomore, which demonstrate effective use of bulleted lists or short outlines to ensure recall of most important points.

2. **Get directly to the point on each essay question.** Avoid elaborate introductions that take up your test time (and your instructor's grading time) but don't earn you any points. For example, an answer that begins with the statement "This is an interesting question that we had a great discussion on in class . . ." is pointless because it will not add points to your test score. The time available to you on essay tests is often limited, so you can't afford flowery introductions that are pointless—both in their content and in what they would add to your score.

One effective way to focus your response is to include part of the question in the first sentence of your answer. For example, suppose the test says, "Argue for or against capital punishment by explaining how it will or will not reduce the nation's murder rate." Your first sentence could read, "Capital punishment will not reduce the murder rate for the following reasons . . ." Thus, your first sentence becomes your thesis statement, which points you directly to the major points you're going to make in your essay and to earning points for your essay.

3. **Answer all essay questions as precisely and completely as possible.** Don't assume that your instructor already knows what you're talking about or will be bored by details. Instead, take the approach that you're writing to someone who knows little or nothing about the subject—as if you're an expert teacher and the reader is a clueless student.

> **! Remember**
>
> As a rule, it's better to overexplain than underexplain your answers to essay questions.

4. **Support your points with evidence—facts, statistics, quotes, or examples.** When taking essay tests, take on the role of a criminal lawyer who makes a case by presenting concrete evidence (exhibit A, exhibit B, etc.). Since timed essay tests can often press you for time, be sure to prioritize and cite your most powerful points and persuasive evidence. If you have time later, you can return to add other points worth mentioning.

5. **Leave space between your answers to each essay question.** This strategy will enable you to easily add information to your original answer if you have time or if you recall something later in the test that you had originally forgotten.

6. **Proofread your test and correct grammar and spelling errors.** When checking your answers to essay questions, before turning in your test, proofread what you've written and correct any spelling or grammatical errors you find. Eliminating them is likely to improve your test score. Even if your instructor doesn't explicitly state that grammar and spelling will be counted in determining your grade, these mechanical mistakes may still subconsciously influence your professor's overall evaluation of your written work.

7. **Remember that neatness matters.** Research indicates that neatly written essays tend to be scored higher than sloppy ones, even if the answers are essentially the same (Klein & Hart, 1968). This is understandable when you consider that grading essay answers is a time-consuming task that requires your weary-eyed instructor to plod through multiple styles of handwriting whose readability may range from crystal clear to cryptic code. Thus, make a point of writing as clearly as possible, and if you finish the test with time to spare, clean up your work by rewriting any sloppily written words or sentences.

8. **Before turning in your test, carefully review and double-check your answers.** This is the critical last step in the process of effective test taking. Sometimes the rush and anxiety of taking a test can cause test takers to overlook details, misread instructions, unintentionally skip questions, or make absentminded mistakes. When you're done, take time to look over your answers to be sure you didn't make any mindless mistakes. Avoid the temptation to immediately cut out because you're pooped out or to take off on an ego trip by trying to be among the first and fastest students in class to finish their test. Instead, take the full amount of time that you have to complete the test. When you consider the amount of time and effort you put into preparing for the exam, it's foolish not to take just a few more minutes to ensure you get maximum mileage out of the time you have to complete the exam.

Pause for Reflection

Rate yourself in terms of how frequently you use these test-taking strategies according to the following scale:

4 = always, 3 = sometimes, 2 = rarely, 1 = never

1. I take tests in the same seat that I usually sit in to take class notes.   4 3 2 1

2. I answer easier test questions first.   4 3 2 1

3. I use a process-of-elimination approach on multiple-choice tests to eliminate choices until I find one that is correct or appears to be the most accurate option.   4 3 2 1

4. For essay questions, I outline or map out my ideas before I begin to write the answer.   4 3 2 1

5. I look for information included on the test that may help me answer difficult questions or that may help me remember information I've forgotten.   4 3 2 1

6. I leave extra space between my answers to essay questions in case I want to come back and add more information later.   4 3 2 1

7. I carefully review my work, double-checking for errors and skipped questions before turning in my tests.   4 3 2 1

Posttest Strategies: What to Do After Receiving Test Results

1. **Use your test results as feedback to improve your future performance.** Your test results are not just an end result; they may also be used as a means to an end—to improve your future test performances and your final course grade. Examine your tests carefully when you get them back, being sure to note any written comments your instructor may have made.

   If your test results are disappointing, don't become mad or sad; instead, get even by using the results as feedback to assess where you went wrong so that you can avoid making the same mistake again. If your test results were positive, use them to see where you went right so that you can do it the same way again.

2. **Ask for additional feedback.** In addition to using your own test results as a source of feedback, actively seek feedback from people whose judgment you trust and value. Three social resources you can use to obtain feedback on how to improve your performance are your instructors, professionals in your Learning or Academic Support Center, and your peers.

   You can make appointments with your instructors to visit them during office hours and get their feedback on how you might be able to improve your performance. You'll likely find it easier to see your instructors after a test than before it, because most students don't realize that it's just as valuable to seek feedback from instructors following an exam as it is to try and get last-minute help before it.

   Tutors and other learning support professionals on your campus can also be excellent sources of feedback about what adjustments to make in your study habits or test-taking strategies to improve your future performance.

   Also, be alert and open to receiving feedback from trusted peers. While feedback from experienced professionals is valuable, don't overlook your peers as another source of feedback on how to improve your performance. You can review your test with other students in class, particularly with students who did exceptionally well. Their tests can provide you with models of what type of work your instructor expects on exams. Also, ask successful students what they did to be successful—for example, what they did to prepare for the test that enabled them to perform so well.

   Whatever you do, don't let a bad test grade get you mad, sad, or down, particularly if it occurs early in the course when you're still learning the rules of the game. Look at mistakes in terms of what they can do for you, rather than to you. A poor test performance can be turned into a valuable learning experience by using test results as feedback or an error detector to locate the source of your mistakes.

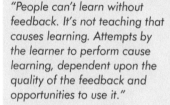

"People can't learn without feedback. It's not teaching that causes learning. Attempts by the learner to perform cause learning, dependent upon the quality of the feedback and opportunities to use it."

–Grant Wiggins, *Feedback: How Learning Occurs*

"When you make a mistake, there are only three things you should do about it: admit it; learn from it; and don't repeat it."

–Paul "Bear" Bryant, college football coach

Remember

Your past mistakes shouldn't be ignored or neglected; they should be detected and corrected so that you don't replay them on future tests.

Strategies for Pinpointing the Reason for Lost Points on Exams

On test questions where you lost points, identify the stage in the learning process at which the breakdown occurred by asking yourself the following questions.

- **Did you have the information you needed to answer the question correctly?** If you didn't have the information, what was the source of the missing information? Was it information presented in class that didn't get into your notes? If so, look at our strategies for improving listening and note-taking habits (**pp. 106–114**). If the missing information was contained in your assigned reading, check whether you're using effective reading strategies (**pp. 114–1189**).

- **Did you have the information but not study it because you didn't think it was important?** If you didn't realize which information would be on the test, then you might want to review the study strategies for finding and focusing on the most important information in class lectures and reading assignments.

- **Did you know the information but not retain it?** Not holding on information may mean one of three things:

  1. You didn't store the information adequately in your brain, so your memory trace wasn't strong enough for you to recall it at the time you took the test. This suggests that more study time needs to be spent on recitation or rehearsal (**p. 139**).

  2. You may have tried to cram too much information in too little time just before the exam and may have not given your brain time enough to digest it and store it in long-term memory. The solution would be to distribute your study time more evenly in advance of the next exam and take advantage of the effective part-to-whole study method (**pp. 124–125**).

  3. You put in enough study time and didn't cram, but you didn't study effectively or strategically. For example, you may have studied for essay questions by just reading over your class and reading notes rather than by writing and rehearsing them. The solution would be to adjust your study strategy so that it better matches or aligns with the type of test you'll be taking (**pp. 137–139**).

- **Did you study the material but not really understand it or learn it deeply?** If deep learning didn't occur, you may need to self-monitor your comprehension more carefully while studying to track whether you truly understand the material at a deeper level.

- **Did you know the information but were not able to retrieve it during the exam?** If you had the information on the "tip of your tongue" during the exam, this indicates that you did retain it and it was stored (saved) in your brain but you couldn't get at it and get it out (retrieve it) when you needed. This error may be corrected by making better use of memory-retrieval cues (**pp. 139–140**).

- **Did you know the answer but just make a careless test-taking mistake?** If your mistake was careless, the solution may be simply to take more time to review your test once you've completed it and check for absent-minded errors before turning it in (**p. 146**).

> ! **Remember**
>
> Just as you learn before tests by preparing for your performance, you can learn after tests by reviewing your performance.

◆ Writing Papers and Reports

The Importance of Writing

Writing is a powerful, transferable skill that you can used to promote your success across the curriculum, including general education courses and courses in your academic major. You may have many great ideas in your head, but unless you can communicate them, your instructors will never know that you have them and you will never receive full credit for them in your college courses. Writing is a major route through which you can communicate your ideas, and it is a route of communication that your instructors will travel often to judge the extent of your knowledge and the quality of your thinking. Thus, if you improve your writing skills, you will improve your ability to demonstrate your knowledge, communicate your ideas, and elevate your grades.

Your ability to write clearly, concisely, and persuasively is a skill that not only will enable you succeed academically but also will help you succeed professionally. In one study, college alumni were asked about the importance of different skills to their current work responsibilities more than 10 years after they graduated, and more than 90 percent of the alumni ranked "need to write effectively" as a skill they considered to be of "great importance" to their current work (Worth, cited in Light, 2001). The first contact and first impression you will make on future employers is likely to be your letter of application or cover letter that you write when applying for positions. Constructing a well-written letter of application may be your first step toward converting your college experience and college degree into a future career.

> ! **Remember**
>
> Writing skills will contribute to your academic success across all subjects throughout all your years in college, and they will promote your professional success in any career you may pursue after college.

Papers and Reports

Studies show that a small percentage of high school students' class and homework time is spent on writing assignments that are as lengthy and demanding as those given in college. For example, in high school, most writing assignments involve summaries or descriptive reports; in college, students are expected to engage in expository (persuasive) writing, which requires the writer to make or prove a case by supporting it with sound evidence (Applebee, 1981; Applebee, Langer, Jenkins, Mullis, & Foertsch, 1990).

Pause for Reflection

Reflect back on your high school experience, and try to recall your writing assignments. What was the longest paper you wrote in high school?

What type of thinking were you usually asked to do on your writing assignments (e.g., memorize, summarize, analyze, criticize, or compare and contrast)?

Dividing large writing assignments into smaller, manageable steps can reduce late-night frustration and the risk of permanent computer damage.

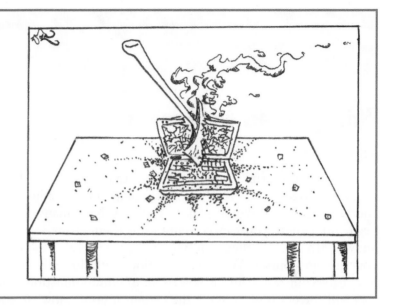

Writing is a multistep process that cannot be completed in one night. Dividing the writing process into a series of shorter steps that are taken in advance of the paper's due date is an effective way to strengthen the quality of your final product.

What follows is a six-step plan for dividing your time and labor that should make the task of writing papers more manageable, less stressful, and more successful.

1. **Know the purpose or objective of the assignment.** Having a clear understanding of the purpose or goal of the writing assignment is the critical first step to completing it successfully. It helps you stay on track and moving in the right direction; it also helps you get on track in the first place, because one major cause of writer's block is uncertainty about the goal or purpose of the writing task (Rennie & Brewer, 1987).

   Before you begin to do any writing, be sure you have a clear understanding of what your instructor expects you to accomplish. You can do this by asking yourself these three questions about the writing assignment:
   - What is the objective or intended outcome of this assignment?
   - What type of thinking am I being asked to demonstrate in this assignment?
   - What criteria (judgment standards) will my instructor use to evaluate and grade my performance on this assignment?

   To help determine what particular form or forms of thinking you are expected to demonstrate in a writing assignment, make special note of any action verbs in the description of the assignment. These verbs can provide valuable clues to the type of thinking that your instructor wants you to demonstrate. Listed in **Box 6.1** are some thinking verbs that you're likely to see college writing assignments and the type of mental action typically called for by each of these verbs.

   As you read the following list, make a short note after each mental action, indicating whether or not you've been asked to use such thinking on any assignments you completed before college.

2. **Generate ideas.** At this stage of the writing process, the only thing you're concerned about is getting the ideas you have in your head out of your head and on to paper. Don't worry about how good or bad the ideas may be. Writing scholars refer to this process as focused freewriting—writing nonstop for a certain period just to generate ideas, without

> "Begin with the end in mind."
>
> –Stephen Covey, *The Seven Habits of Highly Effective People*

Take Action!

Ten Mental-Action Verbs Commonly Found in College Writing Assignments

1. Analyze. Break it down into its key parts and evaluate those parts (e.g., strengths and weaknesses).
2. Compare. Identify the similarities and differences between major ideas.
3. Contrast. Identify the differences between ideas, particularly sharp differences and opposing viewpoints.
4. Describe. Provide details (e.g., who, what, where, and when).
5. Discuss. Analyze (break apart) and evaluate the parts (e.g., strengths and weaknesses).
6. Document. Support your judgment and conclusions with evidence.
7. Explain. Provide reasons that answer the questions "why?" and "how?"
8. Illustrate. Supply concrete examples or specific instances.
9. Interpret. Draw your own conclusion about something, and explain why you came to that conclusion.
10. Support. Back up your ideas with factual evidence or logical arguments.

6.1

worrying about writing complete or correct sentences (Bean, 2001). Remember that the act of writing itself can stimulate ideas, so if you're not sure what ideas you have, start writing because it will likely trigger ideas, which, in turn, will lead to additional ideas. One way to overcome writer's block is to start writing something (Zinsser, 1990). It could be anything, as long as it jump-starts the process.

3. **Organize your ideas.** Ideas should be organized in a paper or written report in one of two ways:

- Separate pieces of specific information related to the same general idea need to be organized conceptually into the same categories.
  Strategy: Review the ideas that you've brainstormed and group together those ideas that may be classified in the same general category. For instance, if your topic is terrorism and you find three ideas on your list referring to different causes of terrorism, group those ideas together under the category of "causes." Similarly, if you find ideas on your list that relate to possible solutions to the problem of terrorism, group those ideas under the category of "solutions." (You could record your separate ideas on sticky notes and stick the notes with ideas pertaining to the same general category on index cards, with the category heading written at the top of the card.)

- General categories of ideas need to be organized sequentially into an order that flows smoothly or logically from start to finish.
  Strategy: Arrange your general categories of ideas into an orderly sequence that creates a beginning, middle, and end. Index cards come in handy when trying to find the best progression of your major ideas because the cards can be arranged and rearranged easily until you discover an order that produces the smoothest, most logical sequence. You can use your sequence of index cards to create an outline for your paper that lists the major categories of your ideas and the order in which they will appear in your paper.

Pause for Reflection

Which of the mental actions in the list in Box 6.1 was most often required on your high school writing assignments?

Which was least often (or never) required?

Strategy: Another effective way to organize and sequence your ideas is by creating a concept map or idea map that represents your main categories of ideas in a visual–spatial format that's similar to a road map. **Figure 6.1** shows a concept map that was used to organize and sequence the main ideas covered in Chapter 7 on higher-level thinking. This type of concept map is called a clock map because its main ideas are organized like the numbers of a clock, beginning at the top and then moving sequentially in a clockwise direction.

4. **Write multiple drafts.** The steps in the writing process discussed thus far are referred to as prewriting because they focus on generating and organizing your ideas before communicating them to anyone else (Murray, 1993). In your first draft, you begin the formal writing process of converting your major ideas into sentences, but you do so without worrying about the mechanics of writing (e.g., punctuation, grammar, or spelling). In your first draft, the goal is to simply "talk through" your key ideas on paper.

Pause for Reflection

When you attempt to organize your ideas, are you more likely to use a map (diagram) format or an outline format—in which you list major ideas as headings (A, B, C, etc.) and related minor ideas as subheadings (1, 2, 3, etc.)?

Why do you think you tend to favor one method over the other?

Which method for organizing ideas appears more natural or comfortable to you?

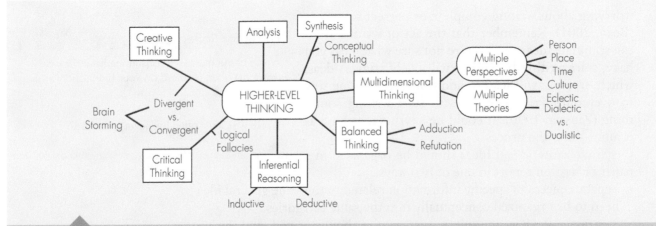

Figure 6.1 Concept Map Used to Organize and Sequence Major Ideas Relating to Higher-Level Thinking

> "I'm not a writer; I'm a rewriter."
>
> –James Thurber, award-winning American journalist and author

Remember

Don't expect to write a perfect draft of your paper on the first try. Even professional writers report that it takes them more than one draft (often three or four) before they produce their final draft. Although the final product of award-winning writers may look spectacular, what precedes it is a messy process that includes lots of revisions between the first try and the final product (Bean, 2001).

> "End with the beginnig in mind."
>
> –Joe Cuseo

• In your final draft be sure that your conclusion and introduction are aligned or interrelated. The most important sentence in your conclusion should be a restatement of your original thesis or should answer the question that was posed in your introduction. Connecting your thesis statement and concluding statement provides a pair of meaningful bookends to your paper, anchoring it at its two most pivotal points—the beginning and the end. It allows you to drive your point home at two influential points of in the communication process—the first and the last impression.

5. **Read and edit your writing.** After you complete a second draft of your paper, take your mind off it for a while and come back to it in a different role—as reader and editor. Up to now, your role has been that of a writer; at this stage, you shift roles from writer to reader; you read your own words as if they were written by someone else, and you critically evaluate the paper's ideas, organization, and writing style. If you find words and sentences that aren't clearly capturing or reflecting what you meant to say, then revision is necessary. At this stage, make sure your paper is double-spaced so that you have ample room for editing and revising.

6. **Proofread your paper carefully for clerical and technical mistakes before submitting it.** Proofreading may be said to be a micro form of editing; it shifts the focus of your editorial attention to the minute mechanics of your paper and detection of details related to referencing, grammar, punctuation, and spelling. Proofreading is a critical last step in the editorial process because small, technical errors are likely to have been overlooked during earlier stages of the writing process when your attention was focused on larger issues related to your paper's content and organizational structure.

When proofing your paper, don't forget that your computer's spell-checker doesn't check whether word are correctly spelled in the context (sentence) in which you're using them. For instance, a spell-checker would not detect the three "correctly" spelled words that are actually misspelled words in the context of the following sentence: "She *war* her high-*healed* sneakers to the *bawl*."

There is another essential element of careful proofreading: Checking to be sure that you've cited all your sources accurately and thoroughly. This will ensure that you demonstrate academic integrity and avoid plagiarism. (See **Box 6.2** for more details.)

> ! **Remember**
>
> Careful proofreading represents the key, final step in the process of writing a high-quality paper. Earlier stages of the writing process are more mentally demanding and time consuming than proofreading, so it would be a shame to overlook this simple last step and lose points for mistakes that can be quickly detected and corrected.

◆ Public Speaking: Making Oral Presentations and Delivering Speeches

The Importance of Oral Communication

In addition to writing, the second major channel used to convey ideas and demonstrate your knowledge is oral communication. Developing your ability to speak in a clear, concise, and confident manner will strengthen your performance in college and your career. The oral communication skills you demonstrate during your job interviews are likely to play a pivotal role in determining whether you're initially hired, and your ability to speak effectively at meetings and when making professional presentations will contribute significantly

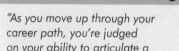

Plagiarism: A Violation of Academic Integrity

What Is Academic Integrity?

There are ethical aspects of writing papers and reports. Academic integrity involves avoiding the unethical practice of stealing the ideas of others, whether they are the ideas of peers (e.g., not cheating on exams) or the words and ideas of authorities that have been borrowed or have influenced the writer's thoughts but for which the writer has failed to give credit. When writing papers and reports, students with academic integrity give credit where credit is due; they carefully cite and reference their sources.

What Is Plagiarism?

Plagiarism is a violation of academic integrity that involves deliberate or unintentional use of someone else's work without acknowledging it, giving the reader the impression it's original work.

Student Perspective

"My intent was not to plagiarize. I realize I was unclear [about] the policy and am actually thankful for now knowing exactly what I can and cannot do on assignments and how to prevent academic dishonesty in the future."

–First-year college student's reflection on a plagiarism violation

Various Forms of Plagiarism

1. Submitting an entire paper, or portion thereof, that was written by someone else,
2. Copying sections of someone else's work and inserting it into your own work,

3. Cutting paragraphs from separate sources and pasting them into the body of your own paper,

Student Perspective

"When a student violates an academic integrity policy no one wins, even if the person gets away with it. It isn't right to cheat and it is an insult to everyone who put the effort in and did the work, and it cheapens the school for everyone. I learned my lesson and have no intention of ever cheating again."

–First-year college student's reflection on an academic integrity violation

4. Paraphrasing (rewording) someone else's words or ideas without citing that person as a source, (For examples of acceptable paraphrasing versus plagiarism, go to www.princeton.edu/pr/pub/integrity/pages/plagiarism.html)

Note: If the source for information included in your paper is listed at the end of your paper in your reference (works cited) section but is not cited in the body of your paper, this still qualifies as plagiarism.

5. Not placing quotation marks around someone else's exact words that appear in the body of your paper,
6. Failing to cite the source of factual information included in your paper that's not common knowledge.

Sources: Academic Integrity at Princeton (2003); Pennsylvania State University (2005); Purdue University Online Writing Lab (1995–2004).

to your prospects for promotion. Research repeatedly shows that employers place high value on oral communication skills and rank them among the top characteristics they seek in prospective employees (AC Nielsen Research Services, 2000; National Association of Colleges & Employers, 2003; Conference Board of Canada, 2000).

National surveys show that fear of public speaking is extremely common among people of all ages, including adolescents and adults (Motley, 1997). Studies also show that many college students experience classroom communication apprehension—that is, they are fearful about speaking in class (Richmond & McCloskey, 1997). If you're at least somewhat nervous about public speaking, welcome to a club that has many members.

Francie reprinted by permission of Sherrie Shepherd.

Surveys reveal that fear of public speaking is very common and ranks high on the list of most intense human fears.

Strategies for Making Effective Oral Presentations and Speeches

In the following section of this chapter, you'll find strategies you can use immediately to improve your ability to make oral presentations and speeches. Since speaking and writing both involve communicating thoughts in the form of words, you'll find that many of the strategies suggested here for improving oral reports will also be useful for improving written reports. You should be able to double dip and transfer the effective strategies you learn for oral presentations to improve your written papers presentations, and vice versa.

Pause for Reflection

Before college, had you ever made an oral presentation or delivered a speech?

Does your college include a course in speech or public speaking as a graduation requirement?

If your college doesn't require it, would you consider taking an elective course in public speaking?

Know the purpose of your presentation. Knowing the intended outcome of your presentation is the critical first step toward making an effective presentation. You can't begin to take the right steps toward doing anything well until you know why you're doing it. If you have any doubt about what your oral presentation should accomplish, seek clarification from your instructor before proceeding.

Similar to formal papers, formal presentations usually fall into one of the following two categories, depending on their purpose or objective:

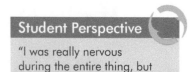

Student Perspective

"I was really nervous during the entire thing, but I felt so relieved and proud afterwards."

—First-year college student commenting on her first public speech

- **Informative presentations,** which are intended to provide the audience with accurate information and explanations
- **Persuasive (expository) presentations,** which are intended to persuade (convince) the audience to agree with a certain position by supporting it with solid evidence and sound arguments

In college, most of your oral presentations will fall into the persuasive category, which means that you will search for information, draw conclusions about your research, and document your conclusions with evidence. Similar to writing research papers, persuasive presentations usually require you to think at a higher level, cite sources, and demonstrate academic integrity.

Strategies for Delivering Your Presentation

1. **Rehearse and revise.** Just as you should write several drafts of a paper before turning it in, your oral presentation should be rehearsed and revised before you deliver it. Rehearsal will improve your memory and increase the clarity of your presentation by reducing long pauses, the need to stop and restart, and the use of distracting fillers (e.g., "uh," "umm," "like," and "you know").

Rehearsing what you plan to say before you start to say it increases the clarity of your oral presentations by reducing the likelihood that you'll fill silent pauses with unnecessary fillers, such as "like," "kind of," and "you know."

"If somebody asked me what my like favorite class is, you know, I'd hafta go, 'Speech'."

During your presentation, you can occasionally look at your notes or slides and use them as cue cards to help you recall the key points you intend to make; however, they shouldn't be used as a script that's read verbatim.

> **!** **Remember**
>
> An oral presentation is a form of public speaking, not a public reading.

On the other hand, a formal presentation is not an impromptu speech that's spontaneously delivered off the top of your head. Instead, it's an extemporaneous presentation, which is something between a formal reading and an impromptu speech; it involves advanced preparation and use of some notes but isn't written out entirely in advance and read (or memorized) word for word (Luotto, Stoll, & Hoglund-Ketttmann,

Take Action!

6.3

Tips for Using (Not Abusing) PowerPoint®

- List information on your slides as bulleted points, not as complete sentences. Wordiness will result in your audience spending more time reading than listening to you. You can further encourage your audience to listen by showing only one of your slide's points at a time. This will keep the audience members focused on the point you're discussing and prevent them from reading ahead.
- Avoid reading your slides. Keep eye contact primarily with your audience.

Remember

The points on the slide are meant to be quick launching pads for more elaborate ideas that you present verbally. PowerPoint should be used to reinforce your oral presentation; it shouldn't become your presentation, nor should it turn public speaking into public reading.

> "A presentation is about explaining things to people that go above and beyond what they get in the slides. If it weren't, they might just as well get your slides and read them in the comfort of their own office, home, boat, or bathroom."
>
> –Jesper Johansson, senior security strategist for Microsoft and author of *Death by PowerPoint* (personal blog) (2005)

- Limit the amount of information on a slide to three to five points. Research indicates that the number of points or bits of information that humans can hold in their short-term memory is about four (plus or minus two; Cowan, 2001).
- Use the title of the slide as a general heading to organize or connect the bullets listed on the slide.
- Use a font size of at least 18 points, or else people in the back of the room will have difficulty reading what's printed on the slide.
- Use color not to decorate or distract but to add meaning to the points on the slide. For example, use a dark or bold blue heading to represent a major category, and list the subcategories beneath it in a lighter (but still visible) shade of blue.
- Use your slides to deliver pictures or visual images that relate to and reinforce the points you're making verbally. This may be the true power of PowerPoint.

Remember

Probably the most powerful advantage of PowerPoint is its ability to enhance your verbal presentation with visual images, which can magnify the impact of your spoken message and expand the attention span of your audience.

- If you include words or an image on a slide that's not your own work, acknowledge its source at the bottom of the slide.
- Proof your slides like you would a written paper before going public with them.

Sources: Johansson (2005); Ten Commandments of PowerPoint Presentations (2005); University of Wisconsin, La Crosse (2001).

2001). Extemporaneous speaking allows you some freedom to ad lib or improvise. If you forget the exact words you intended to use, some improvising can prevent you from getting struck by silence, and it can prevent your audience from even noticing that you forgot what you were planning to say.

2. **Incorporate visual elements into your presentation.** Visual aids can be a powerful way to illustrate or reinforce your points and stimulate

Student Perspective

"The only time I get nervous is when I am not very familiar with my topic or if I'm winging my assignment and I'm not prepared."

–First-year college student commenting on her previous oral presentations

audience interest. You can use pictures, images, graphs, or cartoons that are relevant to the content of your presentation. Or you can bring in objects or artifacts that relate points you'll make in your presentation.

> **Remember**
>
> The more organized and prepared you are for speaking in public, the less anxiety you'll experience when speaking in public.

During Delivery of Your Speech

- Don't remain motionless; move around a bit. When you're experiencing even moderate stress, your body releases adrenaline—an energy-generating hormone. Thus, it may be natural for your body to want to move during your speech, so move it. Trying to inhibit your body's natural tendency to move can increase your level of tension. Furthermore, research shows that some movement and gesticulation on the part of the speaker help hold the audience's attention and interest more effectively than standing still (Andersen, 1985). Perhaps this is because movement suggests energy, which may send the message that you're not emotionless but passionate about the topic you're talking about.

- Focus attention on the *message* you're delivering (the content of your speech), not the *messenger* who's delivering it (yourself). By remaining conscious of the ideas you're communicating to your listeners, you become less self-conscious about the impression you're making on them and their impression (evaluation) of you.

- If you continue to experience high levels of speech anxiety after implementing these strategies, seek advice and help from a professional in your Learning Center or Counseling Center.

◆ Summary and Conclusion

Improving performance on college exams involves strategies used in advance of the test, during the test, and after test results are returned. Good test performance begins with good test preparation and adjustment of your study strategy to the type of test you'll be taking (e.g., multiple-choice or essay test).

You can learn and improve your grades not only by preparing for tests but also by reviewing your tests and using them as feedback to apply as you continue in the course. Past mistakes shouldn't be ignored or neglected; they should be detected and corrected so that they're not replayed on future tests.

Since speaking and writing both involve communicating thoughts in the form of words, many of the strategies for strengthening written reports are effective for strengthening oral presentations (e.g., knowing the purpose of the presentation, revising and editing, and developing a strong introduction and conclusion).

Writing and speaking are essential skills for effective performance in all academic and professional fields. The time and energy you invest in developing these communication skills will pay huge dividends toward promoting your success in college and beyond.

Learning More Through the World Wide Web

Internet-Based Resources for Further Information on Research, Writing, and Speaking

For additional information related to ideas discussed in this chapter, we recommend the following Web sites:

Test-Taking Strategies: www.muskingum.edu/~cal/database/general/testtaking.html

Writing Strategies: www.enhancemywriting.com/

Public Speaking Skills: www.public-speaking.org

6.1 Midterm Self-Evaluation

Since you are near the midpoint of this text book, you may be near the midpoint of your first term in college. At this time of the term you are likely to experience the midterm crunch—a wave of midterm exams and due dates for certain papers and projects. This may be a good time to step back and assess your academic progress thus far.

Use the form that follows to list the courses you're taking this term and the grades you are currently receiving in each of these courses. If you do not know what your grade is, take a few minutes to check your syllabus for your instructor's grading policy and add up your scores on completed tests and assignments; this should give you at least a rough idea of where you stand in your courses. If you're having difficulty determining your grade in any course, even after checking your course syllabus and returned tests or assignments, then ask your instructor how you could estimate your current grade.

Course No.   Course Title   Instructor   Grade

1. _____

2. _____

3. _____

4. _____

5. _____

Self-Assessment Questions

1. Were these the grades you were hoping for? Are you pleased or disappointed by them?

2. Were these the grades you expected to get? If not, were they better or worse than expected?

3. Do you see any patterns in your performance that suggest things you are doing well or things that you need to improve?

4. If you had to pinpoint one action you could immediately take to improve your lowest course grades, what would it be?

6.2 Calculating Your Midterm Grade Point Average

Use the information in the following box to calculate what your grade point average (GPA) would be if these grades turn out to be your final course grades for the term.

Snapshot Summary

6.1

How to Compute Your Grade-Point Average (GPA)

Most colleges and universities use a grading scale that ranges from 0 to 4.0 to represent a student's grade-point average (GPA) or quality-point average (QPA). Some schools use letter grades only, while other institutions use letter grades with pluses and minuses.

Grading System Using Letters Only

Grade = Point value

A = 4
B = 3
C = 2
D = 1
F = 0

GRADE POINTS Earned Per Course = Course Grade Multiplied by the Number of Course Credits

$$\text{GRADE POINT AVERAGE (GPA)} = \frac{\text{Total Number of Grade Points for all Courses}}{\text{Divided by Total Number of Course Units}}$$

SAMPLE/EXAMPLE

Course	Units	×	Grade	=	Grade Points
Roots of Rock 'n' Roll	3	×	C (2)	=	6
Daydreaming Analysis	3	×	A (4)	=	12
Surfing Strategies	1	×	A (4)	=	4
Wilderness Survival	4	×	B (3)	=	12
Sitcom Analysis	2	×	D (1)	=	2
Love and Romance	3	×	A (4)	=	12
	16				48

$$GPA = \frac{48}{16} = 3.0$$

1. What is your overall GPA at this point in the term?

2. When this term began, what GPA were you hoping to attain?

3. Do you think your actual GPA the end of the term will be higher or lower than it is now? Why?

Notes

It's normal for GPAs to be lower in college than they were in high school, particularly after the first of college. Here are the results of one study that compared students' high school GPAs with the GPAs after their first year of college:

- 29% of beginning college students had GPAs of 3.75 or higher in high school, but only 17% had GPAs that high at the end of their first year of college.
- 46% had high school GPAs between 3.25 and 3.74, but only 32% had GPAs that high after the first year of college (National Resource Center for the First-Year Experience and Students in Transition, 2004).

6.3 Preparing an Oral Presentation on Student Success

1. Scan this textbook and identify a chapter topic or chapter section that you find most interesting or most important.

2. Create an introduction for a class presentation on this topic that

   a. provides an overview or sneak preview of what you will cover in your presentation;

   b. grabs the attention of your audience (your classmates); and

   c. demonstrates the topic's relevance or importance for your audience.

3. Create a conclusion to your presentation that

   a. relates back to your introduction;

   b. highlights your most important point or points; and

   c. leaves a memorable last impression.

Bad Feedback: Shocking Midterm Grades

Joe Frosh has enjoyed his first weeks on campus. He has met lots of interesting people and feels that he fits in socially. He also likes that his college schedule does not require him to be in class for 5 to 6 hours per day, like it did in high school. This is the good news. The bad news is that unlike high school, where his grades were all As and Bs, his first midterm grades in college are three Cs, one D, and one F. He is stunned and a bit depressed by his midterm grades because he thought he was doing well. Since he never received grades this low in high school, he's beginning to think that he is not college material and may flunk out.

Reflection and Discussion Questions

1. What factors may have caused or contributed to Joe's bad start?

2. What are Joe's options at this point?

3. What do you recommend Joe do now to get his grades up and avoid being placed on academic probation?

4. What might Joe do in the future to prevent this midterm setback from happening again?

Crime and Punishment: Plagiarism and Its Consequences

In an article that appeared in an Ohio newspaper, titled "Plagiarism persists in classrooms," an English professor was quoted as saying: "Technology has made it easier to plagiarize because students can download papers and exchange information and papers through their computers. But technology has also made it easier to catch students who plagiarize." This professor's college now subscribes to a Web site that matches the content of students' papers with content from books and online sources. Many professors now require students to submit their papers through this Web site. If students are caught plagiarizing, for a first offense, they typically receive an F for the assignment or the course. A second offense can result in dismissal or expulsion from college, which has already happened to a few students.

Source: Mariettatimes.com (March 22, 2006).

Reflection and Discussion Questions

1. Why do you think students plagiarize? What do you suspect are the primary motives, reasons, or causes?

2. What do you think is a fair or just penalty for those found guilty of a first violation plagiarism? What is fair for those who commit a second violation?

3. How do you think plagiarism could be most effectively reduced or prevented from happening?

4. What could students do to minimize or eliminate plagiarism?

5. What could professors do to minimize or eliminate plagiarism?

Higher-Level Thinking

Moving Beyond Factual Knowledge to Higher
Levels of Critical and Creative Thinking

7

ACTIVATE YOUR THINKING   Journal Entry   **7.1**

To me, critical thinking means . . .

(At a later point in this chapter, we discuss critical thinking and have you
flashback to the response you made here.)

_____

_____

_____

LEARNING GOAL

To increase awareness of
what it means to think at
a higher level and to use
higher-level thinking for
achieving excellence in
college and beyond.

What Is Higher-Level Thinking?

The term "higher-level thinking" refers to a more advanced level of thought
than that used for basic learning. Higher-level thinking takes place when you
reflect on the knowledge you've acquired and take additional mental action
on it, such as evaluating its validity and practicality or integrating it with
something else you've learned to create a more comprehensive or creative
product.

    Contestants performing on TV quiz shows such as *Jeopardy* or *Who Wants
to Be a Millionaire?* respond with factual knowledge to questions asking for
information about who, what, when, and where. If game-show contestants
were to be tested for higher-level thinking, they would not be recalling facts;
they would be engaged in thinking about such questions as "Why?" "How?"
and "What if?" Your previous experiences in school or at work may have
trained you to answer questions asked by others. However, in college, it's as
important to ask the right question as it is to give the right answer.

> ### Student Perspective
>
> "To me, thinking at a higher
> level means to think and
> analyze something beyond the
> obvious and find the deeper
> meaning."
>
> —First-year college student

> "What is the hardest task in
> the world? To think."
>
> —Ralph Waldo Emerson, nineteenth-
> century American essayist and lecturer

! Remember

The focus of higher-level thinking is not just to answer questions but also to
question answers.

As its name implies, higher-level thinking involves raising the bar and jacking up your thinking to levels that go beyond merely remembering, reproducing, or regurgitating factual information. "Education is what's left over after you've forgotten all the facts" is an old saying that carries a lot of truth. Studies show that students' memory of facts learned in college often fades with time (Pascarella & Terenzini, 1991, 2005). Factual information that has been memorized has a short life span; learning to think at a higher level is a durable, lifelong learning skill that you will retain and use throughout life.

Compared to high school, college courses focus less on memorizing information and more on thinking about issues, concepts, and principles (Conley, 2005). Remembering information in college may get you a C grade, demonstrating comprehension of that information may give you a B, and going beyond comprehension to demonstrate higher-level thinking should earn you an A. Simply stated, college professors are more concerned with teaching you *how* to think than with teaching you *what* to think (i.e., what facts to remember).

> **!**
>
> **Remember**
>
> Your college professors will often expect you to do more than just retain or reproduce information; they'll ask you to demonstrate higher levels of thinking with respect to what you've learned, such as analyze it, evaluate it, apply it, or connect it with other concepts that you've learned.

This is not to say that basic knowledge and comprehension are unimportant. They supply you with the raw material needed to manufacture higher-level thinking. The deep learning and broad base of knowledge you experience in college will provide the stepping stones you need to climb to higher levels of thinking (as illustrated in **Figure 7.1**).

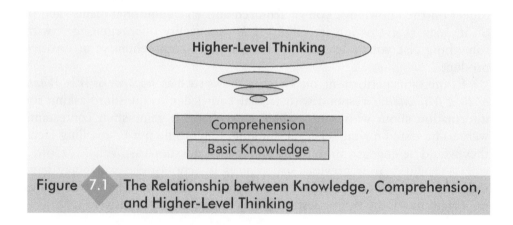

Figure 7.1   The Relationship between Knowledge, Comprehension, and Higher-Level Thinking

◆ Defining and Describing the Major Forms of Higher-Level Thinking

In national surveys of college professors teaching freshman- through senior-level courses in various fields, more than 95 percent of them report that the most important goal of a college education is to develop students' ability to think critically (Gardiner, 2005; Milton, 1982). Similarly, college professors who teach introductory courses to freshmen and sophomores indicate that the primary educational purpose of their courses is to develop students' critical thinking skills (Stark et al., 1990).

When your college professors ask you to "think critically," they're usually asking you to use one or more of the eight forms of thinking listed in the **Snapshot Summary 7.1**. As you read the descriptions of each form of thinking, note whether or not you've heard of it before.

Snapshot Summary   7.1

Major Forms of Higher-Level Thinking

1. **Application (Applied Thinking).** Putting knowledge into practice to solve problems and resolve issues;
2. **Analysis (Analytical Thinking).** Breaking down information to identify its key parts and underlying elements;
3. **Synthesis.** Building up ideas by integrating separate pieces of information into a larger whole or more comprehensive product;
4. **Multidimensional Thinking.** Taking multiple perspectives (i.e., viewing issues from different vantage points);

5. **Inferential Reasoning.** Making arguments or judgment by inferring (stepping to) a conclusion that is supported by empirical (observable) evidence or logical consistency;
6. **Balanced Thinking.** Carefully considering arguments for and against a particular position or viewpoint;
7. **Critical Thinking.** Evaluating (judging the quality of) arguments, conclusions, and ideas;
8. **Creative Thinking.** Generating ideas that are unique, original, or distinctively different.

Application (Applied Thinking)

When you learn something deeply, you transform information into knowledge; when you translate knowledge into action, you're engaging in a higher-level thinking process known as application. Applied thinking moves you beyond simply knowing something to actually doing something with the knowledge you possesses; you use it to solve a problem or resolve an issue. For example, when you use knowledge you've acquired in a human relations course (or from Chapter 8 of this text) to resolve an interpersonal conflict, you're engaging in application. Similarly, you're

Pause for Reflection

Look back at the eight forms of thinking described in the Snapshot Summary 7.1. Which of these forms of thinking had you heard before? Did you use any of these forms of thinking on high school exams or assignments?

using applied thinking when you use knowledge acquired in a math course to solve a problem that you haven't seen before. Application is a powerful form of higher-level thinking because it allows you to transfer your knowledge to new situations or contexts and put it into practice.

Always be on the lookout for ways to apply the knowledge you acquire to your personal life experiences and current events or issues. When you use your knowledge for the practical purpose of doing something good, such as bettering yourself or fellow humans, you not only demonstrate application but also demonstrate wisdom (Staudinger & Baltes, 1994).

Analysis (Analytical Thinking)

The mental process of analysis is like the physical process of peeling an onion. When you analyze something, you break it down, take it apart, and identify its main points, key parts, or underlying elements. For example, if you were to analyze a textbook chapter, you would go beyond simply reading it just to cover the content; instead, you would read it to uncover the author's main ideas—finding the core ideas by separating them from background information and surface details.

You use analysis to identify the components or elements that should be examined in a work of art (e.g., its structure, texture, tone, and form). Analysis is also used to identify underlying reasons or causes, commonly referred to as causal analysis. For instance, a causal analysis of the September 11, 2001, attack on the United States would involve identifying the factors that led to the attack or the underlying reasons for which the attack took place.

Synthesis

A higher-level thinking process that's basically the opposite of analysis is synthesis. When you analyze, you break information into its parts; when you synthesize, you take parts or pieces of information and build them into an integrated whole or comprehensive product (like piecing together a puzzle). You would be engaging in synthesis if you were to connect ideas presented in different courses—for instance, if you were to integrate ethical concepts you learned in a philosophy course with marketing concepts you learned in a business course to produce a set of ethical guidelines for marketing and advertising products.

Synthesis involves more than a summary. It goes beyond just condensing information to finding and forming meaningful connections among separate pieces of information, weaving them together to form a unified picture. When you're synthesizing, you're thinking conceptually by converting isolated facts and separated bits of information and integrating them into a concept—a larger system or network of related ideas.

Although synthesis and analysis are virtually opposite thought processes, they complement each other. When you analyze, you disassemble wholes into their key parts. When you synthesize, you reassemble parts into a new whole. For instance, when writing this book, we analyzed published material in many fields (e.g., psychology, history, philosophy, and biology) and identified information from parts of these fields that were most relevant to promoting the success of beginning college students. We then synthesized or reassembled these parts to create a new whole—the textbook you're now reading.

Multidimensional Thinking

When you engage in multidimensional thinking, you view yourself and the world around you from different angles or vantage points. In particular, a multidimensional thinker is able to think from four perspectives:

1. Person (self)
2. Place

3. Time
4. Culture

Multidimensional thinkers consider how these perspectives influence, and are influenced by, the issue they're discussing or debating. For example, they would ask the following questions:

- How does this issue affect me as an individual? (the perspective of person)
- What impact does this issue have on people living in different countries? (the perspective of place)
- How will future generations of people be affected by this issue? (the perspective of time)
- How is this issue likely to be interpreted or experienced by groups of people who share different social customs and traditions? (the perspective of culture)

Each of these perspectives has different elements embedded within it. The four major perspectives, along with the elements that comprise each of them, are listed and described in the **Snapshot Summary 7.2**. Note how these perspectives are consistent with those developed by the liberal arts (discussed in Chapter 2).

Important issues, problems, and challenges do not exist in isolation but as parts of an interconnected, multiple-perspective system. For example, global warming is a current issue that involves the earth's atmosphere gradually

Snapshot Summary

7.2

Perspectives Associated with Multidimensional Thinking

Perspective 1: PERSON
Perspectives of the individual or self

Components:
- **Intellectual (Cognitive).** Personal knowledge, thoughts, and self-concept;
- **Emotional.** Personal feelings, emotional adjustment, and mental health;
- **Social.** Personal relationships and interpersonal interactions;
- **Ethical.** Personal values and moral convictions;
- **Physical.** Personal health and wellness;
- **Spiritual.** Personal beliefs about the meaning or purpose of life and the hereafter;
- **Vocational (Occupational).** Personal means of making a living or earning an income.

Perspective 2: PLACE
Broader perspectives representing progressively larger circles of social and spatial distance beyond the self

Components:
- **Family.** Parents, children, and relatives;
- **Community.** Local communities and neighborhoods;
- **Society.** Societal institutions (e.g., schools, churches, and hospitals) and groups within society (e.g., groups differing in age, gender, race, or social class);
- **National.** Country or place of citizenship;
- **International.** Different nations or countries;

- **Global.** The earth (e.g., all its life forms and natural resources);
- **Universal.** The relationship between earth and its place in a galaxy that includes planets and heavenly bodies.

Perspective 3: TIME
The chronological perspective

Components:
- **Historical.** The past;
- **Contemporary.** The present;
- **Futuristic.** The future.

Perspective 4: CULTURE
The distinctive way or style of living of a group of people who share the same social heritage and traditions

Components:
- **Linguistic (Language).** How group members communicate through written or spoken words and through nonverbal communication (body language);
- **Political.** How the group organizes societal authority and uses it to govern itself, make collective decisions, and maintain social order;
- **Economic.** How the material wants and needs of the group are met through the allocation of limited resources, and how wealth is distributed among its members;

- **Geographical.** How the group's physical location influences the nature of social interactions and affects the way group members adapt to and use their environment;
- **Aesthetic.** How the group appreciates and expresses artistic beauty and creativity through the fine arts (e.g., visual art, music, theater, literature, and dance);
- **Scientific.** How the group views, understands, and investigates natural phenomena through systematic research (e.g., scientific tests and experiments);
- **Ecological.** How the group views the interrelationship between the biological world (humans and other living creatures) and the natural world (the surrounding physical environment);
- **Anthropological.** How the group's culture originated, evolved, and developed over time;
- Sociological. How the group's society is structured or organized into social subgroups and social institutions;
- **Psychological.** How group members tend to think, feel, and interact, and how their attitudes, opinions, or beliefs have been acquired;
- **Philosophical.** The group's ideas or views on wisdom, goodness, truth, and the meaning or purpose of life;
- **Theological.** Group members' conception and beliefs about a transcendent, supreme being, and how they express their shared faith in a supreme being.

Pause for Reflection

Briefly explain how each of the perspectives of person, place, time, and culture may be involved in causing and solving one the following problems:

1. War and terrorism

2. Poverty and hunger

3. Prejudice and discrimination

4. Any world issue of your choice

thickening and trapping more heat due to a collection of greenhouse gases, which are being produced primarily by the burning of fossil fuels. It's theorized that the increase of manmade pollution is causing temperatures to rise (and sometimes fall) around the world and is contributing to natural disasters, such as droughts, wildfires, and dust storms (Joint Science Academies Statement, 2005; National Resources Defense Council, 2005). A comprehensive understanding and solution to this global problem involves interrelationships among many of the perspectives depicted in **Figure 7.2**. It's an issue that involves:

- Ecology. The interrelationship between humans and their natural environment;

- Science. The need for research and development of alternative sources of energy;
- Economics. The cost incurred by industries to change their existing sources of energy;
- National politics. Laws may need to be created to encourage or enforce changes in industries' use of energy sources; and
- International relations. The collaboration needed among all countries that are contributing to the current problem and could contribute to its future solution.

	IMPLICATION
Person	Global warming involves us on an individual level because our personal efforts at energy conservation in our homes and our willingness to purchase energy-efficient products can play a major role in solving this problem.
Place	Global warming is an international issue that extends beyond the boundaries of one's own country to all countries in the world, and its solution will require worldwide collaboration.
Time	If the current trend toward higher global temperatures caused by global warming continues, it could seriously threaten the lives of future generations of people who inhabit our planet.
Culture	The problem of global warming has been caused by industries in technologically advanced cultures, yet the problem of rising global temperatures is likely to have its most negative impact on less technologically advanced cultures that lack the resources to respond to it (Joint Science Academies Statement, 2005). To prevent this from happening, technologically advanced cultures will need to use their advanced technology to devise alternative methods for generating energy that does not continue to release heat-trapping gases into the atmosphere.

Figure 7.2

Inferential Reasoning

When people make arguments or arrive at conclusions, they do so by starting with a premise (a statement or an observation) and using it to infer (step to) a conclusion. The following sentence starters demonstrate the process of inferential reasoning:

"Because this is true, it follows that . . ."
"Based on this evidence, I can conclude that . . ."

In college, you will often be required to draw conclusions and support those conclusions with evidence. If you're asked to formulate an argument, you're being asked to use inferential reasoning to reach a conclusion and support your conclusion. In a sense, you're being asked to take on the role of a lawyer who's trying to prove a case through documentation by providing supporting arguments and evidence (e.g., exhibit A, exhibit B, and exhibit C).

The following are two major ways in which you use inferential reasoning to support your points or arguments:

1. Citing empirical (observable) evidence (e.g., specific examples, personal experiences, facts, figures, statistical data, scientific research findings, expert testimonies, supporting quotes, or statements from leading authorities in the field);
2. Using principles of logical consistency (i.e., demonstrating that your conclusion follows or flows logically from an established premise or general statement).

The following are examples of logical consistency:

- The constitution guarantees all U.S. citizens the right to vote (established premise);
- U.S. citizens include women and people of color; therefore,
- Denying women and people of color the right to vote was illogical (and unconstitutional).

Here's how these two strategies for supporting an argument have been used by some to conclude that the drinking age in the United States should be lowered to 18:

1. **Citing empirical (observable) evidence.** In other countries where drinking is allowed at age 18, statistics show that they have fewer binge-drinking and drunk-driving problems than the United States.
2. **Using the principle of logical consistency.** The 18-year-olds in the United States are considered to be legal adults with respect to such rights and responsibilities as voting, serving on juries, joining the military, and being held responsible for committing crimes; therefore, 18-year-olds should have the right to drink.

Pause for Reflection

Can you think of any arguments against lowering the drinking age to 18 that are based on empirical (observable) evidence or logical consistency?

Inferential reasoning represents the primary thought processes humans use to reach conclusions about themselves and the world around them. This is also the form of thinking that you will use to make arguments and reach conclusions about ideas presented in your college courses.

Unfortunately, errors can be made in the inferential reasoning process; these errors are often referred to as logical fallacies. Some of the more common logical fallacies are summarized in the **Snapshot Summary 7.3**. As you read each of these reasoning errors, briefly note in the margin whether you've ever witnessed it or experienced it.

Snapshot Summary

Logical Fallacies: Inferential-Reasoning Errors

- **Dogmatism.** Stubbornly clinging to a personally held viewpoint that's unsupported by evidence and remaining closed minded (nonreceptive) to other viewpoints that are better supported by evidence (e.g., believing that America's version of capitalism is the only economic system that can work in a successful democracy and refusing to acknowledge that other successful countries do not have a capitalistic economy).

> "Facts do not cease to exist because they are ignored."
>
> –Aldous Huxley, English writer and author of Brave New World.

- **Selective Perception.** Seeing only examples and instances that support a position while overlooking or ignoring those that contradict it (e.g., believing in astrology and only noticing and pointing out people whose personalities happen to fit their astrological sign, not those who don't).

> "A very bad (and all too common) way to misread a newspaper: To see whatever supports your point of view as fact, and anything that contradicts your point of view as bias."
>
> –Daniel Okrent, first public editor of The New York Times and inventor of Rotisserie League Baseball, the best-known form of fantasy baseball

- **Double Standard.** Having two sets of standards for judgment: a higher standard for judging others and a lower standard for judging oneself. This is the classic "do as I say, not as I do" hypocrisy (e.g., critically evaluating and challenging the opinions of others but not your own).
- **Wishful Thinking.** Thinking that something is true not because of logic or evidence but because the person wants it to be true (e.g., a teenage girl not wanting to become pregnant and believing that she will not even though she and her boyfriend always have sex without using a contraceptive).

> "Belief can be produced in practically unlimited quantity and intensity, without observation or reasoning, and even in defiance of both by the simple desire to believe."
>
> –George Bernard Shaw, Irish playwright and Nobel Prize winner for literature

- **Hasty Generalization.** Reaching a limited number of instances or experiences (e.g., concluding that people belonging to a group are all or nearly all "that way" on the basis of personal experiences with only one or two individuals).
- **Jumping to a Conclusion.** Making a leap of logic to reach a conclusion that's based on only one reason or factor while ignoring other possible reasons or contributing factors (e.g., concluding, after being rejected for a date or a job, that "I must be a real loser").

- **Glittering Generality.** Making a positive general statement without supplying details or evidence to back it up (e.g., writing a letter of recommendation describing someone as a "wonderful human" with a "great personality" but not providing any reasons or evidence for these claims).
- **Straw Man Argument.** Distorting an opponent's argument position and then attacking it (e.g., attacking an opposing political candidate for supporting censorship and restricting civil liberties when the opponent supported only a ban on violent pornography).
- **Ad Hominem Argument.** Aiming an argument at the person rather than the person's argument (e.g., telling a younger person, "You're too young and inexperienced to know what you're talking about," or telling an older person, "You're too old-fashioned to understand this issue"). Literally translated, the term *ad hominem* means "to the man."
- **Red Herring.** Bringing up an irrelevant issue that disguises or distracts attention from the real issue being discussed or debated (e.g., responding to criticism of former President Richard Nixon's involvement in the Watergate scandal by arguing, "He was a good president who accomplished many good things while he was in office"). The term "red herring" derives from an old practice of dragging a herring—a strong-smelling fish—across a trail to distract the scent of pursuing dogs. (In the example, Nixon's effectiveness as a president is an irrelevant issue or a red herring; the real issue being discussed is Nixon's behavior in the Watergate scandal.)
- **Smoke Screen.** Intentionally disguising or covering up true reasons or motives with reasons that are designed to confuse or mislead others (e.g., opposing gun control legislation by arguing that it is a violation of the constitutional right to bear arms without revealing that the opponent of the legislation is receiving financial support from gun manufacturing companies).
- **Slippery Slope.** Using a fear tactic and arguing that not accepting a position will result in a domino effect—that is, it will result in something negative happening that will inevitably lead to another negative event, and so on, like a series of falling dominoes (e.g., saying, "If someone experiments with marijuana, it

will automatically lead to harder drugs, loss of motivation, withdrawal from college, and a ruined life").
- **Rhetorical Deception.** Using deceptive language to conclude that something is true without providing reasons or evidence (e.g., confidently making such statements as "Clearly this is . . ." "It is obvious that . . ." or "Any reasonable person can see . . ." without explaining why it's so clear, obvious, or reasonable).
- **Circular Reasoning (a.k.a. "Begging the Question").** Drawing a conclusion that is merely a rewording or restatement of a position on the issue without any supporting reasons or evidence, which leaves the original question unanswered and the issue still unsolved (e.g., concluding that "Stem cell research should remain illegal because it's research that shouldn't be done").
- **Appealing to Authority or Prestige.** Believing that if an authority figure or celebrity says it's true then it must be true or should be done (e.g., buying product X simply because a famous actor or athlete uses it or believing that if someone in authority, such as the U.S. president, says something should be done then it must be the right or best thing to do).
- **Appealing to the Traditional or the Familiar.** Concluding that if something has been thought true or done the same way for a long time then it must be a valid or the best method (e.g., stating that "This is the way it's always be done, so it's the way it should be done").
- **Appealing to Popularity or the Majority (a.k.a. Jumping on the Bandwagon).** That if a belief is popular or is held by the majority then it must be true (e.g., arguing "So many people believe in psychics, it has to be true; they can't all be wrong").
- **Appealing to Emotion.** Reaching a conclusion based on the intensity of feelings experienced or expressed, rather than the quality of reasoning used to reach the conclusion (e.g., believing that "If I feel strongly about something, it must be true"). The expressions, "always trust your feelings" and "just listen to your heart" may not always lead to the most accurate conclusions and the best decisions because they are based on emotion rather than reason.

Balanced Thinking

Balanced thinking involves seeking out and carefully considering evidence for and against a particular position. The process of supporting a position with evidence is technically referred to as *adduction*; when you adduce, you offer reasons *for* a position. The process of arguing against a position by presenting contradictory evidence or reasons is called *refutation*; when you refute, you provide a rebuttal by supplying evidence *against* a particular position.

Balanced thinking involves both adduction and refutation. The goal of a balanced thinker is not to stack up evidence for one position or the other but to be an impartial investigator who looks at supporting and opposing evidence for both sides of an issue and attempts to reach a conclusion that is neither biased nor one sided. The opposing positions' stronger arguments are acknowledged, and its weaker ones are refuted (Fairbairn & Winch, 1995). Thus, your first step in the process of seeking truth should not be to immediately jump in and take an either–or (for-or-against) stance on a debatable issue. Instead, your first step should be to look at arguments for and against each position, acknowledge the strengths and weaknesses of these arguments, and identify what additional information may still be needed to make a judgment or reach a conclusion.

Balanced thinking requires more than just adding up the number of arguments for and against a position; it also involves weighing the strength of those arguments. Arguments can vary in terms of their level or degree of support. When evaluating arguments, ask yourself, "How sure am I about the conclusion made by this argument?" Determine whether the evidence is:

1. **Definitive.** So strong or compelling that a definite conclusion can be reached;
2. **Suggestive.** Strong enough to suggest that a tentative conclusion may be reached; or
3. **Inconclusive.** Too weak to reach any conclusion.

> ! **Remember**
>
> A characteristic of balanced thinking is being mindful of the weight (degree of importance) you assign to different arguments and articulating how their weight has been factored into your final conclusion (e.g., in a written report or class presentation).

In some cases, after reviewing both supporting and contradictory evidence for opposing positions, balanced thinking may lead you to suspend judgment and to withhold making a firm decision that favors one position over the other. A balanced thinker may occasionally reach the following conclusions: "Right now, I can't be sure; the evidence doesn't strongly favor one position over the other" or "More information is needed before I can make a final judgment or reach a firm conclusion." This isn't being wishy-washy; it's a legitimate conclusion to draw, as long as

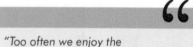

it is an informed conclusion that's supported with sound reasons and solid evidence. In fact, it's better to hold an undecided but informed viewpoint based on balanced thinking than to hold a definite opinion that's uninformed, biased, or based on emotion—such as the opinions offered loudly and obnoxiously by people on radio and TV talk shows.

Personal Story

For years I really didn't know what I believed. I always seemed to stand in the no man's land between opposing arguments, yearning to be won over by one side or the other but finding instead degrees of merit in both. But in time I came to accept, even embrace, what I called "my confusion" and to recognize it as a friend and ally, with no apologies needed. I preferred to listen rather than to speak; to inquire, not crusade.

"In Praise of the 'Wobblies'" by Ted Gup (2005), journalist who has written for Time, National Geographic, and The New York Times

---

Remember

When you combine balanced thinking with multidimensional thinking, you become a more complex and comprehensive thinker who is capable of viewing any issue from both sides and all angles.

Student Perspective

"Critical thinking is an evaluative thought process that requires deep thinking."

—First-year college student

Pause for Reflection

Flash back to the journal entry at the start of this chapter. How does your response to the incomplete sentence compare with the definition of critical thinking we just provided?

How are they similar?

How do they differ?

(If you wrote that critical thinking means "being critical" or negatively criticizing something or somebody, don't feel bad. Many students think that critical thinking has this negative meaning or connotation.)

Critical Thinking

Critical thinking is a form of higher-level thinking that involves evaluation or judgment. The evaluation can be either positive or negative; for example, a movie critic can give a good (thumbs up) or bad (thumbs down) review of a film.

However, critical thinking involves much more than simply stating, "I liked it" or "I didn't like it." Specific reasons or evidence must be supplied to support the critique (critical evaluation). Failing to do so makes the criticism unfounded (i.e., it has no foundation to support it).

Critical thinking is used to evaluate many things besides films, art, or music; it's also used to judge the quality of ideas, beliefs, choices, and decisions—whether they be your own or those of others.

Since thinking skills are so highly valued by professors teaching students at all stages in the college experience and all subjects in the college curriculum, working on these skills now should significantly improve you academic performance throughout college.

You can develop critical thinking skills by always thinking about how you may evaluate ideas and arguments with respect to the following dimensions:

1. **Validity (Truthfulness).** Is it true or accurate?
2. **Morality (Ethics).** Is it fair or just?
3. **Beauty (Aesthetics).** Is it beautiful or artistic?
4. **Practicality (Usefulness).** Can it be put to use for practical purposes?
5. **Priority (Order of Importance or Effectiveness).** Is it the best option or alternative?

Personal Story

When I teach classes or give workshops, I often challenge students or participants to debate me on either politics or religion. I ask them to choose a political party affiliation, a religion or a branch of religion for their debate topic, and their stance on a social issue for which there are political or religious viewpoints. The ground rules are as follows: They choose the topic for debate; they can only use facts to pose their argument, rebuttal, or both; and they can only respond in a rational manner, without letting emotions drive their answers. This exercise usually reveals that the topics people feel strongly about are often topics that they have not critically evaluated. People often say they are Democrat, Republican, independent, and so on, and argue from this position. However, few of them have taken the time to critically examine whether their stated affiliation is actually consistent with their personal viewpoints. For example, they almost always answer "no" to the following questions: "Have you read the core document (e.g., party platform) that outlines the party stance?" and "Have you engaged in self-examination of your party affiliation through reasoned discussions with others who say they have the same or a different political affiliation?"

—*Aaron Thompson*

Creative Thinking

To think creatively is to generate something new or different, whether it is a product, an idea, or a strategy. Creative thinking leads you to ask the question, "Why not?" (e.g., "Why not try doing it a different way?"). It could be said that when you think critically you look "inside the box" and evaluate the quality of its content. When you think creatively, you look "outside the box" to imagine other packages containing different content.

Anytime you combine two old ideas to generate a different idea or a new product, you're engaging in creative thinking. Creative thinking can be viewed as an extension or higher form of synthesis, whereby parts of separate ideas are combined or integrated, resulting in a final product that turns out to be different (and better) than what previously existed (Anderson & Krathwohl, 2001). Even in the arts, what is created isn't totally original or unique. Instead, creativity typically involves a combination or rearrangement of previously existing elements to generate a new "whole"—a final product that is distinctive or noticeably different. For instance, hard rock was created by combining elements of blues and rock and roll, and folk rock took form when Bob Dylan combined musical elements of acoustic blues and amplified rock (Shelton, 2003).

Creative and critical thinking are two of the most important forms of higher-level thinking, and they work well together. You use creative thinking to ask new questions and generate new ideas, and you use critical thinking to evaluate or critique the ideas you create (Paul & Elder, 2004). A creative idea must not only be different or original; it must also be effective (Sternberg, 2001; Runco, 2004). If critical thinking reveals that the quality of what you've created is poor, you then shift back to creative thinking to generate something new and improved. Or, you may start by using critical thinking to evaluate an old idea or approach and come to the judgment that it's not very good. This unfavorable evaluation naturally leads to and turns on the creative thinking process, which tries to come up with a new idea or different approach that is better than the old one.

Brainstorming is a problem-solving process that effectively illustrates of how creative and critical thinking complement each other. The steps or stages involved in the process of brainstorming are summarized in **Box 7.1**.

As the brainstorming process suggests, creativity doesn't just happen suddenly or effortlessly, like the so-called stroke of genius; instead, it takes

> "The principle mark of genius is not perfection but originality, the opening of new frontiers."
>
> –Arthur Koestler, Hungarian novelist and philosopher

> "The blues are the roots. Everything else are the fruits."
>
> –Willie Dixon, blues songwriter; commenting on how all forms of contemporary American music contain elements of blues music, which originated among African American slaves

> "Creativity is allowing oneself to make mistakes; art is knowing which ones to keep."
>
> –Scott Adams, creator of the Dilbert comic strip and author of *The Dilbert Principle*

7.1

The Process of Brainstorming

1. List as many ideas as you can, generating them rapidly without stopping to evaluate their validity or practicality. Studies show that worrying about whether an idea is correct often blocks creativity (Basadur, Runco, & Vega, 2000). So, at this stage of the process, let your imagination run wild; don't worry about whether the idea you generate is impractical, unrealistic, or outrageous.
2. Use the ideas on your list as a springboard to trigger additional ideas, or combine them to create new ideas.

3. After you run out of ideas, review and evaluate the list of ideas you've generated and eliminate those that you think are least effective.
4. From the remaining list of ideas, choose the best idea or best combination of ideas.

Note: The first two steps in the brainstorming process involve creative thinking that goes off in different directions to generate multiple ideas. In contrast, the last two steps in the process involve critical thinking, which focuses on and narrows down the ideas, evaluating them to identify the one that's most effective.

I'm in the middle of an intense brainstorm; ideas are pouring out of my mind at lightning speed! Write 'em down fast!!

Personal Story   Several years ago, I was working with a friend to come up with ideas for a grant proposal. We started out by sitting at his kitchen table, sipping coffee; then we both got up and began to pace back and forth, walking all around the room while bouncing different ideas off each other. Whenever a new idea was thrown out, one of us would jot it down (whoever was pacing closer to the kitchen table at the moment).

After we ran out of ideas, we shifted gears, slowed down, and sat at the table to carefully review each of the ideas we just generated during our "binge-thinking" episode. After some debate, we finally settled on an idea that we judged to be the best one of all the ideas we produced, and we used this idea for the grant proposal.

Although I wasn't fully aware of it at the time, the stimulating thought process we were using was called brainstorming, which involved creative thinking (our fast-paced walking and idea-production stage) followed by critical thinking (our slower-paced sitting and idea-evaluation stage).

—Joe Cuseo

considerable mental effort (Paul & Elder, 2004; Torrance, 1963). Although creative thinking may include some sudden breakthroughs or intuitive leaps, it also involves carefully reflecting on those leaps and critically evaluating whether any of them landed you on a good idea.

Lastly, keep in mind that creative thinking is not restricted to the arts; it can occur in all subject areas, even in fields that seek precision and definite answers. For example, in math, creative thinking may involve using new approaches or strategies for arriving at a correct solution to a problem. In science, creative thinking takes place when a scientist uses imaginative thinking to create a hypothesis or logical hunch ("What might happen if . . . ?") and then conducts an experiment and collects evidence to test whether the hypothesis is true.

> "Imagination should give wings to our thoughts, but imagination must be checked and documented by the factual results of the experiment."
>
> –Louis Pasteur, French microbiologist, chemist, and founder of pasteurization (a method for preventing milk and wine from going sour)

◆ Strategies for Developing Higher-Level Thinking Skills and Applying Them to Improve Academic Performance

Thus far, this chapter has been devoted to helping you get a clear idea about what higher-level thinking is and what its major forms are. The remainder of this chapter focuses on helping you develop habits of higher-level thinking and apply these habits to improve your performance in the first year of college and beyond.

1. Cross-reference and connect any ideas you acquire in class with related ideas you acquire from your assigned reading.

When you discover information in your reading that relates to something you've learned about in class (or vice versa), make a note of it in the margin of your textbook or your class notebook. By integrating knowledge you've obtained from these two major sources, you're using synthesis—a higher-level thinking skill, which you can then demonstrate on your course exams and assignments to improve your academic performance.

2. When listening to lectures and completing reading assignments, pay attention not only to the content but also to the thinking process being used with respect to the content.

Periodically ask yourself what form of higher-level thinking your instructors are using during major segments of a class presentation and what your textbook authors are using in different sections of a chapter. The more conscious you are of the type of higher-level thinking you're being exposed to, the better you'll be able to apply it to the material you're learning and to demonstrate it on exams and assignments.

3. Periodically pause to reflect on your own thinking process.

Ask yourself what type of thinking you are doing (e.g., analysis, synthesis, or evaluation). When you think about your own thinking, you're engaging in a mental process known as metacognition—that is, you're aware of how you are thinking while you are thinking (Flavell, 1985). Metacognition is a mental habit that's been found to promote higher-level thinking and improve problem-solving (Halpern, 2003; Resnick, 1986).

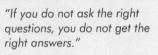

Asking yourself higher-level thinking questions during lectures should prevent you from asking questions like this one.

4. Develop habits of higher-level thinking by asking yourself higher-level thinking questions.

One simple but powerful way to think about your thinking is through self-questioning. Since questions have the power to activate and elevate your thinking and thinking often involves talking silently to yourself, make an intentional

Asking yourself a good question can stimulate your higher-level thinking about almost any experience, whether it takes place inside or outside the classroom.

effort to ask yourself good questions that can train your mind to think at a higher level. Good questions serve as spark plugs for igniting mental action and launching thinking to higher levels in a quest to answer them. The higher the level of thinking called for by the questions you regularly ask yourself, the higher the level of thinking you will display in class discussions, on college exams, and in written assignments.

In **Box 7.2**, you'll find numerous questions that have been intentionally designed to promote higher-level thinking. The questions are constructed in a way that will allow you to easily fill in the blank and apply the type of thinking called for by the question to ideas or issues being discussed in any course you may take. Considerable research indicates that students can learn to use questions such as these to improve their higher-level thinking ability in various subject areas (King, 1990, 1995).

As you read each set of trigger questions, place a checkmark next to one question in the set that could be applied to a concept or issue being covered in a course you're taking this term.

Pause for Reflection

Look back at the forms of thinking described in Box 7.2. Identify one question listed under each set of trigger questions and fill in the blank with an idea or issue being covered in a course you're taking this term.

Take Action!

7.2

Self-Imposed Questions for Triggering Forms of Higher-Level Thinking

Application (Applied Thinking). Putting knowledge into practice to solve problems and resolve issues

Trigger Questions:
- ☑ How can this idea be used to _____?
- ☑ How could this concept be implemented to _____?
- ☑ How can this theory be put into practice to _____?

Analysis (Analytical Thinking). Breaking down information into its essential elements or parts

Trigger Questions:
- ☑ What are the main ideas contained in _____?
- ☑ What are the important aspects of _____?
- ☑ What are the issues raised by _____?
- ☑ What are the major purposes of _____?
- ☑ What assumptions or biases lie hidden within _____?
- ☑ What were the reasons behind _____?

Synthesis. Integrating separate pieces of information to form a more complete product or pattern

Trigger Questions:
- ☑ How can this idea be joined or connected with _____ to create a more complete or comprehensive understanding of _____?
- ☑ How could these different _____ be grouped together into a more general class or category?
- ☑ How could these separate _____ be reorganized or rearranged to produce a more comprehensive understanding of the big picture?

Multidimensional Thinking. Thinking that involves viewing yourself and the world around you from different angles or vantage points

Trigger Questions:
- ☑ How would _____ affect different dimensions of myself (emotional, physical, etc.)?
- ☑ What broader impact would _____ have on the social and physical world around me?
- ☑ How might people living in different times (e.g., past and future) view _____?

☑ How would people from different cultural backgrounds interpret or react to _____?

☑ Have I taken into consideration all the major factors that could influence _____ or be influenced by _____?

Inferential Reasoning. Making arguments or judgment by inferring (stepping to) a conclusion that is supported by empirical (observable) evidence or logical consistency

Trigger Questions Seeking Empirical Evidence:

☑ What examples support the argument that _____?

☑ What research evidence is there for _____?

☑ What statistical data document that this _____ is true?

Trigger Questions Seeking Logical Consistency:

☑ Since _____ is true, why shouldn't _____ also be true?

☑ If people believe in _____, shouldn't they practice _____?

☑ To make the statement that _____, wouldn't it have to be assumed that _____?

Balanced Thinking. Carefully considering reasons for and against a particular position or viewpoint

Trigger Questions:

☑ Have I considered both sides of _____?

☑ What are the strengths or advantages and weaknesses or disadvantages of _____?

☑ What evidence supports and contradicts _____?

☑ What are the arguments for and the counterarguments against _____?

Trigger Questions for Adduction (arguing for a particular idea or position by supplying supporting evidence):

☑ What proof is there for _____?

☑ What are logical arguments for _____?

☑ What research evidence supports _____?

Trigger Questions for Refutation (arguing against a particular idea or position by supplying contradictory evidence):

☑ What proof is there against _____?

☑ What logical arguments indicate that _____ is false?

☑ What research evidence contradicts _____?

☑ What counterarguments would provide an effective rebuttal to _____.

Critical Thinking. Making well-informed evaluations or judgments

Trigger Questions for Validity (truthfulness):

☑ Is _____ true or accurate?

☑ Is there sufficient evidence to support the conclusion that _____?

☑ Is the reasoning behind _____ strong or weak?

Trigger Questions for Morality (ethics):

☑ Is _____ fair?

☑ Is _____ just?

☑ Is this action consistent with the professed or stated values of _____?

Trigger Questions for Beauty (aesthetics):

☑ What is the artistic merit of _____?

☑ Does _____ have any aesthetic value?

☑ Does _____ contribute to the beauty of _____?

Trigger Questions for Practicality (usefulness):

☑ Will _____ work?

☑ How can _____ be put to good use?

☑ What practical benefit would result from _____?

Trigger Questions for Priority (order of importance or effectiveness):

☑ Which one of these _____ is the most important?

☑ Is this _____ the best option or choice available?

☑ How should these _____ be ranked from first to last (best to worst) in terms of their effectiveness?

Creative Thinking. Generating ideas that are unique, original, or distinctively different.

Trigger Questions:

☑ What could be invented to _____?

☑ Imagine what would happen if _____?

☑ What might be a different way to _____?

☑ How would this change if _____?

☑ What would be an ingenious way to _____.

Note: Save these higher-level thinking questions so that you can use them while completing different academic tasks required by your courses (e.g., preparing for exams, writing papers or reports, and participating in class discussions or study-group sessions).

5. To stimulate creative thinking, use the following strategies.

- **Be flexible.** Think about ideas and objects in unusual or unconventional ways. The power of flexible and unconventional thinking is well illustrated in the movie *Apollo 13*, which is based on the real story of an astronaut saving his life by creatively using duct tape as an air filter. Johannes Gutenberg made his discovery of the printing press while watching a machine being used to crush grapes at a wine harvest. He thought that the same type of machine could be used to press letters onto paper (Dorfman, Shames, & Kihlstrom, 1996).

- **Be experimental.** Play with ideas, trying them out to see whether they'll work and work better than the status quo. Studies show that creative people tend to be mental risk-takers who experiment with ideas and techniques (Sternberg, 2001). Consciously resist the temptation to settle for the security of familiarity. Doing things the way they've always been done doesn't mean you're doing them the best way possible. It may mean that it's just the most habitual (and mindless) way to do them. When people cling rigidly or stubbornly to what is conventional or traditional, they may be clinging to the comfort or security of what's most familiar and predictable, which blocks originality, ingenuity, and openness to change.

- **Get mobile.** Get up and move around. By just standing up, studies show that the brain gets approximately 10 percent more oxygen than it does when a person is sitting down (Sousa, 1998). Since oxygen provides fuel for the brain, your ability to think creatively is likely to be enhanced when you think on your feet and move around rather than when you think while sitting down for extended periods.

- **Get it down.** Carry a pen and a small notepad or packet of sticky notes with you at all times because creative ideas often come to mind at the most unexpected moments. The process of creative ideas suddenly popping into your mind is sometimes referred to as incubation—like an egg, an idea can suddenly hatch and emerge from your subconscious after you've sat on it for a while. Unfortunately, however, as suddenly as ideas pop into your mind, they can just as suddenly slip out of your mind when you start thinking about something else. You can prevent this from happening by having the right equipment on hand to record your creative ideas as soon as you have them. That equipment could be pen and paper, or it could be your cell phone. You can go to Jott.com and provide your cell number and e-mail address. Whenever you get a creative idea you want to jot down, speed-dial 866-JOTT123 and you get a voice message that asks you who you want to "jott." After saying "myself," you can state your idea; within 5 minutes, it's transcribed into a typed message that appears in your e-mail inbox.

- **Get diverse.** Seek ideas from diverse sources and subjects of study. Bouncing your ideas off of different people and getting their ideas about your idea is a good way to generate energy, synergy, and serendipity (accidental discoveries). Studies show that creative people have a range of knowledge and interests, and they capitalize on their breadth to create new ideas by combining knowledge from different sources (Riquelme, 2002). They go well beyond the boundaries of their particular area of training or specialization (Baer, 1993; Kaufman & Baer, 2002). Be on the lookout to combine the knowledge and skills you acquire from different subject areas and different people to create bridges to new ideas.

> "
> "I make progress by having people around who are smarter than I am—and listening to them. And I assume that everyone is smarter about something than I am."
>
> —Henry Kaiser, successful industrialist, known as the father of American shipbuilding

- **Take a break.** When working on a problem that you can't seem to solve, stop working on it for a while and come back to it later. Creative solutions often come to mind after you stop thinking about the problem. When you're trying so hard and working so intensely on a problem or challenging task, your attention may become mentally set or rigidly fixed on one aspect of it (Maier, 1970). Taking your mind off of it and returning to it at a later point allows the problem to incubate in your mind at a lower level of consciousness and stress. This can sometimes give birth to a sudden solution. Furthermore, when you come back to the task later, your focus of attention is likely to shift to a different feature or aspect of the problem. This new focus may enable you to view the problem from a different angle or vantage point, which can lead to a breakthrough idea that was blocked by your previous perspective (Anderson, 2000).

- **Reorganize the problem.** When you're stuck on a problem, try rearranging its parts or pieces. Rearrangement can transform the problem into a different pattern that provides you with a new perspective. The new perspective may position you to suddenly see a solution that was previously overlooked, much like changing the order of letters in a word jumble suddenly enables you to see the hidden, scrambled word. By changing the wording of any problem you're working on, or by recording ideas on index cards (or sticky notes) and laying them out in different orders and arrangements, you may suddenly see a solution.

- If you're having trouble solving problems that involve a sequence of steps (e.g., math problems), try reversing the sequence and start by working from the end or middle. The new sequence changes your approach to the problem by forcing you to come at it from a different direction, which may provide you with an alternative path to its solution.

- **Be persistent.** Studies show that creativity takes time, dedication, and hard work (Ericsson & Charness, 1994). Creative thoughts often do not emerge in one sudden stroke of genius but evolve gradually after repeated reflection and persistent effort.

Pause for Reflection

The popularity of sticky notes is no doubt due to their versatility—you can post them on almost anything, remove them from where they were stuck (without a mess), and restick them somewhere else.

Think creatively for a minute. In what ways could college students use sticky notes to help complete the academic tasks they face in college? Think of as many ways as possible.

◆ Summary and Conclusion

Since higher-level thinking is the number one educational goal of college professors, developing this skill is crucial for achieving academic excellence. In addition improving academic performance in college, however, developing higher-level thinking skills have three other critical benefits.

1. Higher-level thinking is essential in today's "information age" in which new information is being generated at faster rates than at any other time in human history.

The majority of new workers in the information age will no longer work with their hands but will instead work with their heads (Miller, 2003), and employers will value college graduates who have inquiring minds and possess higher-level thinking skills (Harvey, Moon, Geall, & Bower, 1997).

2. Higher-level thinking skills are vital for citizens in a democracy.

Authoritarian political systems, such as dictatorships and fascist regimes, suppress critical thought and demand submissive obedience to authority. In contrast, citizens living in a democracy are expected to control their political destiny by choosing (electing) their political leaders; thus, judging and choosing wisely are crucial civic responsibilities in a democratic nation. Citizens living and voting in a democracy must use higher-level reasoning skills, such as balanced and critical thinking, to make wise political choices.

3. Higher-level thinking is an important safeguard against prejudice, discrimination, and hostility.

Racial, ethnic, and national prejudices often stem from narrow, self-centered, or group-centered thinking (Paul & Elder, 2002). Prejudice often results from oversimplified, dualistic thinking that can lead individuals to categorize other people into either "in" groups (us) or "out" groups (them). This type of dualistic thinking can lead, in turn, to ethnocentrism—the tendency to view one's own racial or ethnic group as the superior "in" group and see other groups as inferior "out" groups. Development of higher-level thinking skills, such as taking multiple perspectives and using balanced thinking, counteracts the type of dualistic, ethnocentric thinking that can lead to prejudice, discrimination, and hatred.

Learning More Through the World Wide Web

Internet-Based Resources for Further Information on Higher-Level Thinking

For additional information related to the ideas discussed in this chapter, we recommend the following Web sites:

Critical Thinking: www.criticalthinking.org

Creative Thinking: www.amcreativityassoc.org

Higher-Level Thinking Skills:
www.wcu.edu/ceap/houghton/Learner/think/thinkhigherorder.html

7.1 Self-Assessment of Higher-Level Thinking Characteristics

Listed here are four general characteristics of higher-level thinkers accompanied by a set of traits related to each characteristic. When you read the traits listed beneath each of the general characteristics, place a checkmark next to any trait that you think is true of you.

Characteristics of a Higher-Level Thinker

1. **Tolerant and Accepting**
   - ☑ Keep emotions under control when someone criticizes your viewpoint
   - ☑ Do not tune out ideas that conflict with your own
   - ☑ Feel comfortable with disagreement
   - ☑ Are receptive to hearing different points of view

2. **Inquisitive and Open Minded**
   - ☑ Are eager to continue learning new things from different people and different experiences
   - ☑ Have an inquiring mind that's genuinely curious, inquisitive, and ready to explore new ideas
   - ☑ Find differences of opinion and opposing viewpoints interesting and stimulating
   - ☑ Attempt to understand why people hold different viewpoints and try to find common ground between them

3. **Reflective and Tentative**
   - ☑ Suspend judgment until all the evidence is in, rather than making snap judgments before knowing the whole story
   - ☑ Acknowledge the complexity, ambiguity, or uncertainty of some issues, perhaps saying things like, "I need to give this more thought" or "I need more evidence before I can draw a conclusion"
   - ☑ Take time to think things through before drawing conclusions, making choices, and reaching decisions
   - ☑ Periodically reexamine personal viewpoints to see whether they should be maintained or changed as a result of new experiences and evidence

4. **Honest and Courageous**
   - ☑ Give fair consideration to ideas that other people may instantly disapprove of or find distasteful
   - ☑ Are willing to express personal viewpoints that may not conform to those of the majority
   - ☑ Are willing to change old opinions or beliefs when they are contradicted by new evidence
   - ☑ Are willing to acknowledge the limitations or weaknesses of your attitudes and beliefs

Look back at the list and count the number of checkmarks you placed in each of the four general areas:

1. Tolerant and Accepting = _____

2. Inquisitive and Open Minded = _____

3. Reflective and Tentative = _____

4. Honest and Courageous = _____

1. Under which characteristic did you have the most checkmarks?

2. Under which did you have the fewest checkmarks?

3. How would you interpret the meaning of this difference?

4. Why do you think this difference occurred?

7.2 Planning to Demonstrate Higher-Level Thinking in Your Current Courses

Look at the syllabus for three courses you're enrolled in this term and find an assignment or exam that carries the greatest weight (counts the most) toward your final course grade. (If you're taking fewer than three courses, you can choose more than one assignment or exam from the same course).

Course	Major Assignment or Test
1.	
2.	
3.	

Using the grid that follows, place a checkmark in each box that represents the form of higher-level thinking you think will be required on each of these major assignments or tests. (For a quick review of the major forms of higher-level thinking, see the higher-level thinking definitions on **p. 167**.)

| | **Major Assignment or Test** | | |
Course 1	**Course 2**	**Course 3**
Applied Thinking			
Analysis			
Synthesis			
Multidimensional Thinking			
Inferential Reasoning			
Balanced Thinking			
Critical Thinking			
Creative Thinking			

Choose one box you checked for each course, and describe how you would demonstrate that particular form of higher-level thinking on that particular assignment or test. For instance, if you checked a box indicating that you will use multidimensional thinking, describe what perspectives or factors you will take into consideration.

Course 1 exam or assignment: _____

Form of higher-level thinking required:

How I plan to demonstrate this form of thinking:

Course 2 exam or assignment: _____

Form of higher-level thinking required:

How I plan to demonstrate this form of thinking:

Course 3 exam or assignment: _____

Form of higher-level thinking required:

How I plan to demonstrate this form of thinking:

Trick or Treat: Confusing or Challenging Test?

Students in Professor Plato's philosophy course just got their first exam back and they're going over the test together in class. Some students are angry because they feel that Professor Plato deliberately made up trick questions to confuse them. Professor Plato states that his test questions were designed not to trick the class but to "challenge them to think."

Reflection and Discussion Questions

1. Why do you think that some of students thought that Professor Plato was trying to trick or confuse them on the exam?

2. What do you think the professor meant when he told his students that his test questions were designed to "challenge them to think"?

3. On future tests, what might the students do to reduce the likelihood that they will feel tricked again?

4. On future tests, what might the Professor Plato do to reduce the likelihood that students will complain about being asked trick questions?

Social and Emotional Intelligence

Relating to Others and Regulating Emotions

A once-popular song included the following lyrics: "People who need people are the luckiest people in the world." Would you agree or disagree with these lyrics? Why?

_____

_____

_____

LEARNING GOAL

To gain social and emotional skills that enhance the quality of your interpersonal relationships and mental health.

Social intelligence (a.k.a. interpersonal intelligence) refers to the ability to communicate and relate effectively to others (Gardner, 1993). It's a major type of human intelligence, which research indicates is a better predictor of personal and professional success than intellectual ability (Goleman, 2006).

The term "emotional intelligence" refers to the ability to identify and monitor emotions and to remain aware of how emotions affect thoughts and actions (Salovey & Mayer, 1990). Emotional intelligence has been found to be a better predictor of personal and occupational success than performance on intellectual intelligence tests (Goleman, 1995).

These two important elements of human intelligence and personal success are the focus points of this chapter.

> "I will pay more for the ability to deal with people than any other ability under the sun."
>
> —John D. Rockefeller, American industrialist and philanthropist and once the richest man in the world

Social Intelligence

Interpersonal relationships can be a source of social support that promotes success, or they may be a source of social conflict that distracts you from focusing on and achieving your personal goals. As a new college student, you may find yourself surrounded by multiple social opportunities. One of the adjustments you'll need to make is finding a healthy middle ground between too much and too little socializing, as well as forming solid interpersonal relationships that support rather than sabotage your educational success.

Student Perspective

"I have often found conflict in living a balanced academic and social life. I feel that when I am enjoying and succeeding in one spectrum, I am lagging in the other."

—First-year college student

Studies show that people who have stronger social support networks have a longer life expectancy (Giles, Glonek, Luszcz, & Andrews, 2005) and are more likely to report being happy (Myers, 1993). The development of a strong social support system is particularly important in today's high-tech world of virtual reality and online (vs. in-person) communication, both of which make it easier to avoid direct contact, neglect connections with others, and increase the risk of isolation, loneliness, and social avoidance (Putman, 2000).

The quality of your interpersonal relationships rests on two skills: (a) communication skills, or how well you send and receive information when interacting with others (verbally and nonverbally), and (b) human relations skills, or how well you relate to and treat people (i.e., people skills).

Listed here are our top recommendations for strengthening your interpersonal communication skills. Some strategies may appear to be basic, but they're also powerful. It may be that because they are so basic people overlook look them and forget to use them consistently. Don't be fooled by the seeming simplicity of the following suggestions, and don't underestimate their social impact.

Strategies for Improving the Quality of Interpersonal Communication

1. Work hard at being a good listener.

Studies show that listening is the most frequent human communication activity, followed, in order, by reading, speaking, and writing (Newton, 1990; Purdy & Borisoff, 1996). One study found that college students spend an average of 52.5 percent of each day listening (Barker & Watson, 2000). Being a good listener is one of the top characteristics mentioned by people when they cite the positive features of their best friends (Berndt, 1992). Listening is also one of the top skills employers look for when hiring and promoting employees (Maes, Weldy, & Icenogle, 1997; Winsor, Curtis, & Stephens, 1997).

Human relations experts often recommend that people talk less, listen more, and listen more effectively (Nichols, 1995; Nichols & Stevens, 1957). Since you're not actively doing something while listening, you can easily fall prey to passive listening, whereby you can give others the impression that you're focused on their words but your mind is partially somewhere else. When listening, you need to remain aware of this tendency to drift off and to actively fight it by devoting your full attention to others when they're speaking.

> **Remember**
>
> When you listen closely to those who speak to you, you send them the message that you respect their ideas and that they're worthy of your undivided attention.

2. Remain conscious of the nonverbal messages you send while listening.

It's estimated that 90 percent of communication is nonverbal, because human body language often communicates stronger and truer messages than spoken language (Mehrabian, 1972).

When it comes to listening, body language may be the best way to communicate interest in the speaker's words, as well as interest in the person who's doing the speaking. Similarly, if you are speaking, awareness of your listeners' body language can provide important clues about whether you're holding or losing their interest.

A good mnemonic device (memory-improvement method) for the nonverbal signals you should send others while listening is the acronym SOFTEN, in which each letter stands for an effective nonverbal message:

S = Smiling. Smile periodically but not continually, as if your smile is an artificial pose.
Sitting Still. Don't fidget and squirm, as if the speaker is making you feel anxious or bored.

O = Opening Your Posture. Avoid a closed posture with arms crossed or hands folded together, as if you're Superman or a Supreme Court justice who's about to pass judgment.

F = Forward Leaning. Leaning back can be interpreted as psychoanalyzing or evaluating the speaker.
Facing the Speaker Directly. Line up both shoulders with the speaker rather than turning one shoulder away, as if to give the speaker the cold shoulder.

T = Touching. A light touch on the arm or hand can be a good way to communicate warmth, but no rubbing, stroking, or touching should be used in ways that could qualify as sexual harassment.

E = Eye Contact. Meet the speaker's eyes periodically but not continually, as if you're staring or glaring, and not infrequently, because the speaker may think that your lack of eye contact means you're looking around for something else more interesting or stimulating than the speaker.

N = Nodding Your Head. Nod slowly and every once in a while but not repeatedly and rapidly, because the latter sends the message that you want the speaker to hurry up and finish so that you can start talking.

An interesting exercise you can use to gain greater awareness of your nonverbal communication habits is to choose a couple of people whom you trust, and who know you well, and ask them to imitate your body language. This is an exercise that can often be revealing (and sometimes hilarious).

3. Be open to different topics of conversation.

Don't be closed-minded or selective by listening to people like you're listening to the radio—selecting or tuning into only those conversational topics that reflect your favorite interests or personal points of view but tuning out everything else.

> **Remember**
>
> People learn most from others whose interests and viewpoints don't necessarily match their own. Ignoring or blocking out information and ideas about topics that don't immediately interest you or support your particular perspective is not only a poor social skill but also a poor learning strategy.

If people express viewpoints that you don't agree with, you don't have to nod in agreement; however, you still owe them the courtesy of listening to what they have to say (rather than shaking your head, frowning, or interrupting them). This isn't just a matter of social etiquette; it's a matter of social ethics. After others finish expressing their point of view, you should then feel free to express your own. Your informed opinions are worth expressing, as long as you don't express them in an opinionated way—that is, stating them so strongly that it sounds like your viewpoints are the only rational or acceptable ones while all others are inferior or insane (Gibb, 1961). Opinionated expression is likely to immediately end a potentially useful discussion or a possible future relationship.

Pause for Reflection

On what topics do you hold strong opinions?

When you express these opinions, how do others usually react to you?

Human Relations Skills (a.k.a. People Skills)

In addition to communicating and conversing well with others, another aspect of social intelligence is how well you relate to and treat people in general. You can use several strategies to improve this broader set of human relations or people skills.

1. Remember the names of people you meet.

Remembering people's names communicates to others that you know them as individuals. It makes each person you meet feel less like an anonymous face in a crowd and more like a special and unique individual with a distinctive identity.

Although people commonly claim they don't have a good memory for names, no evidence shows that the ability to remember names is an inherited trait that people are born with and cannot control; instead, it's a skill that can be developed through personal effort and employment of effective learning and memory strategies.

You can use the following strategies for remembering names:

- Consciously pay attention to the name of each person you meet. Listen for the person's name rather than focusing on the impression you're making on that person, the impression the individual is making on you, or what you're going to say next.
- Reinforce your memory for a new name by saying it or rehearsing it within a minute or two after you first hear it. For instance, if your friend Gertrude has just introduced you to Geraldine, you might say: "Geraldine, how long have you known Gertrude?" By using a person's name soon after you've heard it, you intercept memory loss when forgetting is most likely to occur—immediately after you acquire new information (Underwood, 1983).
- Strengthen your memory of an individual's name by associating it with other information learned about the person. For instance, you can associate the person's name with (a) your first impression of the individual's personality, (b) a physical characteristic of the person, (c) your topic of conversation, (d) the place where you met, or (e) a familiar word that rhymes with the person's name. By making a mental connection between the person's name and some other piece of information, you help your brain form a physical connection, which is the biological foundation of human memory.
- People write down things that they want to be sure to remember. You can use this same strategy for learning names by keeping a name journal that includes the names of new people you meet plus some information about them (e.g., what they do and what their interests are). You could make it a

> "We should be aware of the magic contained in a name. The name sets that individual apart; it makes him or her unique among all others. Remember that a person's name is to that person the sweetest and most important sound in any language."
>
> –Dale Carnegie, author of the best-selling book *How to Win Friends and Influence People* (1936) and founder of The Dale Carnegie Course, a worldwide program for business based on his teachings

> "When I joined the bank, I started keeping a record of the people I met and put them on little cards, and I would indicate on the cards when I met them, and under what circumstances, and sometimes [make] a little notation which would help me remember a conversation."
>
> –David Rockefeller, prominent American banker, philanthropist, and former CEO of the Chase Manhattan Bank

goal to meet one new person every day and remember that person's name by recording it in your journal.

> **! Remember**
>
> Developing the habit of remembering names not only is a social skill that can improve your interpersonal interactions and bring you friends' but also is a powerful professional tool that can promote your career success in whatever field you may pursue.

In business, remembering people's names can help recruit and retain customers; in politics, it can win votes; and in education, it can promote the teacher's connection and rapport with students.

2. Refer to people by name when you greet and interact with them.

When you greet a person, be sure to use the person's name in your greeting. Saying, "Hi, Waldo," will mean a lot more to Waldo than simply saying "Hi" or, worse yet, saying "Hi, there"—which sounds like you're just acknowledging something out there that could be either a human or an inanimate object. By continuing to use people's names after you've learned them, you continue to send them the message that you haven't forgotten their unique identity and you continue to strengthen your memory of their names.

> "If we obey this law, [it] will bring us countless friends. The law is this: Always make the person feel important."
>
> –Dale Carnegie, *How to Win Friends and Influence People* (1936)

3. Show interest in others by remembering information about them.

Ask people questions about their personal interests, plans, and experiences. Listen closely to their answers, especially to what seems most important to them, what they care about, or what intrigues them, and introduce these topics when you have conversations with them. For one person that topic may be politics, for another it may be sports, and for another it may be relationships. When you see people again, ask them about something they brought up in your last conversation. Try to get beyond the standard, generic questions that people routinely ask after they say "Hello" (e.g., "What's going on?"). Instead, ask about something specific you discussed with them last time you spoke (e.g., "How did that math test go that you were worried about last week?"). This sends a clear message to others that you remember them and care about them. Your memory often reflects your priorities—you're most likely to remember what's most important to you. When you remember people's names and something about them, it lets them know that they're a high priority to you. Furthermore, you're likely to find that others start showing more interest in you after you show interest in them. Another surprising thing may happen when you ask questions that show interest in others: People are likely to say you're a great conversationalist and a good friend.

> "You can make more friends in 2 months by becoming interested in other people than you can in 2 years by trying to get other people interested in you."
>
> –Dale Carnegie, *How to Win Friends and Influence People* (1936)

Strategies for Meeting People and Forming Friendships

An important aspect of the college experience is meeting new people, learning from them, and forming new friendships. Here are some practical strategies for increasing the quantity, quality, and variety of the people you meet and the friendships you form.

1. Place yourself in situations and locations where you will come in regular contact with others.

Studies show that friendships form when people regularly cross paths and find themselves in the same place at the same time (Latané et al., 1995). You can apply this principle by spending as much time on campus as possible and spending time in places where others are likely to be present (e.g., by eating your meals in the student cafeteria and studying in the college library). If you have the opportunity to live on campus, do so; studies show that it helps students make social connections and increases their satisfaction with the college experience (Pascarella & Terenzini, 2005; Tinto, 1993). If you are a commuter student, try to make your college experience as similar as possible to that of a residential student; for example, try to spend more than just class time on campus by spending study time and social time (e.g., attending campus social or cultural events) on campus.

An important aspect of the college experience is meeting new people and forming lasting friendships.

Pause for Reflection

Have you been to college parties on or off campus?

If yes, what were they like?

If no, why haven't you attended one?

Student Perspective

"I have observed different kinds of people. There are the ones that party and flunk, then there are the kind that party rationally and don't flunk, and the kinds that just don't party."

—First-year college student

2. Put yourself in social situations where you're likely to meet people who have similar interests, goals, and values.

Research supports the proverb, "Birds of a feather flock together." People tend to form friendships with others who share similar interests, values, or goals (AhYun, 2002). When two people have something in common, they're more likely to form friendships because they're more likely to enjoy spending time together doing things that relate to their common interests. They're also more likely to get along with each other because they reinforce or validate each other's personal interests and values (Festinger, 1954).

One straightforward way to find others with whom you have something in common is by participating in clubs and organizations on campus that reflect your personal interests and values. If you cannot find one, start one of your own. Also, regularly check your college newspaper, posted flyers on campus, and the Student Information Desk in your Student Activities Center to keep track of social events that are more likely to attract others who share your interests, values, or goals.

3. Meeting others through a social Web site.

Facebook and other social Web sites represent another type of venue through which you can network with other college students. Through Facebook, you can interact with anyone who has a dot-edu e-mail address. You can use this electronic medium to meet new people, join groups on campus, and check for announcements of parties or other social events. However, be careful about the people you respond to, and be careful about what you post on your page or "wall." Reports indicate that both schools and employers are checking students' Facebook and MySpace entries and using that information to help them decide whether to accept or reject applicants (Palank, 2006).

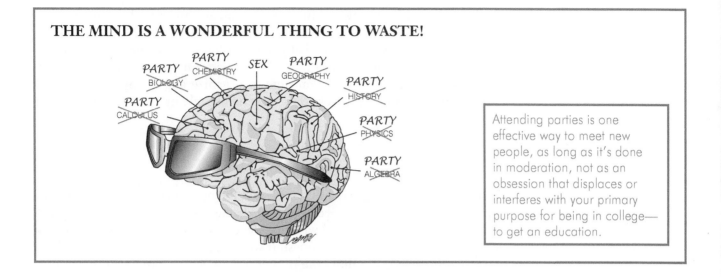

THE MIND IS A WONDERFUL THING TO WASTE!

Attending parties is one effective way to meet new people, as long as it's done in moderation, not as an obsession that displaces or interferes with your primary purpose for being in college—to get an education.

Interpersonal Conflict

Disagreement and conflict among people are inevitable aspects of social life. Research shows that even the most happily married couples don't experience continual marital bliss but have occasional disagreements and conflicts (Gottman, 1994). Thus, conflict is something you cannot expect to escape or eliminate; you can only hope to contain it, defuse it, and prevent it from reaching unmanageable levels. The effective interpersonal communication and human relations skills discussed in this chapter can help minimize conflicts. In addition to these general skills, the following set of strategies may be used to handle interpersonal conflict constructively and humanely.

1. Pick the right place and time to resolve conflicts.

Don't discuss sensitive issues when you're fatigued, in a fit of anger, or in a hurry (Daniels & Horowitz, 1997), and don't discuss them in a public arena; deal with them only with the person involved. As the expression goes, "Don't air your dirty laundry in public." Addressing a conflict in public is akin to a public stoning; it's likely to embarrass or humiliate the person with whom you are in conflict and cause the other person to resist or resent you.

2. Decompress yourself before you expressing yourself.

When you have a conflict with someone, your ultimate objective should be to solve the problem, not to unload your anger and have an emotionally cathartic experience. Impulsively dumping on the other person and saying the first thing that comes to your mind may give you an immediate sense of relief, but it's not likely to produce permanent improvement in the other person's attitude or behavior toward you. Instead of unloading, take the load off—cool down and give yourself a little down time to reflect rationally before you react emotionally. For example, count to 10 and give your emotions time to settle down and think carefully about what you're going to say before saying it. Pausing for reflection also communicates to the other person that you're giving careful thought and attention to the matter rather than lashing out randomly.

If the conflict is so intense that you're feeling incensed or enraged, it may be a good idea to slow things down by writing out your thoughts ahead of time. This strategy will give you time to organize and clarify your ideas by first talking silently to yourself (on paper) before talking out loud to the other person (in person).

3. Give the person a chance to respond.

Just because you're angry doesn't mean that the person you're angry with must forfeit the right to free speech and self-defense. Giving the other person a chance to speak and be heard will increase the likelihood that you'll receive a cooperative response to your request. It will also prevent you from storming in, jumping the gun, and pulling the trigger too quickly before being sure you've got all the facts straight.

After listening to the other person's response, check your understanding by summarizing it in your own words (e.g., "What I hear you saying is . . ."). This is an important first step in the conflict-resolution process because conflicts often revolve around a simple misunderstanding, a failure to communicate, or a communication breakdown. Sometimes just taking the time to hear where the other person is coming from before launching into a full-scale complaint or criticism can reduce or resolve the conflict.

4. Acknowledge the person's perspectives and feelings.

After listening to the person's response, if you disagree with it don't dismiss or discount the person's feelings. For instance, don't say, "That's ridiculous" or "You're not making any sense." Instead, say, "I see how you might feel that way, but . . ." or "I feel badly that you are under pressure, but . . ."

5. If things begin to get nasty, call for a time-out or cease-fire and postpone the discussion to allow both of you time to cool off.

When emotion and adrenalin run high, logic and reason often run low. This can result in someone saying something during a fit of anger, which, in turn, stimulates an angry response from the other person; then the anger of both combatants continues to escalate and turns into an intense volley of verbal punches and counterpunches. For example, the conversation may end up go something like this:

Person A: "You're out of control."
Person B: "No, I'm not out of control, you're just overreacting."
Person A: "*I'm* overreacting, you're the one who's yelling!"
Person B: "I'm not yelling, *you're* the one who's raising your voice!"

Blow-by-blow exchanges such as these are likely to turn up the emotional heat so high that resolving the conflict is out of the question until both fighters to back off, retreat to their respective corners, cool down, and try again later when neither one of them is ready to throw a knockout punch.

> "Seek first to understand, then to be understood."
>
> –Stephen Covey, international best-selling author of *Seven Habits of Highly Effective People* (1990)

6. Make your point assertively (not passively, aggressively, or passive–aggressively).

When you're passive, you don't stand up for your personal rights; you allow others to take advantage of you by letting them push you around. You say nothing when you should say something. You say "yes" when you want to say "no." When you handle conflict passively, you become angry, anxious, or resentful about doing nothing and keeping it all inside.

When you're aggressive, you stand up for your rights but you also violate the rights of the other person by threatening, dominating, humiliating, or bullying that person. You use intense, emotionally loaded words to attack the person (e.g., "You spoiled brat" or "You're a sociopath"). You manage to get what you want but at the other person's expense. Later, you tend to feel guilty about overreacting or coming on too strong (e.g., "I knew I shouldn't have said that").

When you're passive–aggressive, you get back or get even with the other person by either (a) withholding or taking away something (e.g., not speaking to the other person or withdrawing all attention or affection), or (b) indirectly hinting that you're angry (e.g., by making cynical comments or using sarcastic humor).

In contrast, when you're assertive, you strike the middle ground between aggression and passivity. You handle conflict in a way that protects or restores your rights without taking away or stepping on the rights of the other person. You approach conflict in an even-tempered way rather than in an angry or agitated manner; you speak in a normal volume rather than yelling or screaming; and you communicate at a normal distance rather than getting up close and into the face of the other person involved in the conflict. You can resolve conflicts assertively by using the following four strategies:

a. Focus on the specific behavior causing the conflict, not the person's general character. Avoid labeling the person as "selfish," "mean," "inconsiderate," and so on. For instance, if you're upset because your roommate doesn't share in cleaning, stay away from aggressive labels such as "slacker" or "lazy bum." Attacking others with negative labels such as these does to the other person just what it sounds like: It gives the feeling of being attack or verbally assaulted. This is likely to put the other person on the defensive and provoke a counterattack on one of your personal characteristics. Before you know it, you're likely to find yourself in a full-out war of words and mutual character assassinations that has escalated well beyond a small-scale skirmish about the specific behavior of one individual.

Rather than focusing on the person's general character, focus on the behaviors that are causing the problem (e.g., failing to do the dishes or leaving dirty laundry around the room). This will enable the other person to know exactly what actions need to be taken to take care of the problem. Furthermore, it's easier for others to change a specific behavior than it is to change their entire character, which would require a radical change in personality (or a frontal lobotomy).

b. Use "I" messages to focus on how the other person's behavior or action affects you. By using "I" messages, which focus on your perceptions and feelings, you send a message that's less accusatory and threatening (Narciso & Burkett, 1975). In contrast, "you" messages are more likely to make the other person defensive and put that person on the offensive—ready to retaliate rather than cooperate (Gibb, 1991).

For instance, suppose you've received a course grade that's lower than what you think you earned or deserved and you decide to question your instructor about it. This conversation should not begin by saying to the instructor, "You gave me the wrong grade" or "You made a mistake." These messages are likely to make your professor immediately ready to defend the grade you received. Your professor will be less threatened and more likely to listen to and consider your complaint if you initiate the conversation with an "I" statement," such as "I don't believe I received the correct grade" or "I think an error may have been made in my final grade."

"I" messages are less aggressive because you're targeting an issue, not a person (Jakubowski & Lange, 1978). By saying, "I feel angry when . . ." rather than "You make me angry when . . . ," you send the message that you're taking responsibility for the way you feel rather than guilt-tripping the individual for making you feel that way (perhaps without the person even being aware of how you feel).

Do the following when using "I" messages:

- Be specific about what emotion you are feeling. For example, saying "I feel neglected when you don't write or call" more specifically identifies what you're feeling than saying, "I wish you'd be more considerate." Describing what you feel in specific terms increases the persuasive power of your message and reduces the risk that the other person will misunderstand or discount it.
- Be specific about what you're requesting of the other person to improve the situation. For example, saying "I would like for you to call me at least once a day" is more specific than saying "I want you to keep in touch with me."
- Express what you want the other person to do in the form of a firm request rather than a demand or ultimatum. For example, saying "I would like you to . . ." is less likely to put the person on the defensive than saying "I insist . . ." or "I demand . . ."

c. **Don't make absolute judgments or blanket statements.** Compare the following three pairs of statements:

- "You're no help at all" versus "You don't help me enough"
- "You never try to understand how I feel" versus "You don't try hard enough to understand how I feel"
- "I always have to clean up" versus "I'm doing more than my fair share of the cleaning"

The first statement in each of the preceding pairs represents an absolute statement that covers all times, situations, and circumstances—without any room for possible exceptions. Such extreme, blanket criticisms are likely to put the criticized person on the defensive because they state that the person is lacking or deficient with respect to the behavior in question. The second statement in each pair states the criticism in terms of degree or amount, which is less likely to threaten the person's self-esteem (and is probably closer to the truth).

d. **Focus on solving the problem, not winning the argument.** Try not to approach conflict with the attitude that you're going to get even or prove that you're right. Winning the argument but not persuading the person to change the behavior that's causing the conflict is like winning a battle but losing the

---

"Precision of communication is important, more important than ever, in our era of hair-trigger balances, when a false or misunderstood word may create as much disaster as a sudden thoughtless act."

–James Thurber, U.S. author, humorist, and cartoonist

Pause for Reflection

Your classmates aren't carrying their weight on a group project that you're all supposed to be working on as a team; you're getting frustrated and angry because you're doing most of the work. What "I" message could you use to communicate your concern in a nonthreatening way that's likely to resolve this conflict successfully?

"Don't find fault. Find a remedy."

–Henry Ford, founder of Ford Motor and one of the richest people of his generation

war. Instead, approach the conflict with the attitude that it's a problem to be solved and that both parties can win—that is, both of you can end up with a better relationship in the long run if the issue is resolved.

7. Conclude your discussion of the conflict on a warm, constructive note.

By ending on a positive note, you assure the other person that there are no hard feelings, that you're optimistic the conflict can be resolved, and that your relationship can be improved.

8. If the conflict is resolved because of some change made by the other person, express your appreciation for the individual's effort.

Even if your complaint was legitimate and your request was justified, the person's effort to accommodate your request shouldn't be taken for granted. At the least, you shouldn't react to a positive change in behavior by rubbing it in with comments such as "That's more like it" or "It's about time!"

Expressing appreciation to the other person for making a change in response to your request is not only a socially sensitive thing to do but also a self-serving thing to do. By recognizing or reinforcing the other person's changed behavior, you increase the likelihood that the positive change in behavior will continue.

> "To keep your marriage brimming with love . . . when you're wrong, admit it; when you're right, shut up."
>
> –Ogden Nash, American poet

◆ Emotional Intelligence

Research on college students indicates that those with higher emotional intelligence, such as the ability to identify their emotions and moods, are (a) less likely to experience boredom (Harris, 2000) and (b) more able to focus their attention and get absorbed (in the zone) when completing challenging tasks (Wiederman, 2007). Succeeding in college is a challenging task that will test your emotional strength and your ability to persist to task completion (graduation).

Research also indicates that experiencing positive emotions, such as optimism and excitement, promotes learning by increasing the brain's ability to take in, store, and retrieve information (Rosenfield, 1988). In one study involving nearly 4,000 first-year college students, it was found that students' level of optimism or hope for success during their first term on campus was a more accurate predictor of their first-year grades than was their SAT score or high school grade point average (GPA; Snyder et al., 1991). In contrast, negative emotions such as anxiety and fear can interfere with the brain's ability to (a) store memories (Jacobs & Nadel, 1985), (b) retrieve stored memories (O'Keefe & Nadel, 1975), and (c) engage in higher-level thinking (Caine & Caine, 1991).

Discussed below are research-based strategies for minimizing the impact of negative emotions that most often sabotage success, and strategies for maximizing the impact of positive emotions that promote success.

◆ Stress and Anxiety

COUNSELING OFFICE
Hours: 24–7

● Anxiety Disorders
Drug Addiction
Internet Addiction
Information Fatigue
Syndrome

Today's technological revolution and information explosion may be making life particularly stressful.

Among the most common emotions that humans have to monitor, manage, and regulate are stress and anxiety. College students report higher levels of stress while in college than they did before college (Bartlett, 2002; Sax, 2003), and students entering college in recent years report higher levels of stress (Astin, Parrot, Korn, & Sax, 1997; Sax, Astin, Korn, & Mahoney, 1999) and lower levels of mental health (Kadison & DiGeronimo, 2004) than they have in years past. An increased level of stress may reflect that you're living in a world experiencing an unprecedented rate of technological change and information overload. Terms such as "Internet addiction" and "information fatigue syndrome" are now being used by psychologists to diagnose disorders involving, respectively, psychological dependency on the Internet and excess stress related to information overload (Waddington, 1996; Young, 1996).

What exactly is stress? The biology of stress originates from the fight-or-flight reaction that's been wired into your body for survival purposes. This automatic reaction prepares you to handle danger or threat by flooding your body with chemicals (e.g., adrenalin) in the same way that ancient humans had to handle threats by engaging in fight or flight (escape) when confronted by life-threatening predators.

The word "stress" derives from a Latin root that means "to draw tight." Thus, stress isn't necessarily bad. For example, a tightened guitar string provides better sound than a string that's too lax or loose, a tightened bow delivers a more powerful arrow shot, and a tightened muscle provides more strength or speed. Such productive stress is sometimes referred to as eustress—deriving from the root *eu* meaning "good" (as in the words "euphoria," meaning good mood, and "eulogy," meaning good words).

If you keep college stress at a moderate level, it can be a productive emotion that promotes your learning and personal development. Stress in moderate amounts can benefit your:

1. Physical performance (e.g., strength and speed);
2. Mental performance (e.g., attention and memory); and
3. Mood (e.g., hope and optimism).

Pause for Reflection

Can you think of a situation in which you performed at a higher level because you were somewhat nervous or experienced a moderate amount of stress?

However, if stress is extreme and continues for a prolonged period, it moves from being a productive to a destructive feeling. Using the guitar string as an analogy, if a guitar is strung too tightly, the string is likely to snap or break—which isn't productive. Unproductive stress is often referred to as distress—from the root *dis* meaning "bad" (as in the words "discomfort" and "disease"). Extreme stress can create feelings of intense anxiety or anxiety disorders (e.g., panic attacks), and if a high level of stress persists for a prolonged period, it can trigger psychosomatic illness—tension-induced bodily disorders (from *psyche*, meaning "mind," and *soma*, meaning "body"). For instance, prolonged distress can trigger indigestion by increasing secretion of stomach acids or contribute to high blood pressure, a.k.a. hypertension. Prolonged stress can also suppress the immune system, leaving you more vulnerable to flu, colds, and other infectious diseases. Studies show that the immune system of college students is suppressed (produces fewer antibodies) at stressful times during the academic term—such as midterms and finals (Jemott & Magloire, 1988; Kielcolt-Glaser & Glaser, 1986).

Research indicates that college students' stress levels tend to rise when they are experiencing a wave of exams, such as finals.

Excess stress can interfere with mental performance because the feelings and thoughts that accompany anxiety begin to preoccupy your mind and take up space in your working memory, leaving it with less capacity to process information you're trying to learn and retain. Studies also show that students experiencing higher levels of academic stress or performance anxiety are more likely to use ineffective surface approaches to learning that rely merely on memorization (Ramsden & Entwistle, 1981) rather than effective deep-learning strategies that involve seeking meaning and understanding. Furthermore, high levels of test anxiety are more likely to result in careless concentration errors on exams (e.g., overlooking key words in test questions) and can interfere with memory for information that's been studied (Jacobs & Nadel, 1985; O'Keefe & Nadel, 1978; Tobias, 1985).

Although considerable research points to the negative effects of excess stress, you still need to keep in mind that stress can work either for or against you; you can be either energized or sabotaged by stress depending on its level of intensity and the length of time it continues. You can't expect to stop or eliminate stress, nor should you want to; you can only hope to contain it and maintain it at a level where it's more productive than destructive. Many years of research indicate that personal performance is best when it takes place under conditions of moderate stress because this creates a sense of challenge. On the other hand, too much stress creates performance anxiety, and too little stress results in loss of intensity or indifference (Sapolsky, 2004; Yerkes & Dodson, 1908). (See **Figure 8.1**.)

Box 8.1 provides a short summary of the signs or symptoms of extreme stress that indicate stress has climbed to a level where it's creating distress or anxiety. If these are experienced, particularly for an extended period during which symptoms continue to occur for 2 or more weeks, action should be taken to reduce them.

Pause for Reflection

How would you rate your level of anxiety in the following situations?

1. Taking tests or exams   high   moderate   low

2. Interacting in social situations   high   moderate   low

3. Making decisions about the future   high   moderate   low

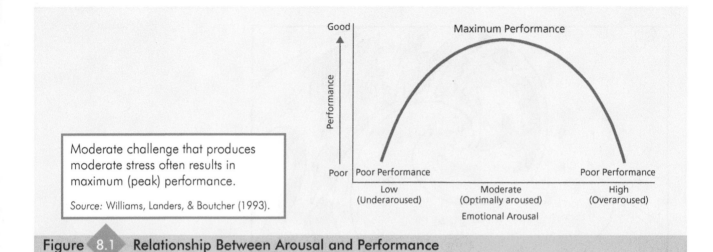

Moderate challenge that produces moderate stress often results in maximum (peak) performance.

Source: Williams, Landers, & Boutcher (1993).

Figure 8.1   Relationship Between Arousal and Performance

Take Action!

High Anxiety: Recognizing the Symptoms (Signs) of Distress

- Jitteriness or shaking. Symptoms that occur, especially the hands.
- Accelerated heart rate or heart palpitations. Irregular heartbeat;
- Muscle tension. Tightness in the chest or upper shoulders or a tight feeling (lump) in the throat (the expressions "uptight" and "choking" stem from these symptoms of upper-body tension);
- Body aches. Heightened muscle tension leading to tension headaches, backaches, or chest pain, which can become so extreme that it can feel as if a heart attack is taking place;
- Sweating. Symptoms seen especially as sweaty (clammy) palms;
- Cold, pale hands or feet. Symptoms that led to the expressions "white knuckles" and "cold feet";

- Dry mouth. Production of less saliva (the expression "cotton mouth" stems from this loss of saliva);
- Stomach discomfort or indigestion. Increased secretion of stomach acid (the expression "feeling butterflies in my stomach" relates to this symptom);
- Elimination problems. Constipation or diarrhea;
- Feeling faint or dizzy. Constriction of blood vessels that decreases oxygen flow to the brain;
- Weakness and fatigue. Sustained (chronic) state of arousal and prolonged muscle tension that becomes tiring;
- Menstrual changes. Symptoms such as missing or irregular menstrual periods;
- Difficulty sleeping. Insomnia or interrupted (fitful) sleep;
- Increased susceptibility to colds, flu, and other infections. Suppression of the body's immune system that leads to more infections.

8.1

Effective Methods for Managing Stress

If you perceive your level of stress to be reaching a point where it's beginning to interfere with the quality of your performance or life, you need to take steps to reduce it. Listed here are three stress-management methods whose positive effects have been well documented by research in psychology and biology (Benson & Klipper, 1990; Everly, 1989; Lehrer & Woolfolk, 1993).

Deep (Diaphragmatic) Breathing

The type of breathing associated with excessive stress is hyperventilation—fast, shallow, and irregular breathing through the mouth rather than the chest. Breathing associated with relaxation is just the opposite—slow, deep, and regular breathing that originates from the stomach.

Breathing is something you usually do automatically or involuntarily; however, with some concentration and effort, you can control your breathing by controlling your diaphragm—the body's muscle that enables you to expand and contract your lungs. By voluntarily controlling your diaphragm muscle, you can slow your breathing rate, which, in turn, can bring down your stress level.

Progressive Muscle Relaxation

A relaxation stress-management method is similar to stretching exercises used to relax and loosen muscles before and after physical exercise. To achieve total-body (head-to-toe) muscle relaxation, progressively tense and release the five sets of muscles listed here. Hold the tension in each muscle area for about 5 seconds, and then release it slowly.

1. Wrinkle your forehead muscles, and then release them.
2. Shrug your shoulders up as if to touch your ears, and then drop them.
3. Make a fist with each hand, and then open both.
4. Tighten your stomach muscles, and then release them.
5. Tighten your toes by curling them under your feet, and then raise them as high as you can.

To help tense your muscles, imagine you're using them to push or lift a heavy object. When relaxing your muscles, take a deep breath and think or say the word "relax." By breathing deeply and thinking or hearing the word "relax" each time you release your muscles, the word becomes associated with your muscles becoming relaxed. Thus, if you find yourself in a stressful situation, you can take a deep breath, think or say the word "relax," and immediately release tension because that's what your muscles have been trained or conditioned to do.

Mental Imagery

Visual imagination can be used to create sensory experiences that promote relaxation. You can create your own relaxing mental movie or imaginary DVD by visually placing yourself in a calm, comfortable, and soothing setting. You can visualize ocean waves, floating clouds, sitting in a warm sauna, or any sensory experience that tends to relax you. The more senses you use, the more real the scene will seem and the more powerful its relaxing effects will be (Fezler, 1989). Try to use all of your senses—try to see it, hear it, smell it, touch it, and feel it. You can also use musical imagination to create calming background music that accompanies your visual image.

My wife, Mary, is a kindergarten teacher. Whenever her young students start misbehaving and the situation becomes stressful (e.g., during lunchtime when the kids are running wildly, arguing vociferously, and screaming at maximum volume), Mary "plays" relaxing songs in her head. She reports that her musical imagination always works to soothe her nerves, enabling her to remain calm and even tempered when she must confront children who need to be scolded or disciplined.

—Joe Cuseo

Simple Stress-Reduction Strategies and Habits

Pause for Reflection

What are the most common sources of stress for you?

Would you say that you deal with stress well?

What strategies do you use to cope with stress?

In addition to formal stress-management techniques, such as diaphragmatic breathing, progressive muscle relaxation, and mental imagery, stress may be managed by simpler strategies and habits, such as those discussed here.

1. Exercise.

Exercise reduces stress by increasing release of serotonin—a mellowing brain chemical that reduces feelings of tension (anxiety) and depression. Thus, psychotherapists prescribe exercise for patients experiencing mild forms of anxiety or depression (Johnsgard, 2004). Studies show that people who exercise regularly tend to report feeling happier (Myers, 1993). Exercise also elevates mood by improving people's sense of self-esteem because it gives them a sense of accomplishment by improving their physical self-image.

2. Keep a journal of feelings and emotions.

Dealing with feelings by writing about them in a personal journal can provide way to identifying your emotions (one element of emotional intelligence), as well as a safe and regular outlet for releasing steam and coping with stress. Writing about your emotions also enables you to become more consciously aware of them, which reduces the risk of pushing them into your subconscious and denying them.

"There are thousands of causes for stress, and one antidote to stress is self-expression. That's what happens to me every day. My thoughts get off my chest, down my sleeves, and onto my pad."

–Garson Kanin, American writer, actor, and film director

3. Take time for humor and laughter.

Research on the power of humor for reducing tension is clear and convincing. In one research study, college students were unexpectedly given an assignment to deliver an impromptu (off the top of their head) speech. This unexpected assignment caused students' heart rate to elevate to an average of 110 beats per minute during their speech. However, if students watched humorous episodes of sitcoms before delivering their impromptu speech, their average heart rate was lower (80–85 beats per minute), which suggests that experiencing humor significantly lowers anxiety (O'Brien, cited in Howard, 2000). Research also shows that if your immune system is suppressed or weakened by stress, humor strengthens it by blocking the body's production of the stress hormone cortisol, the body chemical responsible for suppressing your immune system when you're stressed (Berk, cited in Liebertz, 2005b).

"The arrival of a good clown exercises a more beneficial influence upon the health of a town than the arrival of twenty asses laden with drugs."

–Thomas Sydenham, seventeenth-century physician

◆ Depression

Along with anxiety, depression is the emotional problem that most commonly afflicts humans and must be managed. Excess stress can turn into anxiety (a heightened state of tension, arousal, and nervous energy), or it can lead to depression (an emotional state characterized by a loss of optimism, hope, and energy). As the term implies, when people are depressed, their mood is lowered or pushed down (like depressing the accelerator in a car). In contrast to anxiety, which typically involves worrying about something that's happening or that's about to happen (e.g., experiencing test anxiety before an upcoming exam), depression more often relates to something that's already happened. In particular, depression is often related to a loss, such as a lost relationship (e.g., departed friend, broken romance, or death of a family member) or a lost opportunity (e.g., losing a job, failing a course, or failing to be accepted into a major; Bowlby, 1980; Price, Choi, & Vinokur, 2002). It's natural and normal to feel dejected after losses such as these. However, if your dejection reaches a point where you can't concentrate and complete your day-to-day tasks, and if this continues for an extended period, you may be experiencing what psychologists call clinical depression (i.e., depression so serious that it requires professional help).

Box 8.2 provides a summary of symptoms or signs that may indicate the presence of depression. If these symptoms continue to occur for two or more weeks, action should be taken to relieve them.

! Take Action!

Recognizing the Symptoms (Signs) of Depression

8.2

- Low, down, dejected, sad, or blue feelings
- Pessimistic feelings about the future (e.g., expecting failure or feeling helpless or hopeless)
- Decreased sense of humor
- Difficulty finding pleasure, joy, or fun in anything
- Lack of concentration
- Loss of motivation or interest in things previously found to be exciting or stimulating
- Stooped posture (e.g., hung head or drawn face)
- Slower and softer speech rate
- Decreased animation and slower bodily movements
- Loss of energy
- Changes in sleeping patterns (e.g., sleeping more or less than usual)
- Changes in eating patterns (e.g., eating more or less than usual)
- Social withdrawal
- Neglect of physical appearance
- Consistently low self-esteem (e.g., thinking "I'm a loser")
- Strong feelings of worthlessness or guilt (e.g., thinking "I'm a failure")
- Suicidal thoughts (e.g., thinking "I can't take it anymore," "People would be better off without me," or "I don't deserve to live")

Pause for Reflection

Have you, or a member of your family, ever experienced clinical depression?

What do you think was the primary cause or factor that triggered it?

> **! Remember**
>
> There is a difference between feeling despondent or down and being depressed. When psychologists use the word "depression," they're usually referring to clinical depression—a mood state so low that it's interfering with a person's ability to cope with day-to-day life tasks, such as getting to school or going to work.

Strategies for Coping with Depression

Depression can vary widely in intensity. Moderate and severe forms of depression often require professional counseling or psychotherapy, and their cause often lies in genetic factors that involve inherited imbalances in brain chemistry.

The following strategies are offered primarily for milder cases of depression that are more amenable to self-help and self-control. These strategies may also be used with professional help or psychiatric medication to reduce the intensity and frequency of depression.

1. Focus on the present and the future, not the past.

Consciously fight the tendency to dwell on past losses or failures because you can no longer change or control them. Instead, focus on things you can still control, which are occurring now and will occur in the future.

2. Deliberately make an effort to engage in positive or emotionally uplifting behavior when you're feeling down.

If your behavior is upbeat, your mind (mood) often follows suit. "Put on a happy face" may be an effective depression-reduction strategy because smiling produces certain changes in your facial muscles, which, in turn, trigger changes in brain chemistry that improve your mood (Liebertz, 2005). In contrast, frowning activates a different set of facial muscles that reduces production of mood-elevating brain chemicals (Myers, 1993).

3. Continue to engage in activities that are fun and enjoyable for you.

For example, continue to socialize with friends and engage in your usual recreational activities. Falling into the downward spiral of withdrawing from doing the things that bring you joy because you're too down to do them will bring you even lower by taking away the very things that bring you up. Interestingly, the root of the word "recreation" means to re-create or create again, which suggests that recreation can revive, restore, and renew you—physically and emotionally.

4. Continue trying to get things done.

By staying busy and getting things done when you feel down, you help boost your mood because you experience a sense of accomplishment and boost your self-esteem. Doing something nice for someone less fortunate than yourself

> "Yesterday is gone. Tomorrow has not yet come. We have only today. Let us begin."
>
> —Mother Teresa of Calcutta, Albanian, Catholic nun, and winner of the Nobel Peace Prize

> "The best way to cheer yourself up is to try to cheer somebody else up."
>
> —Samuel Clemens, a.k.a. Mark Twain, writer, lecturer, and humorist

can be a particularly effective way to elevate your mood because it helps you realize that your issues are often far less serious and more manageable than the problems faced by others.

5. Intentionally seek out humor and laughter.

In addition to reducing anxiety, laughter can lighten and brighten a dark mood. Furthermore, humor improves memory (Nielson, cited in Liebertz, 2005), which is an important advantage for people experiencing depression, because depression interferes with concentration and memory. Research supporting the benefits of humor for the body and mind is so well established that humor has become a legitimate academic field of study known as gelontology—the study of laughter (from the Greek word *gelos* for "laughter" and *ology*, meaning "study of").

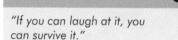

"If you can laugh at it, you can survive it."

–Bill Cosby, American comedian, actor, and activist

6. Make a conscious effort to focus on your personal strengths and accomplishments.

Another way to drive away the blues is by keeping track of the good developments in your life. You can do this by keeping a positive events journal in which you note the good experiences in your life, including things you're grateful for, as well as your accomplishments and achievements. Positive journal entries will leave you with a visible, uplifting record that you can review anytime you're feeling down. Furthermore, a positive events journal can provide you with a starting point for developing a formal résumé, portfolio, and personal strengths sheet, which you can provide to those who serve as your personal references and who write your letters of recommendation.

One strategy for coping with depression is to write down the positive events in your life in a journal.

© Galina Barskay, 2010. Under license from Shutterstock, Inc.

7. If you're unable to overcome depression on your own, seek help from others.

College students are more likely than ever to seek professional help if they're feeling depressed (Kadison & DiGeronimo, 2004). This is good news because it suggests that seeking help is no longer viewed as a source of embarrassment or a sign of personal weakness; instead, today's college students are willing to share their feelings with others and improve the quality of their emotional life.

In some cases, you may be able to help yourself overcome emotional problems through personal effort and effective coping strategies. This is particularly true if you experience depression or anxiety in milder forms and for limited periods. However, overcoming more serious and long-lasting episodes of clinical depression or anxiety isn't as simple as people make it out to be when they glibly (and insensitively) say, "Just deal with it," "Get over it," or "Snap out of it."

In mild cases of anxiety and depression, it's true that a person may be able to deal with or get over it, but in more serious cases, depression and anxiety may be strongly related to genetic factors that are beyond the person's control.

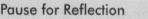

Pause for Reflection

If you thought you were experiencing a serious episode of anxiety or depression, would you feel comfortable seeking help from a professional?

If yes, why? If no, why not?

◆ Summary and Conclusion

Interpersonal relationships are strengthened by communication skills (verbal and nonverbal), and human relations or people skills. You can improve the quality of your interpersonal communication and social relationships by working hard at being a good listener, being open to different topics of conversation, and remembering the names and interests of people you meet.

Interpersonal conflict occurs throughout social life. However, you can minimize and manage such conflict by decompressing emotionally before expressing yourself verbally and by airing your concerns assertively rather than aggressively, passively, or passive–aggressively.

Today's college students report higher levels of stress than did students in years past. Strategies for reducing excess stress include formal stress-management techniques (e.g., diaphragmatic breathing and progressive muscle relaxation), good physical habits (e.g., exercising and reducing intake of caffeine or other stimulants), and positive ways of thinking (e.g., focusing on the present and the future, not the past, and making a conscious effort to focus on your personal strengths and accomplishments)

Intellectual ability is only one form of human intelligence. Social and emotional intelligence are at least as important for being successful, healthy, and happy. The strategies discussed in this chapter are not just soft skills; they are hard "core" skills that are essential for success in college and beyond.

Learning More Through the World Wide Web

Internet-Based Resources for Further Information on Social and Emotional Intelligence

For additional information related to the ideas discussed in this chapter, we recommend the following Web sites:

Social Intelligence and Interpersonal Relationships:

www.Humanresources.about.com/od/interpersonalcommunication1/qt/com_com5.htm

www.articles911.com/Communication/Interpersonal_Communication/

http://hodu.com/ECS-Menu1.shtml

Emotional Intelligence and Mental Health:

www.socialresearchmethods.net/Gallery/Young/emotion.htm

www.eqi.org/eitoc.htm

www.nimh.nih.gov/publicat/index.cfm (National Institute of Mental Health)

www.activeminds.org (national, student-run organization that supports mental health awareness)

8.1 Identifying Ways of Handling Interpersonal Conflict

Think of the social situation or relationship that is currently causing you the most conflict in your life. Describe how this conflict might be approached in each of the following ways:

1. Passively:

2. Aggressively:

3. Passive–aggressively:

4. Assertively:

(See **pp. 197–201** for descriptions of each of these four approaches.)

Consider practicing the assertive approach by role-playing it with a friend or classmate and then applying it to the actual situation or relationship in your life in which you're experiencing conflict.

8.2 College Stress: Identifying Potential Sources and Possible Solutions

Read through the following 29 college stressors and rate them in terms of how stressful each one is for you on a scale from 1 to 5 (1 = lowest, 5 = highest):

Potential Stressors	*Stress Rating*				
Tests and exams	1	2	3	4	5
Assignments	1	2	3	4	5
Class workload	1	2	3	4	5
Pace of courses	1	2	3	4	5
Performing up to expectations	1	2	3	4	5
Handling personal freedom	1	2	3	4	5
Time pressure (e.g., not enough time)	1	2	3	4	5
Organizational pressure (e.g., losing things)	1	2	3	4	5
Living independently	1	2	3	4	5
The future	1	2	3	4	5
Decisions about a major or career	1	2	3	4	5
Moral and ethical decisions	1	2	3	4	5
Finding meaning in life	1	2	3	4	5
Emotional issues	1	2	3	4	5
Physical health	1	2	3	4	5
Social life	1	2	3	4	5
Intimate relationships	1	2	3	4	5
Sexuality	1	2	3	4	5
Family responsibilities	1	2	3	4	5
Family conflicts	1	2	3	4	5
Family pressure	1	2	3	4	5
Peer pressure	1	2	3	4	5
Loneliness or isolation	1	2	3	4	5
Roommate conflicts	1	2	3	4	5
Conflict with professors	1	2	3	4	5
Campus policies or procedures	1	2	3	4	5
Transportation	1	2	3	4	5
Technology	1	2	3	4	5
Safety	1	2	3	4	5

Review your ratings and write down three of your top (highest-rated) stressors. Identify (a) a coping strategy you may use on your own to deal with that source of stress and (b) a campus resource you could use to obtain help with that source of stress.

Stressor: _____

Individual coping strategy:

Campus coping resource:

Stressor: _____

Individual coping strategy:

Campus coping resource:

Stressor: _____

Individual coping strategy:

Campus coping resource:

Caught Between a Rock and a Hard Place: Romantic versus Academic Commitments

Lauren has been dating her boyfriend (Nick) for about 2 months. She's convinced this is the real thing and that she's definitely in love. Lately, Nick has been asking her to skip class to spend more time with him. He tells Lauren, "If you really love me, you would do it for our relationship." Lauren feels that Nick truly loves her and wouldn't do anything to hurt her or interfere with her goals. So she figures that skipping a few classes to spend time with her boyfriend is the right choice. However, Lauren's grades soon start to slip; at the same time, Nick starts to demand that she spend even more time with him.

Reflection and Discussion Questions

1. What concerns you most about Lauren's behavior?

2. What concerns you most about Nick's behavior?

3. Would you agree with Lauren's decision to start skipping classes?

4. What might Lauren do to keep her grades up and still keep her relationship with Nick strong?

5. If you were Lauren's friend, what advice would you give her?

6. If you were Nick's friend, what advice would you give him?

Diversity

Learning About and from Human Differences

Complete the following sentence:

When I hear the word "diversity," the first thoughts that come to my mind are . . .

_____

_____

_____

LEARNING GOAL

To help you appreciate the value of human differences and acquire skills for making the most of diversity in college and beyond.

◆ The Spectrum of Diversity

The word "diversity" derives from the Latin root *diversus*, meaning "various." Thus, human diversity refers to the variety of differences that exist among the people who comprise humanity (the human species). In this chapter, we use "diversity" to refer primarily to differences among the major groups of people who, collectively, comprise humankind or humanity. The relationship between diversity and humanity is represented visually in **Figure 9.1**.

The relationship between humanity and human diversity is similar to the relationship between sunlight and the spectrum of colors. Just as the sunlight passing through a prism is dispersed into all groups of colors that make up the visual spectrum, the human species that's spread across the planet is dispersed into all groups of people that make up the human spectrum (humanity).

As you can see in Figure 9.1, groups of people differ from one another in numerous ways, including physical features, religious beliefs, mental and physical abilities, national origins, social backgrounds, gender, and sexual orientation.

Since diversity has been interpreted (and misinterpreted) in different ways by different people, we begin by defining some key terms related to diversity that should lead to a clearer understanding of its true meaning and value.

> "We are all brothers and sisters. Each face in the rainbow of color that populates our world is precious and special. Each adds to the rich treasure of humanity."
>
> –Morris Dees, civil rights leader and cofounder of the Southern Poverty Law Center

What Is Race?

A racial group (race) is a group of people who share some distinctive physical traits, such as skin color or facial characteristics. The U.S. Census Bureau (2000) identifies three races: White, Black, and Asian. However, as Anderson

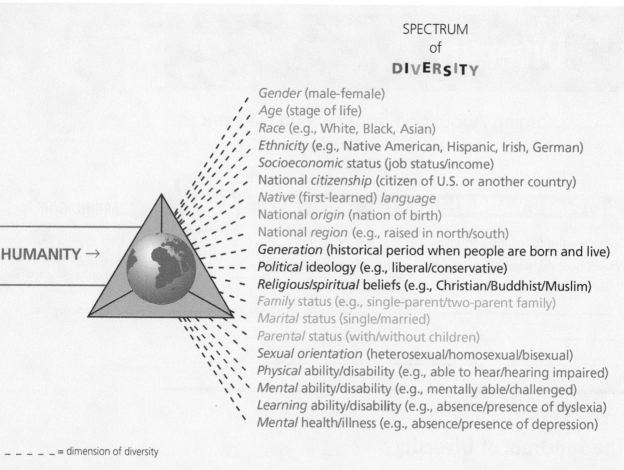

SPECTRUM
of
DIVERSITY

Gender (male-female)
Age (stage of life)
Race (e.g., White, Black, Asian)
Ethnicity (e.g., Native American, Hispanic, Irish, German)
Socioeconomic status (job status/income)
National *citizenship* (citizen of U.S. or another country)
Native (first-learned) *language*
National *origin* (nation of birth)
National *region* (e.g., raised in north/south)
Generation (historical period when people are born and live)
Political ideology (e.g., liberal/conservative)
Religious/spiritual beliefs (e.g., Christian/Buddhist/Muslim)
Family status (e.g., single-parent/two-parent family)
Marital status (single/married)
Parental status (with/without children)
Sexual orientation (heterosexual/homosexual/bisexual)
Physical ability/disability (e.g., able to hear/hearing impaired)
Mental ability/disability (e.g., mentally able/challenged)
Learning ability/disability (e.g., absence/presence of dyslexia)
Mental health/illness (e.g., absence/presence of depression)

HUMANITY →

_ _ _ _ _ _ = dimension of diversity

*This list represents some of the major dimensions of human diversity; it does not represent a complete list of all possible forms of human diversity. Also, disagreement exists about certain dimensions of diversity (e.g., whether certain groups should be considered races or ethnic groups).

Figure 9.1   Humanity and Diversity

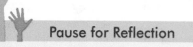

Pause for Reflection

Look at the diversity spectrum in Figure 9.1 and look over the list of groups that make up the spectrum. Do you notice any groups that are missing from the list that should be added, either because they have distinctive backgrounds or because they have been targets of prejudice and discrimination?

and Fienberg (2000) caution, racial categories are social–political constructs (concepts) that are not scientifically based but socially determined. There continues to be disagreement among scholars about what groups of people constitute a human race or whether distinctive races exist (Wheelright, 2005). No genes differentiate one race from another. In other words, you couldn't do a blood test or any type of internal genetic test to determine a person's race. Humans have simply decided to categorize people into races on the basis of certain external differences in physical appearance, particularly the color of their outer layer of skin. The U.S. Census Bureau could just as easily have divided people into categories based on such physical characteristics as eye color (blue, brown, and green) or hair texture (straight, wavy, curly, and frizzy).

The differences in skin color that now occur among humans are likely due to biological adaptations that evolved over long periods among

Personal Experience	My mother was from Alabama and was dark in skin color, with high cheek

bones and long curly black hair. My father stood approximately 6 feet and had light brown straight hair. His skin color was that of a Western European with a slight suntan. If you did not know that my father was of African American descent, you would not have thought of him as Black. All of my life I have thought of myself as African American, and all of the people who are familiar with me thought of me as African American. I have lived half of a century with that as my racial description. Several years ago, after carefully looking through records available on births and deaths in my family history, I discovered that fewer than 50 percent of my ancestors were of African lineage. Biologically, I am no longer Black. Socially and emotionally, I still am. Clearly, race is more of a social concept than a biological fact.

—Aaron Thompson

groups of humans who lived in regions of the world with different climatic conditions. For instance, darker skin tones developed among humans who inhabited and reproduced in hotter regions nearer the equator (e.g., Africans), where darker skin enabled them to adapt and survive by providing their bodies with better protection from the potentially damaging effects of the sun (Bridgeman, 2003) and allowing their bodies to better use the vitamin D supplied by sunlight (Jablonski & Chaplin, 2002). In contrast, lighter skin tones developed over time among humans inhabiting colder climates that were farther from the equator (e.g., Scandinavia) to enable their bodies to absorb greater amounts of sunlight, which was in shorter supply in their region of the world.

While humans may display diversity in skin color or tone, the biological reality is that all members of the human species are remarkably similar. More than 98 percent of the genes that make up humans from different racial groups are the same (Bridgeman, 2003; Molnar, 1991). This large amount of genetic overlap among humans accounts for the many similarities that exist, regardless of what differences in color appear at the surface of skin. For example, all people have similar external features that give them a human appearance and clearly distinguish people from other animal species, all humans have internal organs that are similar in structure and function, and regardless of the color of their outer layer of skin, when it's cut, all humans bleed in the same color.

What Is Culture?

"Culture" may be defined as a distinctive pattern of beliefs and values learned by a group of people who share a social heritage and traditions. In short, culture is the whole way in which a group of people has learned to live (Peoples & Bailey, 1998); it includes style of speaking (language), fashion, food, art, music, values, and beliefs.

Cultural differences can exist within the same society (multicultural society), within a single nation (domestic diversity), or across different nations (international diversity).

Pause for Reflection

What race do you consider yourself to be? Would you say you identify strongly with your race, or are you rarely conscious of it?

I was proofreading this chapter while sitting in a coffee shop in the Chicago O'Hare airport. I looked up from my work for a second and saw what appeared to be a while girl about 18 years old. As I lowered by head to return to my work, I did a double-take to look at her again because something about her seemed different or unusual. When I looked at her more closely the second time, I noticed that although she had white skin, the features of her face and hair appeared to be those of an African American. After a couple of seconds of puzzlement, I figured it out: she was an albino African American. That satisfied me for the moment, but then I began to wonder: Would it still be accurate to say that she is Black even though her skin is white? Would her hair and facial features be sufficient for her to be considered or classified as Black? If yes, then what about someone who had a black skin tone but did not have the typical hair and facial features characteristic of Black people? Is skin color the defining feature of being African American, or are other features equally important? I was unable to answer these questions, but I found it amusing that these thoughts were taking place while I was working on a book dealing with diversity. Later, on the plane ride home, I thought again about that albino African American girl and realized that she was a perfect example of how classifying people into races is based not on objective, scientifically determined evidence but on subjective, socially constructed categories.

—Joe Cuseo

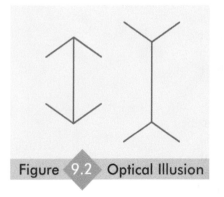

Figure 9.2 Optical Illusion

A major advantage of culture is that it helps bind its members together into a supportive, tight-knit community; however, it can blind them to other cultural perspectives. Since culture shapes the way people think, it can cause groups of people to view the world solely through their own cultural lens or frame of reference (Colombo, Cullen, & Lisle, 1995). Optical illusions are a good illustration of how cultural perspectives can blind people, or lead them to inaccurate perceptions. For instance, compare the lengths of the two lines in **Figure 9.2**.

If you perceive the line on the right to be longer than the line on the left, welcome to the club. Virtually all Americans and people from Western cultures perceive the line on the right to be longer. Actually, both lines are equal in length. (If you don't believe it, take out a ruler and check it out.) Interestingly, this perceptual error is not made by people from non-Western cultures who live in environments populated with circular structures rather than structures with linear patterns and angled corners, like Westerners use (Segall, Campbell, & Herskovits, 1966).

The key point underlying this optical illusion is that cultural experiences shape and sometimes distort perceptions of reality. People think they are seeing things objectively or as they really are, but they are often seeing things subjectively from their limited cultural vantage point. Being open to the viewpoints of diverse people who perceive the world from different cultural vantage points widens the range of perception and helps people overcome their cultural blind spots. As a result, people tend to perceive the world around them with greater clarity and accuracy.

"We see what is behind our eyes."

—Chinese proverb

Remember

One person's reality is not everyone's reality; current perceptions of the outside world are shaped (and sometime distorted) by prior cultural experiences.

What Is an Ethnic Group?

An ethnic group (ethnicity) is a group of people who share the same culture. Thus, culture refers to what an ethnic group has in common and an ethnic group refers to people who share the same culture. Unlike a racial group, whose members share physical characteristics that they are born with and that have been passed on biologically, an ethnic group's shared characteristics have been passed on through socialization—that is, their common characteristics have been learned or acquired through shared social experiences.

Major ethnic groups in the United States include the following:

Culture is a distinctive pattern of beliefs and values that develop among a group of people who share the same social heritage and traditions.

- Native Americans (American Indians)
  - Cherokee, Navaho, Hopi, Alaskan natives, Blackfoot, etc.
- African Americans (Blacks)
  - People who have cultural roots in the continent of Africa, the Caribbean islands, etc.
- Hispanic Americans (Latinos)
  - People who have cultural roots in Mexico, Puerto Rico, Central America, South America, etc.
- Asian Americans
  - Cultural descendents from Japan, China, Korea, Vietnam, etc.
- European Americans (Whites)
  - Descendents from Scandinavia, England, Ireland, Germany, Italy, etc.

Currently, European Americans are the majority ethnic group in the United States because they account for more than 50 percent of the American population. Native Americans, African Americans, Hispanic Americans, and Asian Americans are considered to be ethnic minority groups because each of these groups represents less than 50 percent of the American population.

As with the concept of race, whether a particular group of people is defined as an ethnic group can be arbitrary, subjective, and interpreted differently by different groups of people. Currently, the only races recognized by the U.S. Census Bureau are White, Black, and Asian; Hispanic is not defined as a race but is classified as an ethnic group. However, among those who checked "some other race" in the 2000 Census, 97 percent were Hispanic. This fact has been viewed by Hispanic advocates as a desire for their ethnic group to be reclassified as a racial group (Cianciotto, 2005).

This disagreement illustrates how difficult it is to conveniently categorize groups of people into particular racial or ethnic groups. The United States will continue to struggle with this issue because the ethnic and racial diversity of its population is growing and members of different ethnic and racial groups are forming cross-ethnic and interracial families. Thus, it is becoming progressively more difficult to place people into distinct categories based on their race or ethnicity. For example, by 2050, the number of people who will identify themselves as being of two or more races is projected to more than triple, growing from 5.2 million to 16.2 million (U.S. Census Bureau, 2008).

Pause for Reflection

Which ethnic group or groups do you belong to or identify with?

What are the most common cultural values shared by your ethnic group or groups?

Student Perspective

"I'm the only person from my 'race' in class."

—Hispanic student commenting on why he felt uncomfortable in his Race, Ethnicity, & Gender class

Personal Experience   As the child of a Black man and a White woman, someone who was born in the racial melting pot of Hawaii, with a sister who's half Indonesian but who's usually mistaken for Mexican or Puerto Rican and a brother-in-law and niece of Chinese descent, with some blood relatives who resemble Margaret Thatcher and others who could pass for Bernie Mac, family get-togethers over Christmas take on the appearance of a UN General Assembly meeting. I've never had the option of restricting my loyalties on the basis of race, or measuring my worth on the basis of tribe.

—Barack Obama (2006)

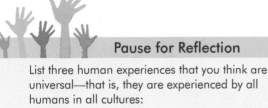

Pause for Reflection

List three human experiences that you think are universal—that is, they are experienced by all humans in all cultures:

1.

2.

3.

What Is Humanity?

It is important to realize that human variety and human similarity coexist and complement each other. Diversity is a "value that is shown in mutual respect and appreciation of similarities and differences" (Public Service Enterprise Group, 2009. Experiencing diversity not only enhances appreciation of the unique features of different cultures but also provides a larger perspective on the universal aspects of the human experience that are common to all humans, no matter what their particular cultural background may be. For example, despite racial and cultural differences, all people express the same emotions with the same facial expressions (see **Figure 9.3**).

Other human characteristics that anthropologists have found to be shared across all groups of people in every corner of the world include storytelling, poetry, adornment of the body, dance, music, decoration of artifacts, families, socialization of children by elders, a sense of right and wrong, supernatural beliefs, explanations of diseases and death, and mourning of the dead (Pinker, 1994). Although different ethnic groups may express these shared experiences in different ways, these universal experiences are common to all humans.

Remember

Diversity represents variations on the common theme of humanity. Although people have different cultural backgrounds, they are still cultivated from the same soil—they are all grounded in the common experience of being human.

"We are all the same, and we are all unique."

–Georgia Dunston, African American biologist and research specialist in human genetics

Thus, different cultures associated with different ethnic groups may be viewed simply as variations on the same theme: being human. You may have heard the question, "We're all human, aren't we?" The answer to this important question is "yes and no." Yes, humans are all the same, but not in the same way.

A good metaphor for understanding this apparent contradiction is to visualize humanity as a quilt in which we are all joined by the common thread of humanity—by the common bond of being human. Yet the different patches that make up the quilt represent diversity—the distinctive or unique cultures

Humans all over the world display the same facial expressions when experiencing certain emotions. See if you can detect the emotions being expressed in the following faces. (To find the answers, turn your book upside down.)

Answers: The emotions shown. Top, left to right; anger, fear, and sadness. Bottom, left to right; disgust, happiness, and surprise.

Figure 9.3

that comprise our common humanity. The quilt metaphor acknowledges the identity and beauty of all cultures. It differs from the old American melting pot metaphor, which viewed differences as something that should be melted down or eliminated, or the salad bowl metaphor, which suggested that America is a hodgepodge or mishmash of cultures thrown together without any common connection. In contrast, the quilt metaphor suggests that the cultures of different ethnic groups should be recognized and celebrated. Nevertheless, differences can be woven together to create a unified whole—as in the Latin expression *E pluribus unum* ("Out of many, one"), the motto of the United States, which you will find printed on all U.S. coins.

To appreciate diversity and its relationship to humanity is to capitalize on the power of differences (diversity) while still preserving collective strength through unity (humanity).

> "
> *"We have become not a melting pot but a beautiful mosaic."*
> —Jimmy Carter, 39th president of the United States and winner of the Nobel Peace Prize

> ! **Remember**
>
> By learning about diversity (differences), people simultaneously learn about their commonality (shared humanity).

Personal Experience

When I was 12 years old and living in New York City, I returned from school one Friday afternoon and my mother asked me if anything interesting happened at school that day. I mentioned to her that the teacher went around the room, asking students what we had eaten for dinner the night before. At that moment, my mother began to become a bit agitated and nervously asked me, "What did you tell the teacher?" I said, "I told her and the rest of the class that I had pasta last night because my family always eats pasta on Thursdays and Sundays." My mother exploded and fired back at me, "Why couldn't you tell her that we had steak or roast beef!" For a moment, I was stunned and couldn't figure out what I had done wrong or why I should have lied about eating pasta. Then it suddenly dawned on me: My mother was embarrassed about being an Italian American. She wanted me to hide our family's ethnic background and make it sound like we were very "American." A few moments later, it also became clear to me why her maiden name was changed from the Italian-sounding DeVigilio to the more American-sounding Vigilis, and why her first name was changed from Carmella to Mildred (and why my father's first name was also changed from Biaggio to Blase). Their generation wanted to minimize discrimination and maximize their assimilation (absorption) into American culture.

I never forgot this incident because it was such an emotionally intense experience. For the first time in my life, I became aware that my mother was ashamed of being a member of the same group to which every other member of my family belonged, including me. After her outburst, I felt a combined rush of astonishment and embarrassment. However, these feelings eventually faded and my mother's reaction ended up having the opposite effect on me. Instead of making me feel inferior or ashamed about being Italian American, her reaction that day caused me to become more aware of, and take more pride in, my Italian heritage.

Student Perspective

When you see me, do not look
    at me with disgrace.
Know that I am an African-
    American
Birthed by a woman of style
    and grace.
Be proud
    To stand by my side.
Hold your head high Like me.
Be proud.
    To say you know me.
Just as I stand by you, proud
    to be me.

—Poem by Brittany Beard, first-year student

As I grew older, I also grew to understand why my mother felt the way she did. She grew up in America's melting pot era—a time when different American ethnic groups were expected to melt down and melt away their ethnicity. They were not to celebrate diversity; they were to eliminate it.

—Joe Cuseo

What Is Individuality?

It's important to keep in mind that the individual differences within the same racial or ethnic group are greater than the average differences between two different groups. For example, although you live in a world that is conscious of differences among races, differences in physical attributes (e.g., height and weight) and behavior patterns (e.g., personality characteristics) among individuals within the same racial group are greater than the average differences among various racial groups (Caplan & Caplan, 1994).

As you proceed through this chapter, keep in mind the following distinctions among humanity, diversity, and individuality:

- **Diversity.** We are all members of *different groups* (e.g., different gender and ethnic groups).
- **Humanity.** We are all members of the *same group* (the human species).
- **Individuality.** Each of us is a *unique person* who is different from any person in any group to which we may belong.

> "Every human is, at the same time, like all other humans, like some humans, and like no other human."
>
> –Clyde Kluckholn, American anthropologist

◆ Major Forms or Types of Diversity

International Diversity

Moving beyond your particular country of citizenship, you are also a member of an international world that includes multiple nations. Global interdependence and international collaboration are needed to solve current international problems, such as global warming and terrorism. Communication and interaction across nations are now greater than at any other time in world history, largely because of rapid advances in electronic technology (Dryden & Vos, 1999; Smith, 1994). Economic boundaries between nations are also breaking down due to increasing international travel, international trading, and development of multinational corporations. Today's world really is a small world after all, and success in it requires an international perspective. By learning from and about different nations, you become more than a citizen of your own country; you become cosmopolitan—a citizen of the world.

Taking an international perspective allows you to appreciate the diversity of humankind. If it were possible to reduce the world's population to a village of precisely 100 people, with all existing human ratios remaining the same, the demographics of this world village would look something like this:

60 Asians, 14 Africans, 12 Europeans, 8 Latin Americans, 5 from the United States and Canada, and 1 from the South Pacific.
  51 males, 49 females
  82 non-Whites, 18 Whites
  67 non-Christians, 33 Christians
  80 living in substandard housing
  67 unable to read
  50 malnourished and 1 dying of starvation
  33 without access to a safe water supply
  39 who lack access to improved sanitation
  24 without any electricity (and of the 76 who do have electricity, most would only use it for light at night)
  7 with access to the Internet
  1 with a college education
  1 with HIV
  2 near birth; 1 near death
  5 who control 32 percent of the entire world's wealth; all 5 would be citizens of the United States
  33 who receive and attempt to live on just 3 percent of the world village's income

Source: Family Care Foundation (2005).

Ethnic and Racial Diversity

America is rapidly becoming a more racially and ethnically diverse nation. In 2008, the minority population in the United States reached an all-time high of 34 percent of the total population. The population of ethnic minorities is now growing at a much faster rate than the White majority. This trend is expected to continue, and by the middle of the twenty-first century, the minority population will have grown from one-third of the U.S. population to more than one-half (54 percent), with more than 60 percent of the nation's children expected to be members of minority groups (U.S. Census Bureau, 2008).

By 2050, the U.S. population is projected to be more than 30 percent Hispanic (up from 15 percent in 2008), 15 percent Black (up from 13 percent), 9.6 percent Asian (up from 5.3 percent), and 2 percent Native Americans (up from 1.6 percent). The native Hawaiian and Pacific Islander population is expected to more than double between 2008 and 2050. In the same time frame, the percentage of Americans who are White will drop from 66 percent (2008) to 46 percent (2050). As a result of these population trends, ethnic and racial minorities will become the new majority because they will constitute the majority of Americans by the middle of the twenty-first century. (See **Figure 9.4**.)

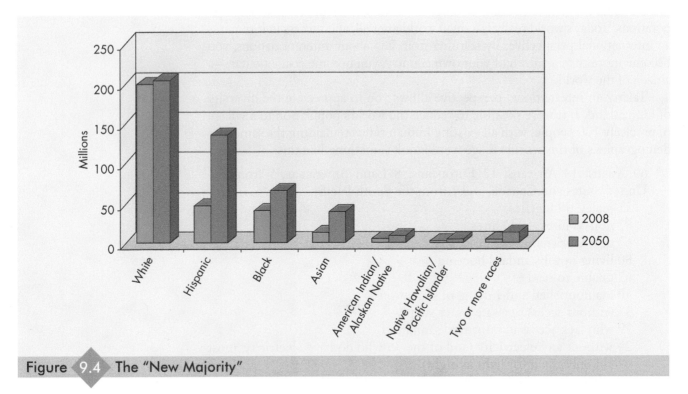

Figure **9.4** The "New Majority"

Generational Diversity

Humans are also diverse with respect to the generation in which they grew up. "Generation" refers to individuals born during the same historical period and may have developed similar attitudes, values, and habits based on the similar events that took place in the world during their formative years of development. Each generation experiences different historical events, so it's likely that generations will develop different attitudes and behaviors as a result.

Snapshot Summary 9.1 provides a brief summary of the major generations, the key historical events that occurred during the formative periods of the people in each generation, and the personal characteristics that have been associated with a particular generation (Lancaster & Stillman, 2002).

Snapshot Summary   9.1

Generational Diversity

- **The Traditional Generation, a.k.a. the Silent Generation** (born 1922–1945). This generation was influenced by events such as the Great Depression and World Wars I and II. Characteristics associated with this generation include loyalty, patriotism, respect for authority, and conservatism.
- **The Baby Boomer Generation** (born 1946–1964). This generation was influenced by events such as the Vietnam War, Watergate, and the human rights movement. Characteristics associated with this generation include idealism, personal fulfillment, and a concern for equal rights.
- **Generation X** (born 1965–1980). This generation was influenced by Sesame Street, the creation of MTV, AIDS, and soaring divorce rates that produced the first generation of latchkey children, who let themselves into their home after school (with their own key) because their parents, or their single parent, would be out working. Characteristics associated with this generation include self-reliance, resourcefulness, and being comfortable with change.

- **Generation Y, a.k.a. Millennials** (born 1981–2002). This generation was influenced by the September 11, 2001, terrorist attack on the United States, the shooting of students at Columbine High School, and the collapse of the Enron Corporation. Characteristics associated with this generation include a preference for working and playing in groups, being technologically savvy, and a willingness to provide volunteer service in their community (the civic generation). They are also the most ethnically diverse generation, which may explain why they are more open to diversity and see it as a positive experience.

"

"I don't even know what that means."

–Comment made by 38-year-old basketball coach after hearing one of his younger players say, "I'm trying to find my mojo and get my swag back."

Source: Lancaster & Stillman (2002).

◆ Diversity and the College Experience

There are more than 3,000 public and private colleges in the United States. They vary in size (small to large) and location (urban, suburban, and rural), as well as in their purpose or mission (research universities, comprehensive state universities, liberal arts colleges, and community colleges). This variety makes the American higher-education system the most diverse and accessible in the world. The diversity of educational opportunities in American colleges and universities reflects the freedom of opportunity in the United States as a democratic nation (American Council on Education, 2008).

Pause for Reflection

Look back at the characteristics associated with your generation. Which of these characteristics most accurately reflect your attitudes, values, or personality traits?

Which clearly do not?

Pause for Reflection

1. What diverse groups do you see represented on your campus?

2. Are there groups on your campus that you did not expect to see or to see in such large numbers?

3. Are there groups on your campus that you expected to see but do not see or see in smaller numbers than you expected?

America's system of higher education is also becoming more diverse with respect to the variety of people enrolled in it. College students in the United States are growing more diverse with respect to age; almost 40 percent of all undergraduate students in America are 25 years of age or older, compared to 28 percent in 1970 (U.S. Department of Education, 2002). The ethnic and racial diversity of students in American colleges and universities is also rapidly rising. In 1960, Whites made up almost 95 percent of the total college population; in 2005, that percentage had decreased to 69 percent. At the same time, the percentage of Asian, Hispanic, Black, and Native American students attending college increased (Chronicle of Higher Education, 2003).

◆ The Benefits of Experiencing Diversity

Diversity Promotes Self-Awareness

Learning from people with diverse backgrounds and experiences sharpens your self-knowledge and self-insight by allowing you to compare and contrast your life experiences with life experiences of others that differ sharply from your own. This comparative perspective gives you a reference point for viewing your own life, which places you in a better position to see more clearly how your unique cultural background has influenced the development of your personal beliefs, values, and lifestyle. By viewing your life in relation to the lives of others, you see more clearly what is distinctive about yourself and how you may be uniquely advantaged or disadvantaged.

When students around the country were interviewed about their diversity experiences in college, they reported that these experiences often helped them learn more about themselves and that their interactions with students from different races and ethnic groups produced unexpected or jarring self-insights (Light, 2001).

Student Perspective

"I remember that my self-image was being influenced by the media. I got the impression that women had to look a certain way. I dyed my hair, wore different clothes, more makeup . . . all because magazines, TV, [and] music videos 'said' that was beautiful. Luckily, when I was 15, I went to Brazil and saw a different, more natural beauty and came back to America more as myself. I let go of the hold the media image had on me."

—First-year college student

Remember

The more opportunities you create to learn from others who are different from yourself, the more opportunities you create to learn about yourself.

Diversity Enriches a College Education

"Without exception, the observed changes [during college] involve greater breadth, expansion, and appreciation for the new and different."

—Ernest Pascarella and Pat Terenzini, How College Affects Students (xxxx)

Diversity magnifies the power of a college education because it helps liberate you from the tunnel vision of ethnocentricity (culture-centeredness) and egocentricity (self-centeredness), enabling you to get beyond yourself and your own culture to see yourself in relation to the world around you. Just as the various subjects you take in the college curriculum open your mind to multiple perspectives, so does your experience with people from varied backgrounds; it equips you with a wide-focus lens that allows you to take a multicultural perspective. A multicultural perspective helps you become aware of cultural blind spots and avoid the dangers of group think—the tendency for tight groups of people to think so much alike that they overlook flaws in their thinking that can lead to poor choices and faulty decisions (Janis, 1982).

Diversity Strengthens Learning and Critical Thinking

Research consistently shows that people learn more from those who are different from them than from those who are similar to them (Pascarella, 2001; Pascarella & Terenzini, 2005). When your brain encounters something that is unfamiliar or different from what you're accustomed to, you must stretch beyond your mental comfort zone and work harder to understand it because doing so forces you to compare and contrast it to what you already know (Acredolo & O'Connor, 1991; Nagda, Gurin, & Johnson, 2005). This mental stretch requires the use of extra psychological effort and energy, which strengthens and deepens learning.

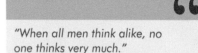

"When all men think alike, no one thinks very much."

–Walter Lippmann, distinguished journalist and originator of the term "stereotype"

A good example of how "group think" can lead to ethnocentric decisions that are ineffective (and unjust).

Diversity Promotes Creative Thinking

Experiences with diversity supply you with broader base of knowledge and wider range of thinking styles that better enable you to think outside your own cultural box or boundaries. In contrast, limiting your number of cultural vantage points is akin to limiting the variety of mental tools you can use to solve new problems, thereby limiting your creativity. When like-minded people only associate with other like-minded people, they're unlikely to think outside the box.

Drawing on different ideas from people with diverse backgrounds and bouncing your ideas off them is a great way to generate energy, synergy, and serendipity—unanticipated discoveries and creative solutions.

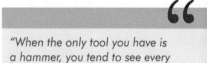

"When the only tool you have is a hammer, you tend to see every problem as a nail."

–Abraham Maslow, humanistic psychologist, best known for his self-actualization theory of achieving human potential

Diversity Enhances Career Preparation and Success

Learning about and from diversity has a practical benefit: It better prepares you for the world of work. Whatever career you choose to pursue, you are likely find yourself working with employers, employees, co-workers, customers, and clients from diverse cultural backgrounds. America's workforce is now more diverse than at any other time in the nation's history, and it will grow ever more diverse. For example, the percentage of America's working-age population that represents members of minority groups is expected to grow from 34 percent in 2008 to 55 percent in 2050 (U.S. Bureau of Labor Statistics, 2009).

In addition to increasing diversity in America, today's work world is characterized by a global economy. Greater economic interdependence among nations, more international trading (imports and exports), more multinational corporations, and almost-instantaneous worldwide communication increasingly occur—thanks to advances in the World Wide Web (Dryden & Vos, 1999; Smith, 1994). Because of these trends, employers of college graduates now seek job candidates with the following skills and attributes: sensitivity to human differences, the ability to understand and relate to people from different cultural backgrounds, international knowledge, and foreign language skills (Fixman, 1990; National Association of Colleges & Employers, 2003; Office of Research, 1994; Smith, 1997). In one national survey, policymakers, business leaders, and employers all agreed that college graduates should be more than just aware or tolerant of diversity; they should have experience with diversity (Education Commission of the States, 1995).

> "Empirical evidence shows that the actual effects on student development of emphasizing diversity and of student participation in diversity activities are overwhelmingly positive."
>
> –Alexander Astin, *What Matters in College* (1993)

Remember

The wealth of diversity on college campuses today represents an unprecedented educational opportunity. You may never again be a member of a community that includes so many people from such a rich variety of backgrounds. Seize this opportunity! You're now in the right place at the right time to experience the people and programs that can infuse and enrich the quality of your college education with diversity.

Pause for Reflection

Have you ever been stereotyped, such as based on your appearance or group membership? If so, how did it make you feel and how did you react?

Have you ever unintentionally perceived or treated someone in terms of a group stereotype rather than as an individual? What assumptions did you make about that person? Was that person aware of, or affected by, your stereotyping?

◆ Stumbling Blocks and Barriers to Experiencing Diversity

Stereotypes

The word "stereotype" derives from a combination of two roots: *stereo* (to look at in a fixed way) and *type* (to categorize or group together, as in the word "typical"). Thus, stereotyping is viewing individuals of the same type (group) in the same (fixed) way.

In effect, stereotyping ignores or disregards a person's individuality; instead, all people who share a similar group characteristic (e.g., race or gender) are viewed as having the same personal characteristics—as in the expression, "You know what they are like; they're all the same." Stereotypes involve bias, which literally means "slant." A bias can be either positive or negative. Positive bias results in a favorable stereotype (e.g., "Italians are great lovers"); negative bias produces an unfavorable stereotype (e.g., "Italians are in the Mafia"). **Box 9.1** lists some common stereotypes.

9.1

Examples of Common Stereotypes

Muslims are terrorists.
Whites can't jump (or dance).
Blacks are lazy.
Asians are brilliant in math.
Irish are alcoholics.
Gay men are feminine; lesbian women are masculine.
Jews are cheap.
Hispanic men are abusive to women.
Men are strong.
Women are weak.

Whether you are male or female, don't let gender stereotypes limit your career options.

Personal Experience

When I was 6 years old, I was told by another 6-year-old from a different racial group that all people of my race could not swim. Since I could not swim at that time and she could, I assumed she was correct. I asked a boy, who happened to be of the same racial group as that little girl, if that statement were true; he responded: "Yes, it is true." Since I was from an area where few other African Americans were around to counteract this belief about Blacks, I bought into this stereotype until I finally took swimming lessons as an adult. I am now a lousy swimmer after many lessons because I did not even attempt to swim until I was an adult. The moral of this story is that group stereotypes can limit the confidence and potential of individuals who are members of the stereotyped group.

—Aaron Thompson

"Let us all hope that the dark clouds of racial prejudice will soon pass away and the deep fog of misunderstanding will be lifted from our fear-drenched communities, and in some not too distant tomorrow the radiant stars of love and brotherhood will shine over our great nation."

–Martin Luther King Jr., civil rights activist and clergyman

Prejudice

If virtually all members of a stereotyped group are judged or evaluated in a negative way, the result is prejudice. (The word "prejudice" literally means to "pre-judge.") Technically, prejudice may be either positive or negative; however, the term is most often associated with a negative prejudgment or stigmatizing—associating inferior or unfavorable traits with people who belong to the same group. Thus, prejudice may be defined as a negative

Pause for Reflection

Prejudice and discrimination can be subtle and only begin to surface when the social or emotional distance among members of different groups grows closer. Rate your level of comfort with the following situations:

Someone from another racial group

1. going to your school;	high moderate low
2. working in your place of employment;	high moderate low
3. living on your street as a neighbor;	high moderate low
4. living with you as a roommate;	high moderate low
5. socializing with you as a personal friend;	high moderate low
6. being your most intimate friend or romantic partner; or	high moderate low
7. being your partner in marriage.	high moderate low

For any item you rated "low," what do you think was responsible for the low rating?

judgment, attitude, or belief about another person or group of people, which is formed before the facts are known. Stereotyping and prejudice often go hand in hand because individuals who are placed in a negatively stereotyped group are commonly prejudged in a negative way.

Someone with a prejudice toward a group typically avoids contact with individuals from that group. This enables the prejudice to continue unchallenged because there is little chance for the prejudiced person to have positive experiences with a member of the stigmatized group that could contradict or disprove the prejudice. Thus, a vicious cycle is established in which the prejudiced person continues to avoid contact with individuals from the stigmatized group, which, in turn, continues to maintain and reinforce the prejudice.

Discrimination

Literally translated, the term "discrimination" means "division" or "separation." Whereas prejudice involves a belief or opinion, discrimination involves an action taken toward others. Technically, discrimination can be either negative or positive—for example, a discriminating eater may be careful about eating only healthy foods. However, the term is most often associated with a negative action that results in a prejudiced person treating another person, or group of people, in an unfair way. Thus, it could be said that discrimination is prejudice put into action. Hate crimes are examples of extreme discrimination because they are acts motivated solely by prejudice against members of a stigmatized group. Victims of hate crimes may have their personal property damaged or they may be physically assaulted, sometimes referred to as gay bashing if the victim is a homosexual. Other forms of discrimination are more subtle and may take place without people being fully aware that they are discriminating. For example, evidence shows that some White, male college professors tend to treat female students and students from ethnic or racial minority groups differently from the way they treat males and nonminority students. In particular, females and minority students in classes taught by White, male instructors tend to:

- Receive less eye contact from the instructor;
- Be called on less frequently in class;
- Be given less time to respond to questions asked by the instructor in class; and
- Have less contact with the instructor outside of class (Hall & Sandler, 1982, 1984; Sedlacek, 1987; Wright, 1987).

In most of these cases, the discriminatory treatment received by these female and minority students was subtle and not done consciously or deliberately by the instructors (Green, 1989). Nevertheless, these unintended actions are still discriminatory, and they may send a message to minority and female students that their ideas are not worth hearing or that they are not as capable as other students (Sadker & Sadker, 1994).

Snapshot Summary

9.2

Stereotypes and Prejudiced Belief Systems About Group Inferiority

- **Ethnocentrism.** Considering one's own culture or ethnic group to be central or normal, and viewing different cultures as deficient or inferior. For example, people who are ethnocentric might claim that another culture is weird or abnormal for eating certain animals that they consider unethical to eat, even though they eat certain animals that the other culture would consider unethical to eat.

- **Racism.** Prejudice or discrimination based on skin color. For example, Cecil Rhodes (Englishman and empire builder of British South Africa), once claimed, "We [the British] are the finest race in the world and the more of the world we inhabit the better it is for the human race." Currently, racism is exemplified by the Ku Klux Klan, a domestic terrorist group that believes in the supremacy of the White race and considers all other races to be inferior.

"The Constitution of the United States knows no distinction between citizens on account of color."

—Frederick Douglass, abolitionist, author, advocate for equal rights for all people, and former slave

- **Classism.** Prejudice or discrimination based on social class, particularly toward people of low socioeconomic status. For example, a classicist might focus only on the contributions made by politicians and wealthy industrialists to America, ignoring the contributions of poor immigrants, farmers, slaves, and pioneer women.

- **Nationalism.** Excessive interest and belief in the strengths of one's own nation without acknowledging its mistakes or weaknesses, the needs of other nations, or the common interests of all nations. For example, blind patriotism blinds people to the shortcomings of their own nation, causing patriots to view any questioning or criticism of their nation as disloyalty or unpatriotic (as in the slogans "America: right or wrong" and "America: love it or leave it!")

- **Regionalism.** Prejudice or discrimination based on the geographical region of a nation in which an individual has been born and raised. For example, a Northerner might think that all Southerners are racists.

Student Perspective

"I would like to change the entire world, so that we wouldn't be segregated by continents and territories."

—College sophomore

- **Religious Bigotry.** Denying the fundamental human right of other people to hold religious beliefs or to hold religious beliefs that differ from one's own. For example, an atheist might force nonreligious (secular) beliefs on others, or a member of a religious group may believe that people who hold different religious beliefs are immoral or sinners.

Student Perspective

"Most religions dictate that theirs is the only way, and without believing in it, you cannot enter the mighty Kingdom of Heaven. Who are we to judge? It makes more sense for God to be the only one mighty enough to make that decision. If other people could understand and see [it] from this perspective, then many religious arguments could be avoided."

—First-year college student

- **Xenophobia.** Extreme fear or hatred of foreigners, outsiders, or strangers. For example, someone might believe that all immigrants should be kept out of the country because they will increase the crime rate.

- **Anti-Semitism.** Prejudice or discrimination toward Jews or people who practice the religion of Judaism. For example, someone could claim to hate Jews because they're the ones who "killed Christ."
- **Genocide.** Mass murdering of one group by another group. An example is the Holocaust during World War II, in which millions of Jews were murdered. Other examples include the murdering of Cambodians under the Khmer Rouge, the murdering of Bosnian Muslims in the former country of Yugoslavia, and the slaughter of the Tutsi minority by the Hutu majority in Rwanda.
- **Terrorism.** Intentional acts of violence against civilians that are motivated by political or religious prejudice. An example would be the September 11, 2001, attacks on the United States.
- **Ageism.** Prejudice or discrimination based on age, particularly prejudice toward the elderly. For example, an ageist might believe that all elderly people are bad drivers with bad memories.

- **Ableism.** Prejudice or discrimination toward people who are disabled or handicapped—physically, mentally, or emotionally. For example, someone shows ableism by avoiding interaction with handicapped people because of anxiety about not knowing what to say or how to act around them.
- **Sexism.** Prejudice or discrimination based on sex or gender. For example, a sexist might believe that no one should vote for a female running for president because she would be too emotional.
- **Heterosexism.** Belief that heterosexuality is the only acceptable sexual orientation. For example, using the slang "fag" or "queer" as an insult or put down or believing that gays should not have the same legal rights and opportunities as heterosexuals shows heterosexism.
- **Homophobia.** Extreme fear or hatred of homosexuals. For example, people who engage in gay bashing (acts of violence toward gays) or who create and contribute to antigay Web sites show homophobia.

Pause for Reflection

Have you ever held a prejudice against a particular group of people?

If you have, what was the group, and how do you think your prejudice developed?

Student Perspective

"I grew up in a very racist family. Even just a year ago, I could honestly say 'I hate Asians' with a straight face and mean it. My senior AP language teacher tried hard to teach me not to be judgmental. He got me to be open to others, so much so that my current boyfriend is half Chinese!"

—First-year college student

The following practices and strategies may be used to accept and appreciate individuals from other groups toward whom you may hold prejudices, stereotypes, or subtle biases that bubble beneath the surface of your conscious awareness.

1. Consciously avoid preoccupation with physical appearances.

Go deeper and get beneath the superficial surface of appearances to judge people not in terms of how they look but in terms of whom they are and how they act. Remember the old proverb "It's what's inside that counts." Judge others by the quality of their personal character, not by the familiarity of their physical characteristics.

2. Perceive each person with whom you interact as having a unique personal identify.

Make a conscious effort to see each person with whom you interact not merely as a member of a same group but as a unique individual. Form your impressions of each person case by case rather than by using some rule of thumb.

This may seem like an obvious and easy thing to do, but research shows that humans have a natural tendency to perceive and conceive of individuals who are members of unfamiliar groups as being more alike (or all alike) than members of their own group (Taylor, Peplau, & Sears, 2006). Thus, you may have to consciously resist this tendency to overgeneralize and lump together individuals into homogenous groups; instead, make an intentional attempt to focus on treating each person you interact with as a unique human.

> **Remember**
>
> While it is valuable to learn about different cultures and the common characteristics shared by members of the same culture, differences exist among individuals who share the same culture. Don't assume that all individuals from the same cultural background share the same personal characteristics.

Interacting and Collaborating with Members of Diverse Groups

Once you overcome your biases and begin to perceive members of diverse groups as unique individuals, you are positioned to take the next step of interacting, collaborating, and forming friendships with them. Interpersonal contact between diverse people takes you beyond multicultural awareness and moves you up to a higher level of diversity appreciation that involves intercultural interaction. When you take this step to cross cultural boundaries, you transform diversity appreciation from a value or belief system into an observable action and way of living.

Your initial comfort level with interacting with people from diverse groups is likely to depend on how much experience you have had with diversity before college. If you have had little or no prior experience interacting with members of diverse groups, it may be more challenging for you to initiate interactions with diverse students on campus.

However, if you have had little previous experience with diversity, the good news is that you have the most to gain from interacting and collaborating with those of other ethnic or racial groups. Research consistently shows that when humans experience social interaction that differs radically from their prior experiences they gain the most in terms of learning and cognitive development (Acredolo & O'Connor, 1991; Piaget, 1985).

Meeting and Interacting with People from Diverse Backgrounds

1. Intentionally create opportunities for interaction and conversation with individuals from diverse groups.

Consciously resist the natural tendency to associate only with people who are similar to you. One way to do this is by intentionally placing yourself in situations where individuals from diverse groups are nearby and potential interaction can take place. Research indicates that meaningful interactions and friendships are more likely to form among people who are in physical

"The common eye sees only the outside of things, and judges by that. But the seeing eye pierces through and reads the heart and the soul, finding there capacities which the outside didn't indicate or promise."

–Samuel Clemens, a.k.a. Mark Twain; writer, lecturer, and humorist

"Stop judging by mere appearances, and make a right judgment."

–Bible, John 7:24

"You can't judge a book by the cover."

–Title of the 1962 hit song by Elias Bates, a.k.a. Bo Diddley (Note: A bo diddley is a one-stringed African guitar)

Student Perspective

"I am very happy with the diversity here, but it also frightens me. I have never been in a situation where I have met people who are Jewish, Muslim, atheist, born-again, and many more."

–First-year college student (Erickson, Peters, & Strommer, 2006)

Pause for Reflection

Rate the amount or variety of diversity you have experienced in the following settings:

1. The high school you attended   high moderate low

2. The college or university you now attend   high moderate low

3. The neighborhood in which you grew up   high moderate low

4. Places where you have worked or been employed   high moderate low

Which setting had the most and which had the least diversity?

What do you think accounts for this difference?

proximity to one another (Latané, Liu, Nowak, Bonevento, & Zheng, 1995). Studies show that stereotyping and prejudice can be sharply reduced if contact between members of different racial or ethnic groups is frequent enough to allow time for the development of friendships (Pettigrew, 1998). You can create this condition in the college classroom by sitting near students from different ethnic or racial groups or by joining them if you are given the choice to select whom you will work with in class discussion groups and group projects.

2. Take advantage of the Internet to chat with students from diverse groups on your campus or with students in different countries.

Electronic communication can be a more convenient and more comfortable way to initially interact with members of diverse groups with whom you have had little prior experience. After you've communicated successfully *online*, you may then feel more comfortable about interacting with them *in person*. Online and in-person interaction with students from other cultures and nations can give you a better understanding of your own culture and country, as well as increase awareness of its customs and values that you may have taken for granted (Bok, 2006).

3. Seek out the views and opinions of classmates from diverse backgrounds.

For example, during or after class discussions, ask students from different backgrounds if there was any point made or position taken in class that they would strongly question or challenge. Seeking out divergent (diverse) viewpoints has been found to be one of the best ways to develop critical thinking skills (Kurfiss, 1988).

4. Join or form discussion groups with students from diverse backgrounds.

You can gain exposure to diverse perspectives by joining or forming groups of students who differ from you in terms of such characteristics as gender, age, race, or ethnicity. You might begin by forming discussion groups composed of students who differ in one way but are similar in another way. For instance, form a learning team of students who have the same major as you do but who differ with respect to race, ethnicity, or age. This strategy gives the diverse

Remember

Including diversity in your discussion groups not only provides social variety but also promotes the quality of the group's thinking by allowing its members to gain access to the diverse perspectives and life experiences of people from different backgrounds.

members of your team some common ground for discussion (your major) and can raise your team's awareness that although you may be members of different groups you can, at the same time, be similar with respect to your educational goals and life plans.

5. Form collaborative learning teams.

A learning team is more than a discussion group or a study group. It moves beyond discussion to collaborative learning—in other words, members of a learning team "co-labor" (work together) as part of a joint and mutually supportive effort to reach the same goal. Studies show that when individuals from different ethnic and racial groups work collaboratively toward the attainment of a common goal it reduces racial prejudice and promotes interracial friendships (Allport, 1954; Amir, 1976). These positive findings may be explained as follows: If individuals from diverse groups work on the same team, no one is a member of an "out" group (them); instead, all are members of the same "in" group (us; Pratto et al., 2000; Sidanius et al., 2000).

◆ Summary and Conclusion

Diversity refers to differences among groups of people who, together, comprise humanity. Experiencing diversity increases appreciation of the features unique to different cultures, and it gives a wider perspective on aspects of the human experience that are common to all people, regardless of their particular cultural background.

Culture is formed by the beliefs and values of a group with the same traditions and social heritage. It helps bind people into supportive, tight-knit communities. However, it can also lead people to view the world solely through their own cultural lens, known as ethnocentrism, which can blind them to other cultural perspectives. Ethnocentrism can contribute to stereotyping—viewing individual members of the same group in the same way and as having similar personal characteristics.

Evaluating members of a stereotyped group negatively results in prejudice—a negative prejudgment about another person or group of people, which is formed before the facts are known. Stereotyping and prejudice often go hand in hand because if the stereotype is negative, individual members of the stereotyped group are then prejudged negatively. Discrimination takes prejudice one step further by converting the negative prejudgment into action that results in unfair treatment of others. Thus, discrimination is prejudice put into action.

If stereotyping and prejudice are overcome, you are then positioned to experience diversity and reap its multiple benefits, which include sharpened self-awareness, social stimulation, broadened personal perspectives, deeper learning, higher-level thinking, and career success.

The increasing diversity of students on campus, combined with the wealth of diversity-related educational experiences found in the college curriculum and cocurriculum, presents you with an unprecedented opportunity to infuse diversity into your college experience. Seize this opportunity and capitalize on the power of diversity to increase the quality of your college education and your prospects for future success.

Internet-Based Resources for Further Information on Diversity

For additional information related to the ideas discussed in this chapter, we recommend the following Web sites:

www.tolerance.org

www.amnesty.org

Chapter 9 Exercises

9.1 Self-Awareness of Multigroup Identities

You can be members of multiple groups at the same time, and your membership in these overlapping groups can influence your personal development and self-identity. In the figure that follows, consider the shaded center circle to be yourself and the six nonshaded circles to be six groups you belong to that you think have influenced your personal development or personal identity.

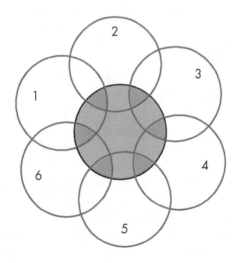

Fill in the nonshaded circles with the names of groups to which you belong that have had the most influence on your personal development. You can use the diversity spectrum that appears on the second page of this chapter to help you identify different groups. Do not feel you have to come up with six groups and fill all six circles. What is more important is to identify those groups that have had a significant influence on your personal development or identity.

Self-Assessment Questions

1. Which one of your groups has had the greatest influence on your personal identity, and why?

2. Have you ever felt limited or disadvantaged by being a member of any group or groups?

3. Have you ever felt that you experienced advantages or privileges because of your membership in any group or groups?

9.2 Intercultural Interview

Find a student, faculty member, or administrator on campus whose cultural background is different from yours, and ask if you could interview that person about his or her culture. Use the following questions in your interview:

1. How is "family" defined in your culture, and what are the traditional roles and responsibilities of different family members?

2. What are the traditional gender (male vs. female) roles associated with your culture? Are they changing?

3. What is your culture's approach to time (e.g., Is there an emphasis on punctuality? Is doing things quickly valued or frowned upon?)

4. What are your culture's staple foods or favorite foods?

5. What cultural traditions or rituals are highly valued and commonly practiced?

6. What special holidays are celebrated?

9.3 Hidden Bias Test

Go to www.tolerance.org/activity/test-yourself-hidden-bias and take one or more of the hidden bias tests on the Web site. These tests assess subtle bias with respect to gender, age, Native Americans, African Americans, Asian Americans, religious denominations, sexual orientations, disabilities, and body weight. You can assess whether you have a bias toward any of these groups.

Self-Assessment Questions

1. Did the results reveal any bias that you were unaware of?

2. Did you think the assessment results were accurate or valid?

3. What do you think best accounts for or explains your results?

4. If your parents and best friends took the test, how do you think their results would compare with yours?

Hate Crime: A Racially Motivated Murder

Jasper County, Texas, has a population of approximately 31,000 people. In this county, 80 percent of the people are White, 18 percent are Black, and 2 percent are of other races. The county's poverty rate is considerably higher than the national average, and its average household income is significantly lower. In 1998, the mayor, president of the Chamber of Commerce, and two councilmen were Black. From the outside, Jasper appeared to be a town with racial harmony, and its Black and White leaders were quick to state that there was racial harmony in Jasper.

However, on June 7, 1998, James Byrd Jr., a 49-year-old African American male, was walking home along a road one evening and was offered a ride by three White males. Rather than taking Byrd home, Lawrence Brewer (age 31), John King (age 23), and Shawn Berry (age 23), three individuals linked to White-supremacist groups, took Byrd to an isolated area and began beating him. They then dropped his pants to his ankles, painted his face black, chained Byrd to their truck, and dragged him for approximately 3 miles. The truck was driven in a zigzag fashion to inflict maximum pain on the victim. Byrd was decapitated after his body collided with a culvert in a ditch alongside the road. His skin, arms, genitalia, and other body parts were strewn along the road, while his torso was found dumped in front of a Black cemetery. Medical examiners testified that Byrd was alive for much of the dragging incident.

While in prison awaiting trial, Brewer wrote letters to King and other inmates. In one letter, Brewer wrote: "Well, I did it and am no longer a virgin. It was a rush and I'm still licking my lips for more." Once the trials were completed, Brewer and King were sentenced to death. Both Brewer and King, whose bodies were covered with racist tattoos, had been on parole before the incident, and they had previously been cellmates. King had spent an extensive amount of time in prison, where he began to associate with White males in an environment in which each race was pitted against the other.

As a result of the murder, Byrd's family created the James Byrd Foundation for Racial Healing in 1998. On January 20, 1999, a wrought iron fence that separated Black and White graves for more than 150 years in Jasper Cemetery was removed in a special unity service. Members of the racist Ku Klux Klan have since visited the gravesite of Byrd several times, leaving racist stickers and other marks that have angered the Jasper community and Byrd's family.

Sources: Houston Chronicle (June 14, 1998); San Antonio Express News (September 17, 1999); Louisiana Weekly (February 3, 2003).

Reflection and Discussion Questions

1. What factors do you think were responsible for causing this incident to take place?

2. Could this incident have been prevented? If yes, how? If no, why not?

3. What do you think will be the long-term effects of this incident on the town?

4. How likely do you think it is that an incident like this could take place in your hometown or near your college campus?

5. If this event took place in your hometown, how would you and members of your family and community react?

Educational Planning and Decision Making

10

Making Wise Choices About Your College Courses and College Major

ACTIVATE YOUR THINKING | Journal Entry **10.1**

Are you decided or undecided about a college major?

_____

_____

_____

If you are undecided, what subjects might be possibilities?

_____

_____

_____

If you are decided, what is your choice and why did you choose this major?

_____

_____

_____

How sure are you about that choice? (Circle one.)

- Absolutely sure
- Fairly sure
- Not too sure
- Likely to change

LEARNING GOAL

To develop strategies for exploring different academic fields and for choosing an educational path that will enable you to achieve your personal and occupational goals.

◆ To Be or Not to Be Decided About a College Major: What the Research Shows

Whether you have or have not decided on a major, here are some research findings related to student decisions about college majors that may be worth keeping in mind:

- Less than 10 percent of new college students feel they know a great deal about the field that they intend to major in.
- As students proceed through the first year of college, they grow more uncertain about the major they chose when they began college.
- More than two-thirds of new students change their mind about their major during the first year of college.
- Only one in three college seniors eventually major in the same field that they chose during their first year of college (Cuseo, 2005).

These findings point to the conclusion that the vast majority of students entering college are truly undecided about a college major. Most students do not make definite and final decisions about their major *before* starting their college experience; instead, they make these decisions *during* the college experience. Being uncertain about a major is nothing to be embarrassed about. The terms "undecided" and "undeclared" don't mean that you have somehow failed or are lost. As a new student, you may be undecided for various good reasons. For instance, you may be undecided simply because you have interests in various subjects. This is a healthy form of indecision because it shows that you have a range of interests and a high level of motivation to learn about different subjects. You may also be undecided simply because you are a careful, reflective thinker whose decision-making style is to gather more information before making any long-term commitments.

In one study of students who were undecided about a major when they started college, 43 percent had several ideas in mind but were not yet ready to commit to one of them (Gordon & Steele, 2003). These students were not clueless; instead, they had some ideas but still wanted to explore them and keep their options open, which is an effective way to go about making decisions.

As a first-year student, it's only natural to be at least somewhat uncertain about your educational goals because you have not yet experienced the variety of subjects and academic programs that make up the college curriculum. You may encounter fields of study in college that you never knew existed. One purpose of general education is to help new students develop the critical thinking skills needed to make wise choices and well-informed decisions, such as their choice of college major. The liberal arts curriculum is also designed to introduce you to various academic subjects, and as you progress through this curriculum, you may discover subjects that captivate you and capture your interest. Some of these subjects may represent fields of study that you never experienced before, and all of them represent possible choices for a college major.

In addition to finding new fields of possible interest, as you gain experience with the college curriculum, you are likely to gain more self-knowledge about your academic strengths and weaknesses. This is important knowledge to take into consideration when choosing a major, because you want to select a field that builds on your academic abilities and talents.

Student Perspective

"The best words of wisdom that I could give new freshmen [are] not to feel like you need to know what you want to major in right away. They should really use their first two years to explore all of the different classes available. They may find a hidden interest in something they never would have considered. I know this from personal experience."

–Advice to new students from a college sophomore (Walsh, 2005)

It's true that people can take too long and procrastinate on reaching decisions; however, it's also true that they can make decisions too quickly that result in premature choices made without sufficient reflection and careful consideration of all options. Judging from the large number of students who end up changing their minds about a college major, it's probably safe to say that more students make the mistake of reaching a decision about a major too quickly rather than procrastinating about it indefinitely. This may be because students hear the same question repeatedly, even before they step a foot on a college campus: "What are you going to major in when you go to college?" You probably also saw this question on your college applications, and you are likely to hear it again during your first term in college. The beginning of your college experience is when you'll meet many new people, and one of the first questions you're likely to hear from them soon after they meet you will be "What's your major?" Family members are also likely to ask you the same question, particularly if they're helping to pay the high cost of a college education, because they want some assurance that their investment will pay off and they feel more assured if they know you have a clear idea about what you're doing in college (your major) and what you'll do after college (your career).

Despite pressure you may be receiving from others to make an early decision, we encourage you not to make it an official and final commitment to a major until you gain more self-knowledge and more knowledge of your options. Even if you think you're sure about your choice of major, before you make a commitment to it, take a course or two in the major to test it out and confirm whether or not your choice is compatible with your personal interests, talents, and values.

Pause for Reflection

If you have chosen a major or are considering a particular major, what or who led you to choose or consider this option?

Student Perspective

"I see so many people switch [their] major like 4 or 5 times; they end up having to take loads of summer school just to catch up because they invest time and money in classes for a major that they end up not majoring in anyway."

—College sophomore (Walsh, 2005)

◆ When Should You Reach a Firm Decision About a College Major?

It's OK to start off not knowing what your major will be and to give yourself some time and college experience before reaching a decision. You can take courses that will count toward your degree and stay on track for graduation, even if you haven't decided or declared your college major.

Similarly, if you've entered college with a major in mind, there's still time to change your mind without falling behind. If you realize that your first choice of a major wasn't a good choice, don't think that you're locked into your original plan and you're only options are to stick with it throughout college or drop out of college. Changing your original educational plans is not necessarily a bad thing. It may mean that you have discovered another field that's more interesting to you or that's more compatible with your personal interests and talents.

The only downside to changing your educational plan is that if you make that change late in your college experience it can result in more time to graduation (and more tuition) because you may need to complete additional courses for your newly chosen field. The key to preventing this scenario from happening later is to be proactive now by engaging in long-range educational planning.

Remember

As a rule, you should reach a fairly firm decision about your major during your second (sophomore) year in college. However, to reach a good decision within this time frame, the process of exploring and planning should begin now—during your first term in college.

◆ The Importance of Long-Range Educational Planning

College will allow you many choices about what courses to enroll in and what field to specialize in. By looking ahead and developing a tentative plan for your courses beyond the first term of college, you will position yourself to view your college experience as a full-length movie and get a sneak preview of the total picture. In contrast, scheduling your classes one term at a time just before each registration period (when everyone else is making a mad rush to get their advisor's signature for the following term's classes) forces you to view your academic experience as a series of short, separate snapshots that lack connection or direction.

Long-range educational planning also enables you to take a proactive approach to your future. Being proactive means you are taking early, preventative action that anticipates events before they sneak up on you, forcing you to react to events in your life without time to plan your best strategy. As the old saying goes, "If you fail to plan, you plan to fail." Through advanced planning, you can actively take charge of your academic future and make it happen *for* you, rather than waiting and passively letting it happen *to* you.

Don't take the denial and avoidance approach to planning your educational future.

"Education is our passport to the future, for tomorrow belongs to the people who prepare for it today."

–Malcolm X, African American Muslim minister, public speaker, and human rights activist

Factors to Consider When Choosing Your Major or Field of Study

Gaining self-awareness is the critical first step in making decisions about a college major, or any other important decision. You must know yourself before you can know what choice is best for you. While this may seem obvious, self-awareness and self-discovery are often overlooked aspects of the decision-making process. In particular, you need awareness of your

- Interests—what you like doing;
- Abilities—what you're good at doing; and
- Values—what you feel good about doing.

Furthermore, research indicates that students are more likely to continue in college and graduate when they choose majors that reflect their personal interests (Leuwerke et al., 2004).

Multiple Intelligences: Identifying Personal Abilities and Talents

One element of the self that you should be aware of when choosing a major is your mental strengths, abilities, or talents. Intelligence was once considered to be one general trait that could be detected and measured by an intelligence quotient (IQ) test. Now, the singular word "intelligence" has been

Pause for Reflection

Consider the following statement: "Choosing a major is a life-changing decision because it will determine what you do for the rest of your life."

Would you agree or disagree with this statement?

Why?

Pause for Reflection

In Chapter 3 (pp. 62–64), you answered self-awareness questions related to each of these three elements of "self." Review your answers to these questions. Do you notice anything about your entries that suggests there might be certain majors or field of study that match your interests, abilities, and values?

replaced by the plural word "intelligences" to reflect that humans can display intelligence or mental ability in many forms other than their paper-and-pencil performance on an IQ test.

Listed in **Box 10.1** are forms of intelligence identified by Howard Gardner (1983, 1993) from studies of gifted and talented individuals, experts in different lines of work, and various other sources. As you read through the types of intelligence, place a checkmark next to the type that you think represents your strongest ability or talent. (You can possess more than one type.) Keep your type or types of intelligence in mind when you're choosing a college major. Ideally, you want to select a major that taps into and builds on your strongest skills or talents. Choosing a major that's compatible with your abilities should enable you to master the concepts and skills required by your major more rapidly and deeply. Furthermore, if you follow your academic talents, you're likely to succeed or excel in what you do, which will bolster your 'academic self-confidence and motivation.

Student Perspective

"I try to do more to please myself, and making good grades and doing well in school helps my ego. It gives me confidence, and I like that feeling."

—First-year college student
(Franklin, 2002)

Take Action!

Multiple Forms of Intelligence

- **Linguistic Intelligence.** Ability to communicate through words or language (e.g., verbal skills in the areas of speaking, writing, listening, or reading)
- **Logical–Mathematical Intelligence.** Ability to reason logically and succeed in tasks that involve mathematical problem solving (e.g., the skill for making logical arguments and following logical reasoning or the ability to think effectively with numbers and make quantitative calculations)
- **Spatial Intelligence.** Ability to visualize relationships among objects arranged in different spatial positions and ability to perceive or create visual images (e.g., forming mental images of three-dimensional objects; detecting detail in objects or drawings; artistic talent for drawing, painting, sculpting, and graphic design; or skills related to sense of direction and navigation)
- **Musical Intelligence.** Ability to appreciate or create rhythmical and melodic sounds (e.g., playing, writing, or arranging music)
- **Interpersonal (Social) Intelligence.** Ability to relate to others; to accurately identify others' needs, feelings, or emotional states

of mind; and to effectively express emotions and feelings to others (e.g., interpersonal communication skills or the ability to accurately "read" the feelings of others or to meet their emotional needs)
- **Intrapersonal (Self) Intelligence.** Ability to self-reflect, become aware of, and understand 'your own thoughts, feelings, and behavior (e.g., capacity for personal reflection, emotional self-awareness, and self-insight into personal strengths and weaknesses)
- **Bodily–Kinesthetic (Psychomotor) Intelligence.** Ability to use 'your own body skillfully and to acquire knowledge through bodily sensations or movements (e.g., skill at tasks involving physical coordination, the ability to work well with hands, mechanical skills, talent for building models and assembling things, or skills related to technology)
- **Naturalist Intelligence.** Ability to carefully observe and appreciate features of the natural environment (e.g., keen awareness of nature or natural surroundings or the ability to understand causes or results of events occurring in the natural world)

Source: Gardner (1993).

10.1

Learning Styles: Identifying Your Learning Preferences

Your learning style is another important personal characteristic you should be aware of when choosing your major. Learning styles refer to individual differences in learning preferences—that is, ways in which individuals prefer to perceive information (receive or take it in) and process information (deal with it after taking it in). Individuals may differ in terms of whether they prefer to take in information by reading about it, listening to it, seeing an image or diagram of it, or physically touching and manipulating it. Individuals may also vary in terms of whether they like to receive information in a structured and orderly format or in an unstructured form that allows them the freedom to explore, play with, and restructure it in their own way. Once information has been received, individuals may also differ in terms of how they prefer to process or deal with it mentally. Some might like to think about it on their own; others may prefer to discuss it with someone else, make an outline of it, or draw a picture of it.

Pause for Reflection

Which type or types of intelligence listed in Box 10.1 represent you strongest area or areas?

Which majors or fields of study do you think may be the best match for your natural talents?

> **Personal Story**
>
> In my family, whenever there's something that needs to be assembled or set up (e.g., a ping-pong table or new electronic equipment), I've noticed that my wife, my son, and myself have different learning styles in terms of how we go about doing it. I like to read the manual's instructions carefully and completely before I even attempt to touch anything. My son prefers to look at the pictures or diagrams in the manual and uses them as models to find parts; then he begins to assemble those parts. My wife seems to prefer not to look at the manual. Instead, she likes to figure things out as she goes along by grabbing different parts from the box and trying to assemble those parts that look like they should fit together—piecing them together as if she were completing a jigsaw puzzle.
>
> —Joe Cuseo

You can take specially designed tests to assess your particular learning style and how it compares with others. If you're interested in taking one, the Learning Center or Career Development Center are the two most likely sites on campus where you will be able to do so.

Probably the most frequently used learning styles test is the Myers-Briggs Type Indicator (MBTI; Myers, 1976; Myers & McCaulley, 1985), which is based on the personality theory of psychologist Carl Jung. The tests consists of four pairs of opposing traits and assesses how people vary on a scale (low to high) for each of these four sets of traits. The four sets of opposing traits are illustrated in **Figure 10.1**.

As you read the following four pairs of opposite traits, place a mark along the line where you think you fall with respect to each set of traits. For example, place a mark in the middle of the line if you think you are midway between these opposing traits, or place a mark at the far left or far right if you think you lean strongly toward the trait listed on either end.

Pause for Reflection

For each of the following four sets of opposing traits, make a note about where you fall—middle, far left, or far right.

	Far Left	Middle	Far Right
Extraversion–Introversion			
Sensing–Intuition			
Thinking–Feeling			
Judging–Perceiving			

What majors or fields of study do you think are most compatible with your personality traits?

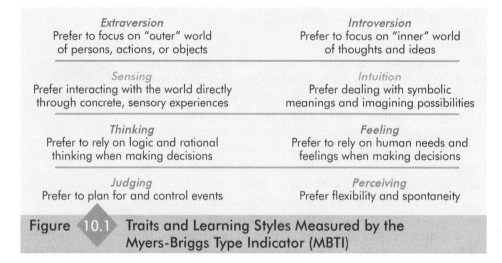

Figure 10.1 Traits and Learning Styles Measured by the Myers-Briggs Type Indicator (MBTI)

It's been found that college students who score high on the introversion scale of the MBTI are less likely to become bored than extroverts while engaging mental tasks that involve repetition and little external stimulation (Vodanovich, Wallace, & Kass, 2005). Students who score differently on the MBTI also have different learning preferences when it comes to writing and the type of writing assignments (Jensen & Ti Tiberio, cited in Bean, 2001). See **Figure 10.2** for the details on the findings.

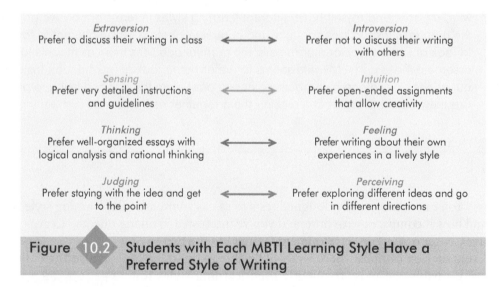

Figure 10.2 Students with Each MBTI Learning Style Have a Preferred Style of Writing

These results clearly indicate that students have different learning styles, which, in turn, influence the type of writing assignments they feel most comfortable performing. This may be important to keep in mind when choosing your major because different academic fields emphasize different styles of writing. Some fields place heavy emphasis on writing that is structured and tightly focused (e.g., science and business), while other fields encourage writing with personal style, flair, or creativity (e.g., English and art). How your writing style meshes with the style emphasized by an academic field may be an important factor to consider when making decisions about your college major.

Another popular learning styles test is the Learning Styles Inventory (Dunn, Dunn, & Price, 1990), which was originally developed by David Kolb, a professor of philosophy (Kolb, 1976, 1985). It is based on how individuals differ with respect to the following two elements of the learning process:

How Information Is *Perceived* (Taken in)

Concrete Experience
Learning through direct involvement or personal experience

Reflective Observation
Learning by watching or observing

How Information Is *Processed* (Dealt with after it has been taken in)

Abstract Conceptualization
Learning by thinking about things and drawing logical conclusions

Active Experimentation
Learning by taking chances and trying things out

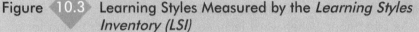

Concrete Experience

Accommodators
Prefer to learn through trial-and-error, hands-on experience; act on gut feelings; get things done; and rely on or accommodate the ideas of others.

Divergers
Prefer to observe, rather than act; generate many creative or imaginative ideas; view things from different perspectives; and pursue broad cultural interests.

Active Experimentation

Reflective Observation

Convergers
Prefer to use logical thinking to focus on solutions to practical problems and to deal with technical tasks rather than interpersonal issues.

Assimilators
Prefer to collect and evaluate lots of information, then systematically organize it into theories or conceptual models; prefer to deal with abstract ideas rather than people.

Abstract Conceptualization

Figure 10.3   Learning Styles Measured by the *Learning Styles Inventory (LSI)*

When these two dimensions are crisscrossed to form intersecting lines, four sectors (areas) are created, each of which represents a different learning style, as illustrated in **Figure 10.3**. As you look at the four areas (styles) in the figure, circle the style that you think reflects your most preferred way of learning.

Research indicates that students majoring in different fields tend to display differences in these four learning styles (Svinicki & Dixon, 1987). For instance, "assimilators" are more often found majoring in mathematics and natural sciences (e.g., chemistry and physics), probably because these subjects stress reflection and abstract thinking. In contrast, academic fields where "accommodators" tend to be more commonly found are business, accounting, and law, perhaps because these fields involve taking practical action and making concrete decisions. "Divergers" are more often attracted to majors in the fine arts (e.g., music, art, and drama), humanities (e.g., history and

Pause for Reflection

Which one of the four learning style appears to most closely match your learning style? (Check one of the following boxes.)

☐ Accommodator

☐ Diverger

☐ Converger

☐ Assimilator

What majors or fields of study do you think would be a good match for your learning style?

The engineering and humanities majors settle their differences in the fine arts quad!

literature), or social sciences (e.g., psychology and political science), possibly because these fields emphasize appreciating multiple viewpoints and perspectives. In contrast, "convergers" are more often found in fields such as engineering, medicine, and nursing, probably because these fields focus on finding solutions to practical and technical problems (Kolb, 1976). This same clustering of fields is found when faculty are asked to classify academic fields in terms of what learning styles they emphasize (Biglan, 1973; Carnegie Commission on Higher Education, cited in Svinicki & Dixon, 1987).

Since students have different learning styles and academic fields emphasize different styles of learning, it's important to consider how your learning style meshes with the style of learning emphasized by the field you're considering as a major. If the match seems to be close or compatible, then the marriage between you and that major could be one that leads to a satisfying and successful learning experience.

We recommend taking a trip to the Learning Center or Career Development Center on your campus to take a learning styles test, or you could try the learning styles assessment that accompanies this text (see the inside of the front cover for details). Even if the test doesn't help you choose a major, it will at least help you become more aware of your particular learning style. This alone could contribute to your academic success, because studies show that when college students gain greater

Personal Story

I first noticed that students in different academic fields may have different learning styles when I was teaching a psychology course that was required for students majoring in nursing and social work. I noticed that some students in class seemed to lose interest (and patience) when we got involved in lengthy class discussions about controversial issues or theories, while others seemed to love it. On the other hand, whenever I lectured or delivered information for an extended period, some students seemed to lose interest (and attention), while others seemed to get "into it" and took great notes. After one class period that involved quite a bit of class discussion, I began thinking about which students seemed most involved in the discussion and which seemed to drift off or lose interest. I suddenly realized that the students who did most of the talking and seemed most enthused during the class discussion were the students majoring in social work. On the other hand, most of the students who appeared disinterested or a bit frustrated were the nursing majors.

When I began to think about why this happened, it dawned on me that the nursing students were accustomed to gathering factual information and learning practical skills in their major courses and were expecting to use that learning style in my psychology course. The nursing majors felt more comfortable with structured class sessions in which they received lots of factual, practical information from the professor. On the other hand, the social work majors were more comfortable with unstructured class discussions because courses in their major often emphasized debating social issues and hearing viewpoints or perspectives.

As I left class that day, I asked myself: Did the nursing students and social work students select or gravitate toward their major because the type of learning emphasized in the field tended to match their preferred style of learning?

—Joe Cuseo

self-aware of their learning styles they improve their academic performance (Claxton & Murrell, 1988).

To sum up, the most important factor to consider when reaching decisions about a major is whether it is compatible with four characteristics of the self: your (a) learning style, (b) your abilities, (c) your personal interests, and (d) your values (see **Figure 10.4**). These four pillars provide the foundation for effective decisions about a college major.

Strategies for Discovering a Major Compatible with Your Interests, Talents, and Values

If you're undecided about a major, there's no need to feel anxious or guilty. You're at an early stage in your college experience. Although you've decided to postpone your decision about a major, this doesn't mean you're a clueless procrastinator as long as you have a plan for exploring and narrowing down your options. Just be sure that you don't put all thoughts about your major on the back burner and simply drift along until you have no choice but to make a choice. Start exploring and developing a game plan now that will lead you to a wise decision about your major.

"Minds differ still more than faces."

–Voltaire, eighteenth-century French author and philosopher

> **Pause for Reflection**
>
> In addition to taking formal tests to assess your learning style, you can gain awareness of your learning styles through some simple introspection or self-examination. Take a moment to complete the following sentences that are designed to stimulate personal reflection on your learning style:
>
> I learn best if …
>
> I learn most from …
>
> I enjoy learning when …

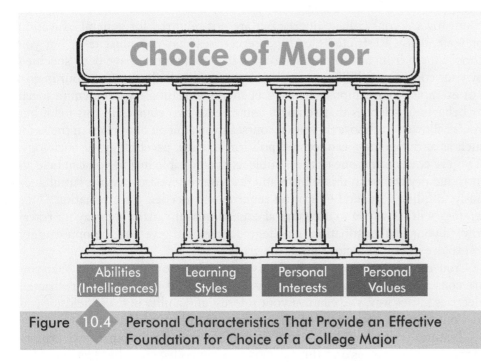

Figure 10.4 Personal Characteristics That Provide an Effective Foundation for Choice of a College Major

Similarly, if you've already chosen a major, this doesn't mean that you'll never have to give any more thought to that decision or that you can just shift into cruise control and motor along a mindless ride in the major you've selected. Instead, you should continue the exploration process by carefully testing your first choice, making sure it's a choice that is compatible with your abilities, interests, and values. In other words, take the approach that it's your *current* choice; whether it becomes your firm and *final* choice will depend on how well you perform, and how interested you are, in the first courses you take in the field.

To explore and identify majors that are compatible with your personal strengths and interests, use the following strategies.

1. Use past experience to help you choose a major.

Think about the subjects that you experienced during high school and your early time in college. As the old saying goes, "Nothing succeeds like success itself." If you have done well and continue to do well in a certain field of study, this may indicate that your natural abilities and learning style correspond well with the academic skills required by that particular field. This could translate into future success and satisfaction in the field if you decide to pursue it as a college major.

You can enter information about your academic performance with high school courses at a Web site (www.mymajors.com), which will analyze it and provide you with college majors that may be a good match for you (based on your academic experiences in high school).

2. Use your elective courses to test your interests and abilities in subjects that you might consider as a major.

As its name implies, "elective" courses are those that you elect or choose to take. In college, electives come in two forms: free electives and restricted electives. Free electives are courses that you may elect (choose) to enroll in; they count toward your college degree but are not required for general education or your major. Restricted electives are courses that you must take, but you choose them from a restricted list of possible courses that have been specified by your college as fulfilling a requirement in general education or your major. For example, your campus may have a general education requirement in social or behavioral sciences that requires you to take two courses in this field, but you're allowed to choose those two courses from a menu of options in the field, such as anthropology, economics, political science, psychology, or sociology. If you're considering one of these subjects as a possible major, you can take an introductory course in this subject and test your interest in it while simultaneously fulfilling a general education requirement needed for graduation. This strategy will allow you to use general education as the main highway for travel toward your final destination (a college degree) and give you the opportunity to explore potential majors along the way.

You can also use your free electives to select courses in fields that you are considering as possible majors. By using some of your free and restricted electives in this way, you can test your interest and ability in these fields; if you find one that is a good match, you may have found yourself a major.

Naturally, you don't have to use all your electives for the purpose of exploring majors. As many as one-third your courses in college may be electives. This leaves you with a great deal of freedom to shape your college experience in a way that best meets your personal needs and future interests. For suggestions on how to make the best use of your free electives, see **Box 10.2.**

Take Action!

Top 10 Suggestions for Making the Most of Your College Electives

At most colleges and universities, approximately one of every three or four courses will be a free elective—your choice of the many courses that are listed in your college catalog. Your elective courses give you academic freedom and personal control of your college coursework. You can exercise this freedom strategically by selecting electives in a way that enables you to make the most of your college experience and college degree. Listed below are 10 suggestions for making strategic use of your college electives. As you read them, identify two suggestions that would be of most interest or use to you.

You can use your electives for the following purposes:

1. Complete a minor or build an area of concentration. Your electives can complement and strengthen your major or allow you to pursue a field of interest other than your major.
2. Help you choose a career path. Just as you can use electives to test your interest in a college major, you can use them to test your interest in a career. For instance, you could enroll in
   - career planning or career development courses; and
   - courses that involve internships or service learning experiences in a field that you're considering as a possible career (e.g., health, education, or business).
3. Strengthen your skills in areas that may appeal to future employers. For example, courses in foreign language, leadership development, and argumentation or debate develop skills that are attractive to future employers and may improve your employment prospects.
4. Develop practical life skills that you can use now or in the near future. You could take courses in managing personal finances, marriage and family, or child development to help you manage your money and your future family.
5. Seek balance in your life and develop yourself as a whole person. You can use your electives strategically to cover all key dimensions of self-development. For instance, you could

take courses that promote your emotional development (e.g., stress management), social development (e.g., interpersonal relationships), mental development (e.g., critical thinking), physical development (e.g., nutrition, self-defense), and spiritual development (e.g., world religions or death and dying).

10.2

Remember

Choose courses that contribute not only to your major and career but also to your quality of life.

6. Make connections across different academic disciplines (subject areas). Courses designed specifically to integrate two or more academic disciplines are referred to as interdisciplinary courses. For example, psychobiology is an interdisciplinary course that combines or integrates the fields of psychology (focusing on the mind) and biology (focusing on the body) and thus helps you see how the mind influences the body, and vice versa. Making connections across subjects and seeing how they can be combined to create a more complete understanding of a subject or issue can be a stimulating mental experience. Furthermore, the presence of interdisciplinary courses on your college transcript may be attractive to future employers because responsibilities and issues in the work world are not neatly packaged into separate majors; they require the ability to combine skills acquired from different fields of study.
7. Help you develop broader perspectives on life and the world in which we live. You can take courses that progressively widen your perspectives. For example, you could select courses that provide you with a societal perspective (e.g., sociology), a national perspective (e.g., political science), an international perspective (e.g., cultural geography), and a global perspective (e.g., ecology). These broadening perspectives widen your scope of knowledge and deepen your understanding of the world.
8. Appreciate different cultural viewpoints and improve your ability to communicate with people from diverse cultural backgrounds. You could take courses related to differences across nations (international diversity), such

as international relations, and you could take courses related to ethnic and racial differences in America (domestic diversity).

9. Stretch beyond your familiar or customary learning style to experience different ways of learning or develop new skills. Your college curriculum is likely to include courses that were never previously available to you and that focus on skills you've never had the opportunity to test or develop. These courses can stretch your mind and allow you to explore new ideas and acquire new perspectives.

10. Learn something about which you were always curious or simply wanted to know more about. For instance, if you've always been curious about how members of the other sex think and feel, you could take a course on the psychology of men and women. Or if you've always been fascinated by movies and how they are made, you might elect to take a course in filmmaking or cinematography.

> **! Remember**
>
> Your elective course in college will give you the opportunity to shape and create an academic experience that is uniquely your own. Seize this opportunity, and exercise your freedom responsibly and reflectively. Don't make your elective choices randomly, or solely on the basis of scheduling convenience (e.g., choosing courses to create a schedule with no early morning or late afternoon classes). Instead, make strategic choices of courses that will contribute most to your educational, personal, and professional development.

3. Be sure you know the courses that are required for the major you're considering.

In college, it's expected that students may know the requirements for the major they've chosen. These requirements vary considerably from one major to another. Review your college catalog carefully to determine what courses are required for the major you're considering. If you have trouble tracking down the requirements in your college catalog, don't become frustrated. These catalogs are often written in a technical manner that can sometimes be hard to interpret. If you need help identifying and understanding the requirements for a major that you are considering, don't be embarrassed about seeking assistance from a professional in your school's Academic Advisement Center.

> **Pause for Reflection**
>
> What were the two primary strategies you selected from the list in Box 10.2?
>
> Write a short explanation about why you chose each of these strategies.

4. Keep in mind that college majors often require courses in fields outside of the major, which are designed to support the major.

For instance, psychology majors are often required to take at least one course in biology, and business majors are often required to take calculus. If you are interested in majoring in particular subject area, be sure you are fully aware of such outside requirements and are comfortable with them.

Once you've accurately identified all courses required for the major you're considering, ask yourself the following two questions:

1. Do the course titles and descriptions appeal to my interests and values?
2. Do I have the abilities or skills needed to do well in these courses?

5. Look over an introductory textbook in the field you're considering as a major.

Find an introductory book in a major that you're considering, review its table of contents, and ask yourself whether the topics are compatible with your academic interests and talents. Also, read a few pages of the text to get some sense of the writing style used in the field and how comfortable you are with it. You should find introductory textbooks for all courses in your college bookstore, in the college library, or with a faculty member in that field.

6. Talk with students majoring in the field you are considering and ask them about their experiences.

Try to speak with several students in the field so that you get a balanced perspective that goes beyond the opinion of one individual. A good way to find students in the major you're considering is to visit student clubs on campus related to the major (e.g., psychology club or history club). You could also check the class schedule to see when and where classes in you major are meeting and then go the classroom where these classes meet and speak with students about the major, either before class begins or after class lets out. The following questions may be good ones to ask students in a major that you're considering:

- What first attracted you to this major?
- What would you say are the advantages and disadvantages of majoring in this field?
- Knowing what you know now, would you choose the same major again?

Also, ask students about the quality of teaching and advising in the department. Studies show that different departments within the same college or university can vary greatly in terms of the quality of teaching, as well as their educational philosophy and attitude toward students (Pascarella & Terenzini, 1991).

Choosing courses that best enable you to achieve your long-term educational and personal goals should take precedence over creating a class schedule that leaves your Fridays free for three-day weekends.

Speaking with students majoring in the discipline you are considering is a good way to get a balanced perspective.

© Jaimie Duplass, 2010. Under license from Shutterstock, Inc.

7. Sit in on some classes in the field you are considering as a major.

If the class you want to visit is large, you probably could just slip into the back row and listen. However, if the class is small, you should ask the instructor's permission. When visiting a class, focus on the content or ideas being covered in class rather than the instructor's personality or teaching style. (Keep in mind that you're trying to decide whether you will major in the subject, not in the teacher.)

8. Discuss the major you're considering with an academic advisor.

It's probably best to speak with an academic advisor who advises students in various majors rather than to someone who advises only students in their particular academic department or field. You want to be sure to discuss the major with an advisor who is neutral and will give you unbiased feedback about the pros and cons of majoring in that field.

9. Speak with faculty members in the department that you're considering as a major.

Consider asking the following questions:

- What academic skills or qualities are needed for a student to be successful in your field?
- What are the greatest challenges faced by students majoring in your field?
- What do students seem to like most and least about majoring in your field?
- What can students do with a major in your field after college graduation?
- What types of graduate programs or professional schools would a student in your major be well prepared to enter?

10. Visit your Career Development Center.

See whether information is available on college graduates who've majored in the field you're considering and what they've gone on to do with that major after graduation. This will give you an idea about the type of careers the major can lead to or what graduate and professional school programs students often enter after completing a major in the field that you're considering.

11. Surf the Web site of the professional organization associated with the field that you're considering as a major.

For example, if you're thinking about becoming anthropology major, check out the Web site of the American Anthropological Association. If you're considering history as a major, look at the Web site of the American Historical Association. The Web site of a professional organization often contains useful information for students who are considering that field as a major. For example, the Web site of the American Philosophical Association contains information about nonacademic careers for philosophy majors, and the American Sociological Association's Web site identifies various careers that sociology majors are qualified to pursue after college graduation. To locate the professional Web site of the field that you might want to explore as a possible major, ask a faculty member in that field or complete a search on the Web by simply entering the name of the field followed by the word "association."

12. Be sure you know what academic standards must be met for you to be accepted for entry into a major.

Because of their popularity, certain college majors may be impacted or over-subscribed, which means that more students are interested in majoring in these fields than there are openings for them. For instance, preprofessional majors that lead directly to a particular career are often the ones that often become oversubscribed (e.g., accounting, education, engineering, premed, nursing, or physical therapy). On some campuses, these majors are called restricted majors, meaning that departments control their enrollment by limiting the number of students they let into the major. For example, departments may restrict entry to their major by admitting only students who have achieved an overall GPA of 3.0 or higher in certain introductory courses required by the majors, or they may take all students who apply for the major, rank them by their GPA, and then count down until they have filled their maximum number of available spaces (Strommer, 1993).

13. Be sure you know whether the major you're considering is impacted or oversubscribed and whether it requires certain academic standards to be met before you can be admitted.

As you complete courses and receive grades, check to see whether you are meeting these standards. If you find yourself failing to meet these standards, you may need to increase the amount of time and effort you devote to your studies and seek assistance from your campus Learning Center. If you're working at your maximum level of effort and are regularly using the learning assistance services available on your campus but are still not meeting the academic standards of your intended major, consult with an academic advisor to help you identify an alternative field that may be closely related to the restricted major you were hoping to enter.

> **Pause for Reflection**
>
> Do you think that the major you're considering is likely to be oversubscribed (i.e., there are more students wanting to major in the field than there are openings in the courses)?

14. Consider the possibility of a college minor in a field that complements your major.

A college minor usually requires about half the number of credits (units) required for a major. Most campuses allow you the option of completing a minor with your major. Check with your academic advisor or the course catalog if your school offers a minor that interests you, find out what courses are required to complete it.

If you have strong interests in two different fields, a minor will allow you to major in one of these fields while minoring in the other. Thus, you can pursue two fields that interest you without having to sacrifice one for the other. Furthermore, a minor can be completed at the same time as most college majors without delaying your time to graduation. (In contrast, a double major will typically lengthen your time to graduation because you must complete the separate requirements of two different majors.) You can also pursue a second field of study alongside your major without increasing your time to graduation by completing a cognate area—a specialization that requires fewer courses to complete than a minor (e.g., four to five courses instead of seven to eight courses). A concentration area may have even fewer requirements (only two to three courses).

Taking a cluster of courses in a field outside your major can be an effective way to strengthen your résumé and increase your employment prospects because it demonstrates your versatility and allows you to gain experience in areas that may be missing or underemphasized in your major. For example, students majoring in the fine arts (e.g., music or theater) or humanities (e.g., English or history) may take courses in the fields of mathematics (e.g., statistics), technology (e.g., computer science), and business (e.g., economics)—all of which are not emphasized by their major.

◆ Summary and Conclusion

Here is a snapshot of the points that were made in this chapter:

* Changing your educational goal is not necessarily a bad thing; it may represent your discovery of another field that's more interesting to you or that's more compatible with your personal interests and talents.

- Several myths exist about the relationship between college majors and career that need to be dispelled:

  - Myth 1. When you choose your major, you're choosing your career.
  - Myth 2. After a bachelor's degree, any further education must be in the same field as your college major.
  - Myth 3. You should major business because most college graduates work in business settings.
  - Myth 4. If you major in a liberal arts field, the only career available is teaching.
  - Myth 5. Specialized skills are more important for career success than general skills.

- You should be aware of two important elements when choosing your major: your form or forms of multiple intelligence (your mental strengths or talents) and your learning style (your preferred way of learning).
- Strategically select your courses in a way that contributes most to your educational, personal, and professional development. Choose your elective courses with one or more of the following purposes in mind:

  - Choose a major or confirm whether your first choice is a good one.
  - Acquire a minor or build a concentration that will complement your major.
  - Broaden your perspectives on the world around you.
  - Become a more balanced or complete person.
  - Handle the practical life tasks that face you now and in the future.
  - Strengthen your career development and employment prospects after graduation.

Higher education supplies you with a higher degree of freedom of choice and a greater opportunity to determine your own academic course of action. Employ it and enjoy it—use your freedom strategically to make the most of your college experience and college degree.

Internet-Based Resources for Further Information on Educational Planning and Decision Making

For additional information related to the ideas discussed in this chapter, we recommend the following Web sites:

Identifying and Choosing College Majors:

www.mymajors.com

www.princetonreview.com/majors.aspx

Careers for Liberal Arts Majors:

www.eace.org/networks/liberalarts.html

10.1 Planning for a College Major

1. Go to your college catalog and use its index to locate pages containing information related to the major you have chosen or are considering. If you are undecided, select a field that you might consider as a possibility. To help you identify possible majors, you can use your catalog or go online and complete the short interview at the www.mymajors.com Web site. (Your learning -style assessment results from Figure 10.1 may also help you identify possibilities.)

   The point of this exercise is not to force you to commit to a major now but to familiarize you with the process of developing a plan, thereby putting you in a position to apply this knowledge when you reach a final decision about the major you intend to pursue. Even if you don't yet know what your final destination may be with respect to a college major, creating this educational plan will keep you moving in the right direction.

2. Once you've selected a major for this assignment, look at you college catalog and identify the courses that are required for the major you have selected. Use the form that follows to list the number and title of each course required by the major.

   You'll find that you must take certain courses for the major; these are often called core requirements. For instance, at most colleges, all business majors must take microeconomics. You will likely discover that you can choose other required courses from a menu or list of options (e.g., "choose any three courses from the following list of six courses"). Such courses are often called restricted electives in the major. When you find restricted electives in the major you've selected, read the course descriptions and choose those courses from the list that appeal most to you. Simply list the numbers and titles of these courses on the planning form. (You don't need to write down all choices listed in the catalog.)

   College catalogs can sometimes be tricky to navigate or interpret, so if you run into any difficulty, don't panic. Seek help from an academic advisor. Your campus may also have a degree audit program available, which allows you to track major requirements electronically. If so, take advantage of it.

College Major Planning Form

Major Selected: _____

Core Requirements in the Major
(Courses in your major that you must take)

Course #	Course Title	Course #	Course Title

Restricted Electives in the Major
(Courses required for your major that you choose to take from a specified list)

Course #	Course Title	Course #	Course Title

Self-Assessment Questions

1. Looking over the courses required for the major you've selected, would you still be interested in majoring in this field?

2. Were there courses required by the major that you were surprised to see or that you did not expect would be required?

3. Are there questions that you still have about this major?

10.2 Developing a Comprehensive Graduation Plan

A comprehensive, long-range graduation plan includes all three types of courses you need to complete a college degree:

1. General education requirements

2. Major requirements

3. Free electives

In exercises 2.1 and 2.2 (**pp. 54–55**) you planned for your required general education courses and required courses in your major. The third set of courses you'll take in college that count toward your degree consists of courses are called free electives—courses that are not required for general education or your major but that you freely choose from any of the courses listed in your college catalog. By combining your general education courses, major courses, and free-elective courses, you can create a comprehensive, long-range graduation plan.

- Use the "long-range graduation planning form" on **pp. 264–265** to develop this complete educational plan. Use the slots to pencil in the general education courses you're planning to take to fulfill your general education requirements, your major requirements, and your free electives. (For ideas on choosing your free electives, see Box 10.2 on **pp. 253–254**.) Since this may be a tentative plan, it 's probably best to use a pencil when completing it in case you need to make modifications to it.

Notes

1. If you have not decided on a major, a good strategy might be to concentrate on taking liberal arts courses to fulfill your general education requirements during your first year of college. This will open more slots in your course schedule during your sophomore year. By that time, you may have a better idea of what you want to major in, and you can fill these open slots with courses required by your major. This may be a particularly effective strategy if you choose to major in a field that has many lower-division (first year and sophomore) requirements that must be completed before you can take upper-division (junior and senior) courses in the major. (These lower-division requirements are often referred to as premajor requirements.)

2. Keep in mind that the course number indicates the year in the college experience that the course is usually taken. Courses numbered in the 100s (or below) are typically taken in the first year of college, 200-numbered courses in the sophomore year, 300-numbered courses in the junior year, and 400-numbered courses in the senior year. Also, be sure to check whether the course you're planning to take has any prerequisites—courses that need to be completed before you can enroll in the course you're planning to take. For example, if you are planning to take a course in literature, it is likely that you cannot enroll in it until you have completed at least one prerequisite course in writing or English composition.

3. To complete a college degree in 4 years, you should complete about 30 credits each academic year.

! Remember

Unlike high school, summer school in college isn't something you do to make up for courses that were failed, or should have been taken during the "regular" school year (fall and spring terms). Instead, it's an additional term that you can use to make further progress toward your college degree and reduce the total time it takes to complete your degree. Adopt the attitude that summer term is a regular part of the college academic year, and make strategic use of it to keep you on a four-year timeline to graduation.

4. Check with an academic advisor to see whether your college has developed a projected plan of scheduled courses, which indicates the academic term when courses listed in the catalog are scheduled to be offered (e.g., fall, spring, or summer) for the next 2 to 3 years. If such a long-range plan of scheduled courses is

available, take advantage of it because it will enable you to develop a personal educational plan that includes not only what courses you will take, but also when you will take them. This can be an important advantage because some courses you may need for graduation will not be offered every term. We strongly encourage you to inquire about and acquire any long-range plan of scheduled courses that may be available, and use it when developing your long-range graduation plan.

5. Don't forget to include out-of-class learning experiences as part of your educational plan, such as volunteer service, internships, and study abroad. (For information on these learning experiences, see Chapter 11.)

Your long-range graduation plan is not something set in stone that can never be modified. Like clay, its shape can be molded and changed into a different form as you gain more experience with the college curriculum. Nevertheless, your creation of this initial plan will be useful because it will provide you with a blueprint to work from. Once you have created slots specifically for your general education requirements, your major courses, and your electives, you have accounted for all the categories of courses you will need to complete to graduate. Thus, if changes need to be made to your plan, they can be easily accommodated by simply substituting different courses into the slots you've already created for these three categories.

Remember

The purpose of this long-range planning assignment is not to lock you into a rigid plan but to give you a telescope for viewing your educational future and a map for reaching your educational goals.

Graduation Planning Form

STUDENT: ID NO:

MAJOR: MINOR:

TERM:		TERM:		TERM:		TERM:	
Course	Units	Course	Units	Course	Units	Course	Units
TOTAL		TOTAL		TOTAL		TOTAL	

TERM:		TERM:		TERM:		TERM:	
Course	Units	Course	Units	Course	Units	Course	Units
TOTAL		TOTAL		TOTAL		TOTAL	

TERM:		TERM:		TERM:		TERM:	
Course	Units	Course	Units	Course	Units	Course	Units
TOTAL		TOTAL		TOTAL		TOTAL	

TERM:		TERM:		TERM:		TERM:	
Course	Units	Course	Units	Course	Units	Course	Units
TOTAL		TOTAL		TOTAL		TOTAL	

		COCURRICULAR EXPERIENCES	SERVICE LEARNING AND INTERNSHIP EXPERIENCES
Advisor's Signature	Date:		
Student's Signature	Date:		
Notes:			

Self-Assessment Questions

1. Do you think this was a useful assignment? Why or why not?

2. Do you see any way in which this assignment could be improved or strengthened?

3. Did completing this long-range graduation plan influence your educational plans in any way?

Whose Choice Is It Anyway?

Ursula, a first-year student, was in tears when she showed up at the Career Center. She had just returned from a weekend visit home, where she informed her parents that she was planning to major in art or theater. When Ursula's father heard about her plans, he exploded and insisted that she major in something "practical," like business or accounting, so that she could earn a living after she graduates. Ursula replied that she had no interest in these majors, nor did she feel she had the skills needed to complete the level of math required by them, which included calculus. Her father shot back that he had no intention of "paying 4 years of college tuition for her to end up as an unemployed artist or actress!" He went on to say that if she wanted to major in art or theater she'd "have to figure out a way to pay for college herself."

Reflection and Discussion Questions

1. What options (if any) do you think Ursula has now?

2. If Ursula were your friend, what would you recommend she do?

3. Do you see any way or ways in which Ursula might pursue a major that she's interested in and, at the same time, ease her father's worries that she will end up jobless after college graduation?

Career Exploration, Planning, and Preparation

Before you start to dig into this chapter, take a moment to answer the following questions:

1. Have you decided on a career, or are you leaning strongly toward one?

_____

_____

2. If yes, why have you chosen this career? (Was your decision influenced by anybody or anything?)

_____

_____

_____

3. If no, are there any careers you're considering as possibilities?

_____

_____

_____

_____

LEARNING GOAL

To acquire strategies that can be used now and throughout the remaining years of your college experience for effective career exploration, preparation, and development.

◆ The Importance of Career Planning

College graduates in the twenty-first century are likely to continue working until age 75 (Herman, 2000). Once you enter the workforce full time, you'll spend most of the remaining waking hours of your life working. The only other single activity that you'll spend more time doing in your lifetime is sleeping. When you consider that such a sizable portion of your life is spent working and that your career can strongly influence your sense of personal identify and self-esteem, it becomes apparent that career choice is a critical process that should begin early in your college experience.

> **Remember**
>
> When you're doing career planning, you're also doing life planning because you are planning how you will spend most of the waking hours of your future.

Even if you've decided on a career that you were dreaming about since you were a preschooler, the process of career exploration and planning is not complete because you still need to decide on what specialization within that career you'll pursue. For example, if you're interested in pursuing a career in law, you'll need to eventually decide what branch of law you wish to practice (e.g., criminal law, corporate law, or family law). You'll also need to decide what employment sector or type of industry you would like to work in, such as nonprofit, for-profit, education, or government. Thus, no matter how certain or uncertain you are about your career path, you'll need to begin exploring career options and start taking your first steps toward formulating a career development plan.

◆ Strategies for Career Exploration and Preparation

Reaching an effective decision about a career involves the same four steps you used in the goal-setting process (see Chapter 3):

1. **Awareness of yourself.** Your personal abilities, interests, needs, and values;
2. **Awareness of your options.** The variety of career fields available to you;
3. **Awareness of what best "fits" you.** The careers that best match your personal abilities, interests, needs, and values;
4. **Awareness of the process.** How to prepare for and gain entry into the career of your choice.

Step 1. Self-Awareness

The more you know about yourself, the better your choices and decisions will be. Self-awareness is a particularly important step to take when making career decisions because the career you choose says a lot about who you are and what you want from life. Your personal identity and life goals should not be based on or built around your career choice; it should be the other way around.

> **Remember**
>
> Your personal attributes and goals should be considered first because they provide the foundation on which you build your career choice and future life.

One way to gain greater self-awareness of your career interests is by taking psychological tests or assessments. These assessments allow you to see how your interests in certain career fields compare with those of other students and professionals who've experienced career satisfaction and success. These comparative perspectives can give you important reference points for assessing whether your level of interest in a career is high, average, or low relative to other students and working professionals. Your Career Development Center is the place on campus where you can find these career-interest tests, as well as other instruments that allow you to assess your career-related abilities and values.

When making choices about a career, you may have to consider one other important aspect of yourself: your personal needs. A need may be described as something stronger than an interest. When you satisfy a personal need, you are doing something that makes your life more satisfying or fulfilling. Psychologists have identified several important human needs that vary in strength or intensity from person to person. Listed in **Box 11.1** are personal needs that are especially important to consider when making a career choice.

Your career choice should make you look forward to going to work each day.

Take Action!

Personal Needs to Consider When Making Career Choices

As you read the needs listed here, make a note after each one, indicating how strong the need is for you (high, moderate, or low).

1. Autonomy. Need to work independently without close supervision or control. Individuals high in this need may experience greater satisfaction working in careers that allow them to be their own boss, make their own decisions, and control their own work schedule. Individuals low in this need may experience greater satisfaction working in careers that are more structured and involve working with a supervisor who provides direction, assistance, and frequent feedback.

2. Affiliation. Need for social interaction, a sense of belonging, and the opportunity to collaborate with others. Individuals high in this need may experience greater satisfaction working in careers that involve frequent interpersonal interaction and teamwork with colleagues or co-workers. Individuals

Student Perspective

"To me, an important characteristic of a career is being able to meet new, smart, interesting people."

—First-year student

11.1

low in this need may be more satisfied working alone or in competition with others.

3. Achievement. Need to experience challenge and a sense of personal accomplishment. Individuals high in this need may be more satisfied working in careers that push them to solve problems, generate creative ideas, and continually learn new information or master new skills. Individuals low in this need may be more satisfied with careers that don't continually test their abilities and don't repeatedly challenge them to stretch their skills with new tasks and different responsibilities.

Student Perspective

"I want to be able to enjoy my job and be challenged by it at the same time. I hope that my job will not be monotonous and that I will have the opportunity to learn new things often."

—First-year student

4. Recognition. Need for high rank, status, and respect from others. Individuals high in this need may crave careers that are prestigious in the eyes of friends, family, or society. Individuals with a low need for recognition would feel comfortable working in a career that they find personally fulfilling, without being concerned

about how impressive or enviable their career appears to others.

5. **Sensory Stimulation.** Need to experience variety, change, and risk. Individuals high in this need may be more satisfied working in careers that involve frequent changes of pace and place (e.g., travel), unpredictable events (e.g., work tasks that vary considerably), and moderate stress (e.g., working under pressure of competition or deadlines). Individuals with a low need for sensory stimulation may feel more comfortable working in careers that involve regular routines, predictable situations, and minimal amounts of risk or stress.

Personal Story

While enrolled in my third year of college with half of my degree completed, I had an eye-opening experience. I wish this experience had happened in my first year, but better late than never. Although I had chosen a career during my first year of college, my decision-making process was not systematic and didn't involve critical thinking. I chose a major based on what sounded prestigious and would pay me the most money. Although these are not necessarily bad factors, my failure to use a systematic and reflective process to evaluate these factors was bad. In my junior year of college I asked one of my professors why he decided to get his PhD and become a professor. He simply answered, "I wanted autonomy." This was an epiphany for me. He explained that when he looked at his life he determined that he needed a career that offered independence, so he began looking at career options that would offer that. After that explanation, "autonomy" became my favorite word, and this story became a guiding force in my life. After going through a critical self-awareness process, I determined that autonomy was exactly what I desired and a professor is what I became.

—*Aaron Thompson*

Pause for Reflection

Which of the five needs in **Box 11.1** did you indicate as being strong personal needs?

What career or careers do you think would best match your strongest needs?

Taken altogether, four aspects of yourself should be considered when exploring careers: your personal abilities, interests, values, and needs. As illustrated in **Figure 11.1**, these four pillars provide a solid foundation for effective career choices and decisions. You want to choose a career that you're good at, interested in, and passionate about and that fulfills your personal needs.

Lastly, since a career choice is a long-range decision that involves life beyond college, self-awareness should involve not only reflection on who you are now but also self-projection—reflecting on how you see yourself in the future. When you engage in the process of self-projection, you begin to see a connection between where you are now and where you want or hope to be.

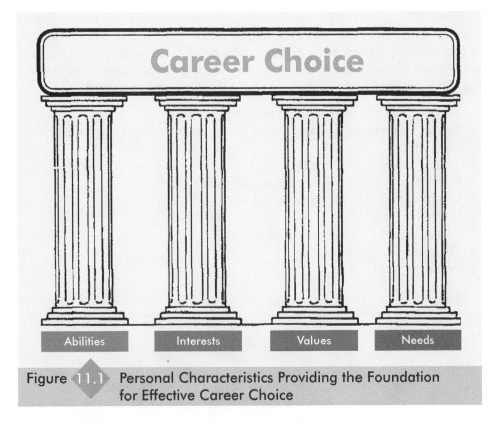

Figure 11.1   Personal Characteristics Providing the Foundation for Effective Career Choice

Ideally, your choice of a career should be one that leads to the best-case future scenario in which your typical day goes something like this: You wake up in the morning and hop out of bed enthusiastically—eagerly looking forward to what you'll be doing at work that day. When you're at work, time flies by, and before you know it, the day's over. When you return to bed that night and look back on your day, you feel good about what you did and how well you did it. For this ideal scenario to have any chance of becoming a reality, or even coming close to reality, you have to select a career path that is true to yourself—a path that leads you to a career that closely matches your abilities (what you do well), your interests (what you like to do), your values (what you feel good about doing), and your needs (what brings you satisfaction and fulfillment in life).

Step 2. Awareness of Your Options

To make effective decisions about your career path, you need to have accurate knowledge about the nature of different careers and the realities of the work world. The Career Development Center is the first place to go for this information and help with career exploration and planning. In addition to helping you explore your personal career interests and abilities, the Career Development Center is your campus resource for learning about the nature of different careers and for strategies on locating career-related work experiences.

Student Perspective

"I think that a good career has to be meaningful for a person. It should be enjoyable for the most part [and] it has to give a person a sense of fulfillment."

—First-year student

Pause for Reflection

Project yourself 10 years into the future and visualize your ideal career and life.

1. What are you spending most of your time doing during your typical workday?

2. Where and with whom are you working?

3. How many hours are you working per week?

4. Where are you living?

5. Are you married? Do you have children?

6. How does your work influence your home life?

If you were to ask people to name as many careers as they can, they wouldn't come close to naming the 900 career titles listed by the federal government in its Occupational Information Network. Many of these careers you may have never heard of, but some of them may represent good career options for you. You can learn about careers through nine major routes or avenues:

- Reading about careers them in books or online
- Becoming involved in cocurricular programs on campus related to career development
- Taking career development courses
- Interviewing people in different career fields
- Observing (shadowing) people at work in different careers
- Interning
- Participating in a co-op program
- Volunteering
- Working part time

"HUNTER OR GATHERER? THOSE ARE MY ONLY OPTIONS?"

There are many more career choices in today's work world than there were for our early ancestors.

Copyright © by Scott Arthur Masear. Reprinted with permission.

Resources on Careers

Your Career Development Center and your College Library are campus resources where you can find a wealth of reading material on careers, either in print or online. Listed here are some of the most useful sources of written information on careers:

- *Dictionary of Occupational Titles* (www.occupationalinfo.org). This is the largest printed resource on careers; it contains concise definitions of more than 17,000 jobs. It also includes information on
  - Work tasks that people in the career typically perform regularly;
  - Types of knowledge, skills, and abilities that are required for different careers;
  - Interests, values, and needs of individuals who find working in particular careers to be personally rewarding; and
  - Background experiences of people working in different careers that qualified them for their positions.

- *Occupational Outlook Handbook* (www.bls.gov/oco). This is one of the most widely available and used resources on careers. It contains descriptions of approximately 250 positions, including information on the nature of work, work conditions, places of employment, training or education required for career entry and advancement, salaries, careers in related fields, and additional sources of information about particular careers (e.g., professional organizations and governmental agencies). A distinctive feature of this resource is that it contains information about the future employment outlook for different careers.
- *Encyclopedia of Careers and Vocational Guidance* (Chicago: Ferguson Press). As the name suggests, this is an encyclopedia of information on qualifications, salaries, and advancement opportunities for various careers.
- **Occupational Information Network (O*NET) Online** (www.online.onetcenter.org). This is America's most comprehensive source of online information about careers. It contains an up-to-date set of descriptions for almost 1,000 careers, plus lots of other information similar to what you would find in the *Dictionary of Occupational Titles*.

There are many resources for finding information on careers, many of which can be accessed on the Internet.

© Robert Kneschke, 2010. Under license from Shutterstock, Inc.

In addition to these general sources of information, your Career Development Center and College Library should have books and other published materials related to specific careers or occupations (e.g., careers for English majors).

You can also learn a lot about careers by simply reading advertisements for position openings in your local newspaper or online, such as at www.careerbuilder.com and college.monster.com. When reading position descriptions, make special note of the tasks, duties, or responsibilities they involve and ask yourself whether these positions are compatible with your personal profile of abilities, interests, needs, and values.

Career Planning and Development Programs

Periodically during the academic year, cocurricular programs devoted to career exploration and career preparation are likely to be offered on your campus. For example, the Career Development Center may sponsor career exploration or career planning workshops that you can attend for free. Also, the Career Development Center may organize a career fair on campus at which professionals working in different career fields are given booths on campus where you can visit with them and ask questions about their careers. Research indicates that career development workshops offered on campus are effective for helping students' plan for and decide on a career (Brown & Krane, 2000; Hildenbrand & Gore, 2005).

Career Development Courses

Many colleges offer career development courses for elective credit. These courses typically include self-assessment of your career interests, information about different careers, and strategies for career preparation. You should be doing career planning, so why not do it by taking a career development course that rewards you with college credit for doing it? Studies show that students who participate in career development courses experience significant benefits in terms of career choice and career development (Pascarella & Terenzini, 2005).

It might also be possible for you to take an independent-study course that will give you the opportunity to investigate issues in the career area you are considering. An independent study is a project that you work out with a faculty member, which usually involves writing a paper or detailed report. It allows you to receive academic credit for an in-depth study of a topic of your choice, without having to enroll with other students in a traditional course that has regularly scheduled classroom meetings. You could use this independent-study option to choose a project related to a career you've considered. To see whether this independent-study option is available at your campus, check the college catalog or consult with an academic advisor. You may be able to explore a career of interest to you in a writing or speech course if your instructor allows you to choose the topic that you'll write or speak about. If you're given this choice, use it to research a career that interests and make that the topic of your paper or presentation.

Information Interviews

One of the best and most overlooked ways to get accurate information about careers is to interview professionals who are working in career fields. Career development specialists refer to this strategy as information interviewing. Don't assume that working professionals would not be interested in taking time out of their day to speak with a student. Most are willing to be interviewed about their careers; they often enjoy it (Crosby, 2002).

Pause for Reflection

If you were to observe or interview a working professional in a career that interests you, what position would that person hold?

Information interviews provide you inside information about what careers are like because you're getting that information directly from the horse's mouth. They also help you gain experience and confidence in interview situations, which may help you prepare for future job interviews. Furthermore, if you make a good impression during information interviews, the people you interview may suggest that you contact them again after graduation in case there are position openings. If there are openings, you might find yourself being the interviewee instead of the interviewer (and you might find yourself a job).

Because interviews are a valuable source of information about careers and provide possible contacts for future employment, we strongly recommend that you complete the information interview assignment included at the end of this chapter.

Career Observation (Shadowing)

In addition to learning about careers from reading and interviews, you can experience careers more directly by placing yourself in workplace situations or work environments that allow you to observe workers performing their daily duties. Two college-sponsored programs may be available on your campus that would allow you to observe working professionals:

- **Job Shadowing Programs.** These programs allow you to follow (shadow) and observe a professional during a typical workday.
- **Externship Programs.** This is basically an extended form of job shadowing, which lasts longer (e.g., 2–3 days).

Visit your Career Development Center to learn about what job shadowing or externship programs may be available on your college campus. If none are available in a career field that interests you, consider finding one on your own by using strategies similar to those we recommend for information interviews at the end of this chapter. The only difference is that instead of asking the person for an interview, you'd be asking whether you could observe that person at work. The same person who gave you an information interview might be willing to allow such observation. Keep in mind that just 1 or 2 days of observation will give you some firsthand information about a career but will not give you firsthand experience in that career.

Internships

In contrast to job shadowing or externships, whereby you observe someone at work, an internship program immerses you in the work itself and gives you the opportunity to perform career-related work duties. A distinguishing feature of internships is that you can receive academic credit and sometimes financial compensation for the work you do. An internship usually totals 120 to 150 work hours, which may be completed at the same time you're enrolled in a full schedule of classes when you're not taking classes (e.g., during summer term). An advantage of an internship is that it enables college students to avoid the classic catch-22 situation they often run into when interviewing for their first career position after graduation. The interview scenario usually goes something like this: The potential employer asks the college graduate, "What work experience have you had in this field?" The recent graduate replies, "I haven't had any work experience because I've been a full-time college student." This scenario can be avoided if you complete an internship during your college experience, which allows you to say, "Yes, I do have work experience in this field." We encourage you to participate in an internship while in college because it will enable you to beat the "no experience" rap after graduation and distinguish yourself from many other college graduates. Research shows that students who have internships while in college are more likely to develop career-relevant work skills and find employment immediately after college graduation (Pascarella & Terenzini, 2005).

"Got Experience?"—The "killer question" that college graduates can't answer after college unless they've had some career-related work experience during college (e.g., internships or volunteer service).

Internships are typically available to college students during their junior or senior year; however, there may be internships available to first- and second-year students on your campus. You can also pursue internships on your own. Published guides describe various career-related internships, along with information on how to apply for them (e.g., *Peterson's Internships* and the *Vault Guide to Top Internships*). You could also search for internships on the Web (e.g., www.internships.com and www.vaultreports.com). Another good resource for possible information on internships is the local chamber of commerce in the town or city where your college is located or in your hometown.

Another option for gaining firsthand work experience is enrolling in courses that allow you to engage in hands-on learning related to your career interest. For instance, if you're interested in working with children, courses in child psychology or early childhood education may offer experiential learning opportunities in a preschool or daycare center on campus.

Cooperative Education (Co-op) Programs

A co-op is similar to an internship but involves work experience that lasts longer than one academic term and often requires students to stop their coursework temporarily to participate in the program. However, some co-op programs allow you to continue to take classes while working part time at a co-op position; these are sometimes referred to as parallel co-ops. Students are paid for participating in co-op programs but do not receive academic credit—just a notation on their college transcript (Smith, 2005).

Typically, co-ops are only available to juniors or seniors, but you can begin now to explore co-op programs by reviewing your college catalog and visiting your Career Development Center to see whether your school offers co-op programs in career areas that may interest you. If you find any, plan to get involved with one because it can provide you with authentic and extensive career-related work experience.

The value of co-ops and internships is strongly supported by research, which indicates that students who have these experiences during college:

- Are more likely to report that their college education was relevant to their career;
- Receive higher evaluations from employers who recruit them on campus;
- Have less difficulty finding an initial position after graduation;
- Are more satisfied with their first career position after college;
- Obtain more prestigious positions after graduation; and
- Report greater job satisfaction (Gardner, 1991; Knouse, Tanner, & Harris, 1999; Pascarella & Terenzini, 1991, 2005).

In one statewide survey that asked employers to rank various factors they considered important when hiring new college graduates, internship or cooperative education program received the highest ranking (Education Commission of the States, 1995). Furthermore, employers report that if full-time positions open up in their organization or company, they usually turn first to their own interns and co-op students (National Association of Colleges & Employers, 2003).

Volunteer Service

Engaging in volunteerism not only helps your community but also helps you by giving you the opportunity to explore different work environments and gain work experience in career fields that relate to your area of service. For example, volunteer service to different age groups (e.g., children, adolescents, or the elderly) and service in different environments (e.g., hospital, school, or laboratory) can provide you with firsthand work experience and simultaneously give you a chance to test your interest in possibly pursuing future careers related to these age groups and work environments. (To get a sense of the range of service opportunities that may be available to you, go to www.usa.service.org.)

Personal Story

As an academic advisor, I was once working with two first-year students, Kim and Christopher. Kim was thinking about becoming a physical therapist, and Chris was thinking about becoming an elementary school teacher. I suggested to Kim that she visit the hospital nearby our college to see whether she could do volunteer work in the physical therapy unit. The hospital did need volunteers, so she volunteered in the physical therapy unit and loved it. That volunteer experience confirmed for her that physical therapy is what she should pursue as a career. She completed a degree in physical therapy and is now a professional physical therapist.

I suggested to Chris, the student who was thinking about becoming an elementary school teacher, that he visit some local schools to see whether they could use a volunteer teacher's aide. One of the schools did need his services, and Chris volunteered as a teacher's aide for about 10 weeks. At the halfway point during his volunteer experience, he came into my office to tell me that the kids were just about driving him crazy and that he no longer had any interest in becoming a teacher. He ended up majoring in communications.

Kim and Chris were the first two students I advised to get involved in volunteer work to test their career interests. Their volunteer experiences proved so valuable for helping both of them make a career decision that I now encourage all students I advise to get volunteer experience in the field they're considering as a future career.

—Joe Cuseo

Volunteer service also enables you to network with professionals outside of college who may serve as excellent references and resources for letters of recommendation for you. Furthermore, if these professionals are impressed with your volunteer work, they may become interested in hiring you part time while you're still in college or full time when you graduate.

It may be possible to do volunteer work on campus by serving as an informal teaching assistant or research assistant to a faculty member. Such experiences are particularly valuable for students intending to go to graduate school. If you have a good relationship with any faculty members who are working in an academic field that interests you, consider asking them whether they would like some assistance (e.g., with their teaching or research responsibilities). Your volunteer work for a college professor could lead to making a presentation with your professor at a professional conference or may even result in your name being included as a coauthor on an article published by the professor.

Pause for Reflection

Have you done volunteer work? If you have, did you learn anything from your volunteer experiences that might help you decide which types of work best match your interests or talents?

Part-Time Work

Jobs that you hold during the academic year or during summer break should not be overlooked as potential sources of career information and as résumé-building experience. Part-time work can provide opportunities to learn or develop skills that may be relevant to your future career, such as organizational skills, communication skills, and ability to work effectively with co-workers from diverse backgrounds or culture.

Also, work in a part-time position may eventually turn into a full-time career. The following personal story illustrates how this can happen.

Personal Story

One student of mine, an English major, worked part time for an organization that provides special assistance to mentally handicapped children. After he completed his English degree, he was offered a full-time position in this organization, which he accepted. While working at his full-time position with handicapped children, he decided to go to graduate school part time and eventually completed a master's degree in special education, which qualified him for a promotion to a more advanced position in the organization, which he also accepted.

—Joe Cuseo

It might also be possible for you to obtain part-time work experience on campus through your school's work–study program. A work–study job allows you to work at your college in various work settings, such as the Financial Aid Office, college library, Public Relations Office, or Computer Services Center, and often allows you to build your employment schedule around your academic schedule. On-campus work can provide you with valuable career-exploration and résumé-building experiences, and the professionals for whom you work can serve as excellent references for letters of recommendation to future employers. To see whether you are eligible for your school's work–study program, visit the Financial Aid Office on your campus.

Learning about careers through firsthand experience in actual work settings (e.g., shadowing, internships, volunteer services, and part-time work) is critical to successful career exploration and preparation. You can take a career-interest test, or you can test your career interest through actual work experiences. There is simply no substitute for direct, hands-on experience for gaining knowledge about careers. These firsthand experiences represent the ultimate career-reality test. They allow you direct access to information about what careers are like—as opposed to how they are portrayed on TV or in the movies, which often paint an inaccurate or unrealistic picture of careers, making them appear more exciting or glamorous than they are.

In summary, firsthand experiences in actual work settings equip you with five powerful career advantages that enable you to:

- Learn about what work is like in a particular field;
- Test your interest and skills for certain types of work;
- Strengthen your résumé by adding experiential learning to academic (classroom) learning;
- Acquire contacts for letters of recommendation; and
- Network with employers who may refer or hire you for a position after graduation.

> "Give me a history major who has done internships and a business major who hasn't, and I'll hire the history major every time."
>
> –William Ardery, senior vice president, investor communications company

Furthermore, gaining firsthand work experience early in college not only promotes your job prospects after graduation but also makes you more a competitive candidate for internships and part-time positions that you may apply for during college.

Be sure to use your campus resources (e.g., the Career Development Center and Financial Aid Office), your local resources (e.g., Chamber of Commerce), and your personal contacts (e.g., family and friends) to locate and participate in work experiences that relate to your career interests. When you land an internship, work hard at it, learn as much as you can from it, and build relationships with as many people as possible at your internship site because these are the people who can provide you with future contacts, references, and referrals.

Step 3. Awareness of What Best Fits You

Effective decision making requires you to identify all important factors that should be considered when evaluating your options and to determine how much weight (influence) each of these factors should carry. As we emphasize throughout this chapter, the factor that should carry the greatest weight in career decision making is the match between your choice and your personal abilities, interests, needs, and values.

Pause for Reflection

1. Have you learned anything from your firsthand work experiences that may influence your future career plans?

2. If you could get firsthand work experience in any career field, what career would it be?

> "Money is a good servant but a bad master."
>
> —French proverb

! Remember

A good career decision should involve more than salary and should take into consideration how the career will affect all of your dimensions of self (social, emotional, physical, etc.) throughout all stages of your adult life: young adulthood, middle age, and late adulthood. It's almost inevitable that your career will affect your identity, the type of person you become, how you balance the demands of work and family, and how well you serve others beyond yourself. An effective career decision-making process requires you to make tough and thoughtful decisions about what matters most to you.

! Remember

A good career choice should be more than financially rewarding; it should be personally fulfilling.

Step 4. Awareness of the Process

Whether you're keeping your career options open or you think you've already decided on a particular career, you can start taking steps to prepare for career success by using the following strategies to prepare for successful career entry and advancement.

Self-Monitoring: Watching and Tracking Your Personal Skills and Positive Qualities

Don't forget that learning skills are also earning skills. The skills you're acquiring in college may appear to be just *academic* skills, but they're also *career* skills. For instance, when you're in the process of completing academic tasks such as taking tests and writing papers, you're using various career-relevant skills (e.g., analyzing, organizing, communicating, and problem solving).

Many students think that a college diploma is an automatic passport to a good job and career success (Ellin, 1993; Sullivan, 1993). However, for most

Pause for Reflection

Answer the following questions about a career that you're considering or have chosen:

1. Why are you considering this career? (What led or caused you to become interested in it?)

2. Would you say that your interest in this career is motivated primarily by intrinsic factors—that is, factors "inside" of you, such as your personal abilities, interests, needs, and values? Or, would you say that your interest in the career is influenced more heavily by extrinsic factors—that is, factors "outside" of you, such as starting salary, pleasing parents, meeting family expectations, or meeting an expected role for your gender (male role or female role)?

3. If money were not an issue and you could earn a comfortable living in any career, would you choose the same career?

employers of college graduates, what matters most is not only the credential but also the skills and personal strengths an applicant brings to the position (Education Commission of the States, 1995). You can start building these skills and strengths by self-monitoring (i.e., watching yourself and keeping track of the skills you're using and developing during your college experience). Skills are mental habits, and like all other habits that are repeatedly practiced, their development can be so gradual that you may not even notice how much growth is taking place—perhaps somewhat like watching grass grow. Thus, career development specialists recommend that you consciously track your skills to remain aware of them and to put you in a position to "sell" them to potential employers (Lock, 2000).

One strategy you can use to track your developing skills is to keep a career-development journal in which you note academic tasks and assignments you've completed, along with the skills you used to complete them. Be sure to record skills in your journal that you've developed in nonacademic situations, such as those skills used while performing part-time jobs, personal hobbies, cocurricular activities, or volunteer services. Since skills are actions, it's best to record them as action verbs in your career-development journal.

The key to discovering career-relevant skills and qualities is to get in the habit of stepping back from your academic and out-of-class experiences to reflect on what skills and qualities these experiences entailed and then get them down in writing before they slip your mind. You're likely to find that many personal skills you develop in college will be the same ones that employers will seek in the workforce. **Box 11.2** contains some important career-success skills that you're likely to develop during your college experience.

Take Action!

Personal Skills Relevant to Successful Career Performance

The following behaviors represent a sample of useful skills that are relevant to success in various careers (Bolles, 1998). As you read these skills, underline or highlight any of them that you have performed, either inside or outside of school.

advising	assembling	calculating	coaching	coordinating
creating	delegating	designing	evaluating	explaining
initiating	measuring	mediating	motivating	negotiating
operating	planning	producing	proving	researching
resolving	sorting	summarizing	supervising	synthesizing

Personal Story

After class one day, I had a conversation with a student (Max) about his personal interests. He said he was considering a career in the music industry and was working part time as a disc jockey at a night club. I asked him what it took to be a good disc jockey, and in less than 5 minutes of conversation, we discovered many more skills were involved in doing his job than either of us had realized. He was responsible for organizing 3 to 4 hours of music each night he worked; he had to read the reactions of his audience (customers) and adapt or adjust his selections to their musical tastes; he had to arrange his selections in a sequence that periodically varied the tempo (speed) of the music he played throughout the night; and he had to continually research and update his music collection to track the latest trends in hits and popular artists. Max also said that he had to overcome his fear of public speaking to deliver announcements that were a required part of his job.

Although we were just having a short, friendly conversation after class about his part-time job, Max wound up reflecting on and identifying multiple skills he was using on the job. We both agreed that it would be a good idea to get these skills down in writing so that he could use them as selling points for future jobs in the music industry or in any industry.

—Joe Cuseo

In addition to tracking your developing skills, track your positive traits or personal qualities. While it's best to record your skills as action verbs because they represent actions that you can perform for anyone who hires you, it may be best to track your attributes as adjectives because they describe who you are and what personal qualities you can bring to the job. **Box 11.3** gives a sample of personal traits and qualities that are relevant to success in multiple careers.

Take Action!

Personal Traits and Qualities Relevant to Successful Career Performance   11.3

The following are some skills that are relevant to success in various careers. As you read these traits, underline or highlight any of them that you feel you possess or will soon possess.

conscientious	considerate	courteous	curious	dependable
determined	energetic	enthusiastic	ethical	flexible
imaginative	industrious	loyal	observant	open minded
outgoing	patient	persuasive	positive	precise
prepared	productive	prudent	punctual	reflective
sincere	tactful	team player	thorough	thoughtful

> **! Remember**
>
> Keeping track of your developing skills and your positive qualities is as important to your successful entry into a future career as completing courses and compiling credits.

Self-Marketing: Packaging and Presenting Your Personal Strengths and Achievements

To convert your college experience into immediate employment, it might be useful to view yourself (a college graduate) as a product and employers as intentional customers who may be interested in making a purchase (of your skills and attributes). As a first-year student, it could be said that you're in the early stages of the product-development process. Begin the process now so that by the time you graduate your finished product (you) will be one that employers notice and become interested in purchasing.

An effective self-marketing plan is one that gives employers a clear idea of what you can bring to the table and do for them. This should increase the number of job offers you receive and increase your chances of finding a position that best matches your interests, talents, and values.

You can effectively advertise or market your personal skills, qualities, and achievements to future employers through the following channels.

Pause for Reflection

Look back at the personal skills and traits listed in Boxes 11.2 and 11.3 that you noted you possess or will soon possess.

1. Do you see your personal skills and traits as being relevant to the career or careers you're considering?

2. Do you see these skills and traits being as relevant, or more relevant, to any career or careers that you haven't yet considered?

College Transcript

A college transcript is a listing of all courses you enrolled in and the grades you received in those courses. Two pieces of information included on your college transcript can influence employers' hiring decisions or admissions committee decisions about your acceptance to a 4-year college, graduate, or professional school: (a) the grades you earned in your courses and (b) the types of courses you completed.

Simply stated, the better your grades in college, the better your employment prospects after college. Research on college graduates indicates that the higher their grades, the higher:

- The prestige of their first job;
- Their total earnings; and
- Their job mobility.

This relationship between college grades and career success exists for students at all types of colleges and universities, regardless of the reputation or prestige of the institution they attend (Pascarella & Terenzini, 1991, 2005).

Cocurricular Experiences

Participation in student clubs, campus organizations, and other types of cocurricular activities can be a valuable source of experiential learning that can complement classroom-based learning and contribute to your career preparation and development. A sizable body of research supports the value of cocurricular experiences for career success (Astin, 1993; Kuh, 1993; Pascarella & Terenzini, 1991, 2005). Strongly consider getting involved cocurricular life on your campus, especially involvement with cocurricular experiences that

- Allow you to develop leadership and helping skills (e.g., leadership retreats, student government, college committees, peer counseling, or peer tutoring);
- Enable you to interact with others from diverse ethnic and racial groups (e.g., multicultural club or international club); and
- Provide you with out-of-class experiences related to your academic major or career interests (e.g., student clubs in your college major or intended career field).

Keep in mind that cocurricular experiences are also résumé-building experiences that provide solid evidence of your commitment to the college community outside the classroom. Be sure to showcase these experiences to prospective employers.

Also, the campus professionals with whom you may interact while participating in cocurricular activities (e.g., the director of student activities or dean of students) can serve as valuable references for letters of recommendation to future employers or graduate and professional schools.

Personal Portfolio

You may have heard the word "portfolio" in reference to a collection of artwork that professional artists put together to showcase or advertise their artistic talents. However, a portfolio can be a collection of any materials or products that illustrates an individual's skills and talents or demonstrates an individual's educational and personal development. For example, a portfolio could include such items as:

- Outstanding papers, exam performances, research projects, or lab reports;
- Artwork and photos from study-abroad, service learning, or internships experiences;
- Video footage of oral presentations or theatrical performances;
- CDs of musical performances;
- Assessments from employers or coaches; and
- Letters of recognition or commendation.

You can start the process of portfolio development right now by saving your best work and performances. Store them in a traditional portfolio folder, or save them on a computer disc to create an electronic portfolio. Another option would be to create a Web site and upload your materials there. Eventually, you should be able to build a well-stocked portfolio that documents your skills and demonstrates your development to future employers or future schools. You can start to develop an electronic portfolio now by completing Exercise 11.2 at the end of this chapter.

Pause for Reflection

What do you predict will be your best work products in college—those that are most likely to appear in your portfolio?

Why?

The ritual of burning completed coursework in high school is not recommended in college. (Instead, save your best work, and include it in a personal portfolio.)

Personal Résumé

Unlike a portfolio, which contains actual products or samples of your work, a résumé may be described as a listed summary of your most important accomplishments, skills, and credentials. If you have just graduated from high school, you may not have accumulated enough experiences to construct a fully developed résumé. However, you can start to build a skeletal résumé that contains major categories or headings (the skeleton) under which you'll eventually include your experiences and accomplishments. (See **Box 11.4** for a sample skeleton résumé.) As you acquire experiences, you can flesh out the résumé's skeleton by gradually filling in its general categories with skills, accomplishments, and credentials.

Take Action!

Constructing a Résumé

11.4

Use this skeletal résumé as an outline or template for beginning construction of your own résumé and for setting your future goals. (If you have already developed a résumé, use this template to identify and add categories that may be missing from your current one.)

Name (First, Middle, Last)

Current Addresses:	Permanent Addresses:
Postal address	Postal address
E-mail address	E-mail address
Phone no.	Phone no.

EDUCATION: Name of College or University, City, State
                       Degree Name (e.g., Bachelor of Science)
                       College Major (e.g., Accounting)
                       Graduation Date, GPA

RELATED WORK   Position Title, City, State   Start and stop dates
EXPERIENCES: (Begin the list with the most recent
(List skills used or developed.)   position dates held.)

VOLUNTEER (COMMUNITY SERVICE)
EXPERIENCES:
(List skills used or developed.)

NOTABLE COURSEWORK:
(e.g., leadership, international, or interdisciplinary courses)

COCURRICULAR EXPERIENCES:
(e.g., student government or peer leadership)
(List skills used or developed.)

PERSONAL SKILLS AND POSITIVE QUALITIES:
(List as bullets. Be sure to include those that are especially relevant to the position for which you're applying.)

HONORS AND AWARDS: (In addition to those received in college, you may include those received in high school.)

PERSONAL INTERESTS: (Include items that showcase any special hobbies or talents that are not directly related to school or work.)

Letters of Recommendation (a.k.a. Letters of Reference)

Personal letters of recommendation can be a powerful way to document your strengths and selling points. To maximize the power of your personal recommendations, give careful thought to:

- Who should serve as your references;
- How to approach them; and
- What to provide them.

Strategies for improving the quality of your letters of recommendation are suggested in **Box 11.5**.

Take Action!

11.5

The Art and Science of Requesting Letters of Recommendation: Effective Strategies and Common Courtesies

1. Select recommendations from people who know you well. Think about individuals with whom you've had an ongoing relationship, who know your name, and who know your strengths; for example, an instructor who you've had for more than one class, an academic advisor whom you see often, or an employer whom you've worked for over an extended period.

2. Seek a balanced blend of letters from people who have observed your performance in different settings or situations. The following are settings in which you may have performed well and people who may have observed your performance in these settings:
    - The classroom—a professor who can speak to your academic performance
    - On campus—a student life professional for a cocurricular reference who can comment on your contributions outside the classroom
    - Off campus—a professional for whom you've performed volunteer service, part-time work, or an internship
3. Pick the right time and place to make your request. Be sure to make your request well in

advance of the letter's deadline date (e.g., at least 2 weeks). First ask whether the person is willing to write the letter, and then come back with forms and envelopes. Do not approach the person with these materials in hand because this may send the message that you have assumed or presumed the person will automatically say "yes." (This is not the most socially sensitive message to send someone whom you're about to ask for a favor.) Lastly, pick a place where the person can give full attention to your request. For instance, make a personal visit to the person's office, rather than making the request in a busy hallway or in front of a classroom full of students.

4. Waive your right to see the letter. If the school or organization to which you're applying has a reference-letter form that asks whether or not you want to waive (give up) your right to see the letter, waive your right—as long as you feel reasonably certain that you will be receiving a good letter of recommendation. By waiving your right to see your letter of recommendation, you show confidence that the letter to be written about you will be positive, and you assure the person who reads the letter that you didn't inspect or screen it to make sure it was a good one before sending it.

5. Provide your references with a fact sheet about yourself. Include your experiences and achievements—both inside and outside the classroom. This will help make your references' job a little easier by providing points to focus on. More importantly, it will help you

because your letter becomes more powerful when it contains concrete examples or illustrations of your positive qualities and accomplishments. On your fact sheet, be sure to include any exceptionally high grades you may have earned in certain courses, as well as volunteer services, leadership experiences, special awards or forms of recognition, and special interests or talents that relate to your academic major and career choice. Your fact sheet is the place and time for you to "toot your own horn," so don't be afraid of coming across as a braggart or egotist. You're not being conceited; you're just showcasing your strengths.

6. Provide your references with a stamped, addressed envelope. This is a simple courtesy that makes their job a little easier and demonstrates your social sensitivity.

7. Follow up with a thank-you note. Thank your references about the time your letter of recommendation should be sent. This is the right thing to do because it shows your appreciation; it's also the smart thing to do because if the letter hasn't been written yet the thank-you note serves as a gentle reminder for your reference to write the letter.

8. Let your references know the outcome of your application (e.g., your admission to a school or acceptance of a job offer). This is the courteous thing to do, and your references are likely to remember your courtesy, which could strengthen the quality of any future letters they may write for you.

◆ Summary and Conclusion

Pause for Reflection

Have you met a faculty member or other professional on campus who knows you well enough to write a personal letter of recommendation for you?

If yes, who is this person, and what position does he or she hold on campus?

In national surveys, employers rank attitude of the job applicant as the number one factor in making hiring decisions; they rate this higher in importance than such factors as reputation of the applicant's school, previous work experience, and recommendations of former employers (Education Commission of the States, 1995; Institute for Research on Higher Education, 1995). Graduating from college with a diploma in hand may make you a more competitive job candidate, but you still have to compete by documenting and selling your strengths and skills. Your diploma doesn't work like a merit badge or passport that you flash to gain automatic access to an ideal job. Your college experience will open career doors, but it's your attitude, initiative, and effort that will enable you to step through those doors and into a successful career.

Internet-Based Resources for Further Information on Careers

For additional information related to the ideas discussed in this chapter, we recommend the following Web sites:

Career Descriptions and Future Employment Outlook: **www.bls.gov/oco**

Internships: **www.internships.com**

www.vaultreports.com

Personalized Career Plan:

www.mapping-your-future.org

Position openings:

www.monster.com

Salaries Associated with Specific Positions:

www.salary.com

11.1 Conducting an Information Interview

To learn accurate information about a career that interests you, interview working professionals in that career—a career-exploration strategy known as information interviewing. An information interview enables you to:

• Learn what a career is really like;

• Network with professionals in the field; and

• Become confident in interview situations and prepare for later job interviews.

1. Select a career that you may be interested in pursuing. Even if you are currently keeping your career options open, pick a career that might be a possibility. You can use the resources cited on **p. 272** in this chapter to help you identify a career that may be most appealing to you.

2. Find someone who is working in the career you selected and set up an information interview with that person.

   To help locate possible interview candidates, consider members of your family, friends of your family members, and family members of your friends. Any of these people may be working in the career you selected and may be good interview candidates, or they may know others who could be good candidates. The Career Development Center on your campus and the Alumni Association (or the Rotaract Club) may also be able to provide you with graduates of your college, or professionals working in the local community near your college, who are willing to talk about their careers with students.

   Lastly, you might consider using the Yellow Pages or the Internet to find names and addresses of possible candidates. Send them a short letter or e-mail asking about the possibility of scheduling a short interview. Mention that you would be willing to conduct the interview in person or by phone, whichever would be more convenient for them.

   If you do not hear back within a reasonable period (e.g., within a couple of weeks), send a follow-up message; if you do not receive a response to the follow-up message, then consider contacting someone else.

3. Conduct an information interview with the professional who has agreed to speak with you. Consider using the following suggested strategies.

- **Thank the person for taking the time to speak with you.** This should be the first thing you do after meeting the person—before you officially begin the interview.

- **Prepare your interview questions in advance.** Here are some questions that you might consider asking:

  1. How did you decide on your career?

  2. What qualifications or prior experiences did you have that enabled you to enter your career?

  3. How does someone find out about openings in your field?

  4. What steps did you take to find your current position?

  5. What advice would you give to beginning college students about things they could start doing now to help them prepare to enter your career?

  6. During a typical day's work, what do you spend most of your time doing?

  7. What do you like most about your career?

  8. What are the most difficult or frustrating aspects of your career?

  9. What personal skills or qualities do you see as being critical for success in your career?

  10. How does someone advance in your career?

  11. Are there any moral issues or ethical challenges that tend to arise in your career?

  12. Are members of diverse groups likely to be found in your career? (This is an especially important question to ask if you are a member of an ethnic, racial, or gender group that is underrepresented in the career field.)

  13. What impact does your career have on your home life or personal life outside of work?

  14. If you had to do it all over again, would you choose the same career?

  15. Would you recommend that I speak with anyone else to obtain additional information or a different perspective on this career field? (If the answer is "yes," you may follow up by asking: "May I mention that you referred me?") This question is recommended because it's always a good idea to obtain more than one person's perspective before making an important choice or decision, especially one that can have a major influence on your life—such as your career choice.

- **Take notes during the interview.** This not only benefits you by helping you remember what was said; it also sends a positive message to the person you're interviewing by showing that the person's ideas are important and worth writing down.

If the interview goes well, you could ask whether it might be possible to observe or shadow your interviewee during a day at work.

Self-Assessment Questions

After completing your interview, take a moment to reflect on it and answer the following questions:

1. What information did you receive that impressed you about this career?

2. What information did you receive that distressed (or depressed) you about this career?

3. What was the most useful thing you learned from conducting this interview?

4. Knowing what you know now, would you still be interested in pursuing this career? (If yes, why?) (If no, why not?)

11.2 Creating an Electronic Portfolio

Using Folio180, create an electronic portfolio of your accomplishments and activities. In this assignment, you will collect information related to the following four areas:

1. Interests

2. Work and professional experiences

3. Awards, honors, and commendations

4. Academic work

You will also have the opportunity to support your entries with documents (e.g., Word, Excel and PowerPoint files) as well as electronic photos, videos and recordings. When completed, you will have a professional-looking electronic portfolio that you can use to showcase in applications for jobs, internships, scholarships and admission to graduate and professional schools.

Detailed instructions for this assignment are found at http://www.folio180.com/customer/KH-Cuseo/Thriving2_11_portfolio1.htm. Just type in this URL in your Internet browser, and follow the instructions.

Career Choice: Conflict and Confusion

Josh is a first-year student whose family has made a great financial sacrifice to send him to college. He deeply appreciates the tremendous commitment his family members have made to his education and wants to pay them back as soon as possible. Consequently, he has been looking into careers that offer the highest starting salaries to college students immediately after graduation. Unfortunately, none of these careers seem to match Josh's natural abilities and personal interests, so he's conflicted, confused, and starting to get stressed out. He knows he'll have to make a decision soon because the careers with high starting salaries involve majors that have many course requirements, and if he expects to graduate in a reasonable period, he'll have to start taking some of these courses during his first year.

Reflection and Discussion Questions

1. If you were Josh, what would you do?

2. Do you see any way that Josh might balance his desire to pay back his family as soon as possible with his desire to pursue a career that's compatible with his interests and talents?

3. What other questions or factors do you think Josh should consider before making his decision?"If you want to earn more, learn more."

Managing Money and Minimizing Debt

12

ACTIVATE YOUR THINKING | Journal Entry **12.1**

Complete the following sentence with the first thought that comes to your mind:

For me, money is . . .

_____

_____

_____

_____

LEARNING GOAL

To become more self-aware, knowledgeable, and strategic with respect to managing your money and financing your college education.

The beginning of college often means the beginning of greater personal independence and greater demands for economic self-sufficiency, critical thinking about consumerism, and effective management of personal finances. The importance of money management for college students is growing for two major reasons. One is the rising cost of a college education, which is causing more students to work while in college and to work more hours per week (Levine & Cureton, 1998). The rising cost of a college education is also requiring students to make more complex decisions about what options (or combination of options) they will use to meet their college expenses. Unfortunately, research indicates that many students today are not choosing financial strategies that contribute most effectively to their educational success in college and their long-term financial success after college (King, 2005).

A second reason money management is growing in importance for college students is the availability and convenience of credit cards. For students today, credit cards are easy to get, easy to use, and easy to abuse. College students can do everything right, such as getting solid grades, getting involved on campus, and getting work experience before graduating, but a poor credit history due to irresponsible use of credit cards in college can reduce students' chances of obtaining credit after college and their chances of being hired after graduation. Credit reporting agencies or bureaus collect information about how well you make credit-card payments and report your credit score to credit-card companies and banks. Potential employers will check your credit score as an indicator or predictor of how responsible you will be as an employee because of a statistical relationship between using credit card responsibly and being a responsible employee. Thus, being irresponsible with credit while you're

in college can affect your ability to land a job after (or during) college. Your credit score report will also affect your likelihood of qualifying for car loans and home loans, as well as your ability to rent an apartment (Pratt, 2008).

Furthermore, research indicates that accumulating high levels of debt while in college is associated with higher levels of stress (Kiecolt et al., 1986), lower academic performance (Susswein, 1995), and greater risk of withdrawing from college (Ring, 1997). On the positive side of the ledger, studies show that when students learn to use effective money-management strategies, they can decrease unnecessary spending, prevent accumulation of significant debt, and reduce personal stress (Health & Soll, 1996; Walker, 1996).

◆ Strategies for Managing Money Effectively

Developing Financial Self-Awareness

Student Perspective

"My money-management skills are poor. If I have money, I will spend it unless somebody takes it away from me. I am the kind of person who lives from paycheck to paycheck."

–First-year student

Developing any good habit begins with the critical first step of self-awareness. Developing the habit of effective money management begins with awareness of your cash flow—the amount of money you have flowing in and flowing out. As illustrated in **Figure 12.1**, you can track your cash flow by monitoring:

- The amount of money you have coming in (income) versus going out (expenses or expenditures); and
- The amount of money you have accumulated and not spent (savings) versus the amount of money you have borrowed and haven't yet paid back (debt).

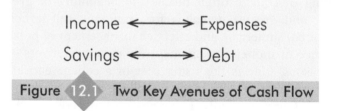

Income ⟷ Expenses

Savings ⟷ Debt

Figure 12.1 Two Key Avenues of Cash Flow

Income for college students typically comes from one or more of the following sources:

- Scholarships or grants, which don't have to be paid back
- Loans, which must be repaid
- Salary earned from part-time or full-time work
- Personal savings
- Gifts or other forms of monetary support from parents and other family members

Yours sources of expenses or expenditures may be classified into three categories:

1. Basic needs or essential necessities—expenses that tend to be fixed because you cannot do without them (e.g., expenses for food, housing, tuition, textbooks, phone, transportation to and from school, and health-related costs)
2. Incidentals or extras—expenses that tend to be flexible because spending money on them is optional or discretionary (i.e., you choose to spend at your own discretion or judgment); these expenses typically include

- Money spent on entertainment, enjoyment, or pleasure (e.g., music, movies, and spring-break vacations); and
- Money spent primarily for reasons of promoting personal status or self-image (e.g., buying expensive, brand name products; fashionable clothes; jewelry; and other personal accessories).

3. Emergency expenses—unpredicted, unforeseen, or unexpected costs (e.g., money paid for doctor visits and medicine resulting from illnesses or accidents)

Developing a Money-Management Plan

Once you're aware of the amount of money you have coming in (and from what sources) and the amount of money you're spending (and for what reasons), the next step is to develop a plan for managing your cash flow. The bottom line is to ensure that the money coming in (income) is equal to or greater than the money going out (expenses). If the amount of money you're spending exceeds the amount you have coming in, you're "in the red" or have negative cash flow.

◆ Strategic Selection and Use of Financial Tools for Tracking Cash Flow

Several financial tools or instruments can be used to track your cash flow and manage your money. These cash-flow instruments include:

- Checking accounts;
- Credit cards;
- Charge cards; and
- Debit cards.

Checking Account

Long before credit cards were created, a checking account was the method most people used to keep track of their money. Many people still use checking accounts in addition to (or instead of) credit cards.

A checking account may be obtained from a bank or credit union; its typical costs include a deposit ($20–$25) to open the account, a monthly service fee (e.g., $10), and small fees for checks. Some banks charge customers a service fee based on the number of checks written, which is a good option if you don't plan to write many checks each month. If you maintain a high enough balance of money deposited in your account, the bank may not charge any extra fees, and if you're able to maintain an even higher balance, the bank may also pay you interest—known as an interest-bearing checking account.

Along with your checking account, banks usually provide you with an automatic teller machine (ATM) card that you can use to get cash. Look for a checking account that does not charge you fees for ATM transactions but provides this as a free service with your account. Also, look for a checking account that doesn't charge you if your balance drops below a certain minimum figure.

Strategies for Using Checking Accounts Effectively

Apply the following strategies to make the best use of your checking account:

- Whenever you write a check or make an ATM withdrawal, immediately subtract its amount from your balance—i.e., amount of money remaining in your account to determine your new balance.
- Keep a running balance in your checkbook; it will ensure that you know exactly how much money you have in your account at all times. This will reduce the risk that you'll write a check that bounces (i.e., a check that you don't have enough money in the bank to cover). If you do bounce a check, you'll probably have to pay a charge to the bank and possibly to the business that attempted to cash your bounced check.
- Double-check your checkbook balance with each monthly statement you receive from the bank. Be sure to include the service charges your bank makes to your account that appear on your monthly statement. This practice will make it easier to track errors—on either your part or the bank's part. (Banks can and do make mistakes occasionally.)

Advantages of a Checking Account

A checking account has several advantages:

- You can carry checks instead of cash.
- You have access to cash at almost any time through an ATM machine.
- It allows you to keep a visible track record of income and expenses in your checkbook.
- A properly managed checking account can serve as a good credit reference for future loans and purchases.

Credit Card (e.g., MasterCard®, Visa®, or Discover®)

A credit card is basically money loaned to you by the credit-card company that issues you the card, which you pay back to the company monthly. You can pay the whole bill or a portion of the bill each month—as long as some minimum payment is made. However, for any remaining (unpaid) portion of your bill, you are charged a high interest rate, which is usually about 18 percent.

Strategies for Selecting a Credit Card

If you decide to use a credit card, pay attention to its annual percentage rate (APR). This is the interest rate you pay for previously unpaid monthly balances, and it can vary depending on the credit-card company. Credit-card companies also vary in terms of their annual service fee. You will likely find companies that charge higher interest rates tend to charge lower annual fees, and vice versa. As a rule, if you expect to pay the full balance every month, you're probably better off choosing a credit card that does not charge you an annual service fee. On the other hand, if you think you'll need more time to make the full monthly payments, you may be better off with a credit-card company that offers a low interest rate.

Another feature that differentiates one credit-card company from another is whether or not you're allowed a grace period (i.e., a certain period after you receive your monthly statement during which you can pay back the company without paying added interest fees). Some companies may allow you a grace period of a full month, while others may provide none and begin charging interest immediately after you fail to pay on the bill's due date.

Credit cards may also differ in terms of their credit limit (a.k.a. a credit line or line of credit), which refers to the maximum amount of money the credit-card company will make available to you. If you are a new customer, most companies will set a credit limit beyond which you will not be granted any additional credit.

Don't let peer pressure determine your spending habits.

Advantages of a Credit Card

If a credit card is used responsibly, it has some advantages as a money-management tool. Its features can provide the following advantages:

- It helps you track your spending habits because the credit-card company sends you a monthly statement that includes an itemized list of all your card-related purchases. This list provides you with a paper trail of what you purchased that month and when you purchased it.
- It provides the convenience of making purchases online, which may save you some time and money that would otherwise be spent traveling to and from stores.
- It allows access to cash whenever and wherever you need, because any bank or ATM machine that displays your credit card's symbol will give you cash up to a certain limit, usually for a small transaction fee. Keep in mind that some credit-card companies charge a higher interest rate for cash advances than purchases.
- It enables you to establish a personal credit history. If you use a credit card responsibly, you can establish a good credit history that can be used later in life for big-ticket purchases such as a car or home. In effect, responsible use of a credit card shows others from whom you wish to seek credit (borrow money) that you're financially responsible.

!

Remember

Do not buy into the belief that the only way you can establish a good credit history is by using a credit card. It's not your only option; you can establish a good credit history through responsible use of a checking account and by paying your bills on time.

Strategies for Using Credit Cards Responsibly

While there may be advantages to using a credit card, you only reap those advantages if you use your card strategically. If not, the advantages of a credit card will be quickly and greatly outweighed by its disadvantages. Listed here are some strategies for using a credit card in a way that maximizes its advantages and minimizes its disadvantages.

1. Use a credit card only as a convenience for making purchases and tracking the purchases you make; do not use it as a tool for obtaining a long-term loan.

A credit card's main money-management advantage is that it allows you to make purchases with plastic instead of cash. The credit card allows you the convenience of not carrying around cash and enables you to receive a monthly statement of your purchases from the credit-card company, which makes it easier for you to track and analyze your spending habits.

The credit provided by a credit card should be seen simply as a short-term loan that must be paid back at the end of every month.

> **!** **Remember**
>
> Do not use credit cards for long-term credit or long-term loans because their interest rates are outrageously high. Paying such a high rate of interest for a loan represents an ineffective (and irresponsible) money-management strategy.

2. Limit yourself to one card.

> **Student Perspective**
>
> "I need to pay attention to my balance more closely and actually allot certain amounts for certain things."
>
> –First-year student

The average college student has 2.8 credit cards (United College Marketing Service, cited in Pratt, 2008). More than one credit card just means more accounts to keep track of and more opportunities to accumulate debt. You don't need additional credit cards from department stores, gas stations, or any other profit-making business because they duplicate what your personal credit card already does (plus they charge extremely high interest rates for late payments).

3. Pay off your balance each month in full and on time.

> **Student Perspective**
>
> "What I don't do that I know I should do is pay my bills on time, i.e., cell phone and credit cards."
>
> –First-year student

If you pay the full amount of your bill each month, this means that you're using your credit card effectively to obtain an interest-free, short-term (1-month) loan. You're just paying principal—the total amount of money borrowed and nothing more. However, if your payment is late and you need to pay interest, you end up paying more for the items you purchased than their actual ticket price. For instance, if you have an unpaid balance of $500 on your monthly credit bill for merchandise purchased the previous month and you are charged the typical 18 percent credit-card interest rate for late payment, you end up paying $590: $500 (merchandise) + $90 (18 percent interest to the credit-card company).

Credit-card companies make their money or profit from the interest they collect from cardholders who do not pay back their credit on time. Just as procrastinating about doing your work is a poor time-management habit, procrastinating about paying your credit-card bills is a poor money-management habit that can cost you dearly in the long run because of the high interest rate you pay.

Pay your total balance on time and avoid paying these huge interest rates to credit-card companies, which allow them to get rich at your expense. If you cannot pay the total amount owed at the end of the month, pay off as much of it as you possibly can—rather than making the minimum monthly payment. If you keep making only the minimum payment each month and continue using your credit card, you'll begin to pile up huge amounts of debt.

> **"**
>
> "You'll never get your credit card debt paid off if you keep charging on your card and make only the minimum monthly payment. Paying only the minimum is like using a Dixie cup to bail water from a sinking boat."
>
> –Eric Tyson, financial counselor and national best-selling author of *Personal Finance for Dummies* (2003)

> **!** **Remember**
>
> If you keep charging on your credit card while you have an unpaid balance or debt, you no longer have a grace period to pay back your charges; instead, interest is charged immediately on all your purchases.

Charge Card

A charge card works similar to a credit card in that you are given a short-term loan for 1 month; the only difference is that you must pay your bill in full at the end of each month and you cannot carry over any debt from one month to the next. Its major disadvantage relative to a credit card is that it has less flexibility—no matter what your expenses may be for a particular month, you must still pay up or lose your ability to acquire credit for the next month. For people who habitually fail to pay their monthly credit-card bill on time, this makes a charge card a smarter money-management tool than a credit card because the cardholder cannot continue to accumulate debt.

Debit Card

A debit card looks almost identical to a credit card (e.g., it has a MasterCard or Visa logo), but it works differently. When you use a debit card, money is immediately taken out or subtracted from your checking account. Thus, you're only using money that's already in your account (rather than borrowing money), and you don't receive a bill at the end of the month. If you attempt to purchase something with a debit card that costs more than the amount of money you have in your account, your card will not allow you to do so. Just like a bounced check, a debit card will not permit you to pay out any money that is not in your account. Like a check or ATM withdrawal, a purchase made with a debit card should immediately be subtracted from your balance.

Like a credit card, a major advantage of the debit card is that it provides you with the convenience of plastic; unlike a credit card, it prevents you from spending beyond your means and accumulating debt. For this reason, financial advisors often recommend using a debit card rather than a credit card (Knox, 2004; Tyson, 2003).

◆ Sources of Income for Financing Your College Education

Free Application for Federal Student Aid

The Free Application for Federal Student Aid (FAFSA) is the application used by the U.S. Department of Education to determine aid eligibility for students. A formula is used to determine each student's estimated family contribution (EFC), which is the amount of money the government has determined a family can contribute to the educational costs of the student. No fee is charged to complete the application, and you should complete

---

Pause for Reflection

1. Do you have a credit card? Do you have more than one?

2. If you have at least one credit card, do you pay off your entire balance each month?

3. If you don't pay off your entire balance each month, what would you say is your average unpaid balance per month?

4. What changes would you have to make in your money-management habits to be able to pay off your entire balance each month?

❝

"Never spend your money before you have it."

—Thomas Jefferson, third president of the United States and founder of the University of Virginia

---

Pause for Reflection

Which of the terms in the preceding list were new to you?

Do any of these terms apply to your current financial situation or money-management plans?

Snapshot Summary

12.1

Financial Literacy: Understanding the Language of Money Management

As you can tell from the variety of financial terms that have already been used in this chapter, you have to acquire a vocabulary of fiscal terms to be able to understand your financial options and transactions; in other words, you have to become financially literate. As you read the financial vocabulary terms listed here, place a checkmark next to any term whose meaning you didn't already know.

Account. A formal business arrangement in which a bank provides financial services to a customer (e.g., checking account or savings account)

Balance. The amount of money in an account or the amount of unpaid debt

Budget. A plan for coordinating income and expenses such that sufficient money is available to cover or pay for expenses

Credit. Money obtained with the understanding that it will be paid back, either with or without interest.

Credit Line (a.k.a. Credit Limit). The maximum amount of money (credit) made available to a borrower.

Debt. The amount of money owed

Default. Failure to meet a financial obligation (e.g., a student who fails to repay a college loan defaults on that loan)

Deferred Student Payment Plan. A plan that allows student borrowers to temporarily defer or postpone loan payments for some acceptable reason (e.g., to pursue an internship or volunteer work after college)

Fixed Interest Rate. A loan with an interest rate that will remain the same for the entire term of the loan

Grant. Money received that does not have to be repaid

Gross Income. Income generated before taxes and other expenses have been deducted

Insurance Premium. The amount paid in regular installments to an insurance company to remain insured

Interest. The amount of money paid to a customer for deposited money (as in a bank account) or money paid by a customer for borrowed money (e.g., interest on a loan); interest is usually calculated as a percentage of the total amount of money deposited or borrowed

Interest-Bearing Account. A bank account that earns interest if the customer keeps a sufficiently large sum of money in the bank

Loan Consolidation. Consolidating (combining) separate student loans into one new, larger loan to make the process of tracking, budgeting, and repayment easier (loan consolidation typically requires the borrower to pay slightly more interest)

Loan Premium. The amount of money loaned without interest

Merit-Based Scholarship. Money awarded to a student on the basis of performance or achievement that does not have to be repaid

Need-Based Scholarship. Money awarded to a student on the basis of financial need that does not have to be repaid

Net Income. Money remaining or earned after all expenses and taxes have been paid

Principal. The total amount of money borrowed or deposited, not counting interest

Variable Interest Rate. An interest rate on a loan that can vary or be changed by the lender

Yield. Revenue or profit produced by an investment beyond the original amount invested (e.g., higher lifetime income and other monetary benefits acquired from a college education that exceed the amount of money invested in or spent on a college education)

it annually to determine your eligibility to receive financial aid, whether you believe you are eligible or not. See the Financial Aid Office on your campus for the FAFSA form and for help in completing the form.

Scholarships

Scholarships are available from many sources, including the institution you choose to attend. They are awarded based on various criteria that may include a written essay, ACT (American College Testing Program) or SAT (formerly Scholastic Aptitude Test or Scholastic Assessment Test) scores, and high school grade point average (GPA). In addition to academic scholarships, scholarships are awarded based on organizations you may have been a part of, race or ethnicity, the region of the country you live in, athletics, artistic talents, and so on. It is important to remember that all scholarships are competitive and deadlines are observed by the awarding agencies or institution. Be aware of the application material deadlines and submit your materials well in advance of these deadlines.

You should contact the Financial Aid Office of the institution you are attending to find available scholarships. You can also conduct an Internet search to find many sites that offer scholarship information, but it is important to remember that you should not enter credit-card or bank account information on any site.

Grants

Grants are considered to be gift aids and generally are not required to be repaid. About two-thirds of all college students receive grant aid, which, on average, reduces their tuition bills by more than half (College Board, 2009).

The Federal Pell Grant is the largest grant program and provides need-based aid to low-income undergraduate students. The amount of the grant depends on certain criteria such as (a) the anticipated contribution of the family to the student's education (EFC), (b) the cost of attending the postsecondary institution, (c) the enrollment status of the student (part time or full time), and (d) whether the student attends for a full academic year or less.

Loans

Student loans are required to be repaid once a student graduates from college. The Federal Perkins Loan is a 5 percent simple-interest loan awarded to exceptionally needy students. The repayment for this loan begins 9 months after a student is no longer enrolled at least half time.

The Federal Subsidized Stafford Loan is available to students enrolled at least half time and has a fixed interest rate that is established each year on July 1, which is based on the 91-day Treasury bill plus 2.5 percent. The federal government pays the interest on the loan while the student is enrolled. The repayment for this loan begins 6 months after a student is no longer enrolled half time.

The Federal Unsubsidized Stafford Loan is not based on need and has the same interest rate as the Federal Subsidized Stafford Loan. You are responsible for paying the interest on this loan while you're enrolled in college. The loan amount limits for Stafford loans are based on the classification of the student (e.g., freshman or sophomore). To apply for each of these loans, you must complete the FAFSA form.

Federal Loan versus Private Loan: A Critical Difference

Private loans and federal loans are different and unrelated types of loans. Here are the key differences:

Federal loans have fixed interest rates that are comparatively low (currently less than 7 percent).

Private loans have variable interest rates that are very high (currently more than 15 percent) and can go higher at any time.

Warning: Despite the high cost of private loans, they are the fastest-growing type of loans taken out by college students, largely because of aggressive, misleading, and sometimes irresponsible or unethical advertising on loan-shopping Web sites. Students sometimes think they're getting a federal loan only to find out later they have taken on a more expensive private loan.

Remember 12.1

Not all loans are the same. Federally guaranteed student loans are relatively low-cost compared to private loans, and they may be paid off slowly after graduation. On the other hand, private lenders of student loans are like credit-card companies; they charge extremely high interest rates (that can go even higher at any time), and should be paid off as quickly as possible. They should not to be used as a primary loan to help pay for college; they should only be used as a last resort—when no other options are available for covering your college expenses.

> "Apply for as much grant aid as possible before borrowing, and then seek lower-interest federal student loans before tapping private one. There is a lot of student aid that can help make the expense [of college] more manageable."
>
> –Sandy Baum, senior policy analyst, College Board (Gordon, 2009)

Source: Kristof (2008).

Keep in mind that federal and state regulations require that if you are receiving financial aid, you must maintain "satisfactory academic progress." In most cases this means that you must do the following:

1. Maintain a satisfactory GPA. (Your entire academic record will be reviewed, even if you have paid for any of the classes with your own resources.)
2. Make satisfactory academic progress. (Your academic progress will be evaluated at least once per year, usually at the end of each spring semester.)
3. Complete a degree or certificate program within an established period of time. (Check with your institution's Financial Aid Office for details.)

Salary Earnings

If you find yourself relying on your salary to pay for college tuition, check with your employer to see whether the company offers tuition reimbursement. You should also check with the Billing Office on your campus to determine whether payment plans are available for tuition costs. These plans may differ in terms of how much is due, deadlines for payments, and how any remaining debt owed to the institution is dealt with at the end of the term. You may find that the institution you are attending will not allow you to register for the following term until the previous term is completely paid for.

Research shows that when students work on campus (versus off campus) they are more likely to succeed in college (Astin, 1993; Pascarella & Terenzini, 1991, 2005). This is probably because students become more connected to the college when they work on campus (Tinto, 1993) and because on-campus employers are more flexible than off-campus employers in allowing students to meet their academic commitments while they are employed. For instance, campus employers are more willing to scheduling students' work hours around their class schedule and allow students to modify their work schedule when their academic workload increases (e.g., midterm and finals). Thus, we strongly encourage you to seek on-campus employment and capitalize on its capacity to promote your academic success.

> **Pause for Reflection**
>
> Do you need to work part time to meet your college expenses?
>
> If yes, do you have to work more than 15 hours per week to make ends meet?
>
> If yes, is there anything you can do to change that?

◆ Money-Saving Strategies and Habits

The ultimate goal of money management is to save money and avoid debt. Here are some strategies for accomplishing this goal.

1. Prepare a personal budget.

A budget is simply a plan for coordinating income and expenses to ensure that your cash flow leaves you with sufficient money to cover your expenses. A budget helps you maintain awareness of your financial state or condition; it enables you to be your own accountant by keeping an accurate account of your money.

Just like managing and budgeting your time, the first step in managing and budgeting your money involves prioritizing. In the case of money management, prioritizing first involves identifying your most important expenses—necessities that are indispensable and that you must have to survive—as opposed to incidentals that are dispensable because you can live without them.

Some people can easily confuse essentials (needs) and incidentals (wants). For instance, if a piece of merchandise happens to be on sale, what this means is that it may be a great bargain for consumers who may want to purchase it; however, it doesn't mean that you need to consume (purchase) it before somebody else does.

> **Student Perspective**
>
> "I shouldn't buy random stuff (like hair dye) and other stuff when I don't need it."
>
> –First-year student

> ! **Remember**
>
> Remaining consciously aware of the distinction between life's *essentials* that must be purchased and *incidentals* that may or may not be purchased is an important first step toward preparing an effective budget that enables you to save money and escape debt.

You need to be aware of whether you're spending money on *impulse* and out of *habit* or out of need and after thoughtful reflection. The truth is that humans spend money for a host of psychological reasons (conscious or subconscious), many of which are unrelated to actual need. For example, they

Since I was a student who had to manage my own college expenses, I became an expert in managing small budgets. The first thing I always took care of was my tuition. I was going to go to school even if I starved. The next thing I budgeted for was my housing, then food (since I worked in a grocery store, someone would feed me), and then transportation and clothing needs. If I ran out of money, I would then work additional hours if it did not interfere with my academics. I clearly understood, that I was working to make a better life for myself and not to just have money to spend at that time. To be successful, I had to be a great money manager because there was so little of it to manage. This took a lot of focus and strong will, but did it ever pay off? Absolutely.

—Aaron Thompson

Student Perspective

"I need to save money and not shop so much and impulse buy."

—First-year student

spend to build their self-esteem or self-image, to combat personal boredom, or to seek stimulation and an emotional "high" (Furnham & Argyle, 1998). Furthermore, people can become obsessed with spending money, shop compulsively, and become addicted to purchasing products. Just as Alcoholics Anonymous (AA) exists as a support group for alcoholics, Debtors Anonymous exists as a support group for shopaholics and includes a 12-step recovery program similar to AA.

2. Make all your bills visible and pay them off as soon as possible.

When your bills are visible, they become memorable and you're less likely to forget to pay them or forget to pay them on time. To increase the visibility of your bill payments, keep a financial calendar on which you record key fiscal deadlines for the academic year (e.g., due dates for tuition payments, residential bills, and financial-aid applications). Also, try to get in the habit of paying a bill as soon as you open it and have it in your hands, rather than setting it aside and running the risk of forgetting to pay it or losing it.

3. Live within your means.

This strategy is simple: Don't purchase what you can't afford. If you are spending more money than you're taking in, it means you're living *beyond* your means. To begin living *within* your means, you have two options:

1. Decrease your expenses (e.g., reduce your spending); or
2. Increase your income.

Since most college students are already working while attending college (Orszag, Orszag & Whitmore, 2001) and working so many hours that it's interfering with their academic performance or progress (King, 2005), the best option for most college students who find themselves in debt is to reduce their spending and begin living within their means.

4. Economize.

By being intelligent consumers who use critical thinking skills when purchasing products, you can be frugal or thrifty without compromising the quality of your purchases. For example, you can pay less to see the same movie in the late afternoon than you would pay at night. Also, why pay more

"We choose to spend more money than we have today. Choose debt, or choose freedom, it's your choice."

–Bill Pratt, *Extra Credit: The 7 Things Every College Student Needs to Know About Credit, Debt & Cash* (2008)

for brand name products that are the same as products with a different name? Why pay 33 percent more for Advil or Tylenol when the same amount of pain-relieving ingredient (ibuprofen or acetaminophen) is contained in generic brands? Often, what you're paying for when you buy brand name products is all the advertising these companies pay to the media and to celebrities to publicly promote their products. (That's why people instantly recognize them as familiar brand name products.)

> **Pause for Reflection**
>
> Are you working for money while attending college?
>
> If you're not working, are you sacrificing anything that you want or need because you lack money?
>
> If you are working,
>
> 1. How many hours per week do you currently work?
>
> 2. Do you think that working is interfering with your academic performance or progress?
>
> 3. Would it be possible for you to reduce the number of weekly hours you now work and still be able to make ends meet?

> **! Remember**
>
> Advertising creates product familiarity, not product quality. The more money manufacturers pay for advertising and creating a well-known or "brand name" product, the more money you pay for the product—not necessarily because you're acquiring a product of higher quality but most often because you're covering its high cost of advertising.

5. Downsize.

Cut down or cut out spending for products that you don't need. Don't engage in conspicuous consumption just to keep up with the "Joneses" (your neighbors or friends), and don't allow peer pressure to determine your spending habits. Let your spending habits reflect your ability to think critically rather than your tendency to conform socially.

> "It is preoccupation with possessions, more than anything else, that prevents us from living freely and nobly."
>
> —Bertrand Russell, British philosopher and mathematician

6. Live with others rather than living alone.

Although you lose privacy when you share living quarters with others, you save money; if you enjoy the company of those you live with, it also has social benefits.

7. Give gifts of time rather than money.

Spending money on gifts for family, friends, and romantic partners is not the only way to show that you care. The point of gift giving is not to show others you aren't cheap or to show off your lavish spending skills. Instead, show off your social sensitivity by doing something special or making something meaningful for them. Gifts of time and kindness can often be more personal and more special than store-bought gifts.

> "The richer your friends, the more they will cost you."
>
> —Elisabeth Marbury, legal agent for theatrical and literary stars in the late nineteenth and early twentieth centuries

> **Personal Story**
>
> When my wife (Mary) and I were first dating, she was aware that I was trying to gain weight because I was on the thin side. (All right, I was skinny.) One day when I came home from school, I found this hand-delivered package in front of my apartment door. I opened it up and there was a homemade loaf of whole wheat bread made from scratch by Mary. That gift didn't cost her much money, but she took the time to do it and remembered to do something that was important to me (gaining weight), which really touched me; it's a gift I've never forgotten. Since I eventually married Mary and we're still happily married, I guess you could say that inexpensive loaf of bread was the "gift that kept on giving."
>
> —Joe Cuseo

8. Develop your own set of money-saving strategies and habits.

You can save money by starting to do little things that eventually turn into become regular money-saving habits, which can and add up to big savings over time. Consider the following list of habit-forming tips for saving money that were suggested by students in a first-year seminar class:

- Don't carry a lot of extra money in your wallet. (It's just like food; if it's easy to get to, you'll be more likely to eat it up.)
- Shop with a list—get in, get what you need, and get out.
- Put all your extra change in a jar.
- Put extra cash in a piggy bank that requires you to smash the piggy to get at it.
- Seal your savings in an envelope.
- Immediately get extra money into the bank (and out of your hands).
- Bring (don't buy) your lunch.
- Take full advantage of your meal plan—you've already paid for it, so don't pay twice for your meals by buying food elsewhere.
- Use e-mail instead of the telephone.
- Hide your credit card or put it in the freezer so that you don't use it on impulse.
- Use cash (instead of credit cards) because you can give yourself a set amount of cash and can clearly see how much of it you have at the start of a week and how much is left at any point during the week.

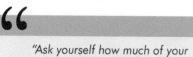

Pause for Reflection

Do you use any of the strategies on the preceding list?

Have you developed any effective strategies that do not appear on the list?

9. When making purchases, always think in terms of their long-term total cost.

It's convenient and tempting for consumers to think in the short term ("I see it; I like it; I want it; and I want it now.") However, long-term thinking is one of the essential keys to successful money management and financial planning. Those small (monthly) installment plans that businesses offer to get you to buy expensive products may make the cost of those products appear attractive and affordable in the short run. However, when you factor in the interest rates you pay on monthly installment plans, plus the length of time (number of months) you're making installment payments, you get a more accurate picture of the product's total cost over the long run. This longer-range perspective can quickly alert you to the reality that a product's sticker price represents its partial and seemingly affordable short-term cost but its long-term total cost is much less affordable (and perhaps out of your league).

Furthermore, the long-term price for purchases sometimes involves additional "hidden costs" that don't relate directly to the product's initial price but that must be paid for the product's long-term use. For example, the sticker price you pay for clothes does not include the hidden, long-term costs that may be involved if those clothes require dry cleaning. By just taking a moment to check the inside label, you can save yourself this hidden, long-term cost by purchasing clothes that are machine washable. Or, to use an

When I was 4 years old living in the mountains of Kentucky, it was safe for a young lad to walk the railroad tracks and roads alone. My mother knew this and would send me to the general store to buy various small items we needed for our household. Since we had little money, she was aware of that we had to be cautious and only spend money on the essential necessities we needed to survive. I could only purchase items from the general store that I could carry back home by myself and the ones my mother strictly ordered me to purchase. Most of these items cost less than a dollar, and in many cases you could buy multiple items for that dollar in the early 1960s. At the store I would hand my mother's handwritten list to the owners. They would pick the items for me, and we would exchange the items for my money. On the checkout counter jars were with different kinds of candy or gum. You could buy two pieces for a penny. As a hardworking boy who was doing a good deed for his parents, I didn't think there would be any harm in rewarding myself with two pieces of candy after doing a good deed. After all, I could devour the evidence of my disobedience on my slow walk home. Upon my return, my mother, being the protector of the vault and the sergeant-of-arms in our household, would count each item I brought home to make sure I had been charged correctly. She always found that I had either been overcharged by 1 cent or that I had spent 1 cent. In those days, parents believed in behavior modification. After she gave me a scolding, she would say "Boy, you better learn how to count your money if you're ever going to be successful in life." I learned the value of saving money and the discomfort of overspending at a young age.

—*Aaron Thompson*

example of a big-ticket purchase, the extra money spent to purchase a new car (instead of a used car) includes not only paying a higher sticker price but also paying the higher hidden costs of licensing and insuring the new car, as well as any interest fees if the new car was purchased on an installment plan. When you count these hidden, long-term costs in a new car's total cost, buying a good used car is a more effective money-saving strategy than buying a new one.

!

Remember

Avoid buying costly items impulsively. Instead, take time to reflect on the purchase you intend to make, do a cost analysis of its hidden or long-term costs, and then integrate these invisible costs with the product's sticker price to generate an accurate synthesis and clearer picture of the product's total cost.

◆ Long-Range Financial Planning: Financing Your College Education

An effective money-management plan should be time sensitive and include the following financial-planning time frames:

- Short-range financial plan (e.g., weekly income and expenses)
- Midrange financial plan (e.g., monthly income and expenses)

- Long-range financial plan (e.g., projected or anticipated income and expenses for the entire college experience)
- Extended long-range financial plan (e.g., expected income and debt after graduation, including a plan for repayment of any college loans)

Thus far, our discussion has focused primarily on short- and midrange financial planning strategies that will keep you out of debt monthly or yearly. We turn now to issues involving long-term financial planning for your entire college experience. While no one "correct" strategy exists for financing a college education that works best for all students, some important research findings relate to the effectiveness of different financing strategies that college students have used, which you should be aware of when doing long-range financial planning for college and beyond.

Research shows that obtaining a student loan and working no more than 15 hours per week is an effective long-range strategy for students to finance their college education and meet their personal expenses. Students who use this strategy are more likely to graduate from college, graduate in less time, and graduate with higher grades than students who work part time for more than 15 hours per week while attending college full time, or students who work full time and attend college part time (King, 2002; Pascarella & Terenzini, 2005).

Studies also show that borrowing money in the form of a student loan and working part time for 15 or fewer hours per week is the most effective financial strategy for students at all income levels, and it is especially effective for students with low incomes. Unfortunately, less than 6 percent of all first-year students use this strategy. Instead, almost 50 percent of first-year students choose a strategy that research shows to be least associated with college success: borrowing nothing and trying to work more than 15 hours per week. Students who use this strategy increase their risk of lowering their grades significantly and withdrawing from college altogether (King, 2005), probably because they have difficulty finding enough time to handle the amount of academic work required by college on top of working outside of college for more than 15 hours per week. Thus, a good strategy for balancing learning and earning would be to try to limit work for pay to 15 hours per week (or as close to 15 hours as possible) because working longer hours may increase your temptation to switch from full-time to part-time enrollment, which can increase your risk of delaying graduation or not graduating (Pascarella & Terenzini, 2005).

Other students decide to finance their college education by working full time and going to college part time. These students believe it will be less expensive in the long run to attend college part time because it will allow them to avoid any debt from student loans. However, studies show that when students go to college part time so that they can work full time it significantly lengthens their time to degree completion and sharply reduces the likelihood that they will ever complete a college degree (Orszag, Orszag, & Whitmore, 2001).

Students who manage to eventually graduate from college, but take longer to do so because they have worked more than 15 hours per week for extra income, eventually lose money in the long run. The longer they take to graduate, the longer they must wait to "cash in" on their college degree and enter higher-paying, full-time positions that a college diploma would allow them to enter. The pay per hour for most part-time jobs that students hold while working in college is less than half what they will earn from working in a full-time position as a college graduate (King, 2005).

Furthermore, studies show that two out of three college students have at least one credit card and nearly one of every two students with credit cards carries an average balance of more than $2,000 per month (Mae, 2005). Debt level this high is likely to push many students into working more than 15 hours a week to pay it off. ("I owe, I owe, so off to work I go."). This often results in their taking longer to graduate and earn a college graduate's salary, because they enroll in fewer courses per term so that they have extra work time and can earn enough money to pay off their credit-card debt.

Instead of these students paying almost 20 percent interest to credit-card companies for their monthly debt, they would be better off obtaining a student loan at a much lower interest rate and which they don't begin to pay back until 6 months after graduation—when they'll be making more money in full-time positions as college graduates. Despite the clear advantages of student loans compared to credit-card loans, only about 25 percent of college students who use credit cards take out a student loan (King, 2002).

"My school sends me portions of my diploma as I make partial payments on my student loans."

Compared to other loans, student loans have a much lower interest rate, and they don't need to be repaid until after students are awarded their college diploma—which, by the way, is awarded in its entirety after graduation—not in parts until the entire load is repaid!

> ## ! Remember
>
> Student loans are provided by the American government with the intent of helping its citizens become better educated. In contrast, for-profit businesses such as credit-card companies lend students money with no intent or interest in helping them become better educated but with the intent of helping themselves make money—from the high rates of interest they collect from students who do not pay their debt in full at the end of each month.

Keep in mind that not all debt is bad. Debt can be good if it represents an investment in something that will appreciate with the time (i.e., something that will gain in value and eventually turn into profit for the investor). Purchasing a college education on credit is a good investment because, over time, it will appreciate—in the form of higher salaries for the remainder of the life of the investor (the college graduate). In contrast, purchasing a new car is a bad long-term investment because it immediately begins to depreciate or lose monetary value once it is purchased. The instant you drive that new car off the dealer's lot, you immediately become the proud owner of a used car that's worth much less than what you just paid for it.

You may have heard the expression that "time is money." One way to interpret this expression is that the more money you spend, the more time you must spend making money. If you're going to college, spending more time to earn money to cover your spending habits often means spending less time

> "Unlike a car that depreciates in value each year that you drive it, an investment in education yields monetary, social, and intellectual profit. A car is more tangible in the short term, but an investment in education (even if it means borrowing money) gives you more bang for the buck in the long run."
>
> –Eric Tyson

Pause for Reflection

In addition to college, what might be other good, long-term investments for you to make now or soon?

studying, learning, completing classes, and earning good grades. You can avoid this vicious cycle by viewing academic work as work that "pays" you back in terms of completed courses and higher grades. If you put in more academic time to complete more courses within less time and earn better grades, you're paid back by increasing the likelihood you will graduate sooner and start earning the full-time salary of a college graduate—which will pay you about twice as much money per hour than you'll earn doing part-time work without a college degree (not to mention fringe benefits such as medical insurance, dental insurance, and paid vacation time). Furthermore, the time you put into earning higher grades while in college should pay off immediately in your first full-time position after college because research shows that students in the same field who graduate with higher grades are offered higher starting salaries (Pascarella & Terenzini, 2005).

◆ Summary and Conclusion

The following strategies for effectively managing money were recommended in this chapter:

- **Develop financial self-awareness.** Become aware of your cash flow—the amount of money flowing in and flowing out of your hands.
- **Develop a money-management plan.** Ensure that your income is equal to or greater than your expenses.
- **Manage your money effectively.** Use available financial tools and instruments to track your cash flow and manage your money, such as checking accounts, credit cards, charge cards, and debit cards.
- **Finance your education wisely.** Explore all sources of income for financing your college education, including FAFSA, scholarships, grants, loans, monetary gifts from family or friends, salary earnings, and personal savings.
- **Build up a cash reserve.** Use available financial tools for saving money, such as savings accounts and money-market accounts.
- **Prepare a personal budget.** A budget helps you make sure that you have sufficient money to cover your expenses. It lets you keep an accurate account of your money.
- **Pay your bills as they arrive.** Pay off your bills as soon as possible. When your bills are visible, you're less likely to forget to pay them on time or at all.
- **Live within your means.** Don't purchase what you can't afford.
- **Economize.** Be an intelligent consumer and use critical thinking skills when purchasing products. You can do so without compromising quality in your purchases.
- **Downsize.** Don't buy products that you don't need or let peer pressure to determine your spending habits. Instead, your spending habits can reflect your ability to think critically.
- **Live with others, not alone.** The reduction in privacy can be offset by the financial savings. Social interactions can be a fringe benefit if you enjoy the company of your roommates or housemates.

- **Give time rather than money.** Gifts of time and kindness can often mean more to the recipient than store-bought gifts.
- **Work for better grades now and better pay later.** Take out a student loan and work part time for 15 or fewer hours per week. This is the most effective financial strategy for students at all income levels.
- **Take full advantage of your Financial Aid Office.** Check periodically to see whether you qualify for additional sources of income, such as part-time employment on campus, low-interest loans, grants, or scholarships.

Money management is a personal skill that can promote or sabotage your success in college and in life beyond college. Similar to time management, if you effectively manage your money and gain control of how you spend it, you can gain greater control over the quality of your life. On the other hand, if you ignore it or abuse it, you raise your level of debt and stress and lower you level of performance. Research shows that accumulating high levels of debt while in college is associated with higher levels of stress, lower academic performance, and greater risk of withdrawing from college. The good news is that students who learn to use effective money-management strategies are able to reduce unnecessary spending and accumulation of debt and stress while improving the quality of their academic performance.

Learning More Through the World Wide Web

Internet-Based Resources for Further Information on Money Management

For additional information related to the ideas discussed in this chapter, we recommend the following Web sites:

Money Management:

www.360financialliteracy.org/Life+Stages/College/

www.youngmoney.com/money_management

Paying for Education:

www.students.gov

Financial Literacy:

www.360financialliteracy.org

12.1 Self-Assessment of Financial Attitudes and Habits

Answer the following questions as accurately and honestly as possible.

		Agree	Disagree
1.	I pay my rent or mortgage on time each month.	_____	_____
2.	I avoid maxing out or going over the limit on my credit cards.	_____	_____
3.	I balance my checkbook each month.	_____	_____
4.	I set aside money each month for savings.	_____	_____
5.	I pay my phone and utility bills on time each month.	_____	_____
6.	I pay my credit-card bills in full each month to avoid interest charges.	_____	_____
7.	I believe it is important to buy the things I want when I want them.	_____	_____
8.	Borrowing money to pay for college is a smart thing to do.	_____	_____
9.	I have a monthly or weekly budget that I follow.	_____	_____
10.	The thing I enjoy most about making money is spending money.	_____	_____
11.	I limit myself to one credit card.	_____	_____
12.	Getting a degree will get me a good job and a good income.	_____	_____

Sources: Cude et al. (2006), Niederjohn (2008).

Give yourself one point for each item that you marked "agree"—except for items 7, 9, and 10. For these items, give yourself a point if you marked "disagree."

A perfect score on this short survey would be 12.

Self-Assessment Questions

1. What was your total score?

2. Which items lowered your score?

3. Do you see any pattern across the items that lowered your score?

4. Do you see any realistic way or ways you could improve your score on this test?

12.2 Financial Self-Awareness: Monitoring Money and Tracking Cash Flow

1. Use the worksheet that follows to estimate what your income and expenses are per month, and enter them in column 2.

2. Track your actual income and expenses for a month and enter them in column 3. (To help you do this accurately, keep a file of your cash receipts, bills paid, and checking or credit records for the month.)

3. After one month of tracking your cash flow, answer the self-assessment questions.

   a. Were your estimates generally accurate?

   b. For what specific items or areas were there the largest discrepancies between what you estimated they would be and what they actually were?

   c. Comparing your bottom-line total for income and expenses, are you satisfied with how your monthly cash flow seems to be going?

   d. What changes could you make to create more positive cash flow—i.e., to increase your income or savings and reduce your expenses or debt?

   e. How likely is it that you would actually make the changes you mentioned in your response to question d?

	Estimate	Actual
Income Sources		
Parents/Family		
Work/Job		
Grants/Scholarships		
Loans		
Savings		
Other:		
TOTAL INCOME		
Essentials (Fixed Expenses)		
Living Expenses:		
Food/Groceries		
Rent/Room & Board		
Utilities (gas/electric)		
Clothing		
Laundry/Dry Cleaning		
Phone		
Computer		
Household Items (dishes, etc.)		
Medical Insurance Expenses		
Debt Payments (loans/credit cards)		
Other:		
School Expenses:		
Tuition		
Books		
Supplies (print cartridges, etc.)		
Special Fees (lab fees, etc.)		
Other:		
Transportation:		
Public Transportation (bus fees, etc.)		
Car Insurance		
Car Maintenance		
Fuel (gas)		
Car Payments		
Other:		
Incidentals (*Variable* Expenses)		
Entertainment:		
Movies/Concerts		
DVDs/CDs		
Restaurants (eating out)		
Other:		
Personal Appearance/Accessories:		
Haircuts/Hairstyling		
Cosmetics/Manicures		
Fashionable Clothes		
Jewelry		
Other:		
Hobbies		
Travel (trips home, vacations)		
Gifts		
Other:		
TOTAL EXPENSES		

Problems Paying for College

A college student posted the following message on the Internet:

I went to college for one semester, failed some my classes, and ended with 900 dollars in student loans. Now I can't even get financial aid or a loan because of some stupid thing that says if you fail a certain amount of classes you can't get aid or a loan. And now since I couldn't go to college this semester they want me to pay for my loans already, and I don't even have a job.

Any suggestions?

Reflection and Discussion Questions

1. What suggestions would you offer this student? Which should the student do right now? Which should the student do eventually?

2. What should the student have done to prevent this from happening?

3. Do you think that this student's situation is common or unusual? Why?

Health and Wellness

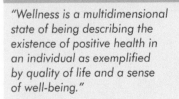

13

ACTIVATE YOUR THINKING | Journal Entry **13.1**

What would you say are the three most important things that humans can do to preserve their health and promote their physical well-being?

1. _____

2. _____

3. _____

LEARNING GOAL

To acquire strategies for physical wellness that can be applied to promote your success during the first year of college and preserve wellness during your later years in college and beyond.

What Is Wellness?

Wellness may be described as a state of good health and positive well-being that promotes peak mental and physical performance by enabling different dimensions of the self to work well together.

While experts disagree on the exact number and nature of the different components of wellness (President's Council on Physical Fitness and Sports, 2001), it's probably simplest to say the spokes of the "wellness wheel" correspond to the dimensions of self discussed in Chapter 2. (See **Figure 13.1**.)

> *"Wellness is an integrated method of functioning, which is oriented toward maximizing the potential of the individual."*
>
> –H. Joseph Dunn, originator of the term "wellness"

- **Intellectual.** Knowledge, perspectives, and ways of thinking;
- **Emotional.** Feelings, self-esteem, emotional intelligence, and mental health;
- **Social.** Interpersonal relationships;
- **Physical.** Bodily health and wellness;
- **Vocational.** Occupational or career development and satisfaction;
- **Ethical.** Values, character, and moral convictions;
- **Spiritual.** Beliefs about the meaning or purpose of life and the hereafter;
- **Personal.** Identity, self-concept, and self-management.

The self is composed of multiple elements or dimensions, and each of them can affect your health, success, and happiness. As can be seen in **Figure 13.1**, numerous elements of the self join together to form the wellness wheel. The development of all these elements is a primary goal of wellness and being a well-rounded person.

The physical component of wellness is the focus of this chapter. It could be said that physical health is the precondition or prerequisite that enables all other elements of wellness to take place. For instance, it's hard to develop intellectually or socially if you're not well physically, and it's hard to become wealthy and wise unless you're first healthy.

> *"Wellness is a multidimensional state of being describing the existence of positive health in an individual as exemplified by quality of life and a sense of well-being."*
>
> –Charles Corbin and Robert Pangrazi, President's Council on Physical Fitness and Sports

However, physical wellness isn't just the absence of illness or something that's done in reaction to illness (e.g., getting well after being sick); it's something that's done proactively to prevent illness from occurring (Corbin, Pangrazi, & Franks, 2000). Wellness puts into practice two classic proverbs: "Prevention is the best medicine" and "An ounce of prevention is worth a pound of cure."

As depicted in **Figure 13.2**, three potential interception points for preventing illness, maintaining health, and promoting peak performance range from the reactive (after illness) to proactive (before illness).

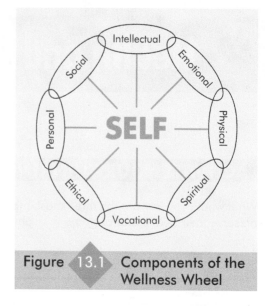

Figure 13.1 Components of the Wellness Wheel

Wellness goes beyond merely maintaining physical health to attaining quality of life to include personal satisfaction, happiness, vitality (energy and vigor), and longevity (a longer life span).

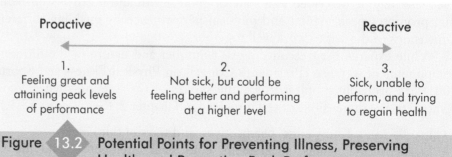

Figure 13.2 Potential Points for Preventing Illness, Preserving Health, and Promoting Peak Performance

The Relevance of Wellness for Today's College Students

When students move directly from high school to college, and move from life at home to life on campus, they're making a major move toward taking sole responsibility for their own wellness. Mom and Dad are no longer around to monitor their health habits and to remind them about what and when to eat, what hours to keep, or when to go to sleep.

In addition to receiving less guidance and supervision, new college students are making a major life transition; during times of change or transition, stress tends to increase. Bad health habits, such as poor eating habits, can further increase stress and moodiness (Khoshaba & Maddi, 1999–2004). In contrast, maintaining good health habits is one way to both cope effectively with college stress and promote peak performance.

In the introduction to this book, we noted research that pointed to the advantages of the college experience and college degree. Among the advantages experienced by college graduates are better physical health, longer lives, and higher levels of both psychological well-being (mental health) and personal happiness (life satisfaction). This suggests that students are learning something about wellness and how to promote it by the time they graduate from college. We want you to begin learning about wellness now so that you can experience its benefits immediately and continue to experience them throughout your college years.

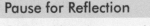

Pause for Reflection

If you could single out one thing about your physical health as something you'd like to improve or learn more about, what would it be?

◆ Elements of Physical Wellness

A healthy physical lifestyle includes four elements:

1. Supplying your body with effective fuel (nutrition);
2. Converting the fuel you consume into bodily energy (exercise);
3. Giving your body adequate rest (sleep) so that it can recover from the energy it has expended;
4. Avoiding risky substances (alcohol and drugs) and risky behaviors that can threaten your health and safety.

◆ Nutrition

Your body needs nutrients to replenish its natural biochemicals and repair its tissues. The food you put into your body supplies it with energy much like fuel does for a car. Just as high-quality gasoline can improve how well and how long your car runs, so can the consumption of high-quality (nutritious) food improve your body and mind, allowing them to function at peak capacity. Unfortunately, however, people often pay more attention to the quality of fuel they put in their cars than to the quality of food they put into their bodies. Humans often eat without any intentional planning about what they eat. They eat at places where they can get food fast, and where they can pick up food on the go, without having to move an inch to get out of their car (and off their butt) to consume it. America has become a fast-food nation, developing the habit of consuming food that can be accessed quickly, conveniently, cheaply, and in large (super-sized) portions (Schlosser, 2001).

Even when people slow down and take time to eat, they often consume food while their attention is divided and consumed by something else (e.g., conversation, reading, or watching TV).

You should eat in a thoughtful, nutritionally conscious way; not just out of convenience, habit, or pursuit of what's most pleasant to your taste buds. You should also "eat to win" (i.e., eat the types of food that will best equip you to defeat disease and allow you to reach peak levels of physical and mental performance).

Studies show that the least nutritious and healthy foods are the very ones that receive the most media advertising (Caroli, Argentieri, Cardone, & Masi, 2004; Hill, 2002). The most frequently advertised food items that people are consuming in the largest quantities tend to be junk food (i.e., food with the least nutrients, the most calories, and the highest health risks). The advertising, availability, and convenience of high-calorie, low-cost food is contributing to Americans being heavier now than at any other time in the nation's history. In 2003, approximately 65 percent of

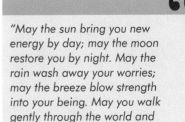

"May the sun bring you new energy by day; may the moon restore you by night. May the rain wash away your worries; may the breeze blow strength into your being. May you walk gently through the world and know its beauty all the days of your life."

—Apache Indian blessing

"If we are what we eat, then I'm cheap, fast, and easy."

—Stephen Wright, Boston-based comedian

Chi mangia bene, vive bene. ("Who eats well, lives well.")

—Italian proverb

© Joy Brown, 2010. Under license from Shutterstock, Inc.

Most people don't take time to slow down and eat. They grab convenient food to go & divide their attention.

Americans 20 years and older were either overweight (20 percent more than the ideal body weight for their height and age) or obese (30 percent more than their ideal weight; American Obesity Association, 2002; Hill, Wyat, Reed, & Peters, 2003). The percentage of Americans who are overweight or obese has risen from 26 percent in 1976 (Hill et al., 2003). The most telling piece of evidence is the finding that when people from other countries move to America and begin to adopt American eating habits, they typically put on a significant amount of weight (Sundquist & Winkleby, 2000).

National surveys of first-year college students indicate that less than 40 percent report that they maintain a healthy diet (Sax, Lindholm, Astin, Korn, & Mahoney, 2004). The phrase "freshman 15" is commonly used to describe the 15-pound weight gain that some students experience during their first year of college (Brody, 2003; Levitsky, Nussbaum, Halbmaier, & Mrdjenovic, 2003). For some first-year students, this weight gain may be temporary and associated with the initial transition to the college eating lifestyle (e.g., all-you-can-eat dining halls, late-night pizzas, and junk-food snacks). However, for other students, it may signal the start of a longer-lasting pattern of gaining and carrying excess weight. The disadvantage of being overweight isn't merely a matter of appearance; it's also a matter of health and survival because excess weight increases susceptibility to the leading life-threatening diseases, such as diabetes, heart disease, and certain forms of cancer.

Pause for Reflection

Have your eating habits changed since you've begun college?

If yes, in what way or ways have they changed?

Snapshot Summary

13.1

Eating Disorders

While some students experience the "freshman 15," others experience eating disorders related to lost weight and loss of control over their eating habits. The disorders described here are more common among females (National Institute of Mental Health, 2001). Studies show that approximately one of every three college females indicates that she worries about her weight, body image, or eating habits (Douglas et al., 1997; Haberman & Luffey, 1998). This is likely because Western cultures place more emphasis and pressure on females than males to maintain lighter body weight and body size. This is an unfortunate social standard (or double standard) because it subjects women to conflict between cultural expectations and biological realities. The female body is genetically constituted or naturally wired with more fat cells, which causes it to store fat more easily than the male body. It's likely that women have been naturally equipped with more ability to store fat because fat is a source of reserve energy that females, as the child-bearing sex, can draw upon during pregnancy to sustain their body, as well as the body of the fetus they're carrying.

What follows is a short summary of the major eating disorders experienced by college students. People experiencing these disorders often deny their problem, and their eating disorder is typically accompanied by emotional issues (e.g., depression and anxiety) that are serious enough to require professional treatment (American Psychiatric Association Work Group on Eating Disorders, 2000). The earlier these disorders are identified and treated, the better the prognosis or probability of complete and permanent recovery. The Counseling Center or Student Health Center is the campus resource to begin the process of seeking help and treatment for any of the following eating disorders.

Anorexia Nervosa

The self-esteem of people who experience anorexia nervosa disorder is often tied closely to their body weight or shape. They see themselves as overweight and have an intense fear of gaining weight, even though they're dangerously thin. Anorexics typically deny that they're severely underweight, and even if their weight drops to the point where they may look like walking skeletons, they may continue to be obsessed with losing weight, eating infrequently, and eating in extremely small portions. Anorexics may also use other methods to lose weight, such as compulsive exercise, diet pills, laxatives, diuretics, or enemas.

Student Perspective

"I've had a friend who took pride in her ability to lose 30 lbs. in one summer because of not eating and working out excessively. I know girls that find pleasure in getting so ill that they throw up and can't eat because the illness causes them to lose weight."

—Comments written in a first-year student's journal

Bulimia Nervosa

The eating disorder known as bulimia nervosa is characterized by repeated episodes of binge eating—eating excessive amounts of food within a limited period. Bulimics tend to lose all sense of self-control during their binges; they then try to compensate for their overeating by engaging in extreme behavior that's designed to purge their guilt and prevent weight gain. For example, they may purge by self-induced vomiting, consuming excessive amounts of laxatives or diuretics, using enemas, or fasting.

The binge–purge pattern typically takes place at least twice a week and continues for 3 or more months.

Unlike anorexia, bulimia is harder to detect because bulimics' binges and purges take place secretly and their body weight looks about normal for their age and height. However, similar to anorexics, bulimics fear gaining weight, aren't happy with their body, and have an intense desire to lose weight.

Binge-Eating Disorder

Like bulimia, the binge-eating disorder involves repeated, out-of-control binging on large quantities of food. However, unlike bulimics, binge eaters don't purge after binging episodes. For someone to be diagnosed as suffering from binge-eating disorder, that person must demonstrate at least three of the following symptoms, two or more times per week, for several months:

1. Eating more rapidly than normal
2. Eating until becoming uncomfortably full
3. Eating large amounts of food when not physically hungry
4. Eating alone because of embarrassment about others seeing how much is eaten
5. Feeling guilty, disgusted, or depressed after overeating

Since those who suffer from these eating disorders usually don't recognize or admit their illness, friends and family members play a role in helping them receive help before the disorder progresses to a life-threatening level. If someone you know is experiencing an eating disorder, consult with a professional at the Student Health Center or Counseling Center about strategies for approaching and encouraging this person to seek help.

Sources: American Psychiatric Association (1994); National Institute of Mental Health (2006).

Nutrition-Management Strategies

Consider this series of nutrition-management strategies for promoting your body's ability to stay well and perform well.

1. Develop a nutrition management plan to ensure your diet has variety and balance.

Take a look at **Figure 13.3**, which lists the basic food groups and the portions of each group recommended by the American Dietetic Association. The Food

Anatomy of MyPyramid

One size doesn't fit all

USDA's new MyPyramid symbolizes a personalized approach to healthy eating and physical activity. The symbol has been designed to be simple. It has been developed to remind consumers to make healthy food choices and to be active every day. The different parts of the symbol are described below.

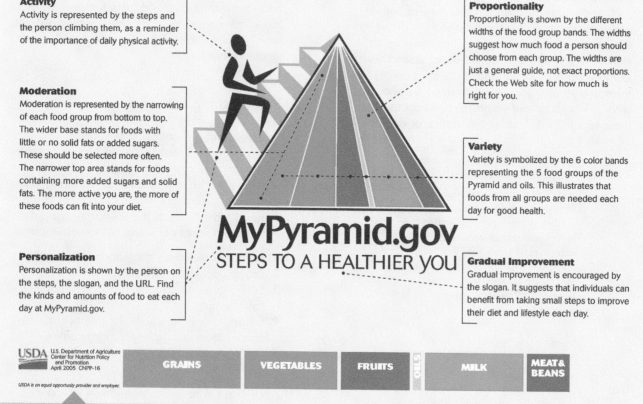

Activity

Activity is represented by the steps and the person climbing them, as a reminder of the importance of daily physical activity.

Moderation

Moderation is represented by the narrowing of each food group from bottom to top. The wider base stands for foods with little or no solid fats or added sugars. These should be selected more often. The narrower top area stands for foods containing more added sugars and solid fats. The more active you are, the more of these foods can fit into your diet.

Personalization

Personalization is shown by the person on the steps, the slogan, and the URL. Find the kinds and amounts of food to eat each day at MyPyramid.gov.

Proportionality

Proportionality is shown by the different widths of the food group bands. The widths suggest how much food a person should choose from each group. The widths are just a general guide, not exact proportions. Check the Web site for how much is right for you.

Variety

Variety is symbolized by the 6 color bands representing the 5 food groups of the Pyramid and oils. This illustrates that foods from all groups are needed each day for good health.

Gradual Improvement

Gradual improvement is encouraged by the slogan. It suggests that individuals can benefit from taking small steps to improve their diet and lifestyle each day.

MyPyramid.gov
STEPS TO A HEALTHIER YOU

USDA U.S. Department of Agriculture
Center for Nutrition Policy
and Promotion
April 2005 CNPP-16

USDA is an equal opportunity provider and employer.

GRAINS   VEGETABLES   FRUITS   OILS   MILK   MEAT & BEANS

Figure 13.3   Food Guide Pyramid

Guide Pyramid divides food into six basic groups. Since foods vary in terms of the nature of nutrients they provide (carbohydrates, protein, and fat), no single food group can supply all nutrients your body needs. Therefore, your diet should be balanced to include all of these food groups but in different proportions or percentages. To find the daily amount of food you should be consuming from each of these major food groups (e.g., your age and gender), go to www.mypyramid.gov.

You can use the food pyramid to create a dietary plan that ensures you consume each of these food groups every day, which will result in a balanced diet that minimizes your risk of experiencing any nutritional deficits or deficiencies. If this guide to nutrition is followed, there should be no need for you to take vitamins or dietary supplements.

Planning what you eat is essential to ensure you eat what's best for preserving health and promoting wellness. If you don't plan ahead to acquire the food you should eat, you're more likely to eat food that can be accessed conveniently and doesn't require advanced preparation.

Pause for Reflection

What type of junk food (if any) do you currently eat? Why?

If you do eat junk food, what's the likelihood that you'll continue to do so? Why?

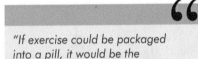

Unfortunately, the types of foods that are readily available, easily accessible, and immediately consumable are usually fast food and packaged food, which are the least healthy foods. If you're serious about eating in a way that's best for your health and performance, you need to do some nutritional planning in advance.

2. Maintain self-awareness of your eating habits.

The first step toward effective nutrition management is to become fully aware of your current eating habits. People often make decisions about what to eat without giving it much thought or even without conscious awareness. You can increase awareness of your eating habits by simply taking a little time to read the labels on the food products before you put them into your shopping cart and into your body. Keeping a nutritional log or journal of what you eat in a typical week to track its nutrients and caloric content is also an effective way to become self-aware of your eating habits.

Another thing to be aware of is your family history. Have members of your immediate and extended family shown tendencies toward heart disease, diabetes, or cancer? If so, intentionally adopt a diet that will reduce your risk for developing the types of illnesses that you may have the genetic potential to develop.

Pause for Reflection

Are you aware of any disease or illness that tends to run in your family?

If yes, is there anything you can do with respect to your diet that may decrease your risk of experiencing this disease or illness?

◆ Exercise and Fitness

Wellness depends not only on fueling the body but also on moving it. The benefits of physical exercise for improving the longevity and quality of human life are simply extraordinary. The health-promoting power of exercise is not surprising because physical activity was something that our early ancestors did daily to stay alive. They had no motorized vehicles to move them from point A to point B, and no one sold or served them food. Exercise was part of their daily survival routine of roaming and rummaging for fruit, nuts, and vegetables to eat or running after and tracking down animals for meat to eat. Just as eating natural (unprocessed) food is better for your health because it's long been part of human history and has contributed to the survival of the human species, so too is exercise a "natural" health-promoting activity that has made the same contribution (Booth & Vyas, 2001). If done regularly, exercise may well be the most effective "medicine" available to humans for preventing disease and preserving lifelong health.

> "If exercise could be packaged into a pill, it would be the single most widely prescribed and beneficial medicine in the nation."
>
> –Robert N. Butler, former director of the National Institute of Aging

Personal Story

I kept in shape when I was young by playing sports such as basketball and baseball. Every chance that made itself available to my schedule, I would play these sports for hours at a time. I enjoyed it so much that I did not realize I was exercising. My body fat was practically nonexistent, energy was ever flowing, and my skills in basketball were always growing. As a middle-aged person, I realize I can no longer do the activities I did for fun as a young person because age has caught up with me. At this point in my life, I attempt to remain active to keep my body fat in a reasonable double-digit category. This takes good scheduling, forethought, and strong will.

—*Aaron Thompson*

Benefits of Exercise for the Body

1. Exercise promotes cardiovascular health.

Exercise makes for a healthy heart. The heart is a muscle, and like any other muscle in the body, its size and strength are increased by exercise. A bigger and stronger heart can pump more blood per beat, which reduces the risk for heart disease and stroke (loss of oxygen to the brain) by increasing circulation of oxygen-carrying blood throughout the body and by increasing the body's ability to dissolve blood clots (Khoshaba & Maddi, 1999–2004).

Exercise further reduces the risk of cardiovascular disease by decreasing the level of triglycerides (clot-forming fats) in the blood and by increasing the levels of "good" cholesterol (high-density lipoproteins) and preventing "bad" cholesterol (low-density lipoproteins) from sticking to and clogging up blood vessels.

2. Exercise stimulates the immune system.

Exercise improves the functioning of the immune system and enables you to better fight off infectious diseases (e.g., colds and the flu) for the following reasons:

- Exercise reduces stress, which normally weakens the immune system.
- Exercise increases breathing rate and blood flow throughout the body; which helps flush out germs from your system by increasing the circulation of antibodies carried through the bloodstream.
- Exercise increases body temperature, which helps kill germs—similar to how a low-grade fever kills germs when you're sick. Nieman & Nehlsen-Cannarella (1994).

Pause for Reflection

Have your exercise habits changed (for better or worse) since you've begun college?

If yes, why do you think this change has taken place?

3. Exercise strengthens muscles and bones.

Exercise reduces muscle tension, which helps prevent muscle strain and pain. For example, strengthening abdominal muscles reduces the risk of developing lower back pain. Exercise also maintains bone density and reduces the risk of osteoporosis (brittle bones that bend and break easily). It's noteworthy that bone density before age 20 affects a person's bone density for the remainder of life. Thus, engaging in regular exercise early in life pays long-term dividends by preventing bone deterioration throughout life.

Student Perspective

"I'm less active now than before college because I'm having trouble learning how to manage my time."

—First-year student

4. Exercising promotes weight loss and weight management.

The increasing national trend toward weight gain is due not only to Americans consuming more calories but also to reduced levels of physical activity (American Obesity Association, 2002). Much of this reduction in physical activity results from the emergence of modern technological conveniences that have made it easier for humans to go about their daily business without exerting themselves in the slightest. For example, almost all TVs now come with remote controls so that you don't have to move to change channels, change volume, or turn it on and off. Children now have video games galore that are played virtually so that they can have fun playing without getting up, running around, or jumping up and down. Consequently, people are playing double jeopardy with their health by eating more and moving less.

Exercise is superior to dieting in one major respect: It raises the body's rate of metabolism (i.e., the rate at which consumed calories are burned as energy rather than stored as fat). In contrast, low-calorie dieting lowers the body's rate of metabolism (Leibel, Rosenbaum, & Hirsch, 1995) and slows the rate at which calories are burned. After 2 to 3 weeks of low-calorie dieting without exercising, the body saves more of the calories it does get by storing them as fat. This happens because long-term low-calorie dieting makes the body "think" it's starving; it therefore tries to compensate and increase its chances of survival by saving more calories as fat so that they can be used for future energy (Bennet & Gurin, 1983). In contrast, exercise speeds up basal metabolism—the body's rate of metabolism when it is resting. Thus, in addition to burning fat directly while exercising, exercise burns fat by continuing to keep the body's metabolic rate higher after you stop exercising and move on to do more sedentary things.

Benefits of Exercise for the Mind

In addition to the multiple benefits of exercise for the body are numerous benefits for the mind. What follows is a summary of the powerful benefits of physical exercise for mental health and mental performance. For people who believe that exercise isn't all that good for them and still cling to this belief after reading the following sections, it may be safe to conclude that they are in denial.

1. Exercise increases mental energy and improves mental performance.

Have you ever noticed how red your face gets when you engage in strenuous physical activity? This rosy complexion occurs because physical activity pumps enormous amounts of blood into your head region, resulting in more oxygen reaching your brain. Exercise increases the heart's ability to pump blood throughout the body and into the brain, and since the brain consumes more oxygen than any other part of the body, it's easy to see why it's the bodily organ that benefits the most from exercise. Moreover, aerobic exercise enlarges the size of the frontal lobe—the part of the brain involved with higher-level thinking (Colcombe et al., 2006; Kramer & Erickson, 2007), and it increases production of brain chemicals that promote formation of physical connections between brain cells (Howard, 2000; Ratey, 2008). As mentioned in Chapter 5, these connections provide the biological basis of learning and memory. Furthermore, exercise is a stimulating activity—it stimulates both the mind and the body. In fact, its stimulating effects are similar to those provided by popular energy drinks (e.g., Red Bull, Full Throttle, and Monster) but without the sugar, caffeine, and negative side effects such as nervousness, irritability, increased blood pressure, and a crash (sharp drop in energy) after the drink's effects wear off (Malinauskas, Aeby, Overton, Carpenter-Aeby, & Barber-Heidal, 2007). Exercise not only increases your energy in the short run but also helps you maintain your overall physical and mental fitness in the long run.

2. Exercise elevates mood.

Exercise increases the release of endorphins (morphine-like chemicals found in the brain that produce a natural high) and serotonin (a mellowing brain chemical that reduces feelings of tension, anxiety, and depression). For these reasons, psychotherapists prescribe exercise for patients experiencing mild

"It is exercise alone that supports the spirits, and keeps the mind in vigor."

—Marcus Cicero, ancient Roman orator and philosopher

Physical exercise provides benefits for the body and the mind.

forms of anxiety or depression (Johnsgard, 2004). Studies show that people who exercise regularly tend to report feeling happier (Myers, 1993).

3. Exercise strengthens self-esteem.

Exercise improves self-esteem by giving you a sense of personal achievement or accomplishment by improving your physical self-image (e.g., improved weight control, body tone, and skin tone).

4. Exercise deepens and enriches the quality of sleep.

Research on the effects of exercise on sleep indicates that if exercise is engaged in at least 3 hours before bedtime it helps people fall asleep, stay asleep, and sleep more deeply (Singh, Clements, & Fiatarone, 1997). Therefore, exercise is a common component of treatment programs for people experiencing insomnia (Dement & Vaughan, 2000).

Guidelines and Strategies for Effective Exercise

Specific exercises vary in terms of what they do to and for the body. Nevertheless, some general guidelines and strategies, such as those discussed here, can be applied to any exercise routine or personal fitness program.

1. Warm up before exercising and cool down after exercising.

Start with a 10-minute warm up of low-intensity movements that are similar to the ones you'll be using in the actual exercise. This increases circulation of blood to the muscles that you'll be exercising and reduces muscle soreness and your risk of muscle pulls.

End your exercise routine with a 10-minute cool down, during which you stretch the muscles that you used while exercising. Stretch the muscle until it burns a little bit, and then release it. Cooling down after exercise improves circulation to the exercised muscles and enables them to return more gradually to a tension-free state, which will minimize the risk of muscle tightness, cramps, pulls, or tears.

2. Engage in cross-training to attain total body fitness.

A balanced, comprehensive fitness program is one that involves cross-training—combining different exercises to achieve overall bodily fitness. For instance, combine exercises that promote:

- Endurance and weight control (e.g., running, cycling, or swimming);
- Muscle strength and tone (e.g., weight training, push-ups, or sit-ups); and
- Flexibility (e.g., yoga, Pilates, or tai chi).

A total fitness plan also includes exercising various muscle groups rotationally (e.g., upper-body muscles one day, lower-body muscles the next), which allows your muscle tissue extra time to rest and fully repair itself before it's exercised again.

3. Exercising with regularity and consistency is as important as exercising with intensity.

Doing exercise regularly, and allowing strength and stamina to increase gradually, is the key to attaining fitness and avoiding injury. One strategy you can use to be sure that you're training your body, rather than straining and overextending it, is to see whether you can talk while you're exercising. If you can't continue speaking without having to catch your breath, you may be overdoing it. Drop the intensity level and allow your body to adapt or adjust to a less strenuous level. After continuing at this lower level awhile, try again at the higher level while trying to talk simultaneously. If you can do both, then you're ready to continue at that level for some time. Thus, you can gradually increase the intensity, frequency, or duration of your exercise routine to a level that produces maximum benefits with minimal postexercise strain or pain.

Personal Story

I had a habit of exercising too intensely—to the point where I overfatigued my muscles and left my body feeling sore for days after I worked out. Like many people, I exercise while listening to music to make the exercise routine more stimulating. I've since discovered that listening to music through headphones while exercising may help me determine whether I'm overdoing it. If I can't sing along with the music without having to stop and catch my breath, then I know I'm overdoing it. This strategy has helped me manage my exercise-intensity level and reduce my day-after-exercise soreness. (Plus, I've gained more confidence as a singer. My singing sounds better to me when my ears are covered with headphones.)

—Joe Cuseo

---

4. Take advantage of exercise and fitness resources on your campus.

You paid for use of the campus gym or recreation center with your college tuition, so take advantage of this and other exercise resources on campus. Also, consider taking physical education courses offered by your college. They count toward your college degree, and typically they carry one unit of credit so that they can be easily added to your course schedule. If exercise-related groups or clubs meet on campus, consider joining them; they can provide you with a motivating support group that can convert your exercise routine from an experience that's done alone to a social experience with others. (It's also a good way to meet and connect with other people.)

5. Take advantage of natural opportunities for physical activity that present themselves during the day.

Exercise can take place outside a gym or fitness center and outside scheduled workout times. Opportunities for exercise often occur naturally as you go about your daily activities. For example, if you can walk or ride your bike to class, do that instead of driving a car or riding a bus. If you can climb some stairs instead of taking an elevator, take the route that's more physically challenging and requires more bodily activity.

Pause for Reflection

Do you have a regular exercise routine?

If no, why not?

If yes, what do you do and how often do you do it?

What more could you do to improve your

1. endurance;

2. strength; and

3. flexibility?

◆ Rest and Sleep

Sleep experts agree that humans in today's information-loaded, multitasking world aren't getting the quantity and quality of sleep needed to perform at peak levels (Mitler, Dinges, & Dement, 1994).

The Value and Purpose of Sleep

Resting and reenergizing the body are the most obvious purposes of sleep (Dement & Vaughan, 1999). However, other benefits of sleep are less well known but equally important for physical and mental health (Dement & Vaughan, 2000; Horne, 1988). Some of these key, less-apparent benefits of sleep are described here.

1. Sleep restores and preserves the power of the immune system.

Studies show that when humans and other animals lose sleep their production of disease-fighting antibodies is reduced and they become more susceptible to illness, such as common colds and the flu (Blakeslee, 1993).

2. Sleep helps you cope with daily stress.

Sleep research shows that the percentage of time people spend in dream sleep increases when they are experiencing stress (Greenberg, Pillard, & Pearlman, 1972). When you lose dream sleep, emotional problems such as anxiety and depression worsen (Voelker, 2004). It's thought that the biochemical changes that take place in your brain during dream sleep restore imbalances in brain chemistry that trigger feelings of anxiety or depression. Getting quality sleep, especially dream sleep, is essential for maintaining a good mood and a positive frame of mind. Indeed, research reveals that people who sleep well are more likely to report that they are happy (Myers, 1993).

3. Sleep helps the brain form and store memories.

Studies show that loss of dream sleep at night results in poorer memory for information learned earlier in the day (Peigneux, Laureys, Delbeuck, & Maquet, 2001). For instance, adolescents who get minimal sleep have a more difficult time retaining new information learned in school (Horne, 1988).

The Importance of Sleep for College Students

College students, in particular, tend to have poor sleep habits. Heavier academic workloads, more opportunities to socialize, and course schedules that provide more opportunity to procrastinate can result in last-minute, late-night, or all-night study binges that lead to irregular sleep schedules and regular sleep loss.

How much sleep do you need or should you get? The answer to this question lies in your genes and varies from person to person. On average, adults need 7 to 8 hours of sleep each day and teenagers need slightly more—about 9 hours (Roffwarg, Muzio, & Dement, 1966). Research shows that college students get an average of less than 7 hours of sleep each night (Hicks, cited in Zimbardo, Johnson, & Weber, 2006), which means that they're not getting the amount of sleep needed for optimal academic performance.

Attempting to train your body to sleep less is likely to be an exercise in futility, because what you're actually trying to do is force your body to do something that it's not naturally (genetically) inclined to do. Eventually, you pay the price for the sleep you've lost with lower energy and poorer performance. When your body is deprived of its needed amount of sleep, it accumulates "sleep debt," which, like financial debt, must be eventually paid back to your body at a later time (Dement & Vaughan, 1999). If your sleep debt isn't repaid, it will catch up with you and you will pay the consequences in terms of impaired health, mood, and performance (Van Dongen, Maislin, Mullington, & Dinges, 2003). For example, studies show that the effects of sleep loss on driving an automobile are similar to the effects of alcohol (Arnedt, Wilde, Munt, & MacLean, 2001; Fletcher, Lamond, van den Heuvel, & Dawson, 2003), and sleep-deprived students have been found to earn lower grades than students who get sufficient sleep (Spinweber, cited in Zimbardo et al., 2006).

Student Perspective

"First of all, you should probably know that your body will not function without sleep. I learned that the hard way."

—Words written by a first-year student in a letter of advice to new college students

Strategies for Improving Sleep Quality

Since sleep has powerful benefits for both the body and the mind, if you can improve the quality of your sleep, you can improve your physical and mental well-being. Listed here is a series of strategies for improving sleep quality that should also improve your health and performance.

Pause for Reflection

What amount of sleep per night do you think you need to perform at your highest level?

How many nights per week do you typically get this amount of sleep?

If you're not getting this optimal amount of sleep each night, what is preventing you from doing so?

1. Increase awareness of your sleep habits by keeping a sleep log or sleep journal.

In your sleep journal, note nights when you slept well or poorly and what you did before going to bed on those nights. Tracking your sleep experiences in a journal may enable you to find patterns that reveal relationships among certain things you do (or don't do) during the day on those nights you sleep well. If you detect such a pattern, you may have detected a routine you could follow regularly to ensure that you consistently get high-quality sleep.

2. Attempt to get into a regular sleep schedule by going to sleep and getting up about the same times each day.

Irregular sleep schedules can disrupt the quality of sleep. This is what happens to people who experience jet lag. Traveling to a new time zone often requires travelers to change their sleep schedule to accommodate the time shift, which can disrupt the quality of their sleep (Rader & Hicks, 1987). Your body likes to work on a biological rhythm of set cycles; if you can get your body on a regular sleep schedule, you're more likely to establish a biological rhythm that makes it easier for you to fall asleep, stay asleep, and wake up naturally from sleep according to your internal alarm clock.

Establishing a stable sleep schedule is particularly important around midterms and finals. Unfortunately, these are the times during the term when students often disrupt their normal sleep patterns by cramming in last-minute studying, staying up later, getting up earlier, or not going to sleep. Sleep research shows that if you want to be at your physical and mental best for upcoming exams, you should get yourself on a regular sleep schedule of going to bed about the same time and getting up about the same time for at least 1 week before your exams (Dement & Vaughan, 1999).

Wellness is built on a balanced foundation of nutrition, exercise, and rest.

3. Attempt to get into a relaxing bedtime ritual each night.

Taking a hot bath or shower, consuming hot milk, or listening to relaxing music are bedtime rituals that can get you into a worry-free state and help you fall asleep sooner. Also, making a list of things you intend to do the next day before going to bed may help you relax and fall asleep because you can go bed with the peace of mind that comes from being organized and ready to handle the following day's tasks.

Light studying or reviewing previously studied material may also be good to do at bedtime because sleep can help you better retain what you've experienced just before going to sleep. Many years of studies show that the best thing you can do after attempting to learn something is to sleep on it, probably because your brain can then focus on processing it without interference from outside distractions (Jenkins & Dallenbach, 1924).

Pause for Reflection

Do you have or need an alarm clock to wake up in the morning?

Why?

4. Make sure the temperature of your sleep room is not too warm (no higher than 70 degrees Fahrenheit).

Warm temperatures often make people feel sleepy, but they usually don't help them stay asleep or sleep well. This is why people have trouble sleeping on hot summer evenings. High-quality, uninterrupted sleep is more likely to take place at cooler, more comfortable room temperatures (Coates, 1977).

5. Avoid intense mental activity just before going to sleep.

Light mental work may serve as a relaxing presleep ritual, but cramming intensely for a difficult exam or doing intensive writing before bedtime is likely to generate a state of mental arousal, which will interfere with your ability to wind down and fall asleep.

6. Avoid intense physical exercise before going to sleep.

Physical exercise generates an increase in muscle tension and mental energy (oxygen flow to the brain), which energizes you and keeps you from falling asleep. If you're going to exercise in the evening, it should be done at least 3 hours before bedtime (Hauri & Linde, 1996).

7. Avoid consuming sleep-interfering foods, beverages, or drugs in late afternoon or evening.

In particular, avoid the following substances near bedtime:

- **Caffeine.** By working as a stimulant drug for most people, caffeine is likely to stimulate your nervous system and keep you awake.
- **Nicotine.** This stimulant drug is also likely to reduce the depth and quality of your sleep.
- **Alcohol.** This drug will make you feel sleepy in larger doses, but smaller doses can have a stimulating effect; furthermore, alcohol in all doses disrupts the quality of sleep by reducing the amount of time you spend in dream-stage sleep (marijuana does the same).
- **Gas-Producing Foods.** Avoid late intake of, for example, peanuts, beans, fruits, raw vegetables, or high-fat snacks, because your stomach has to

work hard to digest them, and this internal energy (and noise) can interrupt or disrupt your sleep. Eating anything near bedtime isn't a good idea because the internal activity your body engages in to digest the food is likely to interfere with the quality of your sleep.

> **Remember**
>
> Things that make you feel sleepy (e.g., warm room temperature or alcohol consumption) often won't improve the depth and quality of your sleep.

◆ Alcohol, Drugs, and Risky Behavior

In addition to putting healthy nutrients into your body, exercising and resting your body, two other elements can help you maintain physical wellness: (a) keeping risky substances out of your body and (b) keeping away from risky behaviors that jeopardize your body.

Alcohol Use Among College Students

In the United States, alcohol is legal for people 21 years of age and older. However, whether you're of legal age or not, it's likely that alcohol has already been available to you and will continue to be available to you when you're in college. Since alcohol is a substance seen often at college parties and social gatherings, you'll be confronted with two sets of decisions about alcohol:

1. To drink or not to drink
2. To drink responsibly or irresponsibly

The best way to avoid irresponsible drinking is to not drink. This is the safest option, particularly if your family has a history of alcohol abuse. If you choose to drink, make sure that it's *your* choice, not a choice imposed on you through social pressure or the need to conform.

Research indicates that first-year college students drink more than they did in high school (Johnston, 2005) and that alcohol abuse is higher among first-year college students than students at more advanced stages of their college experience (Bergen-Cico, 2000). The most common reason first-year students drink is to fit in, or be socially accepted (Meilman & Presley, 2005). However, college students overestimate the number of their peers who drink and the amount they drink; this overestimation can lead them to believe that if they don't drink they're not doing what's expected or normal (DeJong & Linkenback, 1999).

Student beliefs that college partying and college drinking go hand in hand may also be strongly influenced by media portrayals of college students as wild party animals. Popular magazines rank the "top party schools," DVDs depict female college students who've "gone wild," and popular movies have been made whose entire plot revolves around the drunken escapades of college students (e.g., *Animal House, Back to School, Spring Break I*, and *Spring Break II*).

The expectation that college students drink and drink to excess may be the primary reason irresponsible drinking is the number one drug problem on college campuses. Although alcohol is a legal substance (if you're 21 years of age or older), and it's a beverage that people drink rather than inject, smoke,

> **"Drunken State University"**
>
> –Logo once appearing on T-shirts sold at a state university

or snort, alcohol is still a mind-altering substance when consumed in large quantities (doses). Just as THC is the mind-altering ingredient in marijuana, ethyl alcohol is the mind-altering ingredient of beer, wine, and hard liquor (see **Figure 13.4**).

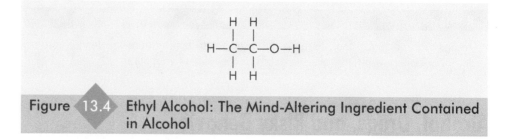

Figure 13.4 **Ethyl Alcohol: The Mind-Altering Ingredient Contained in Alcohol**

Also, like any other drug, alcohol abuse is a form of drug abuse. Approximately 7 to 8 percent of people who drink develop alcohol addiction or dependency (alcoholism; Julien, 2004). However, among college students, the most frequent form of alcohol abuse is binge drinking—consuming a large amount of alcohol in a short amount of time, resulting in a state of intoxication or inebriation (a.k.a. a drunken state).

Binge drinking is a form of alcohol abuse because it has direct, negative effects on the drinker's:

- Behavior (e.g., missing classes; Engs, 1977; Engs & Hanson, 1986);
- Body (e.g., acute alcohol withdrawal syndrome, better known as a hangover); and
- Mind (e.g., memory loss (a.k.a. blackouts in extreme form).

Research indicates that repeatedly getting drunk can reduce the size and effectiveness of the part of the brain involved with memory formation (Brown, Tapert, Granholm, & Delis, 2000), which suggests that the more often people get drunk, the dumber they get (Weschsler & Wuethrich, 2002).

Furthermore, binge drinking can have indirect negative effects on health and safety by reducing the drinker's inhibitions about engaging in risk-taking behavior, which increases the risk of personal accidents, injuries, and illnesses. Arguably, no other drug reduces a person's inhibitions as dramatically as alcohol. After consuming a significant amount of alcohol, people can become much less cautious about doing things they normally wouldn't do. This chemically induced sense of courage (sometimes referred to as liquid courage) can override the process of logical thinking and decision making, thereby increasing drinkers' willingness to engage in irrational, risk-taking behavior. In some cases, they act as if they're invincible and immortal (and infertile). They become more willing to partake in behaviors that increase their risk of physical accidents—for example, reckless driving that increases their risk of serious injury or death and reckless sex (unprotected sex) that increases their risk of such social accidents as accidental pregnancy or sexually transmitted infections (STIs).

It's noteworthy that the legal age for consuming alcohol was once lowered to 18 years; it was raised back to 21 because the number of drunk-driving accidents and deaths among teenage drinkers increased dramatically when the legal age was reduced (Mothers Against Drunk Driving, 2006). Traffic accidents still account for more deaths of Americans between the ages of 15 and 24 than any other single cause (U.S. National Center for

"If you drink, don't park. Accidents cause people."

–Stephen Wright, American comedian

Health Statistics, 2003). When teenagers gain independence and acquire their first taste of new freedoms, they often take the newfound freedom beyond moderation and push it to the outer limits (e.g., drive as fast as they can and drink as much as they can). Perhaps this is a way to prove to themselves and others how much freedom they now have. It's as if the more risks they take with their new freedom, the more of if they think they have. In the case of freedom to drink and freedom to drive, when the two are combined, it can result in a dangerous (or deadly) combination.

Since alcohol is a drug that depresses (slows) the nervous system, it can increase aggressive and sexual behavior by slowing signals normally sent from the upper, front part of the brain (the "human brain") that is responsible for rational thinking and inhibits or controls the lower, middle part of the brain (the "animal brain") that is responsible for basic animal drives, such as sex and aggression (see **Figure 13.5**). When the upper brain's messages are slowed by alcohol, the animal brain is freed from the signals that normally restrain or inhibit it, allowing its basic drives to be released or expressed. Thus, the less inhibited drinker is more likely to engage in aggressive or sexual behavior.

> **Pause for Reflection**
>
> During Prohibition (1920–1933) laws were passed in America that made alcohol illegal for anyone to consume at any age. Why do you think prohibition laws were passed?
>
> Why do you think that alcohol still continued to be produced illegally during Prohibition (as bootleg liquor), which eventually led to the abolition or elimination of prohibition laws?

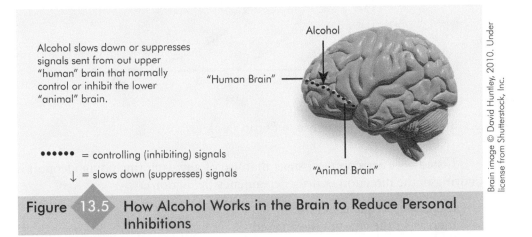

Alcohol slows down or suppresses signals sent from out upper "human" brain that normally control or inhibit the lower "animal" brain.

•••••• = controlling (inhibiting) signals

↓ = slows down (suppresses) signals

Brain image © David Huntley, 2010. Under license from Shutterstock, Inc.

Figure 13.5   How Alcohol Works in the Brain to Reduce Personal Inhibitions

Illegal Drugs

In addition to alcohol, other substances are likely to be encountered on college campuses that are illegal for anyone to use at any age. Among the most commonly used illegal drugs are the following:

- **Marijuana (a.k.a. weed or pot).** Primarily a depressant or sedative drug that slows the nervous system and produces a mellow feeling of relaxation;
- **Ecstasy (a.k.a. X).** A stimulant typically taken in pill form that speeds up the nervous system and reduces social inhibitions;
- **Cocaine (a.k.a. coke or crack).** A stimulant that's typically snorted or smoked and produces a strong rush of euphoria;
- **Amphetamines (a.k.a. speed or meth).** A strong stimulant that increases energy and general arousal; it is usually taken in pill form but may also be smoked or injected;
- **Hallucinogens (a.k.a. psychedelics).** Drugs that alter or distort perception and are typically swallowed (e.g., LSD or acid and hallucinogenic mushrooms or shrooms);

- **Narcotics (e.g., heroin and prescription pain pills).** Depressant or sedative drugs that slow the nervous system and produce feelings of relaxation; heroin is injected or smoked and typically produces a quick, intense euphoria.

All of these drugs are potentially habit forming, particularly if they're injected (shot directly into a vein) or smoked (inhaled through the lungs). These routes of drug delivery are especially dangerous because they allow the drug to reach the brain faster and with more intense impact, resulting in the drug's effect to be experienced more rapidly and at a higher peak level of intensity; however, this is followed by a rapid and sharp drop (crash) after the drug's peak effect has been experienced (see **Figure 13.6**). This peak-to-valley, roller-coaster effect creates a greater risk for craving and repeating use of the drug again, which increases the user's risk of dependency or addiction.

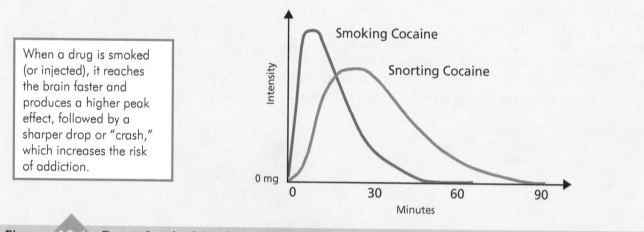

When a drug is smoked (or injected), it reaches the brain faster and produces a higher peak effect, followed by a sharper drop or "crash," which increases the risk of addiction.

Figure 13.6   Drugs Smoked Produce a Higher and More Rapid Peak Effect

Listed here are common signs that use of any drug (including alcohol) is moving in the direction of drug dependency (addiction):

- Increasing frequency of use
- Increasing the amount (dose) used
- Difficulty cutting back (e.g., unable to use it less frequently or in smaller amounts)
- Difficulty controlling or limiting the amount taken after starting
- Using the drug alone
- Hiding or hoarding the drug
- Lying about drug use
- Reacting angrily or defensively when questioned about drug use
- Being in denial about abusing the drug (e.g., "I don't have a problem")
- Rationalizing drug abuse (e.g., "Everyone's doing it" and "It's no big deal")
- Continuing to use the drug means more to the user than the personal and interpersonal problems caused by its use

Addiction is one major motive for repeated use of any drug. However, there are multiple motives or reasons humans do drugs. A summary of the major motives for drug use is provided in **Snapshot Summary 13.2**. Being aware of what motivates people to use drugs (in general) can promote self-awareness of your own motive or motives for drug use, as well as greater awareness of healthier ways to reach the same goal or experience being sought through drug use.

Snapshot Summary

13.2

Drug Use Among College Students: Common Causes and Major Motives

1. **Social Pressure.** To fit in or be cool (e.g., smoking marijuana because it's available at parties and everyone else is doing it, or because it's just "what college students do")
2. **Recreational (Party) Use.** For fun, stimulation, or pleasure (e.g., drinking alcohol at parties to loosen inhibitions and have a good time)
3. **Experimental Use.** Out of curiosity to test out its effects (e.g., experimenting with LSD to see what it's like to have a psychedelic or hallucinogenic experience)
4. **Therapeutic Use.** As treatment, in the form of a prescription or over-the-counter drug, for a mental or emotional disorder (e.g., taking Prozac for depression or Ritalin to treat attention deficit disorder)
5. **Performance Enhancement.** To improve physical or mental performance (e.g., taking steroids to improve athletic performance or stimulants to stay awake all night and cram for an exam)

> **Student perspective**
>
> "For fun." "To party." "To fit in." "To become more talkative, outgoing, and flirtatious."
>
> "To try anything once." "To become numb." "To forget problems." "Being bored."
>
> —Responses of freshmen and sophomores to the question, "Why do college students take drugs?"

6. **Escapism.** To escape or eliminate a personal problem or an unpleasant emotional state (e.g., taking amphetamines to escape depression or boredom)
7. **Addiction.** Out of physical or psychological dependence that results from habitual use of a drug (e.g., continuing to use nicotine or cocaine because stopping will result in withdrawal symptoms such as anxiety or depression)

Strategies for Minimizing or Eliminating the Negative Effects of Alcohol, Drugs, and Risky Behavior

1. Don't let yourself be pressured into drinking.

Keep in mind that college students tend to overestimate the number of their peers who drink, so don't feel you're uncool, unusual, or abnormal if you prefer not to drink.

2. If you drink, maintain awareness of how much you're drinking while you're drinking by monitoring your physical and mental state.

Don't continue to drink after you've reached a state of moderate relaxation or a mild loss of inhibition. Drinking to the point where you're drunk, or bordering on intoxication, doesn't improve your physical health or your social life.

> **Pause for Reflection**
>
> What drugs (if any) have you seen being used on your campus?
>
> How would the type and frequency of drug use on your campus compare to what you saw in high school?
>
> Which motives for drug use listed in Snapshot Summary 13.2 would you say are the most common reasons for drug use on your campus?

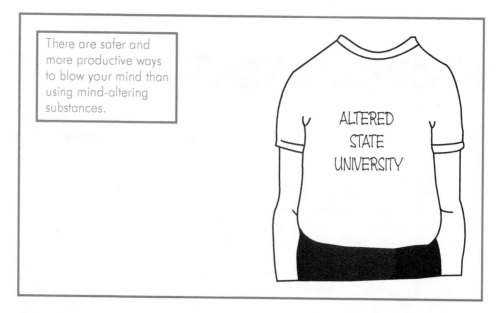

There are safer and more productive ways to blow your mind than using mind-altering substances.

ALTERED STATE UNIVERSITY

You're not exactly the life of the party if you're slurring your speech, vomiting in the restroom, nodding out, or on the verge of falling sound asleep.

The key to drinking responsibly and in moderation is to have a plan for managing your drinking. Your plan should include strategies such as:

- Drinking slowly;
- Eating while drinking;
- Alternating between drinking alcoholic and nonalcoholic beverages; and
- Tapering off your drinking after the first hour of a party or social gathering (Vogler & Bartz, 1992).

Lastly, don't forget that alcohol is costly, both in money and in calories. Thus, reducing or eliminating your drinking not only is a good way to manage your health but also is a good money- and weight-management strategy.

3. If you're a woman who drinks, or who frequents places where others drink, remain aware of the possibility of date-rape drugs being dropped into your drink.

Drugs such as gamma-hydroxybutyric acid (a.k.a. GHB or G) and Rohypnol (a.k.a. roofies or roaches) induce sleep and memory loss, and their effects are particularly powerful when taken with alcohol. To guard against this risk, don't let others give you drinks, and hold onto your drink at all times (e.g., don't leave it, go to the restroom, and come back to drink it again).

4. If you find yourself in a situation where an illegal drug is available to you, our bottom-line recommendation is this: If you're in doubt, keep it out—don't put anything into your body that you're unsure about.

We acknowledge that the college years are a time for exploring and experimenting with different ideas, experiences, feelings, and states of consciousness. However, doing illegal drugs just isn't worth the risk. Even if you're aware of how an illegal drug affects people in general, you don't know how it's going to affect you in particular, because each individual has a unique genetic makeup. Furthermore, unlike legal drugs that have to pass through rigorous testing by the Federal Drug Administration before they're approved for public consumption, you can't be sure how an illegal drug has been produced and packaged from one time to the next and you don't know if, or what, it may have been "cut" (mixed) with during the production process. Thus, you're not just taking a criminal risk by using a drug that's illegal; you're also taking a physical risk by consuming a drug that may have unpredictable effects on your body and mind.

◆ Minimize Your Risk of Contracting Sexually Transmitted Infections

STIs represent a group of contagious infections that are spread through sexual contact. More than 25 types of STIs have been identified, and virtually all of them are easily treated if detected early.

Latex condoms provide the best protection against STIs (Holmes, Levine, & Weaver, 2004). You can also reduce your risk of contracting an STI by having sex with fewer partners. Naturally, not engaging in sexual intercourse is the most foolproof way to eliminate the risk of an STI (and unwanted pregnancy). When it comes to sex, you've got three basic options: do it recklessly, do is safely, or don't do it. Abstinence is one option, and if you choose this option, it doesn't mean you're disinterested in sex, incapable of being physically affectionate, or a prude. It simply means that you're electing not to have sexual intercourse at this particular time in your life.

Virtually all forms of STIs are treatable; however, if ignored, some of them can progress to the point where they result in infection and possibly infertility (Cates, Herndon, Schulz, & Darroch, 2004). Experiencing pain during or after urination, or unusual discharge from the penis or vaginal areas, may be early signs of an STI. However, sometimes the symptoms can be subtle; if you have any doubt, play it safe and check it out immediately by visiting the Health Center on your campus. Any advice or treatment you receive there will remain confidential. If you happen to contract a form of STI, immediately inform anyone you've had sex with, so that he or she may receive early treatment before the disease progresses. This isn't just the polite thing to do; it's the right (ethical) thing to do.

◆ Summary and Conclusion

The research studies and scholarly wisdom reviewed in this chapter suggest that physical wellness is most effectively promoted if you adopt the following strategies with respect to your body:

- **Pay more attention to nutrition.** In particular, you should increase consumption of natural fruits, vegetables, legumes, whole grains, fish, and water and decrease consumption of processed, fatty, and fried foods. Although the expression, "you are what you eat" may be a bit of an exaggeration, it contains a kernel of truth because the food you consume influences your health, your emotions, and your performance.
- **Become more physically active.** To counteract the sedentary lifestyle created by life in modern society and to attain total fitness, you should

engage in a balanced blend of exercises that build stamina, strength, and flexibility.

- **Be careful not to cheat on sleep.** Humans typically do not get enough sleep to perform at their highest levels. Most college students in particular need to get more sleep and develop more regular or consistent sleep habits.
- **Drink alcohol responsibly or not at all.** You should avoid excessive consumption of alcohol or use of other mind-altering substances that can threaten your physical health, impair your mental judgment, and increase your tendency to engage in dangerous, risk-taking behavior.
- **Minimize the risk of contracting sexually transmitted infections.** You have basically three options for doing so: using latex condoms during sex, limiting the number of sexual partners you have, or choosing not to be sexually active.

In the introduction to this book, research was cited about the advantages of the college experience and college degree. Among the many benefits experienced by college graduates are physical benefits: they live healthier and longer lives. This suggests that students are learning something about physical wellness and how to promote it by the time they graduate from college. This chapter provides wellness strategies that you can put into practice immediately to promote optimal health and peak performance during your first term in college and beyond.

Learning More Through the World Wide Web

Internet-Based Resources for Further Information on Health and Wellness

For additional information related to the ideas discussed in this chapter, we recommend the following Web sites:

Nutrition:

www.eatright.org

Fitness:

www.fitness.gov/home_resources.htm

Sleep:

www.sleepfoundation.org

Alcohol and Drugs:

www.nida.nih.gov

13.1 Wellness Self-Assessment and Self-Improvement

For each aspect of wellness listed here, rate yourself in terms of how close you think you are to doing what you should be doing (1 = furthest from the ideal, 5 = closest to the ideal).

	Nowhere Close to What I Should Be Doing		Not Bad but Should Be Better		Right Where I Should Be
	1	2	3	4	5
Nutrition	1	2	3	4	5
Exercise	1	2	3	4	5
Sleep	1	2	3	4	5
Alcohol and Drugs	1	2	3	4	5

For each area in which there's a wide gap between where you are now and where you should be, identify the best action you could take to reduce or eliminate this gap.

13.2 Nutritional Self-Assessment and Self-Improvement

1. Go online to www.mypyramid.gov.

2. Fill in the boxes with information about your age, weight, sex, height and physical activity.

3. Click "select" to get a nutritional guide that is customized to your age, gender, and exercise habits.

4. For each of the five food groups listed here, record the amount recommended for you to consume daily. Next to it, estimate the amount you now consume.

Basic Food Type Consumed	Amount Recommended	Amount Consumed
Grains		
Vegetables		
Fruits		
Milk Products		
Meat and Beans		

5. For any food group for which you're consuming less than the recommended amounts, click on that group on the Web page to find foods you could consume to meet the recommended daily amount. In the space that follows, record any items that you'd be willing to consume in greater amounts to meet the daily recommendation.

_____

_____

_____

_____

_____

6. How likely is it that you'll add these food items to your regular diet? (Circle one.)

Very Likely   Possibly   Unlikely

7. If you didn't answer "very likely," what would interfere or prevent you from adding these food items to your regular diet?

Drinking to Death: College Partying Gone Wild

At least 50 college students nationwide die each year as a result of drinking incidents on or near campus. During a 1-month period in fall 1997, three college students died as a result of binge drinking at college parties. One involved an 18-year-old, first-year student at a private university who collapsed after drinking a mixture of beer and rum, fell into a coma at his fraternity house, and died 3 days later. He had a blood-alcohol level of more than .40, which is about equal to gulping down 20 shots of liquor in 1 hour.

The second incident involved a student from a public university in the South who died of alcohol poisoning (overdose). The third student died at another public university in the Northeast United States where, after an evening of partying and heavy drinking, he accidentally fell off a building in the middle of the night and fell through the roof of a greenhouse. Some colleges in the Northeast now have student volunteers roaming the campus on cold, winter nights to make sure that no students freeze to death after passing out from an intense bout of binge drinking.

The following are some strategies that are being considered to stop or reduce the problem of dangerous binge drinking:

1. A state governor has announced that he is going to launch a series of radio ads designed to discourage underage drinking.

2. A senator has filed bills to toughen penalties for those who violate underage drinking laws, such as producing and using fake identification cards.

3. A group of city council members is going to look into stiffening penalties for liquor stores that deliver directly to fraternity houses.

Source: Los Angeles Times (1997, 2000).

Reflection and Discussion Questions

1. How would you rank the potential effectiveness of the three strategies for stopping or reducing the problem of binge drinking mentioned in the last paragraph (1 = the most effective strategy, 3 = the least effective)?

   1. _____

   2. _____

   3. _____

2. Comparing your highest ranked and lowest ranked choices, what reason or reasons do you have for

   a. ranking the first one as most effective; and

   b. ranking the last one as least effective?

3. What other strategies do you think would be effective for stopping or reducing dangerous binge drinking among college students?

Glossary

Ability (Aptitude) the capacity to do something well or to have the potential to do it well.

Academic Advisor a professional who advises college students on course selection, helps students understand college procedures, and helps guide their academic progress toward completion of a college degree.

Academic Dismissal denying a student continued college enrollment because of a cumulative GPA that remains below a minimum level (e.g., below 2.0).

Academic Probation a period (usually one term) during which students with a GPA that is too low (e.g., less than 2.0) are given a chance to improve their grades; if the student's GPA does not meet or exceed the college's minimum requirement after this probationary period, that student may be academically dismissed from the college.

Academic Support Center the place on campus where students can obtain individual assistance from professionals and trained peers to support and strengthen their academic performance.

Administrator someone whose primary responsibility is the governance of the college or a unit within the college, such as an academic department or student support service.

Career the sum total of vocational experiences throughout an individual's work life.

Career Advancement working up the career ladder to higher levels of decision-making responsibility and socioeconomic status.

Career Development Center a key campus resource for learning about the nature of different careers and strategies on how to locate career-related work experiences.

Career Development Course a college course that typically includes self-assessment of career interests, information about different careers, and strategies for career preparation.

Career Entry gaining entry into a career and beginning a career path.

Citation an acknowledgment of the source of any piece of information included in a written paper or oral report that doesn't represent original work or thoughts.

Cocurricular Experience the learning and development that occur outside the classroom.

Communication Skills skills necessary for accurate comprehension and articulate expression of ideas, which include reading, writing, speaking, listening, and multimedia skills.

Commuter Student a college student who does not live on campus.

Concentration a cluster of approximately three courses in the same subject area.

Concept a larger system or network of related ideas.

Concept (Idea) Map a visual diagram that represents or maps out main categories of ideas and their relationships in a visual–spatial format.

Cooperative Education (Co-op) Program a program in which students gain work experience relating to their college major, either by stopping their coursework temporarily to work full time at the co-op position or by continuing to take classes while working part time at the co-op position.

Core Course a course required of all students, regardless of their particular major.

Cover (Application) Letter a letter written by an applicant who is applying for an employment position or admission to a school.

Cramming packing study time into one session immediately before an exam.

Creative Thinking a form of higher-level thinking that involves producing a new and different idea, method, strategy, or work product.

Critical Thinking a form of higher-level thinking that involves making well-informed evaluations or judgments.

Culture a distinctive way or style of living that characterizes a group of people who share the same social system, heritage, and traditions.

Cum Laude graduating with honors (e.g., achieving a cumulative GPA of at least 3.3).

Cumulative Grade Point Average a student's GPA for all academic terms combined.

Curriculum the total set of courses offered by a college or university.

Dean's List achieving an outstanding GPA for a particular term (e.g., 3.5 or higher).

Diversity interacting with and learning from peers of varied backgrounds and lifestyles.

Diversity Appreciation becoming interested in and valuing the experiences of different groups of people and willingness to learn more about them.

Diversity (Multicultural) Course a course designed to promote diversity awareness and appreciation of multiple cultures.

Documentation information sources that serve as references to support or reinforce conclusions in a written paper or oral presentation.

Elective a course that students are not required to take but that they elect or choose to take.

Experiential Learning out-of-class experiences that promote learning and development.

Faculty the collection of instructors on campus whose primary role is to teach courses that comprise the college curriculum.

Free Elective a course that students may elect to enroll in, which counts toward a college degree but is not required for either general education or academic major.

Freshman 15 a phrase commonly used to describe the 15-pound weight gain that some students experience during their first year of college.

Graduate Assistant (GA) a graduate student who receives financial assistance to pursue graduate studies by working in a university office or college professor.

Grade Points the amount of points earned for a course, which is calculated by multiplying the course grade by the number of credits carried by the course.

Grade Point Average (GPA) the translation of students' letter grades into a numerical system, whereby the total number of grade points earned in all courses is divided by total number of course units.

Graduate School a university-related education pursued after completing a bachelor's degree.

Grant money received that does not have to be repaid.

Greek Life a term that refers to both fraternities (usually all male) and sororities (usually all female).

Hazing a rite of induction to a social or other organization, most commonly associated with fraternities.

Higher-Level Thinking thinking at a higher or more complex level than merely acquiring factual knowledge or memorizing information.

Holistic (or Whole-Person) Development the development of the total self, which includes intellectual, social, emotional, physical, spiritual, ethical, vocational, and personal development.

Human Diversity the variety of differences that exist among people who comprise humanity (the human species).

Humanity common elements of the human experience that are shared by all humans.

Hypothesis an informed guess that might be true but still needs to be tested to confirm or verify its truth.

Illustrate to provide concrete examples or specific instances.

Independent Study a project that allows a student to receive academic credit for an in-depth study of a topic of his or her choice by working independently with a faculty member without enrolling in a formal course that meets in a classroom according to a set schedule.

Information Interview an interview with a professional working in a career to obtain inside information on what the career is like.

Information Literacy the ability to find, evaluate, and use information.

Intellectual (Cognitive) Development acquiring knowledge and learning how to learn and how to think deeply.

Interdisciplinary courses or programs that are designed to help students integrate knowledge from two or more academic disciplines (fields of study).

Interest something someone likes or enjoys doing.

International Student a student attending college in one nation who is a citizen of a different nation.

International Study (Study Abroad) Program doing coursework at a college or university in another country that counts toward graduation, and which is typically done for one or two academic terms.

Internship a work experience related to a college major for which students receive academic credit and, in some cases, financial compensation.

Interpret to draw a conclusion about something and support that conclusion with evidence.

Job Shadowing a program that allows a student to follow (shadow) and observe a professional during a typical workday.

Justify to back up arguments and viewpoints with evidence.

Leadership the ability to influence people in a positive way (e.g., motivating peers to do their best) or the ability to produce positive change in an organization or institution (e.g., improving the quality of a school, business, or political organization).

Leadership Course a course in which students learn how to advance and eventually assume important leadership positions in a company or organization.

Learning Community a program offered by some colleges and universities in which the same group of students takes the same block of courses together during the same academic term.

Learning Style the way in which individuals prefer to perceive information (receive or take it in), and process information (deal with it once it has been taken in).

Liberal Arts the component of a college education that provides the essential foundation or backbone for the college curriculum and is designed to equip students with a versatile set of skills to promote their success in any academic major or career.

Lifelong Learning Skills skills that include learning how to learn and how to continue learning that can be used throughout the remainder of personal and professional life.

Magna Cum Laude graduating with high honors (e.g., achieving a cumulative GPA of at least 3.5).

Major the academic field students choose to specialize in while in college.

Mentor someone who serves as a role model and personal guide to help students reach their educational or occupational goals.

Merit-Based Scholarship money awarded on the basis of performance or achievement that does not have to be repaid.

Metacognition thinking about the process of thinking.

Midterm the midpoint of an academic term.

Minor a second field of study that is designed to complement and strengthen a major, which usually consists of about half the number of courses required for a college major (e.g., six to seven courses are usually needed for a minor).

Mnemonic Device (Mnemonics) a specific memory-improvement method designed to prevent forgetting, which often involves such memory-improvement principles as meaning, organization, visualization, or rhythm and rhyme.

MLA Style a style of citing references in a research report that is endorsed by the Modern Language Association and is commonly used by academic fields in the humanities and fine arts (e.g., English and philosophy).

Multicultural Competence the ability to understand cultural differences and to interact effectively with people from multiple cultural backgrounds.

Multidimensional Thinking a form of higher-level thinking that involves taking multiple perspectives and considering multiple theories.

Multiple Intelligences the notion that humans display intelligence or mental skills in many other forms besides their ability to perform on intellectual tests such as IQ and SAT tests.

Need a key element of life planning that represents something stronger than an interest and makes a person's life more satisfying or fulfilling.

Need-Based Scholarship money awarded to students on the basis of financial need that does not have to be repaid.

Netiquette applying the principles of social etiquette and interpersonal sensitivity when communicating online.

Online Resource a resource that can be used to search for and locate information, including online card catalogs, Internet search engines, and electronic databases.

Oral Communication Skills the ability to speak in a concise, confident, and eloquent fashion.

Oversubscribed (Impacted) Major a major that has more students interested in it than there are openings for students to be accepted.

Paraphrase restating or rephrasing information in original words.

Part-to-Whole Method a study strategy that involves dividing study time into smaller parts or units and then learning these parts in several short, separate study sessions in advance of exams.

Persuasive Speech an oral presentation intended to persuade or convince the audience to agree with a certain conclusion or position by providing supporting evidence.

Plagiarism the deliberate or unintentional use of someone else's work without acknowledging it, giving the impression that it is original work.

Portfolio a collection of work materials or products that illustrates an individual's skills and talents or demonstrates that individual's educational and personal development.

Prewriting an early stage in the writing process where the focus is on generating and organizing ideas rather than expressing or communicating ideas to someone else.

Primary Source the information obtained from a firsthand source or original document.

Process-of-Elimination Method a multiple-choice test-taking strategy that involves weeding out or eliminating choices that are clearly wrong and continuing to do so until the choices are narrowed down to one answer that seems to be the best choice available.

Procrastination the tendency to postpone making a decision or taking action until the last moment.

Professional School a formal education pursued after a bachelor's degree in school that prepare students for an "applied" profession (e.g., pharmacy, medicine, or law).

Prerequisite Course a course that must be completed before students can enroll in a more advanced course.

Proofreading a final microscopic form of editing that focuses on detecting mechanical errors relating to such things as referencing, grammar, punctuation, and spelling.

Recall Test Question a type of test question that requires students to generate or produce the correct answer on their own, such as a short-answer question or an essay question.

Recitation (Reciting) a study strategy that involves verbally stating information to be remembered without looking at it.

Recognition Test Question a type of test question that requires students to select or choose a correct answer from answers that are provided to them (e.g., multiple-choice, true–false, and matching questions).

Reconstruction a process of rebuilding a memory part by part or piece by piece.

Reentry Student a student who matriculated as a traditional (just out of high school) student but who left college to meet other job or family demands and has returned to complete a degree or obtain job training.

Reference (Referral) Letter a letter of reference typically written by a faculty member, advisor, or employer for students who are applying for entry into positions or schools after college or for students during the college experience when they apply for special academic programs, student leadership positions on campus, or part-time employment.

Reflection a thoughtful, personal review of what a person has already done, is in the process of doing, or is planning to do.

Research Skills the ability to locate, access, retrieve, organize, and evaluate information from various sources, including library- and technology-based (computer) systems.

Restricted Elective a course that falls into an area of study students must complete but can be chosen from a restricted set or list of possible courses that have been specified by the college.

Résumé a written summary or outline that effectively organizes and highlights an individual's strongest qualities, personal accomplishments, and skills, as well as personal credentials and awards.

Rough Draft an early stage in the writing process whereby a first (rough) draft is created that converts the writer's major ideas into sentences, without worrying about the mechanics of writing (e.g., punctuation, grammar, or spelling).

Scholarly a criterion or standard for critically evaluating the quality of an information source; typically, a source is considered to be scholarly if it has been reviewed by a panel or board of impartial experts in the field before being published.

Secondary Source a publication that relies on or responds to a primary source that has been previously published (e.g., a textbook that draws its information from published research studies or an article that critically reviews a published novel or movie).

Self-Assessment the process of evaluating personal characteristics, traits, or habits and their relative strengths and weaknesses.

Self-Monitoring the ability to watch yourself and maintain self-awareness of how you're learning, what you're learning, and whether you're learning.

Semester (Term) Grade Point Average a GPA for one semester or academic term.

Senior Seminar (Capstone) Course course designed to put a cap or final touch on the college experience, helping seniors to tie ideas together in their major, make a smooth transition from college to life after college, or both.

Service Learning a form of experiential learning in which students serve or help others while they acquire skills through hands-on experience that can be used to strengthen their résumé and explore fields of work that may relate to their future career interests.

Sexually Transmitted Infections (STIs) a group of contagious infections that are spread through sexual contact.

Shadow Majors students who have been admitted to their college or university but have not yet been admitted to their intended major.

Shallow (Surface-Oriented) Learning an approach to learning in which students spend most of their study time repeating and memorizing information in the exact form that it was presented to them.

Student Development (Cocurricular) Transcript an official document issued by the college that validates a student's cocurricular achievements which the student can have sent to prospective employers or schools.

Summa Cum Laude graduating with highest honors (e.g., achieving a cumulative GPA of at least 3.8).

Syllabus an academic document that serves as a contract between instructor and student, which outlines course requirements, attendance policies, grading scale, course topic outlines by date, dates of tests and for completing reading and other assignments, and information about the instructor (e.g., office location and office hours).

Synthesis a form of higher-level thinking that involves building up ideas by integrating (connecting) separate pieces of information to form a whole or more comprehensive product.

Teaching Assistant (TA) a graduate student who receives financial assistance to pursue graduate studies by teaching undergraduate courses, leading course discussions, and helping professors grade papers or conduct labs.

Test Anxiety a state of emotional tension that can weaken test performance by interfering with memory and thinking.

Test Wise the ability to use the characteristics of the test question itself (such as its wording or format) to increase the probability of choosing the correct answer.

Theory a body of related concepts and general principles that help a student organize, understand, and apply knowledge that has been acquired in a particular field of study.

Thesis Statement an important sentence in the introduction of a paper that is a one-sentence summary of the key point or main argument a writer intends to make, and support with evidence, in the body of the paper.

Transferable Skills skills that can be transferred or applied across a range of subjects, careers, and life situations.

Values what a person strongly believes in and cares about or feels is important to do and should be done.

Visual Aids charts, graphs, diagrams, or concept maps that improve learning and memory by enabling the learner to visualize information as a picture or image and connect separate pieces of information to form a meaningful whole.

Visual Memory the type of memory that relies on the sense of vision.

Visualization a memory-improvement strategy that involves creating a mental image or picture of what is to be remembered or imagining it being placed at a familiar site or location.

Vocational (Occupational) Development exploring career options, making career choices wisely, and developing skills needed for career success.

Waive to give up a right to access information (e.g., waiving the right to see a letter of recommendation).

Wellness a state of optimal health, peak performance, and positive well-being that is produced when different dimensions of the self (body, spirit and mind) are attended to and effectively integrated.

Work–Study Program a federal program that supplies colleges and universities with funds to provide on-campus employment for students who are in financial need.

Written Communication Skills the ability to write in a clear, creative, or persuasive manner.

A Dictionary of College Vocabulary

Academic Affairs the unit or division of the college that deals primarily with the college curriculum, course instruction, and campus services that support academic success (e.g., library and learning center).

Academic Calendar the scheduling system used by a college or university to divide the academic year into shorter terms (e.g., semesters, trimesters, or quarters).

Academic Credits (Units) what students are credited with after completing courses that are counted toward completion of their college degree; course credit is typically counted in terms of how many hours the class meets each week (e.g., a course that meets for 3 hours per week counts for three credits).

Academic Standing where a student stands academically (cumulative grade point average) at a given point in their college experience (e.g., after a term or a year).

Academic Transcript a list of all courses a student has enrolled in, the grades received in those courses, and the student's grade point average.

Advanced Placement (AP) Tests tests designed to measure college-level work that are taken while a student is in high school; if the student scores high enough, then college credit is awarded in the subject area tested or the student is granted advanced placement in a college course.

American Psychological Association (APA) Style a particular style of citing references in a research report or term paper that is endorsed by the APA and is most commonly used in fields that comprise the behavioral sciences (e.g., psychology and sociology) and natural sciences (e.g., biology and chemistry).

Analysis (Analytical Thinking) a form of higher-level thinking that involves breaking down information and identifying its key parts or underlying elements and detecting what is most important or relevant.

Associate (A.A. or A.S.) Degree a 2-year college degree that represents completion of general education requirements and prepares students for transfer to a 4-year college or university.

Bachelor's (Baccalaureate) Degree a degree awarded by 4-year colleges and universities, which represents the completion of general education requirements plus completion of an academic specialization in a particular major.

Breadth Requirements the required general education courses that span a range of subject areas.

Certificate a credential received by students at a community college or technical college who have completed a 1- or 2-year vocational or occupational training program, which allows them entry into a specific occupation or career.

College Catalog (a.k.a. College Bulletin) an official publication of a college or university that identifies its mission, curriculum, and academic policies and procedures, as well as the names and educational backgrounds of the faculty members.

Combined Bachelor–Graduate Degree Program a program offered by some universities that allows students to apply for simultaneous admission to both undergraduate and graduate school in a particular field and to receive both a bachelor's degree and a graduate degree in that field after completing the combined program (e.g., a bachelor's and master's degree in physical therapy).

Counseling Services the personal counseling provided by professionals on campus that is designed to promote self-awareness and self-development in emotional and social aspects of life.

Cross-registration a collaborative program offered by two colleges or universities that allow students who are enrolled at one institution to register for and take courses at another institution.

Dean a college or university administrator who is responsible for running a particular unit of the college.

Distance Learning enrolling in and completing courses online rather than in person.

Doctoral Degree an advanced degree obtained after completion of the bachelor's (baccalaureate) degree, which typically requires 5 to 6 years of full-time study in graduate school, including completion of a thesis or doctoral dissertation.

Double Major attaining a bachelor's degree in two majors by meeting the course requirements of both academic fields.

Drop–Add the process of changing an academic schedule by dropping courses or adding courses to a preexisting schedule; at most colleges and universities, adding and dropping courses can be done during the first week of the academic term.

Fine Arts a division of the liberal arts curriculum that focuses largely on artistic performance and appreciation of artistic expression by pursuing such questions as "What is beautiful?" and "How do humans express and appreciate aesthetic (sensory) experiences, imagination, creativity, style, grace, and elegance?"

Full-Time Student a student who typically enrolls in and completes at least 24 units per academic year.

General Education Curriculum a collection of courses designed to provide a broad rather than narrow education and develop skills needed for success in any major or career.

Graduate Record Examination (GRE) a standardized test for admission to graduate schools, which is used in a manner similar to the way that the SAT and ACT tests are used for admission to undergraduate colleges and universities.

Graduate Student a student who has completed a 4-year (bachelor's) degree and is enrolled in graduate school to obtain an advanced degree (e.g., master's degree or PhD).

Health Services on-campus services provided to help students who are experiencing physical illnesses or injuries and to educate students on matters relating to health and wellness.

Higher Education formal education beyond high school.

Honors Program a special program of courses and other learning experiences designed for college students who have demonstrated exceptionally high levels of academic achievement.

Humanities a division of the liberal arts curriculum that focuses on the human experience, human culture, and questions that arise in a human's life, such as "Why are we here?" "What is the meaning or purpose of our existence?" "How should we live?" "What is the good life?" and "Is there life after death?"

Impacted Major an academic major in which there are more students wishing to enter the program than there are spaces available in the program;

thus, students must formally apply and qualify for admission to the major by going through a competitive screening process.

Interterm (a.k.a. January Interim or Maymester) a short academic term, typically running 3 to 4 weeks, during which students enroll in only one course that is studied intensively.

Learning Habits the usual approaches, methods, or techniques a student uses while attempting to learn.

Living–Learning Environment an on-campus student residence that is designed and organized in such a way that students' learning experiences are integrated into their living environment (e.g., study groups, tutoring, and student development workshops).

Lower-Division Courses courses taken by college students during their freshman and sophomore years.

Master's Degree a degree obtained after completion of the bachelor's (baccalaureate) degree, which typically requires 2 to 3 years of full-time study in graduate school.

Matriculation the process of initially enrolling in or registering for college. (The term is derived from the term *matricula*, a list or register of people belonging to a society or community.)

Multicultural Center a place on campus that is designed for interaction among and between members of diverse cultural groups.

Natural Sciences a division of the liberal arts curriculum that focuses on observing the physical world and explaining natural phenomena, asking such questions as "What causes physical events in the natural world?" and "How can we predict and control physical events and improve the quality of interaction between humans and the natural environment?"

Nonresident Status the status of out-of-state students who typically pay higher tuition than in-state students because they are not residents of the state in which their college is located.

Orientation an educational program designed to help students make a smooth transition to college that is delivered to students before their first academic term.

Part-Time Student a student who typically enrolls in and completes less than 24 units per academic year.

Pass–Fail (Credit–No Credit) Grading a grading option offered in some courses whereby students do not receive a letter grade (A–F) but only a grade of pass (credit) or fail (no credit).

Phi Beta Kappa a national honor society that recognizes outstanding academic achievement of students at 4-year colleges and universities.

Phi Theta Kappa a national honor society that recognizes outstanding academic achievement of students at 2-year colleges.

Placement Tests tests administered to new students upon entry to a college or university designed to assess their basic academic skills (e.g., reading, writing, and mathematics) to place them in courses that are neither too advanced nor too elementary for their particular level of skill development.

Postsecondary Education formal education beyond secondary (high school) education.

Preprofessional Coursework undergraduate courses that are required or strongly recommended for gaining entry into professional school (e.g., medical school or law school).

Proficiency Tests tests given to college students before graduation that are designed to assess whether they can perform certain academic skills (e.g., writing) at a level advanced enough to qualify them for college graduation.

Quarter System a system for scheduling courses in which the academic year is divided into four quarters (fall, winter, spring, and summer terms), each of which lasts approximately 10 or 11 weeks.

Registrar's Office the campus office that maintains college transcripts and other official records associated with student coursework and academic performance.

Resident Assistant a undergraduate student (sophomore, junior, or senior) whose role is to enforce rules in student residences and help new students adjust successfully to residence hall life.

Resident Director a student development professional who is in charge of residential (dormitory) life and the person to whom resident assistants report.

Resident Status the status of in-state students who typically pay lower tuition than out-of-state students because they are residents of the state in which their college is located.

Residential Students students who live on campus or in a housing unit owned and operated by the college.

Semester System a system for scheduling courses in which the academic year is divided into two terms (fall and spring) that are approximately 15 or 16 weeks long.

Self-Regulation adjusting learning strategies in a way that best meets the specific demands of the subject being learned.

Social and Behavioral Sciences a division of the liberal arts curriculum that focuses on the observation of human behavior, individually and in groups, asking such questions as "What causes humans to behave the way they do?" and "How can we predict, control, or improve human behavior and interpersonal interaction?"

Student Activities cocurricular experiences offered outside the classroom that are designed to promote student learning and student involvement in campus life.

Student-Designed (Interdisciplinary) Major an academic program offered at some colleges and universities in which a student works with a college representative or committee to develop a major that is not officially offered by the institution.

Student Development Services (Student Affairs) the division of the college that provides student support on issues relating to social and emotional adjustment, involvement in campus life outside the classroom, and leadership development.

Student Handbook an official publication of a college or university that identifies student roles and responsibilities, violations of college rules and policies, and opportunities for student involvement in cocurricular programs, such as student clubs, campus organizations, and student leadership positions.

Summer Session courses offered during the summer between spring and fall terms that typically run for 4 to 6 weeks.

Transfer Program a 2-year college program that provides general education and premajor coursework to prepare students for successful transfer to a 4-year college or university.

Trimester System a system for scheduling courses in which the academic year is divided into three terms (fall, winter, and spring) that are approximately 12 or 13 weeks long.

Undeclared students who have not committed to a college major.

Undergraduate a student who is enrolled in a 2- or 4-year college.

University an educational institution that offers not only undergraduate degrees but graduate degrees as well.

Upper-Division Courses courses taken by college students during their junior and senior years.

Vocational–Technical Programs community college programs of study that train students for a particular occupation or trade and immediate employment after completing a 2-year associate degree (e.g., Associate of Applied Science) or a 1-year certificate program.

Volunteerism volunteering personal time to help others.

Withdrawal dropping a class after the drop–add deadline, which results in a student receiving a W for the course and no academic credit.

Writing Center a campus support service where students can receive assistance at any stage of the writing process, whether it be collecting and organizing ideas, composing a first draft, or proofreading a final draft.

References

Abbey, A. (2002). Alcohol-related sexual assault: A common problem among college students. *Journal of Studies on Alcohol, 14,* 118–128.

AC Nielsen Research Services. (2000). *Employer satisfaction with graduate skills.* Department of Education, Training and Youth Affairs. Canberra: AGPS. Retrieved October 25, 2006, from http://www.dest.gov.au/ty/publications/employability_skills/final_report.pdf

Academic Integrity at Princeton. (2003). *Examples of plagiarism.* Retrieved October 21, 2006, from http://www.princeton.du/pr/pub/integrity/pages/plagiarism.html

Acredolo, C., & O'Connor, J. (1991). On the difficulty of detecting cognitive uncertainty. *Human Development, 34,* 204–223.

AhYun, K. (2002). Similarity and attraction. In M. Allen, R. W. Preiss, B. M. Gayle, & N. A. Burrell (Eds.), *Interpersonal communication research* (pp. 145–167). Mahwah, NJ: Erlbaum.

Ainslie, G. (1975). Specious reward: A behavioral theory of impulsiveness and impulse control. *Psychological Bulletin, 82,* 463–496.

Ainslie, G. (1992). *Picoeconomics: The strategic interaction of successive motivational states within the person.* New York: Cambridge University Press.

Alkon, D. L. (1992). *Memory's voice: Deciphering the brain-mind code.* New York: HarperCollins.

Allport, G. W. (1954). *The nature of prejudice.* Cambridge, MA: Addison-Wesley.

American College Testing. (2009). *National college dropout and graduation rates, 2008.* Retrieved June 4, 2009, from http://www.act.org/news

American Heart Association. (2006). *Fish, levels of mercury and omega-3 fatty acids.* Retrieved January 13, 2007, from http://americanheart.org/presenter.jthml?identifier=3013797

American Obesity Association. (2002). *Obesity in the U.S.* Retrieved April 26, 2006, from http://www.obesity.org/subs/fastfacts/obesity_US.shtml

Amir, Y. (1976). The role of intergroup contact in change of prejudice and ethnic relations. In P. A. Katz (Ed.), *Towards the elimination of racism* (pp. 245–308). New York: Pergamon Press.

Andersen, P. A. (1985). Nonverbal immediacy in interpersonal communication. In A. W. Siegmean &

S. Feldstein (Eds.), *Multichannel integrations of nonverbal behavior* (pp. 1–36). Hillsdale, NJ: Lawrence Erlbaum.

Anderson, J. R. (2000). *Cognitive psychology and its implications.* Worth Publishers.

Anderson, J. R., & Bower, G. H. (1974). Interference in memory for multiple contexts. *Memory and Cognition, 2,* 509–514.

Anderson, M., & Fienberg, S. E. (2000). Race and ethnicity and the controversy over the U.S. census. *Current Sociology, 48*(3), 87–110.

Anderson, L. W., & Krathwohl, D. R. (Eds.). (2001). *A taxonomy for learning, teaching, and assessing: A revision of Bloom's taxonomy of educational objectives.* New York: Addison Wesley Longman.

Applebee, A. N., Langer, J. A., Jenkins, L. B., Mullis, I. V. S., & Foertsch, M. A. (1990). *Learning to write in our nation's schools: instruction and achievement in 1988 at grades 4, 8, and 12.* Princeton, NJ: The National Assessment of Educational Progress.

Appleby, D. C. (2008, June). *Diagnosing and treating the deadly 13th grade syndrome.* Paper presented at the Association of Psychological Science Convention, Chicago, IL.

Arnedt, J. T., Wilde, G. J. S., Munt, P. W., & MacLean, A. W. (2001). How do prolonged wakefulness and alcohol compare in the decrements they produce on a simulated driving task? *Accident Analysis and Prevention, 33,* 337–344.

Association of American Colleges & Universities. (2002). *Greater expectations: A new vision for learning as a nation goes to college.* Washington, DC: Author.

Astin, A. W. (1993). *What matters in college?* San Francisco: Jossey-Bass.

Astin, A. W., Parrot, S. A., Korn, W. S., & Sax, L. J. (1997). *The American freshman: Thirty year trends, 1966–1996.* Los Angeles: Higher Education Research Institute, University of California.

Baer, J. M. (1993). *Creativity and divergent thinking.* Hillsdale, NJ: Erlbaum.

Bandura, A. (1986). *Social foundations of thought and action: A social cognitive theory.* Englewood Cliffs, NJ: Prentice Hall.

Bandura, A. (1994). Self-efficacy. In V. S. Ramachaudran (Ed.), *Encyclopedia of human behavior* (Vol. 4, pp. 71–81). New York: Academic Press.

Bandura, A. (1997). *Self-efficacy: The exercise of control*. New York: Freeman.

Bandura, A., & Cervone, D. (1983). Self-evaluative and self-efficacy mechanisms governing the motivational effects of goal systems. *Journal of Personality and Social Psychology, 45*(5), 1017–1028.

Barefoot, B. O., Warnock, C. L., Dickinson, M. P., Richardson, S. E., & Roberts, M. R. (Eds.). (1998). *Exploring the evidence: Vol. 2. Reporting outcomes of first-year seminars* (Monograph No. 29). Columbia: National Resource Center for the First-Year Experience and Students in Transition, University of South Carolina.

Bargdill, R. W. (2000). A phenomenological investigation of being bored with life. *Psychological Reports, 86*, 493–494.

Barker, L., & Watson, K. W. (2000). *Listen up: How to improve relationships, reduce stress, and be more productive by using the power of listening*. New York: St. Martin's Press.

Bartlett, T. (2002). Freshman pay, mentally and physically, as they adjust to college life. *Chronicle of Higher Education, 48*, 35–37.

Basadur, M., Runco, M. A., & Vega, L. A. (2000). Understanding how creative thinking skills, attitudes, and behaviors work together. *Journal of Creative Behavior, 34*(2), 77–100.

Bassham, G., Irwin, W., Nardone, H., & Wallace, J. M. (2005). *Critical thinking* (2nd ed.). New York: McGraw-Hill.

Bates, G. A. (1994). *The next step: College*. Bloomington, IN: Phi Delta Kappa.

Baumeister, R. F., Heatherton, T. F., & Tice, D. M. (1994). *Losing control: How and why people fail at self-regulation*. San Diego, CA: Academic Press.

Bellah, R. N., Madsen, R., Sullivan, W. M., Swidler, A., & Tipton, S. M. (1985). *Habits of the heart: Individualism and commitment in American life*. Berkeley: University of California Press.

Benjamin, L. T., Jr., Cavell, T. A., & Shallenberger, W. R., III. (1984). Staying with initial answers on objective tests: Is it a myth? *Teaching of Psychology, 11*, 133–141.

Benjamin, M., McKeachie, W. J., Lin, Y. G., & Holinger. D. (1981). Test anxiety: Deficits in information processing. *Journal of Educational Psychology, 73*, 816–824.

Bennet, W., & Gurin, J. (1983). *The dieter's dilemma*. New York: Basic Books.

Benson, H., & Klipper, M. Z. (1990). *The relaxation response*. New York: Avon.

Bergen-Cico, D. (2000). Patterns of substance abuse and attrition among first-year students. *Journal of the First-Year Experience and Students in Transition, 12*(1), 61–75.

Berndt, T. J. (1992). Friendship and friends' influence in adolescence. *Current Directions in Psychological Science, 1*(5), 156–159.

Biglan, A. (1973). The characteristics of subject matter in different academic areas. *Journal of Applied Psychology, 57*, 195–203.

Bishop, S. (1986). Education for political freedom. *Liberal Education, 72*(4), 322–325.

Bjork, R. (1994). Memory and metamemory considerations in the training of human beings. In J. Metcalfe & A. P. Shimamura (Eds.), *Metacognition: Knowing about knowing* (pp. 185–206). Cambridge, MA: MIT Press.

Blakeslee, S. (1993, August 3). Mystery of sleep yields as studies reveal immune tie. *The New York Times*, pp. C1, C6.

Boekaerts, M., Pintrich, P. R., & Zeidner, M. (2000). *Handbook of self-regulation*. San Diego: Academic Press.

Bok, D. (2006). *Our underachieving colleges*. Princeton, NJ: Princeton University Press.

Bolles, R. N. (1998). *The new quick job-hunting map*. Toronto, Ontario, Canada: Ten Speed Press.

Booth, F. W., & Vyas, D. R. (2001). Genes, environment, and exercise. *Advances in Experimental Medicine and Biology, 502*, 13–20.

Boudreau, C., & Kromrey, J. (1994). A longitudinal study of the retention and academic performance of participants in a freshman orientation course. *Journal of College Student Development, 35*, 444–449.

Bowen, H. R. (1977). *Investment in learning: The individual and social value of American higher education*. San Francisco: Jossey-Bass.

Bowen, H. R. (1997). *Investment in learning: The individual and social value of American higher education* (2nd ed.). Baltimore: Johns Hopkins Press.

Bowlby, J. (1980). *Attachment and loss: Vol. 3. Loss, sadness, and depression*. New York: Basic Books.

Boyer, E. L. (1987). *College: The undergraduate experience in America*. New York: Harper & Row.

Bradshaw, D. (1995). Learning theory: Harnessing the strength of a neglected resource. In D. C. A. Bradshaw (Ed.), *Bringing learning to life: The learning revolution, the economy and the individual* (pp. 79–92). London: Falmer Press.

Bransford, J. D., Brown, A. L., & Cocking, R. R. (1999). *How people learn: Brain, mind, experience and school*. Washington, DC: National Academy Press.

Braskamp, L. A. (2008). Developing global citizens. *Journal of College & Character, 10*(1), 1–5.

Bridgeman, B. (2003). *Psychology and evolution: The origins of mind.* Thousand Oaks, CA: Sage.

Brody, J. E. (2003, August 18). Skipping a college course: Weight gain 101. *The New York Times,* p. D7.

Brown, R. D. (1988). Self-quiz on testing and grading issues. *Teaching at UNL (University of Nebraska–Lincoln), 10*(2), 1–3.

Brown, S. A., Tapert, S. F., Granholm, E., & Delis, D. C. (2000). Neurocognitive functioning of adolescents: Effects of protracted alcohol use. *Alcoholism: Clinical & Experimental Research, 24*(2), 164–171.

Brown, S. D., & Krane, N. E. R. (2000). Four (or five) sessions and a cloud of dust: Old assumptions and new observations about career counseling. In S. D. Brown & R. W. Lent (Eds.), *Handbook of counseling psychology* (3rd ed., pp. 740–766). New York: Wiley.

Bruffee, K. A. (1993). *Collaborative learning: Higher education, interdependence, and the authority of knowledge.* Baltimore: Johns Hopkins University Press.

Burka, J. B., & Yuen, L. M. (1983). *Procrastination: Why you do it, what to do about it.* Reading, MA: Addison-Wesley.

Bushman, B. J., & Cooper, H. M. (1990). Effects of alcohol on human aggression: An integrative research review. *Psychological Bulletin, 107*(3), 341–354.

Business/Higher Education Round Table. (1991). *Aiming higher: The concerns and attitudes of leading business executives and university heads to education priorities in Australia in the 1990s* (Commissioned Report No. 1). Melbourne, Australia.

Business/Higher Education Round Table. (1992). *Educating for excellence part 2: Achieving excellence in university professional education* (Commissioned Report No. 2). Melbourne, Australia.

Caine, R. N., & Caine, G. (1991). *Teaching and the human brain.* Alexandria, VA: Association for Supervision and Curriculum Development.

Cameron, L. (2003). *Metaphor in educational discourse.* London: Continuum.

Campbell, T. A., & Campbell, D. E. (1997, December). Faculty/student mentor program: Effects on academic performance and retention. *Research in Higher Education, 38,* 727–742.

Caplan, P. J., & Caplan, J. B. (1994). *Thinking critically about research on sex and gender.* New York: HarperCollins College Publishers.

Caroli, M., Argentieri, L., Cardone, M., & Masi, A. (2004). Role of television in childhood obesity prevention. *International Journal of Obesity Related Metabolic Disorders, 28*(Suppl. 3), S104–S108.

Cates, J. R., Herndon, N. L., Schulz, S. L., & Darroch, J. E. (2004). *Our voices, our lives, our futures: Youth and sexually transmitted diseases.* Chapel Hill, NC: University of North Carolina at Chapel Hill School of Journalism and Mass Communication.

Cheney, L. V. (1989). *50 hours: A core curriculum for college students.* Washington, DC: National Endowment for the Humanities.

Chi, M., de Leeuw, N., Chiu, M. H., & LaVancher, C. (1994). Eliciting self-explanations improves understanding. *Cognitive Science, 18,* 439–477.

Chickering, A. W., & Schlossberg, N. K. (1998). Moving on: Seniors as people in transition. In J. N. Gardner, G. Van der Veer, et al. (Eds.), *The senior year experience* (pp. 37–50). San Francisco: Jossey-Bass.

Chronicle of Higher Education. (2003, August 30). Almanac 2003–04. *Chronicle of Higher Education, 49*(1).

Claxton, C. S., & Murrell, P. H. (1988). *Learning styles: Implications for improving practice.* ASHE-ERIC Educational Report No. 4. Washington, DC: Association for the Study of Higher Education.

Coates, T. J. (1977). *How to sleep better: A drug-free program for overcoming insomnia.* Englewood Cliffs, NJ: Prentice Hall.

Colcombe, S. J., Erickson, K., Scalf, P. E., Kim, J. S., Prakash, R., McAuley, E., et al. (2006). Aerobic exercise training increases brain volume in aging humans. *Journal of Gerontology: Medical Sciences, 61A*(11), 1166–1170.

College Board (2009). Economic challenges lead to lower non-tuition revenues and higher prices at colleges and universities. Retrieved November 4, 2009, from http://www.collegeboard.com/press/releases/ 208962.html

College Board. (2008). *Education pays 2007.* Washington, DC: Author.

Collins, A. M., & Loftus, E. F. (1975). A spreading activation theory of semantic processing. *Psychological Review, 82,* 407–428.

Colombo, G., Cullen, R., & Lisle, B. (1995). *Rereading America: Cultural contexts for critical thinking and writing.* Boston: Bedford Books of St. Martin's Press.

Corbin, C. B., Pangrazi, R. P., & Franks, B. D. (2000). Definitions: Health, fitness, and physical activity. *President's Council on Physical Fitness and Sports Research Digest, 3*(9), 1–8.

Covey, S. R. (1990). *Seven habits of highly effective people* (2nd ed.). New York: Fireside.

Cowan, N. (2001). The magical number 4 in short-term memory: A reconsideration of mental storage capacity. *Behavioral and Brain Sciences, 24,* 87–114.

Coward, A. (1990). *Pattern thinking*. New York: Praeger Publishers.

Crawford, H. J., & Strapp, C. H. (1994). Effects of vocal and instrumental music on visuospatial and verbal performance as moderated by studying preference and personality. *Personality and Individual Differences, 16*(2), 237–245.

Cronon, W. (1998). "Only connect": The Goals of a Liberal Education. *The American Scholar* (Autumn), 73–80.

Crosby, O. (2002). Informational interviewing: Get the scoop on careers. *Occupational Outlook Quarterly* (Summer), 32–37.

Cross, K. P. (1982). Thirty years passed: Trends in general education. In B. L. Johnson (Ed.), *General education in two-year colleges* (pp. 11–20). San Francisco: Jossey-Bass.

Cude, B. J., Lawrence, F. C., Lyons, A. C., Metzger, K., LeJeune, E., Marks, L., & Machtmes, K. (2006). College students and financial literacy: What they know and what we need to learn. *Proceedings of the Eastern Family Economics and Resource Management Association Conference* (pp. 102–109).

Cuseo, J. B. (1996). *Cooperative learning: A pedagogy for addressing contemporary challenges and critical issues in higher education*. Stillwater, OK: New Forums Press.

Cuseo, J. B. (2003a). Comprehensive academic support for students during the first year of college. In G. L. Kramer et al. (Eds.), *Student academic services: An integrated approach* (pp. 271–310). San Francisco: Jossey-Bass.

Cuseo, J. B. (2005). "Decided," "undecided," and "in transition": Implications for academic advisement, career counseling, and student retention. In R. S. Feldman (Ed.), *Improving the first year of college: Research and practice* (pp. 27–50). Mahwah, NJ: Lawrence Erlbaum.

Cuseo, J. B., & Barefoot, B. O. (1996). A natural marriage: The extended orientation seminar and the community college. In J. Henkin (Ed.), *The community college: Opportunity and access for America's first-year students* (pp. 59–68). Columbia: National Resource Center for the First-Year Experience and Students in Transition, University of South Carolina.

Dalton, J. C., Eberhardt, D., Bracken, J., & Echols, K. (2006). Inward journeys: Forms and patterns of college student spirituality. *Journal of College & Character, 7*(8), 1–21. Retrieved December 17, 2006, from http://www.collegevalues.org/pdfs/Dalton.pdf

Daly, W. T. (1992, July/August). The academy, the economy, and the liberal arts. *Academe,* pp. 10–12.

Damrad-Frye, R., & Laird, J. (1989). The experience of boredom: The role of self-perception of attention. *Journal of Personality & Social Psychology, 57,* 315–320.

Daniels, D., & Horowitz, L. J. (1997). *Being and caring: A psychology for living*. Prospect Heights, IL: Waveland Press.

DeJong, W., & Linkenback, J. (1999). Telling it like it is: Using social norms marketing campaigns to reduce student drinking. *AAHE Bulletin, 52*(4), pp. 11–13, 16.

Dement, W. C., & Vaughan, C. (1999). *The promise of sleep*. New York: Delacorte Press.

Dement, W. C., & Vaughan, C. (2000). *The promise of sleep: A pioneer in sleep medicine explores the vital connection between health, happiness, and a good night's sleep*. New York: Dell.

Demmert, W. G., Jr., & Towner, J. C. (2003). *A review of the research literature on the influences of culturally based education on the academic performance of Native American students* Retrieved from the Northwest Regional Educational Laboratory, Portland, Oregon, Web site: http://www.nrel.org/indianaed/cbe.pdf

Donald, J. G. (2002). *Learning to think: Disciplinary perspectives*. San Francisco: Jossey-Bass.

Dorfman, J., Shames, J., & Kihlstrom, J. F. (1996). Intuition, incubation, and insight. In G. Underwood (Ed.), *Implicit cognition*. New York: Oxford University Press.

Doyle, S., Edison, M., & Pascarella, E. (1998). *The "seven principles of good practice in undergraduate education" as process indicators of cognitive development in college: A longitudinal study*. Paper presented at the annual meeting of the Association for the Study of Higher Education, Miami, FL.

Druckman, D., & Bjork, R. A. (Eds.). (1991). *In the mind's eye: Enhancing human performance*. Washington, DC: National Academy Press.

Dryden, G., & Vos, J. (1999). *The learning revolution: To change the way the world learns*. Torrance, CA: Learning Web.

Dunn, R., Dunn, K., & Price, G. (1990). *Learning style inventory*. Lawrence, KS: Price Systems.

Dupuy, G. M., & Vance, R. M. (1996, October). *Launching your career: A transition module for seniors*. Paper presented at the Second National Conference on Students in Transition, San Antonio, TX.

Eble, K. E. (1966). *The perfect education*. New York: Macmillan.

Eckman, P., & Friesen, W. V. (1969). Nonverbal leakage and clues to deception. *Psychiatry, 32,* 88–106.

Education Commission of the States. (1995). *Making quality count in undergraduate education*. Denver, CO: ECS Distribution Center.

Education Commission of the States. (1996). *Bridging the gap between neuroscience and education*. Denver, CO: Author.

Einstein, G. O., Morris, J., & Smith, S. (1985). Note-taking, individual differences, and memory for lecture information. *Journal of Educational Psychology, 77*(5), 522–532.

Ellin, A. (1993, September). Post-parchment depression. *Boston Phoenix*.

Ellis, A. (1995). Changing rational-emotive therapy (RET) to rational emotive behavior therapy (REBT). *Journal of Rational-Emotive & Cognitive Behavior Therapy, 13*(2), 85–89.

Ellis, A. (2000). *How to control your anxiety before it controls you*. New York: Citadel Press/Kensington Publishing.

Engs, R. C. (1977). Drinking patterns and drinking problems of college students. *Journal of Studies on Alcohol, 38,* 2144–2156.

Engs, R., & Hanson, D. (1986). Age-specific alcohol prohibition and college students' drinking problems. *Psychological Reports, 59,* 979–984.

Entwistle, N. J., & Marton, F. (1984). Changing conceptions of learning and research. In F. Marton et al. (Eds.), *The experience of learning*. Edinburgh: Scottish Academic Press.

Entwistle, N. J., & Ramsden, P. (1983). *Understanding student learning*. London: Croom Helm.

Erickson, B. L., Peters, C. B., & Strommer, D. W. (2006). *Teaching first-year college students*. San Francisco: Jossey-Bass.

Erickson, B. L., & Strommer, D. W. (1991). *Teaching college freshmen*. San Francisco: Jossey-Bass.

Erickson, B. L., & Strommer, D. W. (2005). Inside the fist-year classroom: Challenges and constraints. In J. L. Upcraft, J. N. Gardner, & B. O. Barefoot (Eds.), *Challenging and supporting the first-year student* (pp. 241–256). San Francisco: Jossey-Bass.

Everly, G. S. (1989). *A clinical guide to the treatment of the human stress response*. New York: Plenum Press.

Ewell, P. T. (1997). Organizing for learning. *AAHE Bulletin, 50*(4), 3–6.

Family Care Foundation. (2005). *If the world were a village of 100 people*. Retrieved December 19, 2006, from http://www.familycare.org.news/if_the_world.htm

Feldman, K. A., & Newcomb, T. M. (1997). *The impact of college on students*. New Brunswick, NJ: Transaction Publishers. (Original work published 1969).

Feldman, K. A., & Paulsen, M. B. (Eds.). (1994). *Teaching and learning in the college classroom*. Needham Heights, MA: Ginn Press.

Festinger, L. (1954). A theory of social comparison processes. *Human Relations, 7,* 117–140.

Fidler, P., & Godwin, M. (1994). Retaining African-American students through the freshman seminar. *Journal of Developmental Education, 17,* 34–41.

Fisher, J. L., Harris, J. L., & Harris, M. B. (1973). Effect of note-taking and review on recall. *Journal of Educational Psychology, 65*(3), 321–325.

Fixman, C. S. (1990). The foreign language needs of U.S. based corporations. *Annals of the American Academy of Political and Social Science, 511,* 25–46.

Flavell, J. H. (1985). *Cognitive development* (2nd ed.). Englewood Cliffs, NJ: Prentice Hall.

Fletcher, A., Lamond, N., van den Heuvel, C. J., & Dawson, D. (2003). Prediction of performance during sleep deprivation and alcohol intoxication using a quantitative model of work-related fatigue. *Sleep Research Online, 5,* 67–75.

Flowers, L., Osterlind, S., Pascarella, E., & Pierson, C. (2001). How much do student learn in college? Cross-sectional estimates using the College Basic Academic Subjects Examination. *Journal of Higher Education, 72,* 565–583.

Ford, P. L. (Ed.). (1903). *The works of Thomas Jefferson*. New York: Knickerbocker Press.

Franklin, K. F. (2002). Conversations with Metropolitan University first-year students. *Journal of the First-Year Experience and Students in Transition, 14*(2), 57–88.

Frost, S. H. (1991). *Academic advising for student success: A system of shared responsibility* (ASHE-ERIC Higher Education Report No. 3). Washington,

DC: School of Education and Human Development, George Washington University.

Furnham, A., & Argyle, M. (1998). *The psychology of money*. New York: Routledge.

Gamson, Z. F. (1984). *Liberating education*. San Francisco: Jossey-Bass.

Gardner, H. (1983). *Frames of mind: The theory of multiple intelligences*. New York: Basic Books.

Gardner, H. (1993). *Frames of mind: The theory of multiple intelligences* (2nd ed.). New York: Basic Books.

Gardner, H. (1999). *Intelligence reframed: Multiple intelligences for the 21st century*. New York: Basic Books.

Gardner, P. D. (1991, March). *Learning the ropes: Socialization and assimilation into the workplace*. Paper presented at the Second National Conference on the Senior Year Experience, San Antonio, TX.

Gibb, J. R. (1961, September). Defensive communication. *Journal of Communication, 11*, 3.

Gibb, H. R. (1991). *Trust: A new vision of human relationships for business, education, family, and personal living* (2nd ed.). North Hollywood, CA: Newcastle.

Giles, L. C., Glonek, F. V., Luszcz, M. A., & Andrews, G. R. (2005). Effect of social networks on 10-year survival in very old Australians: The Australia longitudinal study of aging. *Journal of Epidemiology and Community Health, 59*, 574–579.

Gladwell, M. (2008). *Outliers: The story of success*. New York: Little, Brown.

Glass, J., & Garrett, M. (1995). Student participation in a college orientation course: Retention, and grade point average. *Community College Journal of Research and Practice, 19*, 117–132.

Glenberg, A. M., Schroeder, J. L., & Robertson, D. A. (1998). Averting the gaze disengages the environment and facilitates remembering. *Memory & Cognition, 26*(4), 651–658.

Goleman, D. (1992, Oct. 27). Voters assailed by unfair persuasion. *The New York Times*, pp. C1–C3.

Goleman, D. (1995). *Emotional intelligence: Why it can matter more than IQ*. New York: Random House.

Goleman, D. (2006). Social intelligence: The new science of human relationships. New York: Dell.

Gordon, L. (2009, Oct. 21). College costs up in hard times. *Los Angeles Times*, p. A13.

Gordon, V. N., & Steele, G. E. (2003). Undecided first-year students: A 25-year longitudinal study. *Journal of the First-Year Experience and Students in Transition, 15*(1), 19–38.

Gottman, J. (1994). *Why marriages succeed and fail*. New York: Fireside.

Graf, P. (1982). The memorial consequence of generation and transformation. *Journal of Verbal Learning and Verbal Behavior, 21*, 539–548.

Green, M. G. (Ed.). (1989). *Minorities on campus: A handbook for enhancing diversity*. Washington, DC: American Council on Education.

Greenberg, R., Pillard, R., & Pearlman, C. (1972). The effect of dream (stage REM) deprivation on adaptation to stress. *Psychosomatic Medicine, 34*, 257–262.

Grunder, P., & Hellmich, D. (1996). Academic persistence and achievement of remedial students in a community college's success program. *Community College Review, 24*, 21–33.

Hall, R. M., & Sandler, B. R. (1982). *The classroom climate: A chilly one for women*. Project on the Status of Women. Washington, DC: Association of American Colleges.

Hall, R. M., & Sandler, B. R. (1984). *Out of the classroom: A chilly campus climate for women*. Project on the Status of Women. Washington, DC: Association of American Colleges.

Halpern, D. F. (2003). *Thought & knowledge: An introduction to critical thinking* (4th ed.). Mahwah, NJ: Lawrence Erlbaum Associates.

Harris, M. B. (2006). Correlates and characteristics of boredom and proneness to boredom. *Journal of Applied Social Psychology, 30*(3), 576–598.

Hartley, J. (1998). *Learning and studying: a research perspective*. London: Routledge.

Hartley, J., & Marshall, S. (1974). On notes and note taking. *Universities Quarterly, 28*, 225–235.

Hashaw, R. M., Hammond, C. J., & Rogers, P. H. (1990). Academic locus of control and the collegiate experience. *Research & Teaching in Developmental Education, 7*(1), 45–54.

Hauri, P., & Linde, S. (1996). *No more sleepless nights*. New York: John Wiley & Sons.

Health, C., & Soll, J. (1996). Mental budgeting and consumer decisions. *Journal of Consumer Research, 23*, 40–52.

Heath, H. (1977). *Maturity and competence: A transcultural view*. New York: Halsted Press.

Herman, R. E. (2000, November). Liberal arts: The key to the future. *USA Today Magazine, 129*, 34.

Hersh, R. (1997). Intentions and perceptions: A national survey of public attitudes toward liberal arts education. *Change, 29*(2), pp. 16–23.

Higbee, K. L. (2001). *Your memory: How it works and how to improve it*. New York: Marlowe.

Hildenbrand, M., & Gore, P. A., Jr. (2005). Career development in the first-year seminar: Best practice versus actual practice. In P. A. Gore (Ed.), *Facilitating the career development of students in transition* (Monograph No. 43, pp. 45–60). Columbia: National Resource Center for the First-Year Experience and Students in Transition, University of South Carolina.

Hill, A. J. (2002). Developmental issues in attitudes toward food and diet. *Proceedings of the Nutrition Society, 61*(2), 259–268.

Hill, J. O., Wyat, H. R., Reed, G. W., & Peters, J. C. (2003). Obesity and environment: Where do we go from here? *Science, 299*, 853–855.

Hobson, J. A. (1988). *The dreaming brain*. New York: Basic Books.

Hollenbeck, J. R., Williams, C. R., & Klein, H. J. (1989). An empirical examination of the antecedents of commitment to difficult goals. *Journal of Applied Psychology, 74*(1), 18–23.

Holmes, K. K., Levine, R., & Weaver, M. (2004). Effectiveness of condoms in preventing sexually transmitted infections. *Bulletin of the World Health Organization, 82*, 254–464.

Horne, J. (1988). *Why we sleep: The functions of sleep in humans and other mammals*. New York: Oxford University Press.

Howard, P. J. (2000). *The owner's manual for the brain: Everyday applications of mind-brain research* (2nd ed.). Atlanta: Bard Press.

Howe, M. J. (1970). Note-taking strategy, review, and long-term retention of verbal information. *Journal of Educational Psychology, 63*, 285.

Hunter, M. A., & Linder, C. W. (2005). First-year seminars. In M. L. Upcraft, J. N. Gardner, B. O. Barefoot, et al. (Eds.), *Challenging and supporting the first-year student: A handbook for improving the first year of college* (pp. 275–291). San Francisco: Jossey-Bass.

Indiana University. (2004). *Selling your liberal arts degree to employers*. Retrieved July 7, 2004, from http://www.indiana.edu/~career/fulltime/selling_liberal_arts.html

Institute for Research on Higher Education. (1995). Connecting schools and employers: Work-related education and training. *Change, 27*(3), 39–46.

Internal Revenue Service. (2004). *Statistics of income 2001–2003*. Washington, DC: Author.

Jablonski, N. G., & Chaplin, G. (2002). Skin deep. *Scientific American* (October), 75–81.

Jakubowski, P., & Lange, A. J. (1978). *The assertive option: Your rights and responsibilities*. Champaign, IL: Research Press.

Janis, I. L. (1982). *Groupthink: Psychological studies of policy decisions and fiascoes* (2nd ed.). Boston: Houghton Mifflin.

Jemott, J. B., & Magloire, K. (1988). Academic stress, social support, and secretory immunoglobulin. *Journal of Personality and Social Psychology, 55*, 803–810.

Jenkins, J. G., & Dallenbach, K. M. (1924). Oblivescence during sleep and waking. *American Journal of Psychology, 35*, 605–612.

Johansson, J. (2005). *Death by PowerPoint*. Retrieved November 11, 2009, from http://articles.tech.republic.com5100-22_11-5875608.html

Johnsgard, K. W. (2004). *Conquering depression and anxiety through exercise*. New York: Prometheus.

Johnston, L. D., O'Malley, P.M., Bachman, J. G., & Schulenberg, J. E. (2005). *Monitoring the future national survey results on drug use, 1975–2004: Vol 2. College students and adults ages 19–45*. National Institute on Drug Abuse: Bethesda, MD: 2005. NIH Publication No. 05-5728.

Johnstone, A. H., & Su, W. Y. (1994). Lectures: a learning experience? *Education in Chemistry, 31*(1), 65–76, 79.

Joint Science Academies Statement. (2005). *Global response to climate change*. Retrieved August 29, 2005, from http://nationalacademies.org/onpi/06072005.pdf

Jones, L., & Petruzzi, D. C. (1995). Test anxiety: A review of theory and current treatment. *Journal of College Student Psychotherapy, 10*(1), 3–15.

Julien, R. M. (2004). *A primer of drug action*. New York: Worth.

Kadison, R. D., & DiGeronimo, T. F. (2004). *College of the overwhelmed: The campus mental health crisis and what to do about it*. San Francisco: Jossey-Bass.

Kagan, S., & Kagan, M. (1998). *Multiple intelligences: The complete MI book*. San Clemente, CA: Kagan Cooperative Learning.

Kaufman, J. C., & Baer, J. (2002). Could Steven Spielberg manage the Yankees? Creative thinking in different domains. *Korean Journal of Thinking & Problem Solving, 12*(2), 5–14.

Kearns, D. (1989). Getting schools back on track. *Newsweek* (November), pp. 8–9.

Kielcolt-Glaser, J. K., & Glaser, R. (1986). Psychological influences on immunity. *Psychosomatics, 27*, 621–625.

Kiecolt, J. K., Glaser, R., Strain, E., Stout, J., Tarr, K., Holliday, J., et al. (1986). Modulation of cellular immunity in medical students. *Journal of Behavioral Medicine, 9*, 5–21.

Kiewra, K. A. (1985). Students' note-taking behaviors and the efficacy of providing the instructor's notes for review. *Contemporary Educational Psychology, 10*, 378–386.

Kiewra, K. A. (2000). Fish giver or fishing teacher? The lure of strategy instruction. *Teaching at UNL (University of Nebraska–Lincoln), 22*(3), 1–3.

Kiewra, K. A., DuBois, N., Christian, D., McShane, A., Meyerhoffer, M., & Roskelley, D. (1991). Note-taking functions and techniques. *Journal of Educational Psychology, 83*(2), 240–245.

Kiewra, K. A., & Fletcher, H. J. (1984). The relationship between notetaking variables and achievement measures. *Human Learning, 3*, 273–280.

Kiewra, K. A., Hart, K., Scoular, J., Stephen, M., Sterup, G., & Tyler, B. (2000). Fish giver or fishing teacher? The lure of strategy instruction. *Teaching at UNL (University of Nebraska–Lincoln), 22*(3).

King, A. (1990). Enhancing peer interaction and learning in the classroom through reciprocal questioning. *American Educational Research Journal, 27*(4), 664–687.

King, A. (1995). Guided peer questioning: A cooperative learning approach to critical thinking. *Cooperative Learning and College Teaching, 5*(2), 15–19.

King, J. E. (2002). *Crucial choices: How students' financial decisions affect their academic success.* Washington, DC: American Council on Education.

King, J. E. (2005). Academic success and financial decisions: Helping students make crucial choices. In R. S. Feldman (Ed.), *Improving the first year of college: Research and practice* (pp. 3–26). Mahwah, NJ: Lawrence Erlbaum.

King, P. N., Brown, M. K., Lindsay, N. K., & VanHencke, J. R. (2007, September/October). Liberal arts student learning outcomes: An integrated approach. *About Campus,* pp. 2–9.

Kintsch, W. (1968). Recognition and free recall of organized lists. *Journal of Experimental Psychology, 78*, 481–487.

Kintsch, W. (1970). *Learning, memory, and conceptual processes.* Hoboken, NJ: John Wiley & Sons.

Kintsch, W. (1994). Text comprehension, memory, and learning. *American Psychologist, 49*, 294–303.

Klein, S. P., & Hart, F. M. (1968). Chance and systematic factors affecting essay grades. *Journal of Educational Measurement, 5*, 197–206.

Knapp, J. R., & Karabenick, S. A. (1988). Incidence of formal and informal academic help-seeking in higher education. *Journal of College Student Development, 29*(3), 223–227.

Knoll, A. H. (2003). *Life on a young planet: The first three billion years of evolution on earth.* Princeton, NJ: Princeton University Press.

Knouse, S., Tanner, J., & Harris, E. (1999). The relation of college internships, college performance, and subsequent job opportunity. *Journal of Employment Counseling, 36*, 35–43.

Knox, S. (2004). *Financial basics: A money management guide for students.* Columbus: Ohio State University Press.

Kolb, D. A. (1976). Management and learning process. *California Management Review, 18*(3), 21–31.

Kolb, D. A. (1985). *Learning styles inventory.* Boston: McBer.

Kramer, A. F., & Erickson, K. I. (2007). Capitalizing on cortical plasticity: Influence of physical activity on cognition and brain function. *Trends in Cognitive Sciences, 11*(8), 342–348.

Kristof, K. M. (2008, December 27). Hooked on debt: Students learn too late the costs of private loans. *Los Angeles Times,* pp. A1, A18–A19.

Kruger, J., Wirtz, D., & Miller, D. (2005). Counterfactual thinking and the first instinct fallacy. *Journal of Personality and Social Psychology, 88*, 725–735.

Kuh, G. D. (1993). In their own words: What students learn outside the classroom. *American Educational Research Journal, 30*, 277–304.

Kuh, G. D. (1995). The other curriculum: Out-of-class experiences associated with student learning and personal development. *Journal of Higher Education, 66*(2), 123–153.

Kuh, G. D., Douglas, K. B., Lund, J. P., & Ramin-Gyurnek, J. (1994). *Student learning outside the classroom: Transcending artificial boundaries.* ASHE-ERIC Higher Education Report No. 8. Washington, DC: George Washington University, School of Education and Human Development.

Kuh, G. D., Kinzie, J., Schuh, J. H., Whitt, E. J., et al. (2005). *Student success in college: Creating conditions that matter.* San Francisco: Jossey-Bass.

Kuhn, L. (1988). What should we tell students about answer changing? *Research Serving Teaching, 1*(8).

Kurfiss, J. G. (1988). *Critical thinking: Theory, research, practice, and possibilities.* ASHE-ERIC Report No. 2. Washington, DC: Association for the Study of Higher Education.

Ladas, H. S. (1980). Note-taking on lectures: An information-processing approach. *Educational Psychologist, 15*(1), 44–53.

Lakein, A. (1973). *How to get control of your time and your life*. New York: New American Library.

Langer, J. A., & Applebee, A. N. (1987). *How writing shapes thinking*. NCTE Research Report No. 22. Urbana, IL: National Council of Teachers of English.

Lankaster, L., & Stilman, D. (2002). *When generations collide*. New York: HarperCollins.

Latané, B., Liu, J. H., Nowak, A., Bonevento, N., & Zheng, L. (1995). Distance matters: Physical space and social impact. *Personality and Social Psychology Bulletin, 21*, 795–805.

Lay, C. H., & Silverman, S. (1996). Trait procrastination, time management, and dilatory behavior. *Personality & Individual Differences, 21*, 61–67.

Lehrer, P. M., & Woolfolk, R. L. (1993). *Principles and practice of stress management* (Vol. 2). New York: Guilford Press.

Leibel, R. L., Rosenbaum, M., & Hirsch, J. (1995). Changes in energy expenditure resulting from altered body weight. *New England Journal of Medicine, 332*, 621–628.

Levitin, D. J. (2006). *This is your brain on music: The science of a human obsession*. New York: Dutton.

Leuwerke, W. C., Robbins, S. B., Sawyer, R., & Hovland, M. (2004). Predicting engineering major status from mathematics achievement and interest congruence. *Journal of Career Assessment, 12*, 135–149.

Levine, A., & Cureton, J. S. (1998). *When hopes and fears collide*. San Francisco: Jossey-Bass.

Levitsky, D. A., Nussbaum, M., Halbmaier, C. A., & Mrdjenovic, G. (2003, July). *The freshman 15: A model for the study of techniques to curb the "epidemic" of obesity*. Annual meeting of the Society of the Study of Ingestive Behavior, University of Groningen, Haren, The Netherlands.

Levitz, R., & Noel, L. (1989). Connecting student to the institution: Keys to retention and success. In M. L. Upcraft, J. N. Gardner, et al. (Eds.), *The freshman year experience* (pp. 65–81). San Francisco: Jossey-Bass.

Lewin, K. (1935). *A dynamic theory of personality*. New York: McGraw-Hill.

Liebertz, C. (2005a). Want clear thinking? Relax. *Scientific American Mind, 16*(3), 88–89.

Light, R. J. (2001). *Making the most of college: Students speak their minds*. Cambridge, MA: Harvard University Press.

Linn, R. L., & Gronlund, N. E. (1995). *Measurement and assessment in teaching* (7th ed.). Englewood Cliffs, NJ: Prentice Hall.

Lock, R. D. (2000). *Taking charge of your career direction* (4th ed.). Belmont, CA: Wadsworth/Thomson Learning.

Locke, E. (1977). An empirical study of lecture note-taking among college students. *Journal of Educational Research, 77*, 93–99.

Locke, E. A., & Latham, G. P. (1990). *A theory of goal setting and task performance*. Englewood Cliffs, NJ: Prentice Hall.

Love, P., & Love, A. G. (1995). *Enhancing student learning: Intellectual, social, and emotional integration*. ASHE-ERIC Higher Education Report No. 4. Washington, DC: Graduate School of Education and Human Development, George Washington University.

Luotto, J. A., Stoll, E. L., & Hoglund-Ketttmann, N. (2001). *Communication skills for collaborative learning* (2nd ed.): Dubuque, IA: Kendall/Hunt.

Mackes (2003). Employers describe perfect job candidate. *NACEWeb Press Releases*. Retrieved July 13, 2004, from http://www.naceweb.org/press

Maddi, S. R. (2002). The story of hardiness: Twenty years of theorizing, research, and practice. *Consulting Psychology Journal: Practice and Research, 54*(3), 175–185.

Mae, N. (2005). *Undergraduate students and credit cards in 2004: An analysis of usage rates and trend*. Wilkes-Barre, PA: Nellie Mae.

Maes, J. D., Weldy, T. G., & Icenogle, M. L. (1997). A managerial perspective: Oral communication competency is most important for business students in the workplace. *Journal of Business Communication, 34*(1), 67–80.

Maier, N. R. F. (1970). *Problem solving and creativity in individuals and groups*. Belmont, CA: Brooks/Cole.

Malvasi, M., Rudowsky, C., & Valencia, J. M. (2009). *Library Rx: Measuring and treating library anxiety, a research study*. Chicago: Association of College and Research Libraries.

Marzano, R. J., Pickering, D. J., & Pollock, J. (2001). *Classroom instruction that works: Research-based strategies for increasing student achievement*. Alexandria, VA: Association for Supervision and Curriculum Development.

Maslow, A. H. (1954). *Motivation and personality*. New York: Harper & Row.

Matsui, T., Okada, A., & Inoshita, O. (1983). Mechanism of feedback affecting task performance. *Organizational Behavior and Human Performance, 31*, 114–122.

McCance, N., & Pychyl, T. A. (2003, August). *From task avoidance to action: An experience sampling study of undergraduate students' thoughts, feelings and coping strategies in relation to academic procrastination.* Paper presented at the Third Annual Conference for Counseling Procrastinators in the Academic Context, University of Ohio, Columbus.

McGuiness, D., & Pribram, K. (1980). The neurophysiology of attention: Emotional and motivational controls. In M. D. Wittrock (Ed.), *The brain and psychology* (pp. 95–139). New York: Academic Press.

Mehrabian, A. (1972). *Nonverbal communication.* Chicago: Adline-Atherton.

Meilman, P. W., & Presley, C. A. (2005). The first-year experience and alcohol use. In M. L. Upcraft, J. N. Gardner, & B. O. Barefoot, & associates, *Challenging and supporting the first-year student: A handbook for improving the first year of college* (pp. 445–468). San Francisco: Jossey-Bass.

Middleton, F., & Strick, P. (1994). Anatomical evidence for cerebellar and basal ganglia involvement in higher brain function. *Science, 226*(51584), 458–461.

Miller, G. (1988). *The meaning of general education.* New York: Teachers College Press.

Miller, M. A. (2003, September/October). The meaning of the baccalaureate. *About Campus,* pp. 2–8.

Millman, J., Bishop, C., & Ebel, R. (1965). An analysis of test-wiseness. *Educational and Psychological Measurement, 25,* 707–727.

Milton, O. (1982). *Will that be on the final?* Springfield, IL: Charles C. Thomas.

Minninger, J. (1984). *Total recall: How to boost your memory power.* Emmaus, PA: Rodale.

Mitler, M. M., Dinges, D. F., & Dement, W. C. (1994). Sleep medicine, public policy, and public health. In M. H. Kryger, T. Roth, & W. C. Dement (Eds.), *Principles and practice of sleep medicine* (2nd ed.). Philadelphia: Saunders.

Moeller, M. L. (1999). History, concept and position of self-help groups in Germany". *Group Analysis, 32*(2), 181–194.

Molnar, S. (1991). *Human variation: race, type, and ethnic groups* (3rd ed.). Englewood Cliffs, NJ: Prentice Hall.

Motley, M. T. (1997). *Overcoming your fear of public speaking: A proven method.* Boston: Houghton Mifflin.

Multon, K. D., Brown, S. D., & Lent, R. W. (1991). Relation of self-efficacy beliefs to academic outcomes: A meta-analytic investigation. *Journal of Counseling Psychology, 38*(1), 30–38.

Murname, K., & Shiffrin, R. M. (1991). Interference and the representation of events in memory. *Journal of Experimental Psychology: Learning, Memory, & Cognition, 17,* 855–874.

Murray, D. M. (1993). *Write to learn* (4th ed.). Fort Worth: Harcourt Brace.

Myers, D. G. (1993). *The pursuit of happiness: Who is happy—and why?* New York: Morrow.

Myers, D. G., & McCaulley, N. H. (1985). *Manual: A guide to the development and use of the Myers-Briggs Type Indicator.* Palo Alto, CA: Consulting Psychologists Press.

Myers, I. B. (1976). *Introduction to type.* Gainesville, FL: Center for the Application of Psychological Type.

Nagda, B. R., Gurin, P., & Johnson, S. M. (2005). Living, doing and thinking diversity: How does pre-college diversity experience affect first-year students' engagement with college diversity? In R. S. Feldman (Ed.), *Improving the first year of college: Research and practice* (pp. 73–110). Mahwah, NJ: Lawrence Erlbaum.

Naisbitt, J. (1982). *Megatrends: Ten new directions transforming our lives.* New York: Warner Books.

Narciso, J., & Burkett, D. (1975). *Disclose yourself: Discover the "me" in relationships.* Englewood Cliffs, NJ: Prentice Hall.

National Association of Colleges & Employers. (2003). *Job Outlook 2003 survey.* Bethlehem, PA: Author.

National Resource Center for the First-Year Experience and Students in Transition (2004). *The 2003 Your First College Year (YFCY) Survey.* Columbia, SC: Author.

National Resources Defense Council. (2005). *Global warming: A summary of recent findings on the changing global climate.* Retrieved Nov. 11, 2005, from http://www.nrdc.org/global/Warming/fgwscience.asp

National Survey of Student Engagement. (2003). *Converting data into action: Expanding the boundaries of institutional improvement.* Bloomington, IN: Author.

Newell, A., & Rosenbloom, P. S. (1981). Mechanisms of skill acquisition of the law of practice. In J. R. Anderson (Ed.), *Cognitive skills and their acquisition.* Hillsdale, NJ: Erlbaum.

Newton, T. (1990, September). *Improving students' listening skills.* IDEA Paper No. 23. Manhattan, KS: Center for Faculty Evaluation and Development.

Nichols, M. P. (1995). *The lost art of listening.* New York: Guilford Press.

Niederjohn, M. S. (2008). First-year experience course improves students' financial literacy. *ESource for College Transitions* (electronic newsletter published by the National Resource Center for the First-Year Experience and Students in Transition), *6*(1), 9–11.

Niles, S. G., & Harris-Bowlsbey, J. (2002). *Career development interventions in the 21st century.* Upper Saddle River, NJ: Pearson Education.

Norman, D. A. (1982). *Learning and memory.* San Francisco: W. H. Freeman.

Nummela, R. M., & Rosengren, T. M. (1986). What's happening in students' brains may redefine teaching. *Educational Leadership, 43*(8), 49–53.

Obama, B. (2006). *The audacity of hope: Thoughts on reclaiming the American dream.* New York: Three Rivers Press.

Office of Research. (1994). *What employers expect of college graduates: International knowledge and second language skills.* Washington, DC: Office of Educational Research and Improvement, U.S. Department of Education.

O'Keefe, J., & Nadel, L. (1978). *The hippocampus as a cognitive map.* Oxford, England: Clarendon Press.

Onwuegbuzie, A. J. (2000). Academic procrastinators and perfectionistic tendencies among graduate students. *Journal of Social Behavior and Personality, 15*, 103–109.

Orszag, J. M., Orszag, P. R., & Whitmore, D. M. (2001). *Learning and earning: Working in college.* Retrieved July 19, 2006, from http://www.brockport.edu/career01/upromise.htm

Paivio, A. (1990). *Mental representations: A dual coding approach.* New York: Oxford University Press.

Palank, J. (2006, July 17). *Face it: "Book" no secret to employers.* Retrieved August 21, 2006, from http://www.washtimes.com/business/20060717-12942-1800r.htm

Park, O. (1984). Example comparison strategy versus attribute identification strategy in concept learning. *American Educational Research Journal, 21*(1), 145–162.

Pascarella, E. T. (2001, November/December). Cognitive growth in college: Surprising and reassuring findings from the National Study of Student Learning. *Change,* pp. 21–27.

Pascarella, E., & Terenzini, P. (1991). *How college affects students: Findings and insights from twenty years of research.* San Francisco: Jossey-Bass.

Pascarella, E., & Terenzini, P. (2005). *How college affects students: A third decade of research* (Vol. 2). San Francisco: Jossey-Bass.

Paul, R., & Elder, L. (2002). *Critical thinking: Tools for taking charge of your professional and personal life.* Upper Saddle River, NJ: Pearson Education.

Paul, R., & Elder, L. (2004). *The nature and functions of critical and creative thinking.* Dillon Beach, CA: Foundation for Critical Thinking.

Peigneux, P. P., Laureys, S., Delbeuck, X., & Maquet, P. (2001, December 21). Sleeping brain, learning brain: The role of sleep for memory systems. *NeuroReport, 12*(18), A111–A124.

Perry, A. B. (2004). Decreasing math anxiety in college students. *College Student Journal, 38*(2), 321–324.

Perry, W. G. (1970, 1999). *Forms of intellectual and ethical development during the college years: A scheme.* New York: Holt, Rinehart & Winston.

Peter D. Hart Research Associates. (2006). *How should colleges prepare students to succeed in today's global economy?* Based on surveys among employers and recent college graduates. conducted on behalf of the Association of American Colleges and Universities. Washington, DC: Author.

Peterson, C., & Seligman, M. E. P. (2004). *Character strengths and virtues: A handbook and classification.* New York: Oxford University Press.

Pettigrew, T. F. (1998). Intergroup contact theory. *Annual Review of Psychology, 49*, 65–85.

Pew Internet & American Life Project. (2002). *The Internet goes to college: How students are living in the future with today's technology.* Retrieved January 30, 2005, from http://www. perinternet. org/reports/pdfs/Report1.pdf

Piaget, J. (1978). *Success and understanding.* Cambridge, MA: Harvard University Press.

Piaget, J. (1985). *The equilibration of cognitive structures: The central problem of intellectual development.* Chicago: University of Chicago Press.

Pinker, S. (1994). *The language instinct.* New York: HarperCollins.

Pintrich, P. R. (Ed.). (1995). *Understanding self-regulated learning* (New Directions for Teaching and Learning, No. 63). San Francisco: Jossey-Bass.

Pope, L. (1990). *Looking beyond the Ivy League.* New York: Penguin Press.

Porter, S. R., & Swing, R. L. (2006). Understanding how first-year seminars affect persistence. *Research in Higher Education, 47*(1), 89–109.

Potts, J. T. (1987). Predicting procrastination on academic tasks with self-report personality measures. (Doctoral dissertation, Hofstra University). *Dissertation Abstracts International, 48*, 1543.

President's Council on Physical Fitness and Sports. (2001). Toward a uniform definition of wellness: A commentary. *Research Digest, 3*(15), 1–8.

Pribram, K. H. (1991). *Brain and perception: Holonomy and structure in figural processing.* Hillsdale, NJ: Erlbaum.

Pratt, B. (2008). *Extra credit: The 7 things every college student needs to know about credit, debt & cash.* Keedysville, MD: ExtraCreditBook.com.

Price, R. H., Choi, J. N., & Vinokur, A. D. (2002). Links in the chain of adversity following job loss: How financial strain and loss of personal control lead to depression, impaired functioning, and poor health. *Journal of Occupational Health Psychology, 7*(4), 302–312.

Purdue University Online Writing Lab. (1995–2004). *Writing a research paper.* Retrieved August 18, 2005, from http://owl.english.purdue.edu/workshops/hypertext/ResearchW/notes.html

Purdy, M., & Borisoff, D. (Eds.). (1996). *Listening in everyday life: A personal and professional approach.* Lanham, MD: University Press of America.

Putman, R. D. (2000). *Bowling alone: The collapse and revival of American community.* New York: Simon & Schuster.

Rader, P. E., & Hicks, R. A. (1987, April). *Jet lag desynchronization and self-assessment of business-related performance.* Paper presented at the meeting of the Western Psychological Association, Long Beach, CA.

Ramsden, P. (2003). *Learning to teach in higher education* (2nd ed.). London: RoutledgeFalmer.

Ramsden, P., & Entwistle, N. J. (1981). Effects of academic departments on students' approaches to studying. *British Journal of Educational Psychology, 51,* 368–383.

Ratcliff, J. L. (1997). What is a curriculum and what should it be? In J. G. Gaff, J. L. Ratcliff, et al. (Eds.), *Handbook of the undergraduate curriculum: A comprehensive guide to purposes, structures, practices, and change* (pp. 5–29). San Francisco: Jossey-Bass.

Ratey, J. J. (2008). *Spark: The revolutionary new science of exercise and the brain.* New York: Little, Brown.

Reed, S. K. (1996). *Cognition: Theory and applications* (3rd ed.). Pacific Grove, CA: Brooks/Cole.

Rennels, M. R., & Chaudhair, R. B. (1988). Eye-contact and grade distribution. *Perceptual and Motor Skills, 67* (October), 627–632.

Rennie, D., & Brewer, L. (1987). A grounded theory of thesis blocking. *Teaching of Psychology, 14*(1), 10–16.

Rhoads, J. (2005). *The transition to college: Top ten issues identified by students.* Retrieved June 30, 2006, from http://advising.wichita.edu/lasac/pubs/aah/trans.htm

Richmond, V. P., & McCloskey, J. C. (1997). *Communication apprehension: Avoidance and effectiveness* (5th ed.). Boston: Allyn & Bacon.

Riesman, D., Glazer, N., & Denney, R. (2001). *The lonely crowd: A study of the changing American character* (rev, ed.). New Haven, CT: Yale University Press.

Ring, T. (1997, October). Issuers face a visit to the dean's office. *Credit Card Management, 10,* 34–39.

Riquelme, H. (2002). Can people creative in imagery interpret ambiguous figures faster than people less creative in imagery? *Journal of Creative Behavior, 36*(2), 105–116.

Roffwarg, H. P., Muzio, J. N., & Dement, W. C. (1966). Ontogenetic development of the human sleep-dream cycle. *Science, 152,* 604–619.

Roos, L. L., Wise, S. L., Yoes, M. E., & Rocklin, T. R. (1996). Conducting self-adapted testing using MicroCAT. *Educational and Psychological Measurement, 56,* 821–827.

Rosenberg, M. (2009). *The number of countries in the word.* Retrieved Nov. 18, 2009, from http://geography.about.com/cs/countries/a/numbercountries.htm

Rosenfield, I. (1988). *The invention of memory: A new view of the brain.* New York: Basic Books.

Rothblum, E. D., Solomon, L. J., & Murakami, J. (1986). Affective, cognitive, and behavioral differences between high and low procrastinators. *Journal of Counseling Psychology, 33*(4), 387–394.

Rotter, J. (1966). Generalized expectancies for internal versus external controls of reinforcement. *Psychological Monographs: General and Applied, 80*(609), 1–28.

Ruggiero, V. R. (2004). *Beyond feelings: A guide to critical thinking.* New York: McGraw-Hill.

Runco, M. A. (2004). Creativity. *Annual Review of Psychology, 55,* 657–687.

Sadker, M., & Sadker, D. (1994). *Failing at fairness: How America's schools cheat girls.* New York: Charles Scribner's Sons.

Sax, L. J. (2003, July–August). Our incoming students: What are they like? *About Campus,* pp. 15–20.

Sax, L. J., Astin, A. W., Korn, W. S., & Mahoney, K. M. (1999). *The American freshman: National norms for fall 1999.* Los Angeles: Higher Education Research Institute, Graduate School of Education & Information Studies, University of California.

Sax, L. J., Bryant, A. N., & Gilmartin, S. K. (2004). A longitudinal investigation of emotional health among male and female first-year college students. *Journal of the First-Year Experience and Students in Transition, 16*(2), 29–65.

Sax, L. J., Lindholm, J. A., Astin, A. W., Korn, W. S., & Mahoney, K. M. (2004). *The American freshman: National norms for fall 2004.* Los Angeles: Higher Education Research Institute, University of California.

Schacter, D. L. (1992). Understanding implicit memory. *American Psychologist, 47*(4), 559–569.

Schlosser, E. (2001). *Fast food nation: The dark side of the all-American meal.* Boston: Houghton Mifflin.

Schneider, W., & Chein, J. M. (2003). Controlled and automatic processing: Behavior, theory, and biological mechanisms. *Cognitive Science, 27,* 525–559.

Schunk, D. H. (1995). Self-efficacy and education and instruction. In J. E. Maddux (Ed.), *Self-efficacy, adaptation, and adjustment: Theory, research, and application* (pp. 281–303). New York: Plenum Press.

Secretary's Commission on Achieving Necessary Skills. (1992). *Learning a living: A blueprint for high performance. SCANS Report for America 2000.* Washington, DC: U.S. Department of Labor.

Sedlacek, W. (1987). Black students on White campuses: 20 years of research. *Journal of College Student Personnel, 28,* 484–495.

Segall, M. H., Campbell, D. T., & Herskovits, M. J. (1966). *The influence of culture on visual perception.* Indianapolis: Bobbs-Merrill.

Seligman, M. E. P. (1991). *Learned optimism.* New York: Knopf.

Shanley, M., & Witten, C. (1990). University 101 freshman seminar course: A longitudinal study of persistence, retention, and graduation rates. *NASPA Journal, 27,* 344–352.

Shatz, M. A., & Best, J. B. (1987). Students' reasons for changing answers on objective tests. *Teaching of Psychology, 14*(4), 241–242.

Shelton, J. T., Elliot, E. M., Eaves, S. D., & Exner, A. L. (2009). The distracting effects of a ringing cell phone: An investigation of the laboratory and the classroom setting. *Journal of Environmental Psychology,* (March). Retrieved October 25, 2009, from http://news-info.wustl.edu/news/page/normal/14225.html

Sidle, M., & McReynolds, J. (1999). The freshman year experience: Student retention and student success. *NASPA Journal, 36,* 288–300.

Singh, N. A., Clements, K. M., & Fiatarone, M. A. (1997). A randomized controlled trial of the effect of exercise on sleep. *Sleep, 20,* 95–101.

Smith, D. (1997). How diversity influences learning. *Liberal Education, 83*(2), 42–48.

Smith, D. D. (2005). Experiential learning, service learning, and career development. In P. A. Gore (Ed.), *Facilitating the career development of students in transition* (Monograph No. 43, pp. 205–222). Columbia: National Resource Center for the First-Year Experience and Students in Transition, University of South Carolina.

Smith, J. B., Walter, T. L., & Hoey, G. (1992). Support programs and student self-efficacy: Do first-year students know when they need help? *Journal of the Freshman Year Experience, 4*(2), 41–67.

Smith, R. L. (1994). The world of business. In W. C. Hartel, S. W. Schwartz, S. D. Blume, & J. N. Gardner (Eds.), *Ready for the real world* (pp. 123–135). Belmont, CA: Wadsworth Publishing.

Snyder, C. R. (1994). *Psychology of hope: You can get from here to there.* New York: Free Press.

Snyder, C. R., Harris, C., Anderson, J. R., Holleran, S. A., Irving, L. M., Sigmon, S. T., et al. (1991). The will and the ways: Development and validation of an individual-differences measure of hope. *Journal of Personality and Social Psychology, 60,* 570–585.

Sprenger, M. (1999). *Learning and memory: The brain in action.* Alexandria, VA: Association for Supervision and Curriculum Development.

Stark, J. S., Lowther, R. J., Bentley, M. P., Ryan, G. G., Martens, M. L., Genthon, P. A., et al. (1990). *Planning introductory college courses: Influences on faculty.* Ann Arbor: National Center for Research to Improve Postsecondary Teaching and Learning, University of Michigan. (ERIC Document Reproduction Services No. 330 277 370)

Starke, M. C., Harth, M., & Sirianni, F. (2001). Retention, bonding, and academic achievement: Success of a first-year seminar. *Journal of the First-Year Experience and Students in Transition, 13*(2), 7–35.

Staudinger, U. M., & Baltes, P. B. (1994). Psychology of wisdom. In R. J. Sternberg (Ed.), *Encyclopedia of intelligence* (Vol. 1, pp. 143–152). New York: Macmillan.

Stein, B. S. (1978). Depth of processing reexamined: The effects of the precision of encoding and testing appropriateness. *Journal of Verbal Learning and Verbal Behavior, 17,* 165–174.

Sternberg, R. J. (2001). What is the common thread of creativity? *American Psychologist, 56*(4), 360–362.

Strommer, D. W. (1993). Not quite good enough: Drifting about in higher education. *AAHE Bulletin, 45*(10), 14–15.

Sullivan, R. E. (1993, March 18). Greatly reduced expectations. *Rolling Stone*, pp. 2–4.

Sundquist, J., & Winkleby, M. (2000, June). Country of birth, acculturation status and abdominal obesity in a national sample of Mexican-American women and men. *International Journal of Epidemiology, 29*, 470–477.

Susswein, R. (1995). College students and credit cards: A privilege earned? *Credit World, 83*, 21–23.

Svinicki, M. D., & Dixon, N. M. (1987). The Kolb model modified for classroom activities. *College Teaching, 35*(4), 141–146.

Ten Commandments of PowerPoint Presentations (2005). Retrieved November 15, 2009, from http://power-points.blogspot.com/2005/09/10-commandments-of-powerpoint.html

Thomson, R. (1998). University of Vermont. In B. O. Barefoot, C. L. Warnock, M. P. Dickinson, S. E. Richardson, & M. R. Roberts (Eds.). (1998). *Exploring the evidence: Vol. 2. Reporting outcomes of first-year seminars* (Monograph No. 29, pp. 77–78). Columbia: National Resource Center for the First-Year Experience and Students in Transition, University of South Carolina.

Tinto, V. (1993). *Leaving college: Rethinking the causes and cures of student attrition* (2nd ed.). Chicago: University of Chicago Press.

Torrance, E. P. (1963). *Education and the creative potential*. Minneapolis: University of Minnesota Press.

Tyson, E. (2003). *Personal finance for dummies*. Indianapolis: IDG Books.

Underwood, B. J. (1983). *Attributes of memory*. Glenview, IL: Scott, Foresman.

University of Wisconsin, La Crosse (2001). *Strategies for using presentation software (PowerPoint)*. Retrieved November 13, 2009, from http://www.uwlax.edu/biology/communication/Powerpoint Strategies.html

U.S. Census Bureau. (2000). *Racial and ethnic classifications in Census 2000 and beyond*. Retrieved December 19, 2006, from http://census.gov/population/www/socdemo/race/racefactcb.html

U.S. Census Bureau. (2004). *The face of our population*. Retrieved December 12, 2006, from http://factfinder.census.gov/jsp/saff/SAFFInfojsp?_pageId=tp9_race_ethnicity

U.S. Department of Education (1999). *The new college course map and transcripts files: Changes in course-taking and achievement, 1972–1993* (2nd ed.). Washington, DC: Author.

U.S. Department of Education, National Center for Education Statistics. (2002). *Profile of undergraduate students in U.S. postsecondary institutions: 1999–2000*. Washington, DC: Government Printing Office.

U.S. National Center for Health Statistics. (2003). *National vital statistics report*, Volume 51, No. 5.

Van Dongen, H. P. A., Maislin, G., Mullington, J. M., & Dinges, D. F. (2003). The cumulative cost of additional wakefulness: Dose–response effects on neurobehavioral functions and sleep physiology from chronic sleep restriction and total sleep deprivation. *Sleep, 26*, 117–126.

Van Overwalle, F. I., Mervielde, I., & De Schuyer, J. (1995). Structural modeling of the relationships between attributional dimensions, emotions, and performance of college freshmen. *Cognition and Emotion, 9*(1), 59–85.

Viorst, J. (1998). *Necessary losses*. New York: Fireside.

Vodanovich, Wallace, & Kass, (2005). A confirmatory approach to the factor structure of the boredom proneness scale: Evidence for a two-factor sort form. *Journal of Personality Assessment, 85*(3), 295–303, 305.

Voelker, R. (2004). Stress, sleep loss, and substance abuse create potent recipe for college depression. *Journal of the American Medical Association, 291*, 2177–2179.

Vogler, R. E., & Bartz, W. R. (1992). *Teenagers and alcohol: When saying no isn't enough*. Philadelphia: The Charles Press.

Vygotsky, L. S. (1978). Internalization of higher cognitive functions. In M. Cole, V. John-Steiner, S. Scribner, & E. Souberman (Eds. & Trans.), *Mind in society: The development of higher psychological processes* (pp. 52–57). Cambridge, MA: Harvard University Press.

Wabash National Study. (2007). Retrieved October 4, 2007, from http://www.liberalarts.wabash.edu/nationalstudy

Waddington, P. (1996). *Dying for information: An investigation into the effects of information overload in the USA and worldwide*. London: Reuters.

Wade, C., & Tavris, C. (1990). Thinking critically and creatively. *Skeptical Inquirer, 14*, 372–377.

Walker, C. M. (1996). Financial management, coping, and debt in households under financial strain. *Journal of Economic Psychology, 17*, 789–807.

Walsh, K. (2005). *Suggestions from more experienced classmates*. Retrieved June 12, 2006, from http://www.uni.edu/walsh/introtips.html

Walter, T. W., Knudsbig, G. M., & Smith, D. E. P. (2003). *Critical thinking: Building the basics* (2nd ed.). Belmont, CA: Wadsworth.

Walter, T. L., & Smith, J. (1990, April). *Self-assessment and academic support: Do students know they need help?* Paper presented at the annual Freshman Year Experience Conference, Austin, Texas.

Webber, R. A. (1991). *Breaking your time barriers: Becoming a strategic time manager*. Englewood Cliffs, NJ: Prentice Hall.

Weschsler, H., & Wuethrich, B. (2002). *Dying to drink: Confronting binge drinking on college campuses*. Emmaus, PA: Rodale.

Weinstein, C. F. (1994). Students at risk for academic failure. In K. W. Prichard & R. M. Sawyer (Eds.), *Handbook of college teaching: Theory and applications* (pp. 375–385). Westport, CT: Greenwood Press.

Weinstein, C. F., & Meyer, D. K. (1991). Cognitive learning strategies. In R. J. Menges & M. D. Svinicki (Eds.), *College teaching: From theory to practice* (New Directions for Teaching and Learning, No. 45, pp. 15–26). San Francisco: Jossey-Bass.

Wesley, J. C. (1994). Effects of ability, high school achievement, and procrastinatory behavior on college performance. *Educational & Psychological Measurement, 54*, 404–408.

Wheelright, J. (2005, March). Human, study thyself. *Discover*, pp. 39–45.

Wiederman, M. (2007). Why it's so hard to be happy. *Scientific American Mind, 18*(1), 36–43.

Wilkie, C. J., & Thompson, C. A. (1993). First-year reentry women's perceptions of their classroom experiences. *Journal of the Freshman Year Experience, 5*(2), 69–90.

Wilhite, S. (1990). Self-efficacy, locus of control, self-assessment of memory ability, and student activities as predictors of college course achievement. *Journal of Educational Psychology, 82*(4), 696–700.

Willingham, W. W. (1985). *Success in college: The role of personal qualities and academic ability*. New York: College Entrance Examination Board.

Winsor, J. L., Curtis, D. B., & Stephens, R. D. (1997). National preferences in business and communication education: A survey update. *JACA, 3* (September), 170–179.

Wright, D. J. (Ed.). (1987). *Responding to the needs of today's minority students*. New Directions for Student Services, No. 38. San Francisco: Jossey-Bass.

Wyckoff, S. C. (1999). The academic advising process in higher education: History, research, and improvement. *Recruitment & Retention in Higher Education, 13*(1), 1–3.

Yerkes, R. M., & Dodson, J. D. (1908). The relationship of strength and stimulus to rapidity of habit formation. *Journal of Neurological Psychology, 184*, 59–82.

Young, K. S. (1996, August). *Pathological Internet use: The emergence of a new clinical disorder*. Paper presented at the annual meeting of the American Psychological Association, Toronto, Ontario, Canada.

Zeidner, M. (1995). Adaptive coping with test situations: A review of the literature. *Educational Psychologist, 30*(3), 123–133.

Zimbardo, P. G., Johnson, R. L., & Weber, A. L. (2006). *Psychology: Core concepts* (5th ed.). Boston: Allyn & Bacon.

Zimmerman, B. J. (1995). Self-efficacy and educational development. In A. Bandura (Ed.), *Self-efficacy in changing societies*. New York: Cambridge University Press.

Zinsser, W. (1988). *Writing to learn*. New York: HarperCollins.

Zull, J. E. (2002). *The art of changing the brain: Enriching the practice of teaching by exploring the biology of learning*. Sterling, VA: Stylus.

Index